Edward M. Spiers

Radical general
Sir George de Lacy Evans
1787–1870

Manchester University Press

Copyright © Edward M. Spiers 1983

Published in Great Britain and the United States of America by
Manchester University Press
Oxford Road, Manchester M13 9PL, UK
51 Washington Street, Dover, N.H. 03820, USA

British Library cataloguing in publication data
Spiers, Edward M.
  Radical general.
  1. Evans, *Sir* George De Lacy – Biography
  2. Great Britain. *Army* – Biography
  I. Title
  355.3′32′0924   DA69.3.E/
  ISBN 0–7190–0929–4

Library of Congress catalog card number
82–62250

Library of Congress cataloging in publication data
Spiers, Edward M.
  Radical general.

  Bibliography: p.
  Includes index.
  1. Evans, George De Lacy, Sir, 1787–1870.
  2. Great Britain. Army – Biography. 3. Generals – Great
  Britain – Biography. I. Title.
  DA68.22.E8S68   1983   355′.0092′4 [B]   83–5421
  ISBN 0–7190–0929–4

Photoset in Plantin by
Northern Phototypesetting Co., Bolton
Printed in Great Britain by
Redwood Burn Ltd, Trowbridge, Wiltshire

Contents

Preface	*page*	vi
Acknowledgements		ix
1 A subaltern's experience		1
2 Russophobe		18
3 An advanced Reformer		40
4 Commanding the Legion		66
5 'Count I-run'		101
6 An ageing Radical		121
7 Crimean hero		146
8 Army reformer		173
9 An assessment		198
Notes and references		212
Bibliography		242
Index		251

List of illustrations

Maps

1. The British advance on Washington and Baltimore, 1814	7
2. The route to India	21
3. The theatre of operations in the Basque provinces	71
4. The advance on Sebastopol	151
5. The battle of the Alma	154

Plates

Evans as lieutenant-general (*by courtesy of the BBC Hulton Picture Library*)	*frontispiece*
In the Crimea: a photograph by Roger Fenton (*by courtesy of the Royal Archives and the Imperial War Museum*)	147

Preface

Sir George de Lacy Evans (1787–1870) was a redoubtable Victorian general. In a military career which spanned nearly half a century he distinguished himself as a subaltern in India and in the Peninsular War, as a staff officer in North America and at Waterloo, and as a field commander in the Carlist War and in the Crimea. He also engaged in an extensive range of political activities. In the 1820s he wrote two influential books, sounding the tocsin over a possible Russian threat to the British Empire. An avowed Reformer, he represented Rye in the pre-reformed Parliament and then Westminster, a Radical bastion, for nearly thirty years (1833–41 and 1846–65). As a Member of Parliament, Evans advocated political, fiscal, and ecclesiastical reform at home and championed the struggle of liberal movements abroad. Throughout his long military and political career, he consistently promoted army reform, specifically the abolition of flogging in the peacetime army, the abolition of the purchase system, and an improvement in the pay, conditions, and terms of service of the rank and file.

Dr A. P. C. Bruce has rightly remarked that 'a study of this remarkable soldier and army reformer is required'.[1] A comprehensive biography has not been written hitherto because Evans left neither memoirs nor a substantial collection of private papers. Nevertheless he wrote expansively, if not always lucidly, to politicians, journalists, and military colleagues. Letters to, from, and about him survive in various archives and personal collections. When coupled with his voluminous writings and speeches, they provide sufficient material for a study of his public career (if not for a full biography, as his childhood and family life remain somewhat obscure).

Evans warrants such a study because his career, aside from its intrinsic interest, may illuminate aspects of military and political life in the early and mid-nineteenth century. He was, for example, a soldier-politician, belonging thereby to one of the largest occupational groups in the House of Commons.[2] The vast majority of these serving and retired officers were linked by a network of cousinage to the governing classes of the country and tended to be Tory or Whig in sentiment. Evans was an exception. If not a solitary exception, he was sufficiently rare to inquire how he managed to forge a successful military career while professing extreme Radical opinions. He neither concealed nor compromised his views (save in respect of a possible invasion threat from France). Even before entering Parliament, he wrote two alarmist books about the 'Russian threat', which prompted a wide-ranging inquiry into the defences of the North West Frontier. By studying his writings and the reaction to them, more insights may be gathered about British Russophobia in the 1820s and 1830s.[3]

Evans sought election to the House of Commons on thirteen occasions, winning ten of the contests. He was never assured of success until his later years. In winning election to the pre-reformed Parliament from Rye, Evans achieved a notable triumph which is worthy of scrutiny. In seeking to represent Westminster, a seat with a famous Radical history, his task might have been less exacting in some respects but was still demanding in others. Westminster Radicals were neither a cohesive nor a docile body. They pursued many divergent causes, frequently quarrelling among themselves. Deeply concerned about particular issues, they periodically split the Radical vote by choosing rival candidates. Evans, who won his first victory in such a contest, would face similar challenges from Radical opponents in future elections. He also faced opposition from a resurgent Conservative party under the leadership of Sir Robert Peel. Within Westminster, the Conservatives mounted increasingly formidable challenges, benefiting from demographic changes in the borough. The extensive redevelopment of the metropolis led to the demolition of many of the poorer houses, while more affluent citizens continued to move into the fashionable parish of St George.[4] The latter had become the borough's largest parish, providing the Conservatives with a substantial base of support. As Evans struggled to overcome these diverse opponents, his campaigns reflected the ever-changing character of Westminster politics.

In his military commands Evans faced a wide array of difficulties in Spain and the Crimea. Commanding the British Auxiliary Legion (1835–37) was the more onerous task. It carried the inordinate hopes of the Whig government, incurred the wrath of the Tory opposition, and received scant support from either the Spanish high command or the political authorities in Madrid. The Legion endured an appalling winter in 1835–36, suffered losses from sickness, desertion, and mutiny, and encountered a ruthless enemy fighting on its own terrain. By examining Evans's achievements as the corps commander, it may be possible to assess the contribution of the Legion to the Carlist War as well as its impact upon British politics. In the Crimea, as commander of the Second Division, he displayed immense personal qualities under the stress of battle and a shrewd grasp of modern tactical requirements. Hailed as a hero on his return to England, he devoted his final years in politics to campaigning for army reform. A review of this largely abortive campaign may assist in explaining the limited achievements of army reformers in the post-Crimean period.

Acknowledgements

I should like to acknowledge my indebtedness to Her Majesty the Queen for her gracious permission to use materials from the Royal Archives at Windsor Castle. I must further thank Sir Robin Mackworth-Young, the Royal Librarian, and his staff for their efforts on my behalf. I am also extremely grateful to several people who helped me to locate the papers of Sir George de Lacy Evans, namely Mr Christopher Hibbert; Mr Charles Niles Jr., the Research and Manuscript Assistant, Mugar Memorial Library (Special Collections), Boston University; Messrs Warmingtons and Hasties; and finally Mr P. C. Metcalfe, who owns the papers and kindly allowed me to use them.

The following individuals and institutions have kindly afforded me access to unpublished manuscripts of which they own the copyright: the Trustees of the Estate of the seventh Duke of Newcastle (deceased), the Trustees of the Broadlands Archives Trust, the Right Honourable the Earl of Dalhousie, the Right Honourable the Earl of Clarendon, and the British Library Board. References from Crown-copyright records in the Public Record Office appear by permission of the Controller of Her Majesty's Stationery Office.

I should like to thank several librarians for their assistance and co-operation, namely Mr C. A. Potts (Ministry of Defence Library), Mr G. Phillips (*The Times* Archive), Mr R. J. Olney (Assistant Keeper, the Royal Commission on Historical Manuscripts), Mr N. Higson (University of Hull), Ms Ruth Anne Becker (Museum and Library of Maryland History), Ms Roisin De Nais (Limerick County Library), Mrs Brigid Dolan (Royal Irish Academy), Mr J. S. Lucas (Imperial War Museum), Mr B. Mollo (National Army Museum) and the staffs of the National Library of Scotland, New York Public Library, the Library of Congress, the Greater London Record Office, Westminster

Public Library, the National Library of Ireland, the Genealogical Office, Dublin Castle, the Public Record Office of Ireland, the Bodleian Library Oxford, the Department of Palaeography and Diplomatic, University of Durham, the Scottish Record Office, Durham County Archives, the Registry of Deeds, Dublin, and the inter-library loan staff of the University of Leeds.

I must also express my gratitude to the librarians and curators of several regimental museums, particularly Col. A. V. Tennuci (Royal Army Medical Corps Historical Museum), Mr B. Rigby (Regimental H.Q., the 22nd (Cheshire) Regiment), Maj. D. I. A. Mack (Regimental H.Q., the Royal Highland Fusiliers), and Maj. J. S. Sutherland, M.B.E. (Home H.Q., the Queen's Own Hussars).

I am deeply obliged to the British Academy for a grant which facilitated my research from the Small Grants Research Fund in the Humanities and for the subsequent award of a publication subvention.

I am particularly grateful to Mr T. R. Hadwin and Mr J. Dixon, School of Geography, Leeds University, for drawing the maps.

I am profoundly indebted to several academic colleagues. Professor David N. Dilks of Leeds University, Professor Geoffrey Best of Sussex University, Dr Roger Bullen of the London School of Economics, and Mr John Keegan of the Royal Military Academy, Sandhurst, supported my research and publication endeavours. Dr E. D. Steele of Leeds University drew my attention to useful correspondence in the Cobden papers, while Professor Best and Dr Bullen commented upon various chapters of my original manuscript. Any remaining blemishes, mistakes, and errors of omission or commission are entirely my own responsibility.

I am grateful to Mrs Elizabeth Seaward for her patience in typing and retyping the drafts of this manuscript. I am also especially obliged to Fiona, my wife, for her scholarly advice during the writing of this book and for her constructive criticism of the final text.

1
A subaltern's experience

George de Lacy Evans was born in Moig, County Limerick, on 7th October, 1787. He was the third son of John and Mary Ann Evans, who had married in 1781. John Evans was a gentleman farmer from Lisready, County Limerick, and Mary Ann was the only child of Elizabeth Lacy of Leamlara, County Cork. At their marriage, the couple had received the townlands[1] of Milltown, in the barony of Connello, County Limerick, from Mary Ann's widowed mother.[2] Subsequently they procured other farms and estates, including 624 acres in East and West Athea from the Earl of Carrick (at a rent of £160 for the first four years, and £200 per annum thereafter).[3] By 1814 the Evanses holdings in Limerick and Kerry, as well as their house in the city of Limerick, were worth £1,000.[4]

Unfortunately little is known of George's early life in these modest, though fairly comfortable, family surroundings. As a public figure, he kept his private life extremely private and bequeathed neither an autobiography nor an extensive collection of family correspondence. His Irish background, however, almost certainly influenced his choice of career and political attitudes. Whereas the paternal side of the family had established itself, after five generations, as small landowners and farmers in Limerick,[5] his mother's family, much more exalted in the annals of the county, had experienced a tempestuous past, riven with internecine strife. By the 1780s the scars of that history had by no means healed.

The De Lacys had come to Ireland at the time of the Anglo-Norman invasion, having left Lascy, Normandy, in the previous century, to follow William the Conqueror to England. During the sixteenth and seventeenth centuries the family had stoutly defended its Catholic heritage. The most Reverend Hugh Lacy, Bishop of Limerick from 1557 to 1581, was deprived of his bishopric by Queen Elizabeth in

1571 and died in gaol ten years later. In 1607 Pierce Lacy of Bruff was executed for his part in the Elizabethan wars. In 1651 Colonel John Lacy, a member of the Supreme Council of Confederate Catholics, was expressly excluded from the amnesty after the siege of Limerick. At the second siege of Limerick, in 1691, Pierce Edmond, known as Peter, Lacy was conspicuously involved, although only thirteen years of age. Thereafter, members of the family either resigned themselves to the new regime or left Ireland for military service in Europe.

Among those who remained in Ireland was Pierce Edmond's nephew, Edmund, the great grandfather of George de Lacy Evans. He not only remained in Limerick but also conformed to the Established Church in 1738, so acquiring estates at Milltown and estranging himself from the rest of the family. Despised by his Catholic relatives, Edmund was left out of his father's will.[6] The animosity persisted over the next two generations. Edmund's descendants were not even befriended by other conformists in the family. On account of a defect in Edmund's conformation, ejectment suits were repeatedly brought over the Milltown estates. Indeed, Milltown was only secured by George's parents after legal struggles with two of his mother's uncles.[7] Reared in a family so divided by religious differences, Evans became a fierce opponent of religious bigotry and a zealous campaigner for the removal of civil disabilities based on religious criteria.

He felt more positively about his family's military past. In the eighteenth century few Irish families rivalled the exploits of the De Lacys in the military history of Europe. Pierce Edmond (1678–1751) had established the tradition, seeking service with Peter the Great and rising to the rank of field-marshal in the armies of Russia and Austria. His son, Francis Maurice de Lacy (1725–1801), became an Austrian field-marshal. From another branch of the family came General Maurice de Lacy of Grodno (1740–1820), a celebrated general of the Russian army, and Count Francis Anthony de Lacy (1731–92), a distinguished general and diplomat in the Spanish service. Equally illustrious were the Brownes, who had married into the Lacy family, particularly Ulysses Browne, a Count of the Holy Roman Empire, and his son, Field-Marshal Ulysses Maximilian Browne (1705–57), who was Commander-in-Chief of the Austrian armies, Governor of Prague and a Knight of the White Eagle of Poland.[8] Although highly respected in Limerick and welcomed during their brief visits (as in 1792–93, when General Count Maurice de Lacy and his kinsman, General Count George de Lacy Browne, visited Rathcahill), the success of these distinguished soldiers contrasted all too sharply with the family's declining fortunes.[9] They set an example which Evans, as the third son of a minor branch of the family, with modest prospects, eagerly followed.

Prior to entering the army, Evans attended the Royal Military Academy, Woolwich, where cadets were prepared for the *scientific* corps and the East India Company. At the turn of the century, the academy accepted cadets at fourteen years of age and provided a two-year course of instruction. Cadets were taught mathematics, military drawing, and some basic principles of fortification, and, in the Upper Academy, some lessons in French. The teaching was formal and pedantic, based upon lectures and textbook learning rather than any personal tuition. Military instruction was even more cursory. Apart from drill, the cadets received little training in either small arms or gunnery.[10] Yet Evans clearly profited from this education; unlike many subalterns who entered the infantry and cavalry, he possessed skills in mathematics and military sketching which would soon be utilised in a staff capacity.

Lacking the benefits of patronage or influence, he joined the army in India as a volunteer in 1806, and was appointed ensign in the 22nd Foot on 1st February 1807. As a subaltern, he was not directly involved in the training and daily routine of the regiment (duties normally undertaken by the adjutant, quartermaster, and senior noncommissioned officers). His main duties were on active service, where he was expected to lead by example, to display bravery and initiative and, if necessary, to die like a gentleman. Evans relished this responsibility. From the outset of his career, in the campaign against Amir Khan, he demonstrated an instinctive boldness and daring, gaining a promotion for gallantry to the rank of lieutenant on 1st December 1808. He served under Major-General the Honourable John Abercromby in the capture of Mauritius (1810) and was then appointed to Sir John Malcolm's mission to Persia. Evans refused the appointment, which promised certain advancement, preferring to join the more perilous operations in the Deccan.[11]

In India, Evans forged his reputation as a dashing and courageous officer. He enjoyed the life of a young subaltern, displaying a genuine enthusiasm for active employment. Although he developed a lasting attachment to the military profession, he disliked aspects of his early career, particularly the use of corporal punishment to maintain discipline. Nearly thirty years later he recalled:

when I first entered the Army, the frequent, the arbitrary, and indiscriminate way in which some commanding officers resorted to this method of maintaining discipline, was highly reprehensible, distressing, and frequently perfectly useless, and tended to harden and destroy, rather than amend, the moral feelings of the men.[12]

As an ambitious lieutenant, however, Evans was more immediately concerned to seek further employment and, if possible, to advance his career. Fortunately, in March 1812 a report on the capture of Mauritius, which had met the approval of the Duke of York, the Commander-in-Chief, secured his transfer to the 3rd Dragoons, then serving in the Iberian Peninsula.[13]

Evans served for two years in the Peninsular army under Lord (later the Duke of) Wellington. He found the experience exhilarating and frustrating. Seeking action, honour and advancement from war, he relished an opportunity for service in the field. During the retreat from Burgos (October 1812) he participated in the rearguard operations. Ordered to check the enemy, who were in close pursuit, he led his cavalry detachment in several audacious charges which delayed the French and facilitated the successful retreat. In the action on the Hermoza river he was wounded but remained in the saddle as an example to his men.[14]

Evans fought in all the principal battles of 1813 and 1814. At Vitoria (21 June 1813) he led several cavalry charges in the final rout, capturing prisoners, an artillery piece and a large sum of money. Praised for his exploits by Lord Charles Manners, his commanding officer, he earned similar plaudits for his judgement and daring in the battles of Sorauren.[15] As the French retreated through the Pyrenees, Evans had a horse shot from under him at Bayonne, and distinguished himself in the actions of Nivelle, Orthez and Tarbes. In the final battle of Toulouse (10 April 1814) he was twice wounded and had another two horses shot from under him.

Despite displaying bravery and endurance under fire, Evans was far from satisfied with his duties as a cavalry subaltern. The cavalry had found its rôle circumscribed by the wooded and mountainous terrain of northern Spain. The 3rd Dragoons had merely supported the infantry during the battle of Vitoria, only intervening to pursue the retreating French and to capture some stragglers.[16] Wellington, moreover, had frequently censured his cavalry commanders for their reckless charges, involving needless casualties in earlier battles. By the later stages of the war the cavalry was largely confined to limited raids, pursuit, and the capture and escort of prisoners. Off the battlefield, it protected foragers, found and sounded river fords, and undertook outpost duties. Evans was too restless to settle for these mundane, though important, tasks. He volunteered for more strenuous action, offering to serve as an engineer in the trenches before San Sebastian and to join the assault on the fortress. He was also active in the siege of Pamplona.[17]

This persistent quest for action merely reflected Evans's more profound disappointment. During his two years in Spain and France he had never once been promoted, and his aggrieved feelings were not alleviated by the general scarcity of official rewards. Few officers were promoted or obtained brevet rank for outstanding gallantry: even Ensign Joseph Dyas, 51st Foot, who twice led the 'forlorn hope' at Badajoz in 1811, remained a subaltern for another decade.[18] Evans's sense of frustration was compounded by the possibilities of promotion which officer mortality bequeathed. Regimental promotion was not slow for officers who could purchase their advancement. In the 3rd Dragoons, Lieutenant Bragge, who had barely completed three years in the regiment, purchased his troop on 20th July 1813, so ranking on a par with officers of ten years' military service.[19] Incensed by the injustice of the purchase system, Evans would campaign vigorously against it in later life. Meanwhile, he had to accept that his Peninsular deeds would only be recognised by a brief attachment to the Quatermaster-General's department (13 March – 25 May 1814) and by the Military General Service medal, with bars for Vitoria, the Pyrenees and Toulouse.[20]

Unlike many of his fellow officers, Evans did not return to Britain after the victory at Toulouse. He was ordered to join the staff of Major-General Robert Ross, the commander of a division sent to join Sir Alexander Cochrane's fleet, then 'employed upon the coasts of the United States'.[21] While three other divisions were sent to reinforce Lieutenant-General Sir George Prevost, the commander-in-chief in Canada, and so enable him to take the offensive against the greater part of the American army, Ross was required to co-operate with Cochrane in launching diversionary attacks against the eastern seaboard.[22] Ordered to avoid any unnecessary risks, Ross was directed to surprise the enemy, strike hard at naval and military stores and installations, and then withdraw. To undertake this task, he was allocated the 4th, 44th and 85th Regiments, a brigade of field artillery, a company of sappers and miners, as well as commissariat and medical services. He later received the 21st Regiment, and a battalion of marines from Cochrane. His effective force totalled about 4,000 men.[23]

Evans, who was appointed Deputy Assistant Quartermaster-General, sailed with General Ross aboard the *Royal Oak*. Departing from the Garonne on 2nd June 1814, the fleet rested briefly at Sao Miguel, the largest island in the Azores, and eventually reached Bermuda on 24th July. During the trans-atlantic voyage Evans became acquainted with some congenial fellow officers, particularly Captain (later General Sir) Harry Smith, the Deputy Adjutant-General, and Captain (later General Sir) Duncan MacDougall, of the 85th. These officers enjoyed each other's company, dined ashore together in Bermuda, and remained friends for the remainder of their service careers.[24]

Once the expedition had rested, and had taken fresh supplies, ammunition and reinforcements on board, it sailed for Chesapeake Bay, arriving on 15th August. Ross consulted the naval commanders on the flagship, *Tonnant*, about the choice of targets. Instinctively cautious, Ross did not favour another series of marauding sorties along the Chesapeake coastline, as Cochrane had mounted in 1813, involving wanton killing and the destruction of property. He was more tempted by the proposal of Rear-Admiral George Cockburn to destroy the flotilla of American gunboats under Captain Barney which had fled from the British armada up the Patuxent river and then to attack Washington. Although the latter was a prestigious and important target, Ross demurred initially. He feared that his army could not hazard an inland march out of range of Cochrane's guns, and against the defences which a national capital might muster. Consequently, he declined to commit himself; he only agreed to land his force at Benedict, on the mouth of the Patuxent river, and to march northwards, so dislodging any American infantry and covering the advance of the British boats.[25]

Evans, who attended the first meeting, would later defend the caution of his commanding officer against the criticisms of Cockburn. The army lacked appropriate maps to embark immediately upon an inland campaign. It had sailed from France with sealed orders, and, on reaching the Chesapeake, possessed 'neither guides, spies, nor intelligence of a local nature ...'. Above all, it lacked any draught horses to haul the guns, horses, and provisions on an extended

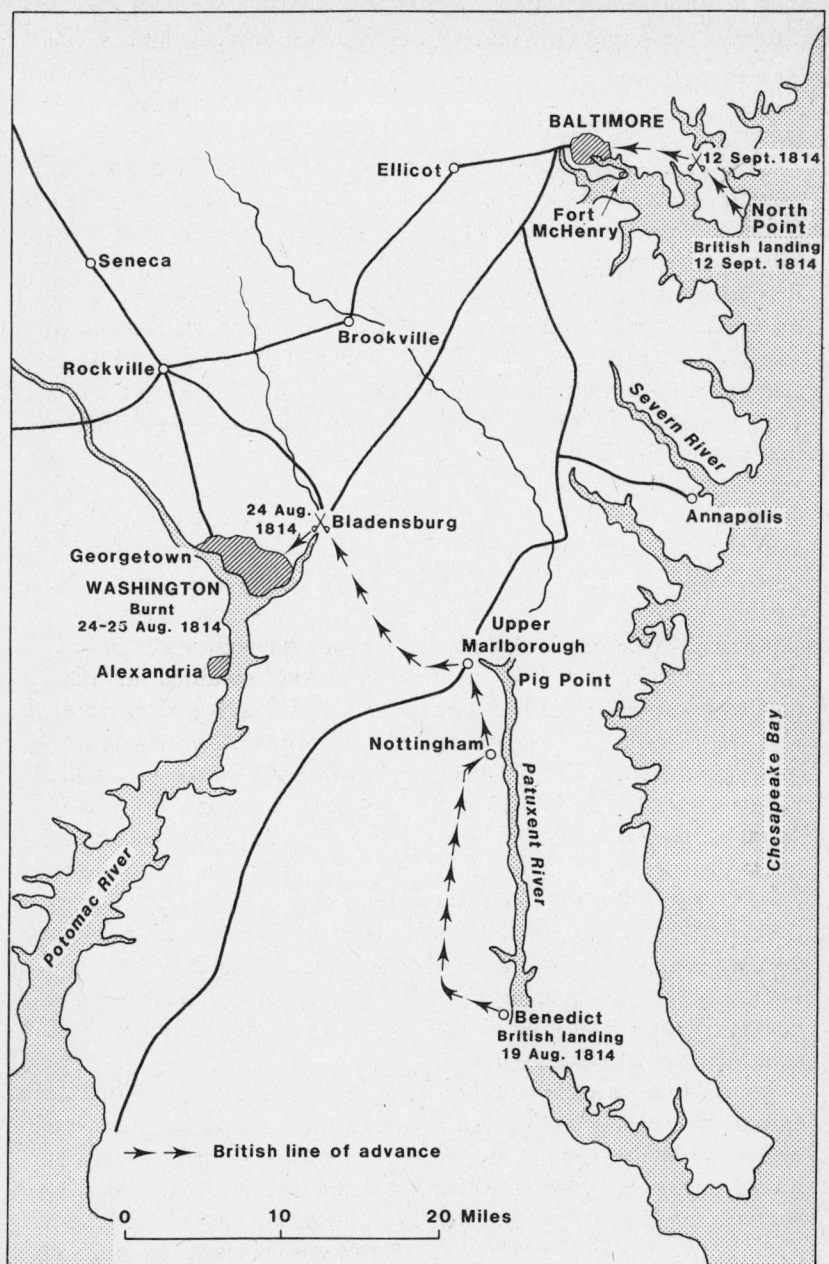

1. The British advance on Washington and Baltimore, 1814

march.[26] As Deputy Assistant Quartermaster-General, Evans was preoccupied with the logistical problems of any march into the hinterland. On 17th August he sent a detailed list of instructions to Colonel William Thornton, the commander of the Light Brigade. Each soldier, wrote Evans, should carry a blanket or greatcoat, an extra shirt, and a pair of shoes and stockings. The sick and weakly would remain on board. The company of sappers and miners, and two three-pounders, would accompany the leading troops under Colonel Thornton. Two hundred seamen would be attached to the artillery 'to aid in drawing the Guns, Ammunition etc.', and, in view of the transport shortage, officers would not be permitted to carry 'private baggage'.[27]

The army landed at Benedict on 19th August. Meeting no resistance, it advanced slowly northwards and reached Upper Marlborough on the 22nd. Meanwhile, Cockburn's naval squadron had come within sight of Captain Barney's flotilla, sheltering at a junction known as Pig's Point, just below Upper Marlborough. Hopelessly trapped, Barney destroyed his sloop and fifteen gunboats to escape capture by the British. Having secured the first objective, Cockburn renewed his pleas for an immediate assault on Washington. Ross eventually agreed, as the enemy had yet to show itself and the capital lay only sixteen miles away. 'I determined to make it,' wrote Ross, 'and accordingly put the troops in movement on the evening of the 23rd.'[28] On the following day the army encountered its first resistance, at Bladensburg, a small village on the main Baltimore–Washington road. After much dithering and confusion, the Americans had chosen to defend this approach to the capital with about 7,000 troops, most of whom were inexperienced militia. Nevertheless, this army, commanded by General Winder, possessed twenty-six field guns (of which twenty were only six-pounders) and held the high ground overlooking the river which the British had to cross. Colonel Thornton led his Peninsular veterans in a reckless dash across the bridge, but was temporarily checked by accurate American fire. When two more brigades advanced, supported by the firing of the spectacular, if inaccurate, Congreve rockets, the Americans fled in disorder. Only the sailors, under Captain Barney, held firm, but they too retreated when the British flanked them. The British had incurred far heavier casualties than the Americans – 64 killed and 185 wounded – but they had swept away Washington's sole means of defence, so prompting the flight of President Madison from the capital.[29]

During the battle Evans had displayed his customary *élan*. Acting as Quartermaster-General, he disposed the troops on the field, and had another two horses shot from under him. On the same day he personally reconnoitred the city of Washington, proposed its capture, and volunteered to lead a storming party of one hundred light infantry in a night attack upon the city. Ross approved this request, since he, Cockburn and some other officers had just been fired upon from the outskirts of the town. Evans led the attack, dislodging a few enemy soldiers, and gaining possession of the Houses of Congress before any other troops arrived.[30] On the night of the 24th August, and the following morning, the British set fire to the Capitol, the President's House, the Treasury, the War Office, the arsenal, Dock Yard, the ropewalk, and the Potomac bridge.[31] By destroying public buildings, and not just military barracks and stores, the army aroused American ire and even more vehement criticism in the Houses of Parliament. But such destruction was neither illegal nor unique. The Americans had sacked public buildings in York (now Toronto), Upper Canada, in April 1813; and the British had limited their destruction: they had not embarked upon an orgy of pillage and plunder. Only three private dwellings were destroyed (two by accident), and the plunder of private property was rigidly prohibited.[32]

For his services at Bladensburg and Washington, Evans was mentioned in despatches and recommended for 'some distinguished mark of approbation'. In a separate despatch Ross was even more complimentary: he claimed that the success of the mission must be attributed 'chiefly' to the 'perseverance and indefatigable exertions' of Evans.[33] The Horse Guards was unmoved, and, in the meantime, Evans had more immediate concerns than promotion. The army had withdrawn from Washington on the 25th, reaching its ships at Benedict five days later. At another planning conference, the naval and military commanders and their staffs discussed the next point of attack. Cochrane, who had formerly doubted that the expeditionary force could attack Baltimore – a larger, richer, and more easily defended city than Washington – now modified his views. According to Captain Harry Smith, who attended the meeting, Cochrane, Cockburn and 'Evans, burning with ambition', urged Ross to move on Baltimore. The general was circumspect, apparently sharing the reservations of Smith, but he eventually gave way.[34] Lacking self-confidence, Ross approved a 'demonstration' against Baltimore, with a view to probing its defences and to launching an assault 'should circumstances appear to justify it'.³⁵

The attack upon Baltimore proved a more daunting proposition than Evans had anticipated. Some preparations for the defence of the city had been made in 1813 and in the spring and summer of 1814. After the fall of Washington, even more trenches and fortifications had been constructed. Some 14,000 men, including 1,000 sailors under Commodore Rodgers, manned these defences. Another 1,000 sailors, regulars and volunteers garrisoned Fort McHenry, which dominated the narrow entrance to Baltimore's harbour on the Patapsco river.³⁶ On 11th September, Cochrane's fleet anchored off the south of the Patapsco river, and Ross's division disembarked on the following morning. Assisted by Cockburn and 600 seamen, the army began the fourteen-mile march to Baltimore. Cochrane, meanwhile, sailed up the Patapsco, intending to breach the defences of Fort McHenry. Major-General Samuel Smith, the American commander, had detached a brigade of Baltimore militia, about 3,500 men, under Brigadier-General John Stricker, to check the British advance. Despite their lack of numbers, Stricker's riflemen briefly checked the British, killing Ross in the process. Under the command of Colonel Arthur Brooke, the British forces regrouped and advanced in battle order; they broke the American line, forcing Stricker to retreat. Nevertheless, the smaller American force had inflicted far heavier casualties on the British (46 killed and 295 wounded) than they had suffered themselves (24 killed, 139 wounded, and 50 prisoners).³⁷ Although Brooke's army was able to continue its march, halting one and a half miles from Baltimore, it could not attempt an assault without naval co-operation. But naval support never materialised, as Cochrane failed to fight his way into Baltimore harbour. On 14th September the British naval and military units withdrew.

Once again, Evans was heartily praised for his performance as a staff officer. Brooke formally requested 'a promotion suitable to the high professional merits of this officer'.³⁸ He also approved of the way in which Evans negotiated with Captain Barney over the exchange of prisoners. By 7th October, Evans had secured an agreement that all prisoners captured at Bladensburg and Baltimore should be 'delivered up without delay'.³⁹ However satisfied with this news, the Horse Guards was preoccupied with gaining a decisive success in America. Even before the abortive assault on Baltimore, and the failure of Prevost's northern offensive, the government had sent fresh instructions to Ross and Cochrane. It had authorised an invasion of

Louisiana to secure command of the mouth of the Mississippi and to obtain some important possession which could be traded subsequently in a peace settlement.[40]

Cochrane, who had always been confident of seizing New Orleans, sailed for the Caribbean. He reached the rendezvous at Negril Bay, Jamaica, in early November, where reinforcements under Major-General John Keane arrived on the 25th. As Major-General Sir Edward Pakenham, who had been appointed to replace Ross, had not yet arrived, Keane assumed command of the army, now totalling about 6,000 officers and men. Having agreed New Orleans as their point of attack, Cochrane and Keane sailed for the Gulf of Mexico. By 10th December the fleet began to anchor near the entrance to Lake Borgne, where the approach to New Orleans via the lake was barred by six American gunboats.

On the night of 12th December, forty-five launches and barges, under the command of Captain Nicholas Lockyer, rowed into the lake in search of the American flotilla. Characteristically, Evans volunteered for the mission and joined one of the launches. After a thirty-six hour chase across the lake, the British boats closed upon the American vessels, and, despite a heavy fire of round and grapeshot, the British boarded and captured the American flagship. Within two hours all the gunboats were taken, at a loss of seventeen killed and seventy-seven wounded.[41] As the only soldier in the action, Evans was awarded the Naval General Service Medal.

Capturing these gunboats proved the only triumph of the campaign. From the outset, operations were bedevilled by logistical difficulties, especially the lack of shallow-draft barges. Troops were laboriously transported across the lake to the swampy and deserted Isle aux Poix, where they suffered from severe frosts and strong winds. Having assisted Major Forrest in moving, disembarking and quartering the troops, Evans accompanied Colonel Thornton, on the morning of the 22nd, in the first advance on New Orleans. The advance guard of 1,600 men set forth in the boats of the fleet, rowing across the lake and up the bayou. By the evening of the 23rd the men, exhausted from weariness, hunger and lack of sleep, camped some eight miles from New Orleans: their situation was precarious. The river flank lay unsecured, reinforcements could not be expected for several hours, and the line of communications stretched through swamp and bayou and across ninety miles of water. The brigade possessed little artillery, having brought only two guns and a few rockets, and lacked any naval support.[42] Warned of this advance, Major-General Andrew Jackson launched a night attack upon the camp while the schooner *Carolina* bombarded the British from the river. After four hours' fighting, the first troops of the second British division began to arrive and the Americans withdrew. The British advance had been halted, with losses of 46 killed, 167 wounded (including Evans) and 64 missing. Keane applauded 'the indefatigable zeal and intelligence' displayed by Evans, claiming that it merited 'the most favourable consideration.'[43]

Evans had little time to recover from injury. As the British, now under the command of Pakenham, consolidated their position, flanked by the Mississippi on the left and a cypress swamp on the right, the troops endured the torrential rain and hard frosts of this exceptional winter. Evans himself fell victim to the frostbite which afflicted many officers and men.[44] Another advance, on the 28th, encountered unexpectedly strong American entrenchments and was quickly withdrawn. Pakenham then summoned additional guns to bombard the American position; but rowing heavy ordnance up the bayou, dragging it through the swamp, and mounting it in batteries merely gave Jackson four days to improve his defences and emplace his guns. In the artillery duel, on New Year's Day, the British failed either to silence the enemy's guns or to reduce Jackson's parapet. Lacking sufficient ammunition and field gun carriages, the artillery withdrew after a three-hour struggle.

Undaunted, Pakenham awaited the arrival of reinforcements under Major-General John Lambert. In the meantime he authorised the arduous digging of a canal through the levee to carry boats from the Bayou Bienvena to the Mississippi, so enabling a flank attack to be attempted in conjunction with a two-pronged frontal assault on Jackson's bulwark. The delay allowed Jackson to strengthen his defences and to receive more reinforcements. When the attack was launched, on 8th January, it proved an utter disaster. Only the flanking column, under Colonel Thornton, achieved any success; the other two columns, commanded by Keane and Major-General Gibbs respectively, were repulsed with heavy losses. Pakenham and Gibbs were mortally wounded, and Keane severely wounded. Lambert took command and prudently withdrew the remaining troops. Having sent some 4,000 men into battle, the British recorded losses of 291 dead, 1,262 wounded and 484 missing.[45] Evans, who had sustained another serious wound, again distinguished himself, particularly in the handling of the retreat. In praising the Quartermaster-General's department, Lambert testified to his 'exertions and indefatigability'.[46]

Despite the débâcle of New Orleans, and the signing of a peace treaty at Ghent on 24th December 1814, the war continued. Unaware of the outcome at Ghent, Lambert resolved to salvage something from the expedition and to revive the morale of his despondent troops. He planned an assault on Fort Bowyer and, if successful, an attack on Mobile. In a methodical operation, the fort was surrounded and batteries were erected in position to bombard it. When these were completed, on 11 February, the garrison surrendered,[47] but as news of the treaty reached Cochrane on the 13th, further operations were suspended.

On 12th January, Evans, who had been mentioned five times in despatches from America, was promoted to a captaincy in the 5th West India Regiment. The appointment, though hardly prestigious, was not a 'gross injustice', as one writer claims, but a fairly typical form of promotion.[48] Evans, in any case, was not destined to remain a captain. When Lambert's army returned to Spithead on 9th May, it found that Wellington was already forming another army to oppose Napoleon, who had recently escaped from Elba and had raised an army in France. For Lambert, Brooke, Smith and Evans this was a fresh opportunity to win military laurels. Awarded a brevet majority, Evans joined Wellington's army as a Deputy Assistant Quartermaster-General.

He saw action almost immediately. Napoleon had hoped to foil the allies (Britain, Prussia, Russia and Austria) by attacking and defeating the British and Prussian forces in Belgium, before the Austrians and Russians could cross the Rhine and join in a concerted march on Paris. By 14th June he had assembled an army of 115,000 men in the area of Beaumont. When he crossed the frontier on the following day, he faced an allied army of 244,000 men and hence sought to separate and defeat the component parts of the allied force. On 16th June, while Marshal Ney engaged the Dutch and Belgian units holding the crossroads at Quatre-Bras, Napoleon attacked and defeated Blücher's Prussian army at Ligny. Wellington rushed reinforcements to Quatre-Bras, where the French columns were eventually held by superior firepower. The vital task of deploying and concentrating battalions during the course of the battle devolved upon the Quartermaster-General's department. Evans was present when the original instructions were issued to Sir William De Lancey, the Quartermaster-General; he was responsible for copying and circulating the orders to corps commanders, and assisted in disposing the troops.⁴⁹

The next morning he performed similar duties, as Wellington commenced his retreat to Mont-Saint-Jean.⁵⁰ He was ordered by Lord Anglesey to accompany Sir John Elley, the Adjutant-General of the cavalry, in a reconnoitre of Genappe. He was instructed 'to examine and report on that defile, but chiefly to select a position on the open high ground above it towards the Waterloo side for the whole of the heavy cavalry & some horse artillery . . .'.⁵¹ Thereafter he remained with Elley, personally directing the regiments to the ground on which they were to form. Evans reported that the Household Brigade and the Union Brigade of heavy cavalry retreated 'in good order', with only slight skirmishing. The brigades bivouacked astride the Brussels–Genappe highway, the Household on the right and the Union (the Royals, Scots Greys and Inniskillings) on the left.⁵²

At the battle of Waterloo, on 18th June, Evans served as an A.D.C. to Sir William Ponsonby, commander of the Union Brigade. Deployed in a long hollow behind a ridge held by the infantry of the 5th Division, the cavalry was concealed from view and screened from cannon fire. Though composed of reliable, battle-hardened Peninsular veterans, the 5th Division, under Sir Thomas Picton, had been severely depleted by the fighting at Quatre-Bras. At 1.30 p.m., on the 18th, it was bombarded by eighty French cannon and then attacked by three full-strength divisions. Facing overwhelming odds, Picton's division checked the French advance by volley firing and a bayonet charge, but only momentarily. It needed cavalry support, which was ordered forth by the Earl of Uxbridge. Ponsonby instructed the brigade to form up, about one hundred yards to the rear of the little sunken road and hedge which traversed the main highway. Evans, who had passed on the order to form,⁵³ also authorised the charge when the enemy crossed the road. Ponsonby, having dismounted to collect his cloak after his untrained mount had reared at the sound of cannon fire, directed Evans to make the signal. He took off his hat and waved the brigade forward.⁵⁴

The charge, as recalled by Evans, was a dashing and decisive affair which degenerated into chaos and confusion, and nearly resulted in disaster. Initially the French, on reaching the crest of the position, appeared to be nearly 'helpless'. They had lost many officers in the assault, were 'incapable of deploying' and had 'very little fire to give' from either front or flanks. The cavalry seized the opportunity; it moved forward and charged down the hill, taking some 2,000 prisoners and two eagles. The enemy, wrote Evans,

fled as a flock of sheep across the valley – quite at the mercy of the Dragoons – in fact, our men were *out of hand*. The Gen[era]l of the Brigade, his staff & every officer within hearing, exerted themselves to the utmost to reform the men – but the helplessness of the enemy offered too great a temptation to the Dragoons – & our efforts were abortive.[55]

In a less vivid account of the battle, published in 1818, Evans qualified this description. He emphasised that the French did not simply surrender or flee: many 'defended themselves to the last', and some arose, after being passed or ridden over by the Dragoons, to fire at the galloping horsemen. He reiterated, nonetheless, that the cavalry had become uncontrollable, pursuing its advantage with excessive zeal.[56]

Officers anticipated that the French cavalry, held in reserve, could exploit the 'disorder'. Evans rode back to the infantry lines, where he persuaded Sir James Kempt, now commander in place of the mortally wounded Picton, to provide infantry cover for the 'inevitable' retreat. In his recollections of the battle, Evans maintained that the cavalry could still have made a 'respectable retreat' had it been able to reform.[57] But the men were animated and undisciplined; they thundered into the rear of the French position, sabring gun teams and overturning guns. Suddenly they were assailed by French lancers on their left and sent into headlong retreat. A brigade of light dragoons, commanded by Sir John Vandeleur, covered their movements and prevented total annihilation. Even so, Ponsonby was killed and nearly half the Household and Union Brigades were lost. Evans escaped, as he was well mounted on a powerful, nearly thoroughbred bay gelding which reached the lines, despite a sabre wound 'from the eye to the mouth'. He changed horses, but his new horse was later shot from under him.[58]

Despite the excessive casualties, the cavalry had gained some respite for Wellington's hard-pressed infantry. It had also inflicted heavy losses on the French, demoralising three infantry divisions, capturing prisoners and eagles, and disabling some twenty-five guns. In his account of the cavalry achievement General Sir A. Clifton praised 'the gallant and admirable conduct of Major Evans'.[59] Even more important, Evans assisted in the reorganisation of the brigade once the remnants had rallied in their overnight position. During the remainder of the battle the three regiments, reformed on a two-squadron basis, rendered assistance where they could. For more than two hours they guarded the rear of squares composed of raw second-line troops, mainly Brunswickers and Hanoverian militia. Compelled to remain stationary under heavy musket and artillery fire, the regiments suffered even more severely than they had done in their earlier charge. Latterly, though reduced to only three squadrons, the brigade joined the counter-attacks against Marshal Ney's cavalry. After ten hours' fighting, the allies finally triumphed when Blücher's army arrived to provide vital assistance in the final battle.

Major-General Sir Denis Pack, who had commanded one of the brigades of the 5th Division, recommended Evans for promotion, particularly for his services in the later part of the battle.[60] The recommendation was acted upon directly. Evans was made a brevet lieutenant-colonel, bearing the date 18th June 1815. He continued to serve on the staff of the army of occupation in France, although he was placed on half-pay on 25th April 1817. When the army returned from the Continent in 1819, Evans briefly served on the staff of Sir Hussey Vivian, the commander of forces then deployed in Glasgow during industrial disturbances. Dissatisfied with this work, he resigned in favour of Harry Smith, preferring to prepare himself for a new career in politics.[61]

Evans still yearned for the action and excitement of military service. He repeatedly offered to serve abroad – in India, Canada, Algiers, Portugal and Sierra Leone – whenever the opportunity arose. He was usually informed that his name had been 'noted for employment'.[62] Evans bitterly resented that the Horse Guards had promoted him so tardily and had neglected his requests for employment: he was still complaining forty years later. He bemoaned the readiness to reward senior commanders while ignoring the qualities of a junior officer.[63] Acutely self-conscious, he attributed this oversight not simply to a system which favoured seniority and the ability to purchase promotion, but also to personal malice. He believed that political reasons, particularly dislike of his pronounced Radical opinions, had blocked his promotion (he was not made colonel until 10th January 1837).[64] In later years such prejudice was possibly a contributory factor, as Evans never concealed his intense dislike of the Duke of Wellington's political views, but his rate of promotion was not unusually slow during the Peninsular, American and Waterloo campaigns.

As a soldier, Evans had revealed remarkable qualities. He had always led by example, relishing action and involvement, and displaying bravery of the highest order. After several rigorous campaigns, in a variety of climates, he had proven his resilience, endurance and physical toughness. A hard-knit, sinewy man, he had continued fighting at New Orleans despite suffering two wounds and frostbite within the previous fortnight. Immensely versatile, he had served in infantry and cavalry regiments, even volunteering, on one occasion, to act as an engineer. He had demonstrated a genuine concern about the welfare of the rank and file, deploring flogging as a degrading and inefficient punishment. As a staff officer he had proved meticulous and competent, with a keen eye for detail. He had erred, particularly in advising the attack upon Baltimore, but he had still exhibited a potential capability as a field commander, a potential which was left unrecognised for nearly twenty years.

2
Russophobe

Evans found that writing compensated, at least partially, for the lack of military employment in the 1820s. It modestly supplemented his half-pay pension of £130 a year (despite brevet promotion to lieutenant-colonel, his pension was based upon his rank of captain). He was not impoverished,[1] but he was not as well endowed as many political aspirants and was described by one contemporary as 'miserly poor'.[2] He certainly welcomed any additional income from his literary endeavours. He also found that writing enhanced his political prospects by establishing his Radical credentials. Motivated by these personal considerations, and by his deep suspicion of Tsarist foreign policy, Evans became one of the foremost Russophobes of the 1820s and early 1830s.

British hostility towards Russia had recurred periodically ever since the late eighteenth century. It had become increasingly apparent, albeit in a gradual and evolutionary fashion, in the years after Waterloo. Although trade flourished between the two countries, the balance largely favoured Russia, which maintained an array of tariffs against foreign imports. Fear of Russia's aims in Europe and Asia surfaced as early as 1817, when Sir Robert Wilson warned of her immense natural resources and of her desire for 'universal dominion'.[3] As the revolutionary movements of 1820 accelerated the process of international change, the differing Russian and British interpretations of the post-war order, as embodied in the Quadruple Alliance of 1815, became more and more evident. A military revolt in Spain, which forced Ferdinand VII to restore the liberal constitution of 1812, prompted Russia to propose international measures of repression. Britain did not agree. Lord Castlereagh, in his memorandum of 5th May 1820, deplored intervention in Spain, and warned against perverting the aims of the Alliance.[4] The distinction between absolutist or despotic, and representative or constitutional, governments was becoming more manifest.

The revolt of the Greeks against their Turkish rulers in 1821 posed a major dilemma for Britain and Russia. Under the direction of Castlereagh and Canning, British foreign policy was concerned primarily with preserving the general peace in Europe and the existing political order. As these objectives would be jeopardised by any Russian intervention on behalf of the Greeks, Britain tried to induce Turkey to compose its difficulties with the Russians and the Greeks before war erupted. Russia had powerful religious, commercial and strategic incentives to intervene; she also had outstanding territorial disputes and differences with Turkey over the treaty of 1812. But Alexander I would not condone the Greek revolt, despite the misgovernment and ill-treatment of the Orthodox Christians by their infidel rulers. The Tsar would not support rebels against their legitimate government. His brother, Nicholas I, who succeeded him in 1825, held similar views. Nevertheless, the efforts of the great powers to bring an end to the fighting by diplomatic means proved abortive. Even the Convention of Akkerman (October 1826), by which the Turks conceded a whole series of Russian demands in the Balkans and the Caucasus, proved inadequate. As the Sultan carried out the terms reluctantly and slowly over the next year, the hostilities continued until the Turkish and Egyptian fleets were destroyed in an unplanned and somewhat fortuitous battle at Navarino. Thereupon, Mahmud II became even more intransigent; by the end of 1827 he had denounced the Convention and declared a holy war on Russia. Nicholas, constrained by military commitments and depleted finances, had to make peace with Persia before joining hostilities with Turkey in April 1828.[5]

Prompted by the onset of Russo-Turkish conflict, Evans wrote his diatribe *On the Designs of Russia* (1828). He feared that Russia, having embarked upon a policy of aggrandisement, would not cease until she had dismembered the Ottoman Empire and captured Constantinople. Neither Britain nor France could accept this state of affairs, as Russia, once established on the Hellespont, would dominate both the Mediterranean and central Asia: she could thereby undermine the trade of Britain and France, imperil British possessions in India, and disturb the balance of power in Europe. British statesmen, argued Evans, had to recognise this threat and to consider the possibility of assuming the offensive against the Russian

Empire.⁶

To substantiate these alarmist views, Evans compared the rival powers in the Balkans. The Ottoman Empire, he affirmed, was already in a state of decay; it was bound to be overwhelmed on account of its military weakness, precarious finances and internal disunity, especially the implacable hostility of the subjugated Greeks. Russia, conversely, was an inherently aggressive and expansionist State. Its 'grandeur', wrote Evans, had been founded upon conquest; in the past hundred years, Russia had never made peace without advancing its frontiers and had 'never lost a conquest by war or rebellion'.⁷ Nor was the country likely to change course, so long as an autocratic ruler commanded 'an immense, well-appointed, and warlike army'. Having triumphed in previous foreign adventures, this army could do so again. Indeed, a large military caste, with 'confirmed habits and separate interests', favoured such operations and was ready to mount them. Nor were there many difficulties to be overcome. The army could be paid and provisioned beyond the Russian borders; 'with good management', argued Evans, the army should cost 'very little more than if it had remained in concentrated cantonments'.⁸

He feared that Russia, once esconced in Constantinople, would transform it into a formidable arsenal and naval base. She would construct a new navy in the Sea of Marmara, financed partly by loans raised on the London stock exchange. Thereupon the Tsar, at some suitable moment, would be able to threaten Britain's interests in the Mediterranean and her possessions in India. Discounting any obstacles which might inhibit such action, Evans envisaged a Russian advance along the valley of the Oxus and through the countries of Khiva and Bokhara. He assumed that the Tsar, encountering no resistance from the local inhabitants, would be able to command their resources and would receive their support for a promised share in the plunder. While India was being attacked, the Tsar could launch an assault on Malta and, in liaison with Spain, invest Gibraltar. The diversion of British naval resources would then enable Andrew Jackson, if President of the United States, to provide the arms, ammunition and stores for an Irish insurgency. Evans doubted that 'a more obvious, and easier, cheaper, or more decisive diversion against British power' could be effected.⁹

Rather than let disaster overwhelm them, Evans urged the governments of Britain and France to act immediately. By decisive initiatives, these countries could still rally the free nations of Europe and save civilisation. In the Balkans, they could consolidate the

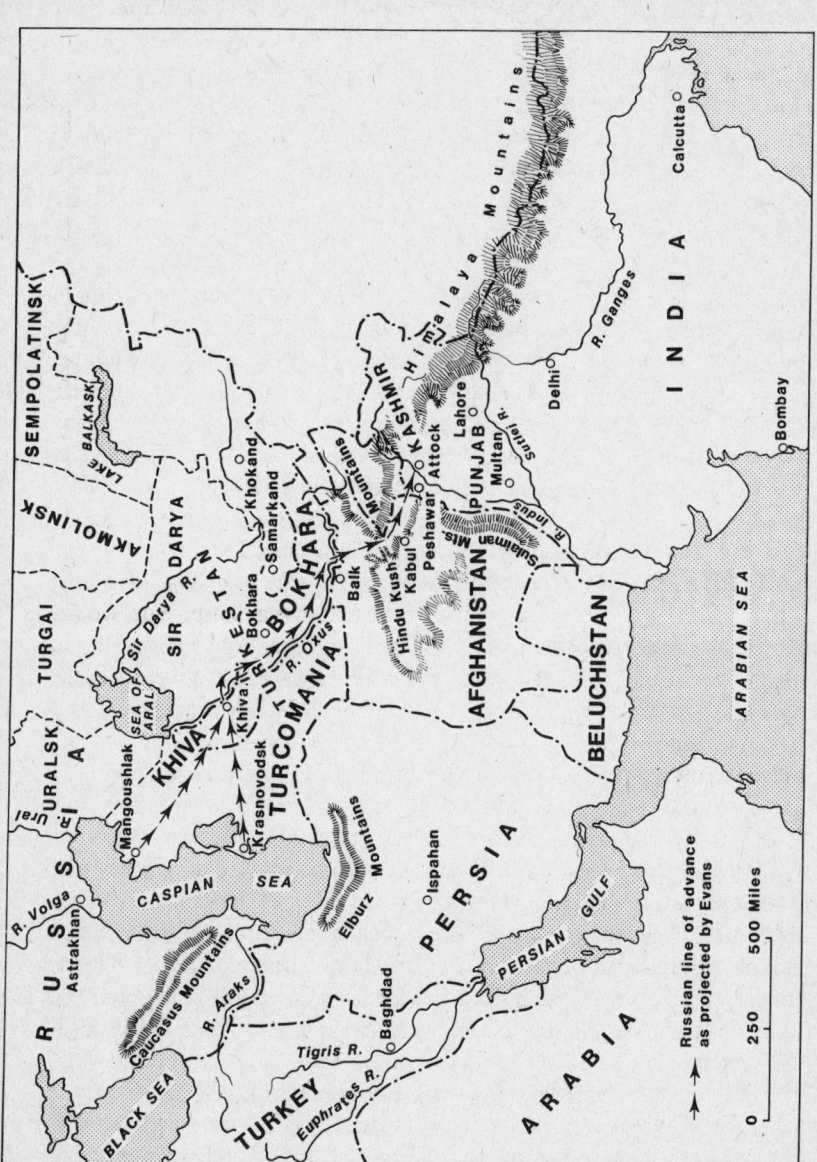

2. The route to India

freedom and power of Greece and so establish a bulwark against further Russian encroachments. Should a war with Russia ensue, they need not fear a recurrence of the fate which befell Charles XII and Napoleon. By a concerted assault on the periphery of the Romanov Empire, they could exploit the vulnerabilities of Russia. They could destroy her commerce, and attack her depots and frontiers in the Black and Baltic Seas. They could aid the Persians to recover their lost possessions and so stretch the military resources of Russia. By sending an allied fleet into the Gulf of Finland they could inspire a Polish insurrection and possibly bombard St Petersburg. As a consequence, Russia would be made to atone for her crimes of the past century and to recognise the liberty and independence of the Polish people in a new peace settlement.[10]

Understandably, Evans was concerned about the credibility of his narrative. Denying any powers of prescience, he stressed that he was merely describing the likely consequences should Russia continue, over several years, to expand her commercial, maritime and territorial power.[11] Despite this disclaimer, the book encountered a mixed reception. *The Times* was impressed. In a lengthy and generally favourable review, it admitted that the book had flaws – poor organisation, an inelegant style, and a curious choice of examples – but still praised the valuable knowledge and forceful reasoning of the author, claiming that the book had drawn attention to important questions of 'universal interest'.[12] *The Times* was inspired by the brochure to re-examine the situation in the Balkans, viewing Russian policy with much more apprehension. Only a day after reviewing Evans's work, it was denouncing any Russian seizure of Turkish territory, speculating upon the fall of Constantinople, and insisting that Britain could not view these contingencies with indifference. Although these fears were doused by the bungling of the Russian army in 1828, they were revived by the more successful campaign of 1829 which culminated in the capture of Adrianople. 'The schemes of Catherine,' wrote *The Times*, 'have abundantly succeeded. What new schemes may grow out of their accomplishment, belongs to a different chapter.'[13]

Complimentary comments by *The Times* almost certainly boosted sales. Some five hundred copies were sold, at 8s 6d each.[14] Other newspapers followed *The Times*; they either reviewed the book, or quoted from it, or gave it a passing mention in leading articles on the Russo-Turkish war. But few reviewers agreed with Evans. *The*

Standard described the work as 'clever though rather fanciful', while *The Globe* dismissed any anti-Russian alliance, headed by Britain, as unnecessary, futile, and only liable to increase the national debt.[15] In two extensive reviews *The Morning Chronicle* challenged both the assumptions and the proposals of Evans. Unconvinced that Constantinople would prove an easily exploitable asset, it reckoned that Russian resources would be drained by the creation of a sizeable navy and by the suppression of the 'barbarous and discontented inhabitants'. It feared that a new Greek State could not be established so long as the Turks retained a foothold in Europe, and that quarrels between the two would merely facilitate the return of Russia. *The Chronicle* argued, too, that Evans had provided the best antidote to his own forebodings, namely his account of Russian vulnerabilities. The paper believed that Russia faced sufficient difficulties in keeping her empire together, without embarking on further adventures against the British position in India.[16]

More critical reviews appeared in some weekly papers and quarterly journals. *The Examiner* described the book as irritating and unsatisfactory – a profound disappointment in view of the author's military reputation. It dismissed Evans's alarmist fears as 'huge shadowy bug-a-boos', based upon vague speculation and little else. It regretted the lack of factual information, and deplored the loose and inaccurate style, especially the author's *penchant* for *non sequiturs*.[17]
The Quarterly Review was equally caustic. 'Our Cassandra-like Colonel,' it claimed, had written too rashly and hastily, without considering the full extent and complexity of his subject. Discounting any Russian threat to the west, *The Quarterly* was even more sceptical about a Russian invasion of India. It doubted that Russia could attempt such a venture across a thousand miles of mountainous and arid terrain, interspersed by extensive deserts. To support this view, it quoted from the recent narratives of their travels in the region by Baron Meyendorff and Captain Muraviev. *The Quarterly* concluded that this was not country over which armies could pass and repass with the facility supposed by Evans.[18]

These reviews, though unfavourable in many respects, at least testified to the widespread interest in the book. Most reviewers agreed that the author had called attention to an issue of immediate and vital significance. Evans even provoked Thomas Tooke, a wealthy merchant who traded with Russia, to write his own account of Anglo-Russian relations under the pseudonym 'Non Alarmist'.[19] Tooke feared that any war with Russia would ruin Anglo-Russian trade, and would prevent some 2,000 British vessels, about 340,000 tons, from carrying more than half Russia's foreign trade.[20] While accepting that Russia would probably submit before an allied onslaught, he doubted that war was either necessary or desirable. Further conquests by Russia, he contended, would only multiply the problems of defending her Empire: the capture of Constantinople, far from augmenting Russian power, would simply drain her resources in the maintenance of any army of occupation, many miles from the Russian border. Moreover, Tooke regarded Russian expansion in the Balkans as a development to be welcomed and not abhorred; he viewed Russia as a civilising power, liable to 'force the rapacious Pasha, and his brutal agents, to respect the property of the peasant'.[21]

Tooke also doubted whether Western countries had any need to fear Russian military might. He correctly noted that the establishment of the Russian army bore little relation to its effective strength. By excluding irregulars, garrison troops, cadet corps, local militia and invalid battalions, and by making allowance for nominal rolls inflated by colonels intent on profiting from the State, he calculated that Russia could put fewer than 400,000 men in the field. He dismissed any possibility of a Russian invasion force marching over the twelve hundred miles to the Indian frontier. Even if an army thirty thousand strong, exclusive of the troops left to guard the lines of communication, could reach India, he believed that any one of the Indian armies, buttressed by local resources and reinforcements, could thwart its advance. For the Russians, he insisted, 'a mere check would entail all the consequences of the most ruinous defeat'.[22]

Evans, a vain and sensitive man, took criticism poorly. He disparaged the military assessments of civilian critics, particularly those of Tooke, describing these writings as 'entirely Russian in spirit', motivated by commercial interests, the product of men 'who are, by birth and connexion, more Muscovite than English'.[23] Nevertheless, he accepted that he had to refute two major criticisms of his work if it was to retain a semblance of credibility. He had to establish that Britain had the resources to join an anti-Russian campaign, and that Russia could threaten British possessions in India. Hence he compiled material for a second pamphlet, *On the Practicability of an Invasion of British India*, which appeared towards the end of 1829, after the conclusion of peace at Adrianople.

In this work Evans refrained from personal predictions, preferring to quote extensively from various authorities. By comparing the views of several eighteenth-century politicians and philosophers with those of David Ricardo, he claimed that the British economy was more solvent in 1829 than in either 1783 or 1793. Completely satisfied about the state of British resources, he insisted that the government must be ready to counter Russian aggression. He argued that Russian hostility towards Britain was likely to endure in view of Russia's tariff policy and her maintenance of an army of a million men (he never distinguished between the 'paper' establishment and the effective strength of the Russian army).[24] He suggested that Russia could despatch an expeditionary force across central Asia, quoting selectively from many authorities, including General Malcolm, Lord Elphinstone, Colonel Kinneir, Baron Meyendorff and Captain Muraviev, to demonstrate the feasibility of an invasion.

But selective quotations could not conceal the military shortcomings of the Russian army. The campaign in the Balkans had taken longer to resolve and had proved less conclusive than Evans had forecast. Disease, inadequate leadership, and deficiencies of organisation and supply had undermined the campaign of 1828. Although the Russians had made more progress in the following year, entering Adrianople in August, their military machine excited less apprehension than formerly. Evans wisely conceded this point, but emphasised that the war was not over, and that it was still too soon to estimate the real strength and resources of the Russian State.[25] On the other hand, he maintained that the North West Frontier was vulnerable to attack, as reflected by the testimony of General Sir John Malcolm and Colonel Kinneir. He depicted the border-States as inherently weak and incapable of offering any resistance to a European force. Quoting from several Russian sources, he asserted that Russia could move 30,000 men, exclusive of lines of communication, from the Caspian and Aral Seas along the valley of the Oxus to the neighbourhood of Attock on the Indus or into the Punjab. He dismissed the likelihood of serious local resistance, even envisaging Persian support. And he insisted that the logistical difficulties could be overcome: horses could feed off the steppes, and the means of transport, both horses and camels, could be procured locally. In short, he could not foresee any insurmountable difficulty which might deter an invasion.[26]

Evans was sanguine, nonetheless. Britain, he argued, had merely to anticipate the direction from which an attack might come in order to prepare the necessary means of repulsing it. He urged the authorities to examine this 'dry but not unimportant' topic, as any quarrel between Britain and Russia would be 'the signal' for an invasion. He recommended that Britain should complete an authoritative topographical survey of the region, appoint political agents in Kabul, Peshawar and Bokhara, and support the unifying elements in Kabul and Lahore. Britain, he claimed, by taking minimal precautions, could prepare effectively to resist any incursions on the North West Frontier.[27]

As the book only elaborated upon the author's already well publicised views, and in a fairly temperate tone, it received little scrutiny from either newspapers or periodicals. But its publication coincided with a revival of fears in official circles of a Russian threat to India. In September 1829 the Russians announced the arrival of an Afghan chief in St Petersburg, along with ambassadors from Runjeet Singh, the ruler of Lahore and Kashmir. The visit alarmed Lord Ellenborough, president of the East India Company, and his board of directors. Ellenborough, who believed that eventually Britain would have to fight the Russians on the Indus,[28] had his fears confirmed by reading Evans's book in late October. He readily accepted that Britain should 'have full information as to Cabul, Bokhara, and China', and so sent copies of the work to Lieutenant-Colonel Sir John McDonald Kinneir, the East India Company's envoy at Teheran, and to Sir John Malcolm, then Governor of Bombay. He awaited their detailed comments upon the Russian threat as described by Evans.[29]

Meanwhile Ellenborough discussed the book with the Duke of Wellington, then Prime Minister. The Duke thought that Britain could defend the North West Frontier, even if Russia reached Kabul with twenty or thirty thousand men. He dreaded, however, the financial implications of a continued Russian presence on the border, especially the 'enormous expense' of sustaining the military preparations and of quelling any insurrections within India. Should Russia move an army towards India, he agreed that the government of India, with British financial support, could act 'as an Asiatic Power'. He also promised 'to take up the question here in Europe, if the Russians move towards India with views of evident hostility'.[30]

Henceforth official investigations, so desired by Evans, proceeded at several different levels. On 18th December 1829, two days after Ellenborough's meeting with the Duke, the India Board requested an account of Russia's trading with Khiva, Bokhara and Khokand from the Foreign Office. Within two months Lord Heytesbury, the British ambassador at St Petersburg, returned comprehensive reports upon Russia's commercial contacts with central Asia, her volume of shipping in the Caspian Sea, and the routes and time taken by caravans through Bokhara.[31] Ellenborough immersed himself in the travel literature of central Asia, reading the works of Meyendorff and J. B. Fraser. He was soon convinced that Britain, by her commerce, could enhance relations with the States in this region, even underselling the Russians in Bokhara, but he also accepted that the region would remain unstable with the Persian monarchy nearing collapse.[32] In these circumstances, the Board required an authoritative assessment of the Russian threat.

Sir John Kinneir obliged. In a lengthy review of Evans's arguments, he examined the feasibility of invasion. Although he accepted that Russia entertained designs against the British Empire, he doubted that there was any immediate likelihood of her acting upon them. He explained his reasons in meticulous fashion. In the first place, Russia had experienced immense difficulties in provisioning her troops during the recent wars with Persia and Turkey. Not only had the Georgian provinces been drained of corn, cattle and beasts of burden, but all additional supplies had had to be brought, at a substantial cost, from Astrachan and the Crimea. Secondly, the projected army of 30,000 Russians, assisted by an equal number of newly raised troops, was too small to mount an effective invasion. Evans had only allowed for the main force and for troops to secure the lines of communication; but troops would also be required to garrison the intermediate towns, to contain the conquered tribesmen, to guard the flanks against Persia, and to sustain the flow of supplies and ammunition. Thirdly, the cost of an operation 'so bold and perilous' would be immense. Although the Russian army, as Evans observed, was levied, clothed, equipped and fed for less than any other army, it never enjoyed these advantages when serving abroad. Russia's military operations had often 'been crippled by want of pecuniary means', a formidable and recurrent problem.[33]

Kinneir also suspected that a host of practical problems would bedevil an expeditionary force. If the army suffered as much from the ravages of heat and disease as it had done recently in Persia, casualties might account for one half of the original number. Fatigue, drunkenness, unwholesome food and a lack of cleanliness would soon induce dysentery and fevers, so thinning the ranks and undermining morale. Mortality would rapidly increase, unchecked by a wholly inadequate medical corps and a defective commissariat. Difficulties would beset the provision of supplies and transport. The boats on the Oxus were poorly constructed, limited in number, and not easily replaced. Cattle and provisions, though plentiful in Khiva and in parts of Bokhara, were not always available, and some regions were bereft of food or water. Camels were numerous in Turkestan, Persia and Afghanistan, but they could not be procured until the local tribesmen were quelled. Some tribesmen, especially Tartars and Afghans, might rally to the Russian banner in the hope of booty and honours, but they could prove more of a liability than an asset: their hatred of discipline, and of each other, might render them an 'unmanageable' rabble.[34]

Kinneir was even more sanguine about the prospects of defending India. He maintained that an army composed of sepoys and Europeans was more suited to the area than an entirely European force. The sepoys, he argued, were more used to the climate and could survive on simpler and more easily obtained provisions. If supported by British reinforcements, the Indian Army retained decisive advantages in its material efficiency and its defensive position. The tactical and logistic problems of the Russian army would only intensify as they approached the Indian border. Tired, depressed, and decimated in numbers, they would be particularly vulnerable to attacks from tribesmen. 'The horrors of a Moscow retreat,' wrote Kinneir, would then 'recoil on the head[s] of the Muscovites themselves.'[35] Moreover, an invasion of India could not be isolated from events in Europe. British attacks on Russian commerce, the impoverishment of the Tsarist exchequer, and the likelihood of revolts by subjugated peoples or of revanchist attacks by the Turks could not be discounted. So formidable were these problems, in Kinneir's opinion, that Britain had 'little to dread from the machinations of Russia'.[36]

In a separate report Sir John Malcolm agreed that Evans's warning had been timely; he accepted that an invasion of India was 'a constant and favourite theme of conversation' within the Russian army, and that any Russian intrigues, alliances, or military operations in central Asia warranted careful attention.[37] Nevertheless, he concurred with Kinneir about the impracticability of an immediate invasion. He suspected that the inhabitants of Khiva, Bokhara and Balkh would prove difficult to suppress without leaving numerous troops to guard the lines of communication. Like Kinneir, he reckoned that the financial and logistical problems would bedevil an invasion and emasculate the strength of the invading army. He stressed, however, that the Russian army, despite its many deficiencies, had triumphed against Asiatic opponents; since 1797 it had extended the Russian frontier from north of the Caucasus to the Aroxes river, and had recently defeated both Persia and Turkey. To Malcolm, it seemed imperative that Britain should prevent Russia from making further advances in Persia, and that this was a more pressing concern than an invasion of India. He doubted that the Tsar would authorise any immediate invasion of India, attended as it was 'with such eminent hazards to Russia'.[38]

Although Kinneir and Malcolm reassured the Indian Directors about invasion, they testified to the unease Evans had evoked and to the impact of his writing. The two books, though devoid of literary merit and containing speculations based more on fantasy than fact, had been widely read and seriously considered. The numerous reviews of his first volume reflected the interest he had aroused over Russian designs in the Balkans and in central Asia. Most reviewers, however critical of his writing, admitted that he had drawn attention to an important issue. The more measured tones of the second work, coupled with extensive quotations from a variety of sources, had occasioned an extensive examination of Russian policy by the government. Admittedly, the investigation had not adduced the same conclusions, but its authorisation remained a remarkable tribute to the timeliness and vigour with which a half-pay captain had expressed his feelings. As a pamphleteer, Evans had proved fairly successful.

European events, which had lent a semblance of credibility to his writings, continued to do so. The Polish revolution (1830–31) provided a new impetus for Russophobia in Britain and for the activities of Evans. British opinion, as expressed in Parliament and in the press, was not indifferent to the Polish struggle for independence. Britain was neither preoccupied entirely with the Reform Bill campaign, nor deterred by 'revolutionary' causes, as has been suggested.[39] From the outset, the Polish revolution was extensively reported and generally acclaimed by the London press. Even Conservative papers like *The Morning Post* and *The Standard* endorsed the Polish cause.[40] *The Times* was particularly belligerent; it advocated foreign intervention to assist the Poles and, by late July, favoured British intervention. Depressed by the resignation of Prince Czartoryski and the fall of Warsaw in September, it deplored British inaction and the demise of Polish liberty.[41]

Earl Grey's government saw little scope for British initiatives during the crisis. Although Grey and Palmerston privately sympathised with the plight of the Poles, they never questioned the Tsar's right to suppress the insurrection. They were mainly concerned to prevent Prussia and Austria from joining the Tsar, in case that should provoke French intervention on behalf of the Poles. As the conflict had arisen at a time when France's foreign policy, following her own revolution of July 1830, was still unclear, Palmerston did not want the Eastern powers to become so embroiled in Poland that they could not resist France in the west, should it prove necessary to do so.[42] British protests on behalf of the Poles were limited to a mild remonstrance in March 1831, and to a disagreement over the Russian interpretation of the Polish clauses in the Treaty of Vienna, by which Russia's connection with Poland was ratified internationally. After the fall of Warsaw, Britain urged the Russians to temper their repressive policies. Throughout the conflict, the government had recognised that Britain could not intervene directly in Poland, and that it was imperative to retain 'the closest relations of friendship' with Russia. Diplomatic protests, therefore, were limited in tone and content and were not sustained once the revolt had been crushed.[43]

Evans, who had been elected Member of Parliament for Rye in March 1830,[44] readily embraced the Polish cause. In March 1831 he was listed as a steward for the dinner in honour of Marquess Wielopolski, the Polish envoy, but he missed the dinner on account of the agitation over the Reform Bill. Though not involved in the crucial parliamentary debate (Evans had lost his seat within five months of his election and did not regain it till April 1831), he was to the forefront of the popular protests in Sussex and Westminster.[45] By missing the dinner, Evans, like several M.P.s, including Sir Francis Burdett, the designated chairman of the occasion, indicated the degree of early interest in the Polish cause. Although there was genuine sympathy and support for the Poles in Britain, attention was not riveted upon them. During the Reform Bill crisis and the subsequent general election, domestic issues assumed a more immediate significance. Moreover, in 1831 there was no organisation that could mobilise support for Poland and co-ordinate the activities of the philo-Poles in Britain.

After the general election of 1831 Evans tried to arouse the House of Commons over the plight of the Poles. As the speech from the throne had barely mentioned the revolt, individual Members like Henry Hunt, Joseph Hume and Evans himself had had to raise the issue.

Incensed by ministerial indifference, Evans endeavoured to rally backbench support for 'the liberal cause throughout Europe'.⁴⁶ On 16th August 1831 he introduced the first parliamentary debate on Poland since the outbreak of the revolution. He declared that the Poles had been promised constitutional rights under the Treaty of Vienna, so reestablishing their country as a component of the European balance of power. By balance, he meant equality neither of power nor of territory, but of 'rights and station in the political society of Europe'. Since 1815, he argued, these rights had never been honoured: the press had been shackled, personal liberty infringed, and taxation inflicted by royal decree. As the Poles were now nobly resisting 'the Russian autocrat', he demanded information from the government about the policy of Prussia, a nominally neutral country, which he feared was assisting the Russian army. Lord Palmerston refused to present papers to Parliament, claiming that comment upon the behaviour of other nations in the conflict would be improper. Although three Members spoke in support of Evans, the prevailing mood of the House was profoundly apathetic, a reflection in Evans's view of 'the cold and feeble manner' in which he had spoken. Undoubtedly his speech, which included lengthy quotations from the Treaty of Vienna, may have bored the House, but an awareness of Britain's inability to influence events in eastern Europe was probably more important in inducing such apathy in the chamber.⁴⁷

Evans, if not an eloquent speaker, was at least tenacious. Passionately committed to Polish independence, he was not deterred by ministerial intransigence. He regarded the cause as above party politics,⁴⁸ one which enjoyed a broad measure of support in the United Kingdom. Within three weeks of his initial failure, he again drew the attention of the House to the war by presenting a petition of protest from the citizens of Westminster. He dwelt upon the consequences of the war — the disruption of trade, the spread of disease, and the possible repression of the Polish people. Supported by Sir Francis Burdett and Daniel O'Connell, he exhorted the government to intervene with the aim of halting 'this calamitous war'.⁴⁹

After the fall of Warsaw he reiterated his protests and his admiration for 'the spirit, bravery and patriotism' of the Poles. He demanded the production of government papers about the cause of the war, the policies pursued by Prussia, the mediation proposals of France, and the promises of Russia to observe Poland's constitutional rights. Lord Althorp, replying on behalf of the government, bluntly refused any papers on these sensitive issues. To produce them, he argued, would only impede the current round of diplomatic exchanges between Poland and Russia, and between Russia and all other countries. Evans promptly withdrew the request, expressing his hope that the House would not remain 'indifferent to the armed occupation of Poland'.[50]

Sympathy for the Poles mounted as reports were received in Britain of the horrendous atrocities perpetrated by the Russian troops. Buttressed by this growing sense of outrage, Evans continued his campaign inside and outside Parliament. Despite his fervent commitment, however, he was never a natural leader of the philo-Polish movement. He was neither a good speaker, nor particularly eminent, nor as well-connected as many of his colleagues. By contemporary standards he was also regarded as an 'advanced' Radical whose leadership would not be welcomed by those Whigs and Tories who identified with the Polish cause. Thomas Campbell, the poet, became the first president of the Literary Association of the Friends of Poland, founded on 25th February 1832. Subsequent presidents included Lord Dudley Stuart, an indefatigable philo-Pole, and Lords Harrowby, Houghton and Lytton. Under this distinguished patronage the association held regular meetings, published a monthly magazine, *Polonia*, annually commemorated the birthday of Kosciusko,[51] collected a library of Poloniana, and provided relief for distressed exiles.[52] Thomas Campbell acknowledged that the aim of the association was to reveal 'all the black and horrid facts of Russian cruelty' towards Poland.[53]

Within the House of Commons, Robert Cutlar Fergusson, a highly articulate M.P., who was then independent of the main parties, took the initiative in promoting Poland's cause. In April 1832, and again the following June, he opened debates on Poland, deploring the repressive policies of Russia since the fall of Warsaw. He enjoyed a wide measure of support in the House. During the debate on 28th June he gained endorsements not only from the Irish and Radical Members, but also from government supporters, Lords Sandon, Morpeth and Ebrington, and from the Opposition benches, notably Alexander Baring and Sir Robert Peel. But Fergusson could only muster a coalition which was so broadly based because he was merely seeking an expression of sympathy for the Polish predicament. Even so, there were disagreements among his supporters. Baring and Peel joined Palmerston and Sir Robert Inglis in deprecating the language with which some Irish and Radical Members had castigated the Tsar. And few Whigs or Tories applauded Evans when he demanded some action 'to vindicate the honour and consistency of this country', even at the risk of war with Russia. To the consternation of several Members, he advocated that Britain should fight alongside France 'in the cause of liberty'.[54] Palmerston, noticeably, did not defend the Tsar; he merely let the motion be carried without dissent, as it committed neither the House nor the government to any specific course of action.

Evans could not rest content with the mere expression of sympathy for the Polish people. Having urged British intervention during the revolution, he now believed that the post-revolutionary policies of Russia warranted retaliation by the Western powers. On 7th August 1832 he formally proposed that Britain should review her financial commitments to Russia, particularly the Russo-Dutch loan which had been arranged in 1815.[55] The idea had been broached in earlier debates; it involved linking two entirely separate aspects of the Treaty of Vienna, both of which had come under review since 1830. In the peace settlement, Castlereagh had gained Russian support for the creation of the Kingdom of the Netherlands by promising to pay, with the Dutch, the interest and sinking fund of part of a loan contracted by Russia in Holland before the Napoleonic Wars. Payment had been dependent upon the union of Holland and Belgium, but, as this had now ceased since the Belgian revolution of 1830, Britain was technically absolved from further payment. Non-payment, however, would have been dishonourable, as Britain had desired the separation, while Russia had opposed it. Accordingly, in a secret agreement between Palmerston and Prince Lieven, the Russian ambassador in London, on 16th November 1831, Britain had promised to continue her payments in return for Russian recognition of an independent Belgium.[56]

Linking the Russo-Dutch loan to the utterly irrelevant question of Poland was a dubious line of reasoning. To justify the connection, Evans argued that Russia had abrogated her treaty commitments to Poland, and had embarked upon a policy of territorial aggrandisement against her neighbours, Persia and Turkey. Denouncing the 'cruelty and perfidy' of the Tsar, he described Poland as languishing in 'misery and desolation' under 'the tyranny of her barbarous oppressor'. Palmerston was unimpressed. He rejected any connection between Poland and the Russo-Dutch loan, and deplored the strictures against Russian foreign policy. He claimed that Russia had been provoked by

Persia and Turkey, and that the Poles, not the Russians, had been the aggressors in the recent conflict. While the government stood fast, the philo-Poles divided among themselves. Radicals like Hume supported Evans, but some Members, like Lord Robert Grosvenor, doubted that any treaty had been broken, and several, including Sir Robert Inglis and Cressett Pelham, feared that Evans's proposal, if implemented, could lead to a war with Russia. Lord Sandon, after a vehement denunciation of Russian policy in Poland, questioned whether the government should change its line. Hitherto, he argued, the government had pursued 'a wise and temperate course', abstaining 'from interference, where the risk was great, and the chance of successful intervention doubtful'. Deserted by so many potential supporters, Evans withdrew his motion.[57]

The debates of 1832 had revealed many of the weaknesses of the philo-Polish group in Parliament. Beyond the expression of sympathy for the Poles, it could neither sway the government nor carry the House. As soon as the more extreme Members began vilifying the Tsar, rifts had opened within the group. Any suggestion of sanctions against Russia, or of interference by Britain, had merely widened those rifts. Several philo-Poles supported the government; they either doubted that Britain could intervene effectively or feared a war with Russia. Ministerial policy, therefore, had never been imperilled.

After the adjournment of Parliament, various groups, more or less affiliated to the Polish Association, mounted a carefully organised campaign throughout the country. They convened protest meetings in the large provincial towns and raised petitions to the King and to the Commons. Although the parliamentary petitions bore only fourteen hundred signatures (a relatively small number compared with contemporary anti-slavery petitions), they enabled the philo-Poles to renew their onslaught on Russian policy. Their agitation reached a climax on 9th July 1833, when Fergusson initiated a long debate in support of petitions from the Glasgow Polish Association and from the inhabitants of Birmingham. He proposed that the House should not recognise 'the present state and condition of Poland', a motion too extreme for philo-Poles, such as P. M. Stewart, Lord Sandon and Lord Ebrington. Fearing the possibility of war with Russia, they joined Opposition Members and ministerial supporters to defeat the motion by 177 votes to 95. Even so the motion had secured substantial support from the Irish and Radical Members, including Evans, and a sprinkling of votes from the Whig and Tory benches. It had prompted a sympathetic response from Palmerston, who explained that the government had protested over the incorporation of Poland into Russia. He also admitted that atrocities had occurred, but disputed that the issue merited the risk of general war. At a time of international tension over Belgium and Turkey, the debate had exacerbated Anglo-Russian relations, destroying the slight improvement which Lord Durham's mission to St Petersburg had effected the previous summer.[58]

Evans was bitterly disappointed. Almost one year previously he had realised that the agitation had flared too slowly to have any impact upon ministerial policy. He now criticised his parliamentary colleagues for failing to rally behind his earlier pronouncements on Poland during the revolution, when the government might have been able to act, had it been prodded into doing so.[59] Consumed by a sense of anticlimax, Evans could only press for some means of relief for the one hundred Polish exiles who were living in Britain. Like O'Connell, Dudley Stuart and Thomas Attwood, he tabled petitions pressing the government to follow the example of France and give aid to the Poles.[60] Initially the government refused, but it yielded eventually to continued pressure, authorising a grant of £10,000 to the exiles. This appropriation was renewed annually until 1852.

Though thwarted over Polish independence, Evans was at least consoled by the drift of British foreign policy under Palmerston's guidance. From 1832–33, Britain became increasingly identified with the so-called liberal cause in Europe. Palmerston seemingly relished the clash between conservative and liberal, or absolutist and constitutional, interests; he assumed the moral leadership of the liberal movement, so long as this served the interests of Great Britain. To ensure British interests in the Low Countries, he supported the Belgian nationalists, even countenancing the use of French troops to subdue the Dutch. To preserve the neutrality of Spain and Portugal during any war in which Britain might be involved, he backed the constitutional forces in the Peninsula. Indeed, he favoured the creation of a Quadruple Alliance between Portugal, Spain, Britain and France in 1834 as a moral blow against absolutism in Europe.[61] Evans heartily approved of these policies, and sought a similarly bold stand by Britain when the Eastern Question re-surfaced in 1833–34.[62]

The weakness of the Ottoman Empire had rekindled fears of Russian aggression. Faced with an ominously successful rebellion by the forces of the Egyptian Pasha, Mehemet Ali, in Syria and Asia Minor,

Mahmud II had appealed to Britain for help. But in 1832 Britain could not intervene in the Near East, as a portion of her fleet was blockading Holland, while other ships were assisting Queen Maria of Portugal against her reactionary uncle, Dom Miguel. Commissioning new ships would have been expensive, and would have enabled the Tories to attack the sanctions policy against Holland. Moreover, some members of Cabinet doubted that the Sultan either would survive or could resist Russia as effectively as Mehemet Ali. Britain did not proffer any assistance, and, as France strongly favoured the Egyptian Pasha, who had enrolled many French officers in his service, Mahmud was abandoned by his traditional allies. He turned to Russia, his historic adversary, and found Nicholas I willing to assist. Fearing the precedent of a successful revolution, and the prospect of a powerful 'Arab empire', under strong French influence, emerging in Asia Minor, Nicholas sent naval and military forces to defend Constantinople. Although this aid could not prevent the loss of Syria and the Adana district to Mehemet Ali, Russo-Turkish links were consummated in the Treaty of Unkiar-Skelessi (8th July 1833).

Evans was horrified by the spectre of Russian troops in Constantinople, apparently confirming his worst fears and trepidations. On 11th July he joined Henry Lytton Bulwer in requesting an account of British policy in the Near East. Understandably, Palmerston replied that publishing papers at this time would be premature. Expressing his 'full confidence in the honour and good faith of Russia', he assured the House that the Russian troops, who had entered the Turkish capital on a temporary basis, would withdraw once the emergency had passed. Evans was astonished. He insisted that Russian policy towards Poland and Turkey had always been 'marked by want of faith and honesty'. By failing to support the Sultan, he argued, Britain and France had missed a vital opportunity. He feared that the Russians would remain in 'continued occupation' of Constantinople, unless France and Britain undertook the necessary measures to preserve Turkey as an independent State. Unwilling to specify these measures, he merely hoped that the government would act with a 'little more vigour'.[63]

He was even more alarmed when the first report of the Treaty of Unkiar-Skelessi appeared in *The Morning Herald* of 21 August. As originally reported, this treaty confirmed the Adrianople agreement and the recent Greek agreement, provided for mutual assistance should either Russia or Turkey be attacked by a third party, and contained some secret articles. *The Herald's* correspondent stressed that the treaty had been furtively agreed between Russia and Turkey, and that it included provisions of an 'offensive and defensive' character.[64] Within three days of *The Herald's* report, Evans demanded an explanation of ministerial policy. Supported by Fergusson and Sir Robert Inglis, he pressed for the publication of papers about the treaty. Palmerston demurred; he assured the House that the government had not been officially informed of the treaty, and that he knew nothing about its contents save for the rumours in the press.[65]

Neither this statement nor subsequent assurances that every 'attention will be carefully directed' to events in the Near East[66] satisfied Evans. As soon as the treaty was ratified, an abstract of its contents was published in *The Morning Herald*, disclosing the promise of the Sultan to close the Straits to foreign warships in time of war.[67] Although this provision merely codified existing practice in international law, as embodied in the Anglo-Turkish Treaty of 1809, some Western observers believed that it would enable Russian warships to move through the Straits without fear of attack.[68] This suspicion, though groundless, had aroused 'great anxiety', a point raised by Evans after the Christmas recess. Concerned about the lack of any British initiative, he criticised the government for letting Russia gain too much influence over Turkey. Advocating a prompt British initiative to prevent further encroachments, he recommended that an alliance should be concluded with Mehemet Ali, so establishing 'a barrier between Russia and our Indian possessions, to the south of Hellespont'.[69] But the suggestion failed to elicit a ministerial response: it had been raised during the debate on the King's Speech, when foreign policy was only one of many topics under discussion.

Evans had to wait until a formal motion was tabled on 17th March 1834 by Richard Sheil, the M.P. for Tipperary, renewing the demand for papers about the Russo-Turkish treaty. Palmerston again refused. In an extensive review of British policy he explained that, since the government had been unable to assist Turkey, it had not complained of Russian intervention. It had accepted Russia's promise to withdraw her forces after the successful defence of Constantinople, and the promise had been honoured. The government, Palmerston admitted, had been concerned initially about the naval clause in the treaty, but had received assurances from both contracting parties that it did not discriminate in favour of Russian warships. Evans was far from mollified. He refused to accept that Britain had lacked the means to intervene on behalf of the Sultan; he insisted that Britain and France 'in close alliance' could have acted decisively in this region. Their failure to do so, he argued, had brought Turkey to a low ebb, a condition merely ratified by the Treaty of Unkiar-Skelessi. He maintained, quite wrongly, that the treaty, by barring the Dardenelles to a British fleet in wartime, had precipitated 'a most serious and injurious change', altering the balance of power in the Near East. Again he urged the government to promote 'the Pasha of Egypt as a counterpoise against Russia in that quarter of the world'.[70]

Evans's preference for dramatic British initiatives, at the side of France, evoked little support from the House and less interest from the government. Palmerston rightly perceived that Russia was unlikely to embark on any immediate aggressive move in the Near East. Nicholas I was more interested in containing the forces of revolution and international discord than in promoting purely Russian interests. As the Tsar still wished to co-operate with Austria and Britain, Palmerston could reasonably expect that the *status quo* would be maintained. He believed that Turkey could be preserved by avoiding further friction between Mahmud and Mehemet Ali. As he assured Earl Granville, 'while we have a good fleet in the Mediterranean we can answer for Mehemet's peaceableness'.[71]

Evans, in sum, had had relatively little influence upon British policy towards Tsarist Russia. In promoting Russophobic views he had proved more effective as a pamphleteer than as a politician. His two books had at least generated a debate about the aims of Russian foreign policy. While the first had stimulated a wide-ranging debate in the metropolitan press and in some periodicals, the second had provoked an official review of Russian capabilities in central Asia and of the defences of the North West Frontier. Admittedly, neither his assumptions nor his proposals had gained ministerial approval. Indeed, his persistent advocacy of intervention by Britain, in collaboration with France, ensured fairly limited support in the House of Commons and the philo-Polish movement. Although Evans never tempered his *penchant* for extreme proposals, he increasingly supported Palmerston's policy, in as much as it identified with the 'liberal cause' in Europe (in June 1835 he accepted command of the British Auxiliary Legion which assisted the Constitutional forces in Spain). Nevertheless, he had displayed a zealous commitment to the Polish cause and a profound fear of Russian intentions: as a

Russophobe, he had blazed a trail which David Urquhart and others would eagerly follow.[72]

3
An advanced Reformer

In May 1830 Evans realised his ambition of becoming a Member of Parliament. Having established his political credentials as a Russophobe and a champion of Polish nationalism, he had more to offer as a prospective politician than merely a distinguished war record. His prospects, nonetheless, were limited. Lacking any property, and thus the influence derived from property, he could only aspire to become the representative of an open borough.[1] Such an opportunity arose when Henry Bonham, the Member for Rye, a freeman borough, accepted the Chiltern Hundreds. Samuel Miller, a prominent member of the Rye Independent Association, and a friend of Evans, asked him to stand for election.

By accepting this request, Evans was not raising the standard of any Radical cause. The Rye Independent Association was a body of respectable citizens, seeking limited electoral reform. William Holloway, chairman of the election committee, denied any Radical intent. While he favoured the removal of rotten boroughs, the restoration of triennial Parliaments, and the enfranchisement of county ratepayers, he insisted that 'the men of Rye were not radicals — they did not wish to subvert the Constitution, but they wished to restore ancient rights and principles'.[2] Rye was a freeman borough in name only. Whereas there had been 102 freemen in 1702, there were only sixteen in 1826, despite a doubling of the population.[3] The town had become little more than a pocket borough, with the corporation under the sway of the Lamb family. The Reverend Dr George Lamb dominated local politics, even installing his brother-in-law, the Reverend William Dodgson, a parson from Lincolnshire, as mayor in 1826. In the same year incensed local citizens, who had been denied their voting rights in the courts, formed the Rye Independent Association. They claimed the right to vote in as much as they paid parochial taxes, the scot-and-lot taxes. Restoring rights and privileges, enshrined in local charters and records, remained their main objective. As Holloway insisted, universal suffrage was not their aim: a restrictive franchise, excluding soldiers, paupers and other disreputable groups, still held its attractions; it would, he thought, encourage paupers 'to strive against their pauperism' and so ease the burden of parish relief.[4]

Evans furtively entered Rye on the eve of the poll. Early next morning, 1st March, 1830, he canvassed the freemen of the borough, securing three promises of support. As he also promised to bring a petition before the House of Commons in the event of his defeat, the association endorsed him. The election was held at the town hall, where Lamb's candidate, Frederick Pusey, duly received the endorsement of his patron and the majority of the corporation. Evans demanded a poll, and speedily obtained the votes of three freemen, three sons of freemen, and of a large body of citizens who paid scot-and-lot taxes. His supporters swamped the fourteen votes for Pusey, but the mayor discounted all votes other than those of the corporation, declaring Pusey duly elected.[5] Displaying commendable persistence, Evans challenged the result before a select committee of the House of Commons. Briefed by Miller and Thomas Edwards, a local expert on the charters and records of Rye, he proved successful – the votes of his supporters were accepted as valid and his election was recognised on 14th May. A month later, Evans returned to Rye to receive a tumultuous reception. Driving through the streets in a barouche, drawn by six greys, and escorted by members of the association on horseback, he received an ecstatic welcome. Hundreds of people thronged the route. Banners, flags and flowers garlanded the town. Speeches and poems were read in his honour; a band played 'See, the conquering hero comes'. After a dinner for 200 supporters at the George Inn, his health was toasted heartily. As Holloway claimed, the new Member of Parliament had crowned the struggles of the past five years: he had brought 'Liberty' to the port of Rye. Moved by these accolades, Evans apologised for his lack of oratorical eloquence, paid tribute to the work of the association, and hoped 'that the noble example set by the borough of Rye may find numerous worthy imitators . . .'.[6]

His triumph was destined not to last. The death of George IV precipitated a general election. The poll in Rye began on Friday 30th July and ended on Monday 2nd August, with nearly all the time consumed in legal argument. The mayor refused to heed the report of the select committee. Acting on the advice of his assessor, he maintained that anyone who wished to vote should have applied to the Court of King's Bench for a *mandamus* (at a cost of about £200), to show that they had done everything in their power to establish their legal rights. Corporation votes, in other words, would decide the outcome of the election. Lamb's candidates, Colonel Baillie and Francis R. Bonham, received fourteen and twelve votes respectively; Evans and his reforming colleague, Benjamin Smith, gained six apiece.[7] A petition against the result was rejected the following December.

Having experienced such success and frustration in a mere six months of political activity, Evans was not about to leave the fray. In the first place, the general election had greatly weakened the government of the Duke of Wellington. The sweeping successes it had so confidently expected had failed to materialise: the government had lost prestige as a consequence. Secondly, the tide seemed to be flowing in favour of Reform. At the hustings, protests had erupted against the electoral system and the dominance of magnates and boroughmongers. Electoral control, which had encountered growing opposition throughout the 1820s, had now become extremely unpopular in many boroughs and counties. In the new Parliament many Whigs and some Tories accepted that opposing Reform would raise more dangers than conceding it. The risings in France and the southern Netherlands, the disruption of trade, and the growth and militance of the trade union movement only increased their alarm.[8] In these circumstances Evans sought to establish himself as the popular champion of Rye.

He cultivated the constituency assiduously. He travelled down from London for the various meetings and dinners of the Rye Independent Association. At the Red Lion Inn, on 24th September 1830, he assured supporters that he would never withdraw until their rights 'were fully obtained and firmly secured'.[9] Less than a month later, he encountered another exuberant welcome on entering the town and was toasted and cheered at a public dinner.[10] He wrote expansive letters to the local press, outlining the peculiar rights and status of the Cinque Ports as embodied in their Great Paramount Charters. Indulging in wild hyperbole, he described his defeat in August as the 'most wanton and unparalleled outrage on the laws and constitution of the country'. He was even more distressed when the Commons overruled his appeal against the result; henceforth, he wrote, Rye could promote its interests most effectively by uniting with other towns and constituencies in demanding Reform – 'this one great common and Constitutional object'.[11]

Evans took the lead in the renewed agitation. Addressing a couple of hundred supporters after a dinner in the Red Lion, on 31 December, he urged them to petition the new King, 'for it was useless, in his opinion, to petition the House of Commons, so long as two thirds of that house was composed of men who were in the same predicament as the present patron of the town of Rye'.[12] He co-ordinated the protests on a regional basis. On 27th January 1831 he attended a Cinque Ports reform dinner with Henry Shirley and William Fraser, the Reform candidates for Winchelsea and Hythe. Influence, argued Evans, was all-pervasive throughout the county of Sussex. Of its twenty-eight Members, he calculated, twenty-four 'were under the dictation of the aristocracy' or, more precisely, 'were nominated by eleven individuals'.[13] He believed that the system was not only unfair and corrupt but the basis of a ruinous and incompetent government. As he informed an audience at Hastings, indulging 'the oligarchial faction' had saddled the country with debt, reduced half the people to pauperism, and plunged the country into needless and expensive wars over American independence and the French Revolution.[14] Evans, in short, had broadened his rhetorical attacks while consolidating his political base. Dubbed 'the idol of the Cinque Ports', he had firmly established himself as a favourite in Rye[15] and had integrated the political demands of his own supporters into a regional, even a national cause.

The terms of the first Reform Bill, published on 1st March 1831, added further impetus to his campaigning. The Duke of Wellington's government had fallen on 16th November, to be replaced by a coalition of Whigs and Canningites under Earl Grey. The Whigs feared social disorder and attacks on property unless parliamentary reform was conceded. To allay the signs of discontent, the Cabinet concluded that the reforms would have to be substantial and sweeping by contemporary standards. Hence the Bill proposed not only a wholesale redistribution of seats, enfranchising many large towns for the first time and removing numerous rotten boroughs, but also a broader franchise, adding £10-a-year copyholders and £50-a-year leaseholders to the county roll while enfranchising £10 householders in the boroughs.[16]

Within two days of the Bill's publication, Evans returned to Rye to mobilise local support. He called upon his supporters – some 300 to 400 attended the meeting – to send an address to the King applauding 'the admirable plan of the Ministers'.[17] He had reservations about the Bill. As he explained to an audience of nearly 3,000 at Hastings, vote by ballot and triennial Parliaments should have been included. Nevertheless, the Bill represented a great improvement over 'the present disgraceful system', and the possibility of adding 500,000 voters to the electoral roll and of abolishing 169 rotten boroughs should be welcomed.[18] Returning to Westminster, he attended the meeting of reformers in the Crown and Anchor tavern in the Strand, on 4th March. He delivered a militant, if not very audible, speech, predicting that 8,000 or 10,000 men might march on London from the south coast should the Bill be defeated. 'The only question', he was reported as saying, was whether the Bill 'should be settled in an amicable manner, or amidst anarchy, confusion and bloodshed'.[19] He later wrote to *The Morning Chronicle*, protesting that he had been misrepresented and noting that the reports of his speech differed from paper to paper. What he had meant to say was 'that with all these alarming symptoms of confusion, and even anarchy, so much to be deprecated and deplored, I did most earnestly hope that a useless opposition might not be persevered in'.[20]

Like reformers throughout the country, Evans recognised that popular clamour was the only means by which parliamentary opinion might be swayed in favour of Reform. These tactics proved successful. A huge majority against the Bill, as forecast by the Tory whips, soon evaporated. On 23rd March the Bill passed its second reading by the barest of majorities – one vote. After the Easter recess the Tories regrouped round an amendment to the motion for going into committee. They defeated the government by eight votes on 20th April, whereupon Grey persuaded the King to grant a dissolution. A general election followed, with the polling in Rye due to occur on 28th April.

Evans, who had spent some £4,000 in campaign expenses, required financial support to enter the lists again. Sir John Cam Hobhouse, Member for Westminster, advised him to seek the nomination at Preston, for which he would receive £1,000 from the Whig funds in Brooks's Club if he displaced the ultra-Radical, Henry Hunt. Evans, however, arrived too late for the Preston contest, and was persuaded by several members of the Rye Association, who had pursued him to Lancashire, to return to Rye.[21] In the ensuing election Lamb resolved upon a last-ditch resistance. He hired eighteen Bow Street runners and a gang of labourers, enrolled as special constables, to escort his supporters to the hustings. He also sent for a detachment of customs officers to come to Mountfield House, where his supporters would assemble on the morning of the election. By mistake, these men marched past the market house, where the local townsfolk had gathered. Incensed, the populace tore down an iron fence and armed themselves with paving stones and iron railings.

The uproar and confusion only compounded the tactics of intimidation used by Holloway and his associates. 'Every obstacle', he recalled, was thrown in the way of corporation members who refused to support the popular candidates.[22] After the first day's polling Evans held a narrow lead, with several corporation freemen too frightened to vote. On the following day Lamb deployed two companies of the 7th Dragoon Guards and a body of customs officers on the outskirts of the town. Refusing to be overawed, Evans's supporters mustered again, erected barricades, and even threatened to ignite a massive bonfire in the streets. Unable to reach the poll, Lamb accepted a compromise: he agreed upon the election of one member from the town and one from the corporation. Evans and Pemberton were duly elected, with seven and five votes respectively. 'No election,' claimed Evans, 'in ancient Greece, nor even in America could be more popular than his was.'[23]

As a Member of Parliament, Evans proved fastidious in his constituency duties. Following the election, he gave a ball at the George Inn for the ladies of Rye. Some 200 people attended, where the colonel was the perfect host, dancing nearly the whole night with his guests. As a local reporter noted, 'Rich and poor were intermixed in a happy maze .... There was neither waltz, gallopade, quadrille nor redonwackzhs; but all joined in the true old English country dance'.[24] Repeatedly over the next eighteen months, Evans returned to Rye to address public meetings, attend dinners, and meet his constituents. His attentiveness contrasted sharply with the indifference and disdain of Pemberton, a point emphasised in the local press.[25] His willingness to keep in touch with his constituents and to attend and vote in Parliament, save where illness interceded, earned him plaudits in Sussex. 'The diligence and exertion' of Evans, wrote the *Brighton Guardian*,

bear a striking contrast to the indifference and thoughtlessness of those pretended Reformers, who are willing, even at this crisis, to sacrifice all their political duties to their own pleasures and the enjoyments of the field.[26]

Evans, however, cut a less impressive figure in the House of Commons. Unversed in its ways, he was not familiar with the procedural requirements and foundered, on several occasions, in presenting petitions and in raising motions for debate.[27] He was not a good speaker and was extremely conscious of making 'very bad' speeches.[28] Lacking powers of imagery and rhetoric, he relied upon factual data and lengthy quotations. He was always liable to misrepresentation, partly because his speeches were not entirely audible, and partly because his points were not clearly and coherently made. His endorsement of the ballot and triennial Parliaments bracketed him with the more extreme Radicals in the House. A comparatively tiny bloc in the unreformed Parliament, the Radicals could exert little influence upon a Whig government which had just been returned to office with a majority of 130 to 140. Given these circumstances, and his own limitations, Evans was unlikely to figure prominently in the proceedings.

Apart from promoting the Polish cause, the main issue he adopted was the maintenance of public order. Having witnessed intimidation and the excessive use of military force at the recent elections, he sounded the tocsin over this question. Although he accepted that the military and the auxiliary forces had a legitimate rôle in preserving public order, he feared that excessive reliance upon them could prove provocative and counter-productive. He deplored the Yeomanry, whose reputation had been blackened by the Peterloo massacre, and believed that regular troops were about 'ten times' more efficient than irregular troops in policing duties; he always preferred using the former, especially during disturbances in Ireland.[29] Nevertheless, he was reluctant to rely upon military force. Indeed, he claimed that the Tories, by eschewing Reform, had provoked public disorder, and would do so again if re-elected without any reforming commitment. He conjured the emotive prospect of a 'government of the sword', a taunt which Sir Robert Peel found deeply offensive and quite irresponsible in view of the ferment raised over parliamentary reform.[30]

Unabashed, Evans continued to champion popular liberties against any semblance of oppression. He had already taken this issue to the forefront of parliamentary attention by raising the recent judgement involving Thomas and Caroline Deacle, a gentleman farmer and his wife, from Marwell Farm, Hampshire. The couple had been arrested on a charge of conspiracy in November 1830, following the agricultural disturbances in the county, when the 'Captain Swing' movement 'attained its greatest momentum'.³¹ Handcuffed, manhandled, and dragged from their home, the Deacles were thrown into jail and later brought before the Winchester assizes. At their trial, all charges against them were dropped as the evidence was revealed as pure fabrication. Deacle pressed charges against six magistrates for unlawful and violent arrest, trespass and assault. The charges were examined at the assizes in July. The Hampshire jury found all the magistrates innocent save Bingham Baring, a wealthy landowner, whom they found guilty of assault. Deacle was awarded £50 damages. The paucity of the award caused surprise locally, and newspaper comment was generally critical of Bingham Baring.³²

On 21st July 1831 Evans raised the case in Parliament, requesting information about the charges which had been laid against the Deacles. Should the verdicts of the two courts be upheld, he argued, Baring should be removed from the magistrates' bench. Francis Baring, the Member for Portsmouth, vigorously defended his cousin. He claimed that the magistrates had had to act as they did, at a time when 'the whole country was full of mobs', in view of detailed evidence against the Deacles and a convicted felon, Boyes. 'It was of no consequence', he added, that the evidence was not substantiated at the trial; indeed, it was significant that there were 'no more outrages in that part of the country' after the warrants were served. Sergeant Wilde, who had assisted in the prosecution, was even more opposed to reopening the case lest it should inhibit the future conduct of other magistrates. Rather than throw obloquy on the magistracy, he believed they should be encouraged to enforce the law in a manner which both 'commanded respect' and 'inspired terror'.³³ These sentiments merely inflamed the controversy. The Deacles were furious that the case, which had been raised in Parliament without their knowledge or consent, should have resulted in a further impugning of their character. Having lost a tenancy as a consequence of the debate, they petitioned Parliament in protest, clearly expecting Evans to press for a committee of enquiry. Initially he delayed tabling a motion, in case of further legal proceedings (so enraging the Deacles further).³⁴ When it was clear that Baring would not appeal the decision Evans moved for the appointment of a select committee, only to find the government solidly arraigned against him. The Attorney-General stated that justice had been done, and that the House could not be turned into a court of appeal. The motion fell by thirty-one votes to seventy-eight.³⁵

Although Evans had raised a highly sensitive issue in a temperate and moderate manner – and was duly thanked on this account by Baring[36] – he had done little to assist the Deacles. Failing to consult them, in the first instance, was a blunder. Equally short-sighted was raising an issue about which 'he knew nothing' save what he had read in the press.[37] Admittedly, he was not primarily concerned with the interests of the couple; he had only raised the case because it involved 'a serious question respecting the liberty of the subject and magisterial authority'.[38] Evans never realised that using their case to draw attention to more abstract issues could further embarrass the Deacles. Once he had raised the issue, he was caught on the horns of a dilemma. While other Radicals, like Joseph Hume, and the Deacles pressed him to seek a committee of enquiry, he knew from the immediate response of the government front bench that any motion was bound to fail. His subsequent prevarications only antagonised the Deacles and ensured a more humiliating *dénouement*. His first parliamentary sortie had not been a success.

Evans rarely participated in the debates over parliamentary reform. Although he had voted in favour of the second and third readings of the Reform Bill, he seldom offered an opinion in the chamber. This silence had been deliberate, as he later explained to a Reform meeting, which had convened in the Covent Garden market for the purpose of petitioning the House of Lords. Parliament, he stated, possessed less power than it imagined in forwarding or retarding the measure. 'All power,' he declared, lay 'with the people'; they had favoured the Bill and would not be thwarted by the House of Lords. Indeed, he doubted that the Lords would defy 'the King, the Government, and the People'.[39] This confidence proved utterly misplaced. On 8th October 1831 the Lords rejected the Bill, precipitating another wave of popular protest and agitation. Evans threw his energies into the protest movement. He joined the committee of the Metropolitan Political Union, chaired by Sir Francis Burdett, one of the M.P.s for Westminster. But, like Burdett, he resigned from this body as it evolved into the more militant working-class body, the National Political Union. Evans feared public disorder; he urged people to refrain from 'turbulence and clamour' lest they assist the anti-reformers.[40] He also took a prominent part in the provincial Reform movement, joining other reformers in Sussex in deploring the veto of the Lords.[41]

As the Reform movement became more and more difficult to

control, with riots erupting in many parts of the country, Evans shared the fears of some Rye constituents for the safety of their property. Swallowing his distaste for irregular troops, he wrote to the Earl of Egremont, the Lord Lieutenant of Sussex, and later to the Duke of Wellington, as Warden of the Cinque Ports, requesting permission to raise a body of Volunteer or Yeomanry infantry. Appalled at the idea of Evans heading a corps of Volunteers, the Duke promptly rejected the request. As the militant tide soon receded, Evans was not too downcast by the rejection. He merely assured the Duke that the inhabitants of Rye would always be ready to assist in preserving 'the public peace' and 'the institutions of their county'.[42]

After the Christmas recess, Evans returned to the Commons ready to embrace an ever-expanding range of Radical causes. He denounced the effects of the purchase system in the army, especially the ability of wealthy young officers to purchase promotion and even regimental command over the heads of older and more experienced men. He supported the abolition of flogging in the peacetime army. And he earned the everlasting distrust of the Horse Guards by advocating the wholesale reduction of the military establishment, including two military hospitals, two schools for military orphans, the waggon train, the Yeomanry, the remainder of the Militia, the regimental depot reserves, district recruiting establishments, the royal arms factories, foreign half-pay lists, the Household Troops of Cavalry and Foot Guards, and the number of officers assigned to each regiment.[43] He also pressed the government to act more vigorously in foreign affairs. Aware that the Whig government supported the claims of Doña Maria over those of her uncle, Dom Miguel, to the throne of Portugal, he urged them to recognise her as queen. As Evans did not realise the desperate plight of the exiled Doña Maria and her supporters, his exhortations were duly ignored.[44]

Apart from voting, he still took little interest in the debates on parliamentary reform. When the crisis erupted in May, as the Lords supported the motion of Lord Lyndhurst to postpone the disfranchising clauses in the Bill and the Cabinet offered to resign, Evans again took his protests to the people. Addressing a crowded and emotive meeting at the Crown and Anchor, he endorsed measures of civil disobedience. Non-payment of taxes, he argued, would be 'infinitely preferable to the prostration of a vast empire before a base and grasping Oligarchy'.[45] He deplored the prospect of another government headed by the Duke of Wellington. The Duke had bartered 'the well earned glories of military victory, for the doubtful honours of a political career'.[46] But it was soon clear that the Tories could not form a government. The Duke and Lyndhurst promised the King that they would not oppose the Bill further. William IV recalled Grey and gave him full authority to create additional peers if necessary. On 4th June 1832 the Lords passed the Reform Bill.

Henceforth the shortcomings of the Reform Act became more and more apparent. Evans was alarmed by the restrictions of the franchise, especially the disfranchisement of scot-and-lot voters who had not paid their rates at the time of registration. He foresaw a massive reduction in the voting roll of Westminster, which had formerly exceeded 18,500 electors.[47] Even more worrying, from his own point of view, were the boundary changes introduced by the English Boundary Act of 1832. By its provisions, the borough of Rye would be expanded from 1·6 square miles to 32·3, incorporating the towns of Rye and Winchelsea, the parishes of Rye, Peasemarch, Iden, Playden, Winchelsea, East Guildford, Icklesham, Udimer and part of Brede. Of the 379 voters, only 217 lived in Rye.[48] Aware that his prospects of re-election were slight in a sprawling, largely agricultural constituency, Evans resolved to stand in both Rye and Westminster in the general election of December 1832.

The result in Rye was never in doubt. In fact Evans spent most of the election campaigning in the capital. Local power in the Rye borough passed from the Lamb family to the Curteis family of Windwell Hill, Hurstmonceux. Captain Edward Barrett Curteis, a younger son of this wealthy land-owning family, contested Rye. The corporation voted solidly against Evans, while the Tories regarded Curteis, a Whig, as the lesser of two evils. Curteis had considerable influence in the agricultural part of the constituency. He was also prepared, according to the local press, to sway voters by bribery and intimidation. Evans, meanwhile, had antagonised some of his own supporters by his extreme Radicalism and his reluctance to devote all his energies to the Rye campaign. In a sixty-nine per cent poll, he was defeated by 162 votes to 128. He never contested Rye again.[49]

In Westminster he experienced even more difficulties. His candidature reflected a split in the constituency over Sir John Hobhouse, one of the Members of Parliament. Hobhouse had first been elected for the Radical bastion of Westminster in 1819. Over the years his views had steadily moderated, with any Radicalism becoming less and less evident once he had accepted office under Lord

Grey. On 18th November a delegation of electors had called on Hobhouse seeking a pledge from him to vote in favour of shorter Parliaments, the ballot, and the repeal of certain taxes. He refused to do so. Like his parliamentary colleague, Sir Francis Burdett, he would not be mandated on how he should vote in the Commons. Dissatisfied constituents, headed by Francis Place and Thomas Prout, a tradesman from the Strand, pressed Evans to stand against Hobhouse.[50]

The colonel opened his campaign with an ingenuous letter to Burdett, offering to unite with him against Hobhouse. Burdett dismissed the notion with contempt.[51] Evans riposted by describing Hobhouse as 'the comparatively silent ornament of the Treasury bench',[52] and by unfurling an extensive list of Radical commitments. At the Crown and Anchor, on 22nd November, he promised his support for shortened Parliaments, the ballot and the repeal of taxes on paper, printing, houses and windows. He favoured the abolition of tithes, and the separation of Church and State, 'some reform' in Ireland, and fiscal retrenchment. He pledged his support for the abolition of slavery and military flogging.[53] Over the next three weeks he toured the parishes, reiterating these themes. He expanded upon his commitments, pledging opposition to the Corn Laws and reminding electors of his support for Polish nationalism. He embraced local issues, condemning the unpopular Metropolitan Police and the new Hackney Coach Act, which had enraged shopkeepers by enabling drivers to stop in any part of the street. He drew clear distinctions between his policies and Hobhouse's, noting that the latter, as Secretary at War, had rejected his proposal to reduce the army by 9,000 men. Above all, he challenged the representative notion of democracy. The 'testiness and fretfulness' exhibited by Hobhouse over the subject of pledging was 'a strong indication of the necessity of demanding pledges'. He envisaged the new reformed Parliament as essentially a 'Peoples' Parliament in which Members gave preference to their constituents' interests over those of any administration.[54]

Evans was an active and hard-working candidate. As the campaign developed he drew larger and more vociferous audiences. He clearly had substantial popular support, albeit a support based largely on hostility to Hobhouse. Evans himself exhibited little charisma on the hustings. He performed poorly at the eve-of-poll nomination meeting in front of St Paul's Church, Covent Garden. Sir Denis Le Marchant, Lord Althorp's private secretary, attended and was profoundly unimpressed. He described Evans as 'Tall and thin, with very sallow complexion, and jet black hair and whiskers, one might almost have mistaken him for an Italian assassin'.[55] Le Marchant thought even less of Evans's hour-long speech, read from notes, which seemed 'ill-adapted to the audience' and received only 'moderate' applause. The crowd had come not to hear Evans but to shout, yell and throw mud at Hobhouse.[56] But the mob was not representative of the Westminster electorate. Burdett and Hobhouse polled 3,248 and 3,214 votes respectively, leaving Evans trailing with 1,076. The superior organisation and canvassing of the constituency loyalists, under Thomas De Vear, helped the incumbents. So, too, did the absence of any Tory candidate, and the extreme Radicalism espoused by Evans. The colonel had stampeded many of the Tory voters, especially in the wealthy St George's parish, into the Hobhouse camp.

Understandably, Evans resented his double defeat at the polls. The size of the Westminster reverse was particularly galling, especially in view of the derisory turn-out (less than 40 per cent). He did not believe that the issues had been 'fairly tested' in view of the support for Hobhouse from the government, several London papers, and from both Tories and some Radicals in the constituency. On 12th March 1833 he aired these feelings in a rambling letter of over forty pages, addressed to the electors of Westminster. The letter, though ostensibly concerned with the prevalence of military and naval sinecures, was essentially a defence of his candidature and a *résumé* of his diatribes against Hobhouse. Evans claimed that he had been misrepresented throughout the campaign. As a Member of Parliament he had never been utterly hostile to the Whig government; he had neither vilified nor reviled them. Although unconnected with the Whigs, he had usually 'endeavoured to render them support'.[57] In short, he was trying to modify his political image without trimming any of his policy commitments.

He would soon be able to test this approach. In a key election promise Sir John Hobhouse had joined Burdett in giving explicit assurances that they would vote for the repeal of the house and window taxes. They believed Lord Althorp, who had promised that the government, if re-elected, would remove the assessments as soon as possible. In late April 1833, however, Althorp announced that the government had reneged on its promise, whereupon Hobhouse resigned not only his ministerial office but also his seat at Westminster. He offered himself for re-election, facing challenges from Evans and from Bickham Escott, a Tory candidate. From 3rd to 11th May a turbulent by-election campaign convulsed the constituency. Voters gathered in the various parishes to pass motions censoring or approving the resignation. Several Members of Parliament joined the fray, with Daniel Whittle Harvey, the M.P. for Colchester, denouncing Hobhouse's failure to vote for repeal of the taxes. A fighting fund was raised for Evans when Colonel Hodges, a former comrade-in-arms, told supporters that Evans could not 'measure his purse' against the opposition: he had to have financial support.[58]

The election proved violent, with the worst scenes occurring on nomination day, 7th May, in Covent Garden. As Sir John Hobhouse recalled:

But the moment I got into the Market the disturbance began: and it was not without difficulty, not to say danger, that I got within the rails of the church portico. The people were ferocious, and, if they had got me down, I should never have arisen again. I saw many of my Committee, 'well tried through many a varying year,' now ranged with my opponents.[59]

To his credit, Evans tried repeatedly to calm the mob and ensure a hearing for his opponent. He had also learnt from his previous nomination meeting, and kept his speech as brief as possible. Nevertheless, he rounded on Hobhouse, criticising him for resigning his seat instead of voting for repeal of the house and window taxes. Indeed, he cast doubt on whether Hobhouse had actually resigned his office, an imputation which the latter deeply resented.[60]

After two days' polling, Evans triumphed completely. He carried seven of the ten parishes, winning by 2,027 votes to Hobhouse's 1,875. The results, as reported in the local press,[61] are shown in Table 1. The outcome reflected a massive swing of opinion since the previous December. Hobhouse had undoubtedly lost votes to the Tory candidate, especially in St George's parish, but he had lost even more support on account of his waning Radicalism and new image as 'an Establishment figure'.[62] Evans had profited accordingly; he had almost doubled his vote, emerging as the new standard-bearer of Radicalism in Westminster. The Radical press rejoiced; the *Morning Advertiser* applauded the return of the 'independent and consistent candidate – Colonel Evans', while *The Freeman's Journal* attributed the result to 'the ascendancy of the people'.[63]

Evans drew appropriate lessons from his victory. He had sensed the depth of feeling and passion in the constituency during the campaign.

Table 1

Parish	Evans	Hobhouse	Escott
St Martin's	457	285	93
St James's	391	343	97
St George's	270	697	339
St John's	246	89	52
St Margaret's	234	182	50
St Clement Dane's	223	116	95
St Paul's	31	37	4
St Anne's	142	110	17
St Mary's	26	8	10
Savoy	7	8	1
Total	2,027	1,875	738

After the final results were announced in Covent Garden, on 11th May, he addressed his delighted supporters upon 'the great cause' of their triumph, namely the furor over the house and window taxes. He pledged that as a Member of Parliament he would 'advert to them and repudiate them on every occasion that was in his power'.[64] At a victory dinner in the Eyre Arms tavern, St John's Wood, on 29th May, he explained his priorities as a newly elected Member. Flanked by several colleagues from the Commons, including Daniel O'Connell and Patrick Lalor, Evans reiterated his campaign promises. He rejected the suggestion, which had circulated on the eve of the election, that he was basically a military officer and not a dedicated politician. He wished to serve the citizens of Westminster; indeed, he declared, in a statement which would rebound upon him two years later, that he had 'no desire to perform any duties for them in his military capacity'. He could not emulate the oratorical eloquence of Fox or Sheridan – previous Members for Westminster – but offered 'good sense and honesty' instead. He disdained any income from government and pledged himself to champion the Radical cause. He feared that Reform had stagnated since 1832 apart from the prospect of the emancipation of the Jewry. The size of the military estimates, the failure to repeal the house and window duties, the retention of the Corn Laws, and the scale of compensation proposed for slave owners simply confirmed that 'the Reformed Parliament ... was not a whit better than the unreformed ...'.[65]

Determined to honour his election pledges, Evans immediately raised the issue of house and window duties in Parliament. These taxes had been a profound source of grievance, particularly to middle-class householders. In 1798 William Pitt had combined the taxes for the purpose of funding the war effort. Although their rate had been considerably reduced and some trade exemptions had been extended in 1825, the taxes still yielded over £2½ million in 1833. Theoretically, the window tax was the more objectionable. It was a tax on light and air, discouraging ventilation and the improvement of poorer dwellings. It was inequitable, as the number of windows in a house indicated neither its value nor the means of its occupier. But the house tax aroused even more fury. It was levied on all houses, excluding farmhouses, valued at £10 a year or more. The assessments seemed less than fair, being based upon the annual value to let. As the annual value to let of very large houses was assumed to be negligible, baronial homes, mansions and country houses were comparatively lightly taxed. The mansion of the Duke of Norfolk in St James's Square was rated at £1,000, precisely the same assessment as the London Tavern. While Northumberland House was rated at £1,500 and paid tax at 4½d per square foot, a neighbouring grocer's shop was charged at 7s per square foot. In short, a disproportionate burden of tax was born by middle-class residents, the core of Evans's political support.[66]

Evans, who had been briefed on these taxes by Francis Place,[67] pressed for their repeal within ten days of his election. He emphasised the distress of his constituents, arguing that the taxation only aggravated the plight of shopkeepers during a period of dwindling receipts. Half the inhabitants of Regent Street were in a state of insolvency, and so were nearly half the tradesmen of the Strand. Almost all the houses and shopkeepers let rooms to lodgers 'from absolute necessity'. He did not accept that repeal could only be implemented by substituting an income tax to raise the same revenue. Massive savings could be realised in expenditure upon the army, the colonies, sinecures and pensions. The reduction of assessed taxes would lead to increased consumption of 'excisable commodities', so swelling the exchequer by an alternative tax.[68]

Throughout the summer of 1833 Evans repeatedly drew the attention of the House to the inequities of assessed taxation. He deplored the disproportionate burden of tax borne by the tradesmen, innkeepers and middle-class householders. He compared the assessments of various mansions and shops in his own constituency, stressing the enormous discrepancies involved. The taxes, he asserted, would always be detested 'while the industrious part of the metropolis groaned under the oppression of their inequality'.[69] Moreover, the tax bill of the metropolis was excessive. One of the parishes in his constituency, St James's, paid more in assessed taxes than Leeds, Birmingham and Manchester. The city of Westminster, with a population of 200,000, was assessed more heavily in house and window taxes than the whole of Scotland (population of $2\frac{1}{2}$ million). Like many Members from urban constituencies, Evans felt that the Whig Ministers, especially Lord Althorp, the Chancellor of the Exchequer, had defaulted on promises to repeal the taxes.[70]

Evans participated vigorously in the repeal campaign, mounted in the various constituencies. He championed the protest movement in Westminster, presenting petitions in Parliament from constituents in the Strand and from parishoners in St Anne's and St James's. He wrote letters to the press, endorsing the formation of associations to seek the repeal of assessed taxes. He attended meetings in Westminster, and joined other Radical Members of Parliament in denouncing the government.[71] He was not impressed by the willingness of Lord Althorp to repeal the house duties in his budget of February 1834. The Chancellor had only bowed before popular pressure and repealed the duties because he had a financial surplus of £1,900,000. Only by weakening 'the moral strength and the political power of the present government', argued Evans, could the people 'expect further relief from the Corn Laws and the window duties'. Indeed, he caused uproar among his constituents at a meeting in the British Coffee House, Cockspur Street, by suggesting that material benefit could only accrue from a rotation of governments, alternating between the 'two Aristocratical powers'.[72] Evans, who had never had much faith in the government of Lord Grey, had plumbed new depths of disillusionment.

His despair merely reflected the widening rift between the Whigs and Radicals in the reformed Parliament. The tiny band of Radicals had seen their proposals crushed by overwhelming votes, often at ministerial behest. Without further measures of parliamentary reform, they saw little prospect for continued 'movement' in politics. Evans shared these sentiments. He advocated vote by ballot as the 'real and effective remedy for corrupt practices' in elections. He favoured a restoration of triennial Parliaments, and he proposed an amendment to the Reform Act removing the payment of rates and taxes as a qualification for voting. Any electoral qualification, he argued, merely served to disfranchise voters and to encourage corruption, in this instance by the collectors of rates and taxes. On all these issues he encountered the blunt rejection of the Whigs.[73]

Baulked on the issue of reform, Evans was even more alarmed by the growth of governmental power, particularly its power of surveillance through the Metropolitan Police. When William Cobbett, the veteran Radical who represented Oldham, denounced the practice of police spies infiltrating political unions, Evans resumed his attacks on the police. He had always feared that the force would develop an inquisitorial rôle ever since the first printed instructions had been issued by the Home Department. 'Nothing,' he argued, 'was more like the establishment of a *gendarmerie*.' He accepted that the French police had preserved life and property, but their intolerable methods in Paris had led to their suppression since the revolution of 1830.[74] He complained, too, that the new police had proved much more expensive than the old watchmen. In the previous year, 1832, the cost of stationing the police was £215,000, compared with £137,000 under the former system. (These statistics were not strictly fair, as the new police had more extensive duties than the old watchmen.) As he doubted that any real improvement had occurred in the rate of detection, Evans believed that the force had not given value for money and that it should be reformed. Using policemen in plain clothes as spies merely increased 'the prejudices against the police-system'. He favoured a curtailment of the powers of the police, by giving some control over their activities to local authorities – another proposal which fell on deaf ears.[75]

Evans had not invariably opposed the government during the parliamentary session of 1833. He had supported the proposed emancipation of the Jews, the renewal of the East India Company charter, and the Factory Act. But he had either spoken or voted in favour of parliamentary reform, the repeal of the Corn Laws and assessed taxation, a reduction of the compensation paid to slave owners, and a diminution of the wealth of the Established Church in Ireland: on all these issues he had found himself in a minority, sometimes a derisory minority. On a tour of the mills in the Manchester area, in November, he joined the local M.P., Joseph Brotherton, in criticising the record of the government. Evans was more critical than Brotherton, deploring the Irish Coercion Act, which had been passed the previous February. Profoundly opposed to the use of any repressive measures in Ireland, he declared that this Act was certainly the very last measure which the people had any right to expect at the hands of this government, and ... [it] would remain as a stain on Earl Grey's administration which it would be difficult to obliterate.[76]

Towards the end of his speech Evans thanked his hosts for showing him round several mills and commercial centres in the locality. He had been impressed with the 'splendour' of these establishments, and considered them indicative of 'the progressive state of the country'. The remark caused surprise locally. A deputation of weavers, tailors, and shoemakers called on him at the Royal Hotel, Manchester. They described the plight of the cotton and silk hand-loom weavers – the high incidence of unemployment, low wages, and appalling living conditions. Evans, who knew little of the industrial north, was appalled by the evidence of misery and destitution. He agreed with the deputation that the remedy lay in the repeal of internal taxes, the abolition of the Corn Laws, and an improvement of the Irish economy (to inhibit the export of cheap labour). But he did not sanction industrial strikes as a means of seeking higher wages. He characterised such action as violent and essentially 'despotic'. He also thought that it liable to prove abortive, as wage rates were dependent upon fiscal and commercial regulations beyond the control of factory owners. Operatives, he argued, should unite and combine with their fellows in other towns and with the 'independent' press; they should then seek to improve their conditions by electing Members of Parliament who would heed their representations.[77]

Endorsing the concept of trade unionism, even in a half-hearted manner, was a bold statement by contemporary standards. The formation of trade unions in the late '20s and early '30s had alarmed employers and the government. In the last few months of 1833, numerous local struggles had occurred between combinations of workers and counter-combinations of employers. There had also been a resurgence of rural unrest, including rick-burning and machine-breaking. The government, particularly Lord Melbourne, the Home Secretary, believed that repression was essential to quell these developments. It supported the arrest, trial and conviction of six Tolpuddle labourers for the 'administering or taking of unlawful oaths'. Under an Act of 1797, the labourers were given the maximum sentence of transportation for seven years.

In the ensuing wave of protest, Evans was again a prominent spokesman. On the evening of 18th April 1834 he took the chair at a densely crowded meeting held in the Crown and Anchor tavern (where the estimated capacity of the 'great room' was 13,000 people). Not for the first time, however, he completely misread his audience and delivered a totally inappropriate speech. He began by correcting press reports of a recent speech he had made in the Commons, in which he had denounced the sentence of the Tolpuddle martyrs, or, as they were then known, 'the Dorchester men'. He then launched into a disquisition about the principles and regulations which should guide the formation of trade unions. This lecture so irritated his audience that they began to heckle and to shout him down with cries of 'the Dorchester men!' Evans eventually gave way and sat down, to be replaced by more fervent orators who had sensed the mood of the meeting. Daniel O'Connell, John Arthur Roebuck and Feargus O'Connor earned rapturous applause by denouncing the government and the trial, and by venerating the 'honest Dorchester labourers'.[78] Evans and O'Connor clashed in the Commons as a consequence of this meeting. Evans deplored O'Connor's harangue, his suggestion that unions should seek political objectives, and the hypocrisy of making wild, impassioned speeches in public, so unlike the sound and temperate ones he made in the House. O'Connor retorted with a reminder of Evans's somewhat theatrical promise, made in the midst of heckling and derision, that he would willingly enrol in a trade union. The retort was not entirely convincing. *The Globe* devoted a long editorial to the quarrel, praising the colonel for 'his rebuke of the mean and designing inconsistency of certain senatorial demagogues . . .'.[79]

Throughout the session of 1834 Evans diligently raised the issues of most concern to his Westminster constituents. He advocated the relief of Dissenters from their various grievances – payment of tithes and the inability either to marry in their own chapels or to enter a university in London. Indeed, he warned the government against half-measures, as the tone and language of the Dissenters' petitions had become more violent than ever before.[80] Military flogging was another issue he aired on account of public 'feeling'. He denounced the practice as ineffectual and counter-productive, more liable to encourage sympathy for the victim than to deter further offences. This punishment, he asserted, dissuaded a better class of recruits from entering the army, the only way, ultimately, of reducing the infractions of military discipline. Although a motion to abolish flogging was defeated by 227 votes to 97 on 7th March, he presented a petition condemning the practice from his parishioners in St Martin's in the Fields the following August. Flogging, he declared, was 'a dishonour and a degradation to the British army', a punishment which could not be continued in view of public sentiment.[81]

Constituency feeling also determined his response to the main legislative measure of the session, the Poor Law Amendment Bill. Having attended several public meetings in Westminster, he had found widespread opposition to the Bill across all shades of political opinion. During the second reading debate, he repeated the main objections of his constituents, particularly about the loss of parish control of relief.[82] He was in a very small minority. Only eight Members voted to move the Bill into committee, and the press were scathing about their tactics. The *Morning Chronicle* deplored

> men, who, from having too low ideas of human nature, imagine that there is no way of standing well with others but by assenting to all they say.
>
> In the long run, however, this seldom fails even to be agreeable. People are seldom displeased to see men show that they have opinions of their own, and that they are not echoes in everything.[83]

This judgement would soon be tested in a general election. In November 1834 Lord Althorp left the leadership of the Commons to succeed his father as Earl Spencer. The King disliked Lord Melbourne's choice of successor, Lord John Russell, and used the occasion to break up the government. He sent for Peel but, as he was on holiday in Italy, invited Wellington to form a caretaker government until his return. Almost at once, protest meetings were convened throughout the country. Differences between the Whigs and Radicals were soon submerged as they faced the prospect of an imminent election against the common foe. In Covent Garden, on 2nd December, the supporters of Hobhouse and Evans coalesced; they had come, in the words of Evans, 'to bury in oblivion the little differences which existed amongst them, for the general good of the country'. Armed with a letter of support from Sir Francis Burdett, Evans castigated any government headed by the Duke of Wellington: he could not accept 'that those who denounced the Reform Bill throughout its progress were the fit and proper men to carry out its principles'.[84]

In fact the hostility between the rival camps of supporters proved more enduring than Evans had anticipated. Burdett had been ill in early December and had not visited the constituency from his home in

Derby. His letters to parishoners and the protestations of his principal supporters, De Vear and Pouncey, did not allay the doubts of the Radical faction. At a Christmas Eve meeting, in the Crown and Anchor, a motion was formally proposed that electors would not support a candidate who did not pledge himself to oppose the Tories, and to vote for triennial Parliaments and the introduction of the ballot. Evans, who desperately wanted a united front in the forthcoming election, assured his supporters that Burdett 'felt nothing but contempt and detestation of the present Government'. He carried the day, so ensuring a daunting task for the Conservative candidate, Sir Thomas Cochrane.[85]

At the nomination hustings on 6th January 1835 Evans appeared in a confident and combative mood. He reminded electors that he had formerly been criticised as 'an anarchist and revolutionist', but such remarks were no longer possible now that he was standing alongside the Duke of Bedford and the Marquis of Westminster. He defended the foreign policy of the late Whig government, and inveighed against the record of the Tories in the unreformed Parliament. He urged voters to unite under the banner of Reform and to trounce the Tory candidate.[86] The victory would prove less spectacular than he obviously expected. Despite an increased electorate of 13,268 voters, neither Burdett nor himself received 3,000 votes. Burdett topped the poll with 2,747, Evans received 2,583 and Cochrane, 1,528. Although Evans had secured a majority of 1,055 over Cochrane, the Conservative candidate was by no means disgraced. He had more than doubled the Conservative vote in the constituency, and had built a substantial base in St George's parish.[87]

Evans could not feel altogether secure in the result. He had fought the election in seemingly favourable circumstances. The constitutional controversy had revived the alliance, if not the fervour, of the Reform Bill movement. For the first time, he had contested Westminster on a common front against the Tories. He was no longer a candidate, disparaged by the Whig press, but a representative with a record of one and a half years of fulfilling election pledges. Yet his majority was less than half the size of Sir John Hobhouse's in 1832, which had melted away in less than six months. He had suffered from a rekindling of Conservative enthusiasm under the leadership of Peel. The latter's election address, commonly known as the Tamworth Manifesto, had accepted the Reform Act as 'a final and irrevocable settlement of a great constitutional question'. Nationally, the Conservatives reduced the Whig majority, gaining 290 seats out of 658, with many others doubtful.[88] Within Westminster, Evans attributed the Conservative revival to systematic bribery and corruption, organised by the local Conservative Society.[89] But other factors were probably as important. Evans was still perceived as an extreme Radical, which ensured a loyal and popular support but also limited his appeal among potential voters. His *rapprochement* with the Whigs was extremely new and was based almost entirely on hostility towards the Tories. He lacked wealth and influence as a Member of Parliament. His powers of oratory had not improved. In short, he was not firmly entrenched as a sitting Member.

Peel remained in office until April 1835. His minority government faced a stormy opposition from the outset, with a keenly contested election over the speakership of the House of Commons. Evans pledged his support to the Whig candidate, James Abercromby, in an open letter to his supporters published in the *Morning Advertiser*.[90] Abercromby narrowly won by 316 votes to 306. Evans stood firm in support of the Whig–Radical realignment, which, after the Lichfield House compact between Russell and O'Connell, would encompass the Irish Members also. When the government fell from office to be replaced by a new Ministry, headed by Lord Melbourne, Evans actively participated in the first test of this Ministry's electoral popularity. In a south Devonshire by-election Lord John Russell faced the challenge of a heavily financed Tory campaign. Government supporters gathered in Manchester and London to raise funds for him. Evans chaired the meeting in the British Coffee House, Cockspur Street, on 22nd April. He lauded Russell's political record, contrasting the clear and specific reforms of his election address with the 'vague and uncertain' promises of the Tamworth Manifesto. Evans endorsed the Whig proposals on municipal reform and the relief of Dissenters' disabilities. He commended Russell for his 'judgment, ability and discretion'.[91] Although Russell lost the election, Evans had loyally supported the government.

In the meantime, Evans had given evidence before the Royal Commission on Military Punishments. He accepted from the composition of the commission (largely senior military officers) that its report was unlikely to favour abolition. Nevertheless, he seized this opportunity to testify against flogging in a more extensive manner than ever before. He claimed that this punishment ought to be abolished because of the growing 'public' feeling that it was essentially degrading and incompatible with the standards of modern civilisation. He advocated a limited and gradual abolition, beginning with the home-based army during the present period of peace. As a replacement for the lash, he proposed more use of fines, more recourse to capital punishment for mutiny, the addition of military cells to all barracks, and the formation of 'correctional corps' for disciplining incorrigible offenders. He also believed that good service could be encouraged by positive inducements. He favoured the introduction of good-conduct badges, the offer of pensions and discharges on the basis of long service and good conduct jointly, the possibility of some civil advantages, such as the franchise, and a greater likelihood of promotion for noncommissioned officers. The ultimate aim, he argued, was to attract a better class of person into the army:

Do away with the lash, and excite emulation in good conduct by promotions from the ranks; and though some of those thus advanced might not, in the first instance, be as completely adequate to the duties of commissioned officers as would be desirable, yet the eventual result would inevitably be that of inducing a better class of the youth of the country to enter into the military service.[92]

As anticipated, these views found little support. The authorities in the Horse Guards believed that the lash was essential for the maintenance of military discipline.

Evans, however, would soon find his military experience more highly regarded in foreign countries. In May 1835 the Carlist War, which had erupted twenty months previously over a disputed succession to the Spanish throne, had reached an apparent watershed. The Constitutionalists, supporters of the Queen Isabella, had suffered a series of defeats in northern Spain. Zumalacárregui, the distinguished general of Don Carlos, the claimant to the throne, had won a decisive victory at Guernica, and Carlist forces had captured Villafranca, Vergara, Tolosa and Estella. Reports confirming the Constitutionalist plight poured into London from George Villiers, the British Minister at Madrid, and from Viscount Eliot and Colonel Gurwood, two emissaries whom Wellington had sent Spain[93] (they had recently secured an agreement between the warring factions – the Eliot Convention – for the more humane treatment of prisoners). Britain had committed herself to the Constitutionalist cause by joining France, Spain and Portugal in the Quadruple Alliance of April 1834. By this alliance Palmerston had hoped to compel the pretenders, Dom

Miguel and Don Carlos, to leave Portugal, so establishing liberal and constitutional regimes in the Iberian peninsula. A Western Confederacy of free States, he argued, would serve 'as a counterpoise to the eastern league of arbitrary governments'.[94] As the military situation worsened in Spain (the Portuguese problem was quickly settled by the departure of Dom Miguel), Britain and France had agreed Additional Articles to the Alliance (18th August 1834). By these articles Britain promised to supply the Spanish government with arms and, if necessary, with a naval force.

Palmerston had anticipated that the articles might not prove adequate. Unlike the Tories, the Whigs were prepared to expand their commitment and to proffer even more assistance.[95] The political division was sharply exposed by the crisis of May 1835. When General Alava, the Spanish ambassador in London, requested permission to raise a force of 10,000 volunteers for service against the Carlists, the government readily concurred. By Orders in Council it suspended the Foreign Enlistment Act, so enabling the Spanish government to recruit soldiers from the United Kingdom. Whereas the Spanish would hope for further military assistance, the Whig government, like its counterpart in France, which also permitted the formation of a legion for Spanish service, viewed the legion as a substitute for intervention. Nevertheless, the Tories deplored this initiative, believing that the provisions of the Quadruple Alliance and the Additional Articles had been entirely fulfilled. Viscount Mahon, who had been Wellington's Under-Secretary at the Foreign Office, disparaged the volunteers as mercenaries, ready to call themselves Englishmen one day and Spaniards the next.[96] Tory displeasure was only heightened by Alava's request on behalf of Juan Mendizábal, the Spanish Premier, that Evans should command the legion.[97]

There were several reasons for the offer of command. Alava had known Evans as a junior officer on the Quartermaster-General's staff during the Peninsular War. He had also heard of Evans's deep personal commitment to the Constitutional cause in Spain and Portugal. Indeed, Evans had advocated British intervention in Portugal as early as June 1833. He had later visited the country and returned with a glowing account of the freedom and liberty apparent in Lisbon.[98] Preserving Spanish freedom was a cause which he had unequivocally endorsed and all too often compared with the struggle between freedom and repression in Britain.[99] In this respect, Evans was merely reflecting the wider debate between Whigs and Tories over the struggle in the Peninsula. Both parties recognised that the conflict had a European dimension. For the Whigs, it was a struggle between 'freedom and tyranny, liberty and despotism'; for the Tories, it was yet another encounter between the forces of 'revolutionary excitement' and the forces of order, tradition, and established institutions. Evans endorsed the ministerial claim that intervention, even in the limited form of a legion, would assist Spain to realise some of the liberties already secured in Britain.

Even so, he accepted Alava's offer for personal as well as political reasons. Financially, he could afford to do so, having married Josette Arbuthnot, a wealthy widow, on 21st June 1834.[100] He was also promised a salary of £5,000 a year from the Spanish authorities. After twenty years of professional inactivity, Evans had a strong desire for military service, especially for field command, not readily obtainable in the British army. Equally appealing was the limited commitment of Spanish service, as he had not secured his base in Westminster. Having promised to desist from military service, he could only reassure his supporters by pledging a prompt return from northern Spain. After a short deliberation, he accepted the offer of command 'willingly and cheerfully'. He rejected any notion of being a mercenary. As he informed the Commons, he had merely accepted an offer to serve in support of principles which he had always upheld.[101]

4
Commanding the Legion

Command of the Auxiliary Legion in Spain proved a difficult and demanding task. It required military expertise, a degree of diplomatic dexterity, and some understanding of the political and economic problems of the Spanish government. Few British officers could have possessed all these attributes. Evans neither spoke Spanish nor had any experience of field command. Untested in diplomacy, he had not proved particularly adroit in the handling of sensitive political issues. On the other hand, he was fully committed to the Constitutional or Cristino cause (named after María Cristina, the Queen Regent). He had seen active service in Spain. At the age of forty-seven he was still physically fit and a capable horseman. He had, too, a presence which would evoke the respect, even the admiration, of the rank and file.[1] Above all, he relished the prospect of his first command.

The Carlist War, which had erupted in October 1833, was not merely a war of succession occasioned by the claim of Don Carlos to the throne of his niece; it was also a provincial revolt in the northern provinces. Carlism represented clerical, agrarian and reactionary interests, and received powerful support from the Basques, in rural areas, who feared incursions on their local privileges from the centralising policies of a liberal government in Madrid. The Carlist troops were intimately acquainted with their own terrain, controlled their own supply lines, and received financial support from the absolutist rulers of eastern Europe. Under the enterprising command of Zumalacárregui, this mobile and well organised striking force inflicted a succession of defeats on the Cristino armies. By May 1835 the revolt had spread to Catalonia, Aragon and Valencia, leaving the road to Madrid open.

These defeats had exacerbated the predicament of the Spanish government. The Ministry of Martínez de la Rosa lacked political support. In 1834 it had introduced a controversial constitution which re-established a partly elected Cortes but left ultimate power to the Crown, or, at its time of promulgation, to the Queen Regent. The progressives were left unsatisfied, while the Carlists deplored any concession to the concept of popular government. Given the inability of the parties to agree, or to support a compromise policy, politically-minded generals were able to intrigue in Madrid or even, on occasions, to issue *pronunciamento* (declarations with the assistance of troops, civilians or both against the government or its policy). As this political instability was compounded by chronic financial weakness and military mismanagement, governments proved of short duration. The Ministry of Martínez de la Rosa fell in spring 1835; its successor, under the Count of Toreno, lasted only ten weeks, to be replaced by a Ministry headed by the radical hero and Jewish financier, Mendizábal. In these circumstances, there was always a faction who believed that the Cristino cause could best be saved by full-scale French intervention.

Despite these unpropitious omens, the Legion was raised extremely quickly. Its formation was sanctioned in June; its first detachments reached Spain on 10th July, and by the end of October some 7,800 recruits had landed along the northern coast at Santander, Bilbao and San Sebastian. The Spanish government had paid their recruiting agents £2 for each man enlisted, accepting a cursory, and in many respects totally inadequate, medical examination. Rutherford Alcock, one of the Legion's medical officers, reckoned that 'one-eighth at least of the whole force was unfit for service and ought never to have been enlisted'.[2] But the Spanish authorities had placed a premium on speed, as the military situation appeared extremely grave in the Basque provinces. They may also have been worried by the declaration of Don Carlos, on 20th June, that any foreign prisoners would not be protected by the terms of the Eliot Convention. Although the pronouncement, which became known as the Durango Decree, had little effect on recruitment, it embarrassed the British government, whose spokesmen had stated that the Convention would apply to British prisoners.[3]

Recruits came forward, lured by promises of pay and martial adventure. Of the first 7,800, about 2,800 were Irish, 1,800 Scots and 3,200 English. Only the Irish were drawn predominantly from agricultural trades; the Scots and English came largely from the ranks of the unemployed in cities like Glasgow, London, Liverpool and

Bristol. It was their 'force of circumstances', wrote Private Somerville, 'that led many of them to go to Spain'.[4] Many of the recruits, coming from deprived urban backgrounds, would experience difficulty in adapting to the climate, food and mode of life on active service. The Irish, on the other hand, would adjust more rapidly to Spanish conditions; they proved hardier and less susceptible to disease: in Alcock's opinion, they 'were physically and morally the best adapted for the service'.[5]

Evans had the responsibility of recruiting officers. From the army list of 13,000 to 14,000 officers, he thought that some 500 would volunteer for Spanish service. This hope was soon confounded. Within days of the publication of the Order in Council, the Duke of Wellington and Lord Hill, the Commander-in-Chief, expressed their opposition to intervention in the Carlist War and their disdain for the Legion. The Commander-in-Chief required all officers on long leave to pledge that they would not go to Spain. As Evans recalled, 'This had the instantaneous effect of deterring great numbers of officers from engaging in the corps.'[6] Notwithstanding these difficulties, he found competent senior officers from among his friends, notably Charles Chichester and William Reid. He enrolled six officers on leave from the East India Company, and about forty who had served as mercenaries in Greece, Portugal and South America. Another forty or fifty officers were commissioned from the ranks, but the bulk of the Legion's 400 officers had seen no service whatsoever. They possessed courage and enthusiasm but little military knowledge: some lacked the rudiments of discipline and were prone to duelling.

This force of largely inexperienced officers and raw recruits engendered extraordinary expectations. Writing to Villiers, on 9th July 1835, Palmerston claimed that 'Evans's ten thousand will turn the fate of the war. The Spaniards ought to give him the chief command, if he acquits himself well when he gets to the ground.'[7] Villiers, though more circumspect, was also optimistic. He believed that the example of the Legion would revitalise the Spanish army, and that the insurrection would eventually be overcome.[8] Pro-Carlists were less convinced. Captain Henningsen, who had served for twelve months in the army of Don Carlos, doubted that the sight of red coats would inspire the Queen's forces and revive memories of the Pensinular War. The Carlists now numbered thirty thousand men, possessed considerable artillery, and were intimately acquainted with the mountainous terrain. Facing this enemy, argued Henningsen, 'what is Colonel Evans, who, after all, is in a subordinate capacity, to do with his six or eight thousand ragamuffins?'[9] Such criticism infuriated the government. Villiers assured Palmerston that he would never miss an opportunity of praising the Legion in his public despatches. He was certain that the corps would disappoint 'the Tories and those who are advised by them'.[10]

To fulfil ministerial hopes would prove exceedingly difficult. Owing to the provisions of one of Sidmouth's 'Six Acts' (1819), the Legion could not be trained in Britain. Evans could authorise the purchase of arms and accoutrements from the Tower of London (the main source of supply for the British army) and uniforms from regular army tailors. But drilling was not permitted, and so he had to send his untrained recruits direct to the Peninsula. When Evans landed in San Sebastian in August, the first detachments were already engaged in training, drills and route marches. Spanish and British observers doubted that the new recruits were fit for immediate service. The Duke of Ahumada, then Minister of War, proposed that they should remain at San Sebastian, performing garrison duty, until properly disciplined and acquainted with each other and their officers. In view of the rapturous welcome of the British troops in San Sebastian, he hoped that a division could be sent to Burgos to bolster local morale and inspire 'old associations'.[11] Villiers accepted that the Legion should not be thrown precipitately into action. 'It must be still some weeks,' he wrote, on 22nd August, 'before the English auxiliaries can be trained sufficiently to give them a fair chance of being useful.'[12]

Evans, who had the local rank of lieutenant-general in the Spanish army, had not come to Spain to mount guard at San Sebastian. He was resolved to grapple with the enemy as quickly as possible. Carlist forces were split, with five battalions before San Sebastian, five before Bilbao, and another five at Hernani. With the approval of Generals Alava and Jáuregui, he proposed an immediate attack on Hernani with eight battalions, half British and half Spanish. He admitted that this might seem 'imprudent . . . with such raw troops'; but he believed that the odds were in his favour, and that the 'Spanish allies are good troops and hearty in the cause'.[13] These assets, however, were not sufficient. On 30th August, General Gómez, the Carlist commander, successfully defended his position, killing six and wounding twenty of the Legion. After the skirmish, several British prisoners were shot under the terms of the Durango Decree.

Despite this reverse, Evans remained optimistic. Only ten days after the defeat, he wrote in a despatch: 'The Legion is flourishing in point of organisation and strength. In one month I shall have a force equal to anything in this country or nearly so.'[14] When the Carlists lifted the siege of Bilbao, on 6th September, before the advancing armies from Miranda and Vitoria, five battalions of the Legion and the troops under Generals Espartero and Espeleta entered the city. Three days later Generals Alava, Espeleta, Espartero and Evans held a council of war. They determined upon an offensive operation, in the hope of seizing Ordũna as a military base. Capturing Ordũna would have drawn Carlist forces from Vitoria, so freeing the main Cristino army under General Córdoba for further offensives. Had this strategy succeeded, it might have rallied the Queen's government, which was on the brink of collapse in Madrid. Unfortunately, neither the Cristino generals nor Evans had any reliable intelligence about the strength and disposition of the Carlist forces. Espeleta and Espartero simply marched out of Bilbao on 11th September at the head of 9,000 troops, covered on their left flank by 3,000 men, including six battalions of the Legion, under Count Mirasol and Evans. Within hours of leaving Bilbao they encountered Carlist fire, and found the main bridges and passes strongly defended. Espeleta, who had rashly withdrawn Mirasol's force, ordered a retreat of the main body, in the course of which Espartero's division was routed. The strength of the Carlists, fighting on their own countryside, using their artillery and light infantry efficiently, had been clearly demonstrated.

After their success of the 11th September, the Carlists left the vicinity of Bilbao to concentrate their forces against Córdoba. Evans contented himself with organising the Legion and supervising the erection of defences around the town and the river Nervion. As battalions arrived in piecemeal fashion from England, he accepted that it would take 'a little time' to complete the organisation.[15] Meanwhile he experienced his first frustrations with Spanish bureaucracy as the construction of Bilbao's defences proceeded at an agonisingly slow pace. Neither the municipality nor the military authorities of the province nor the government itself would finance the project.[16]

The Legion remained for nearly two months in Bilbao, until ordered by General Córdoba, on 29th October, to move into the interior. As Córdoba wanted the Legion's support in his blockade of the Carlists during the winter months, he directed Evans to march his troops via the Durango road to a new base at Vitoria. Evans refused to follow the

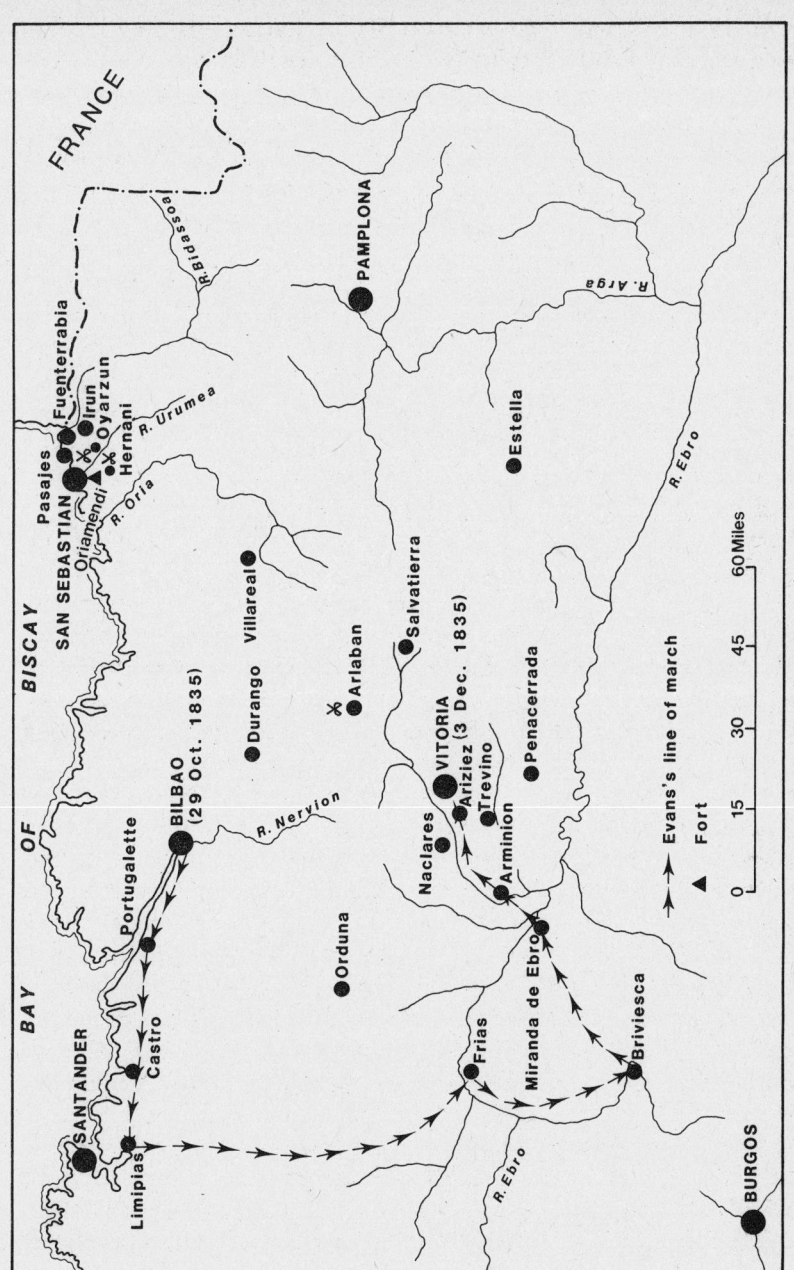

3. The theatre of operations in the Basque provinces

route, as it led through the heart of Carlist country. Wisely, he chose a much longer route through Portugalette, Castro, Limpias, Frias, Briviesca and Miranda de Ebro, a distance of nearly 150 miles. This line of march skirted the enemy-held territory, and enabled the Legion to transport its voluminous baggage and impedimenta in comparative safety. The Carlists exploited the propaganda value of this cautious detour, while an angry Córdoba had to be mollified by Colonel William Wylde, the British commissioner with the Cristino armies.[17] Marching about fifteen to twenty miles a day, the Legion reached Briviesca on the tenth day (having halted at Castro for a day). At Briviesca, Evans and Córdoba met for the first time, on 7th November, where Evans was immediately impressed by 'the kindness and good nature' of the Spanish commander-in-chief. He admitted that Córdoba had 'the immeasurable advantages over me of youth and experience of this peculiar war ... a man of most remarkable talent – I should say – genius'.[18] Initially, relations were harmonious between the two commanders, even if they had not forged any real understanding.

By early November 1835 Evans was already concerned about a problem which would bedevil the Legion throughout the war, namely mounting arrears of pay. Generous loans of 35,000 and 50,000 dollars (about £7,000 and £10,000 respectively) from Córdoba stemmed the immediate shortage, but Evans, concerned about the discipline and order of his newly formed force, pressed for more regular payments from the Spanish authorities. He asked Villiers to raise the issue on his behalf, and sent Colonel Wylde to Madrid to represent the wants of the army generally and of the auxiliaries in particular.[19] After a rest of three weeks in Briviesca, Evans took the Legion on to Vitoria, covering a move by Córdoba's forces in the direction of Aragon. On 3rd December the Legion entered Vitoria, having completed the last twenty-four to twenty-eight miles without a single straggler. It received a tumultuous welcome from the town authorities, inhabitants and garrison. Córdoba had organised a formal military reception, with bands playing Riego's Hymn, the famous liberal marching song, as Evans entered town. Córdoba inspected the Legion three days later, whereupon Evans reported the troops as ready to undertake any operation within the general plan of campaign. He was not too dismayed, however, when Córdoba indicated that he did not plan any further movements for two or three weeks. 'The delay,' wrote Evans, 'will not be without advantage as regards the further instruction of the Legion.'[20]

For the rest of the winter, the majority of the Spanish and British troops were quartered in or near Vitoria, which had become the focal point of Córdoba's blockade. The living conditions were deplorable. Bereft of adequate accommodation during December and January, the Legion occupied large convents, churches and ruined houses. The soldiers had a scanty supply of wood, bedding and straw (as some three to four thousand blankets had not arrived). They slept on boards, many on flagstones, without any covering save their clothes, which were frequently saturated with rain or snow. A severe winter compounded the discomforts, with the ground either covered by two to three feet of snow, or clogged by mud in the thaws and rain. The food, which stretched to one meal a day, was generally disgusting. The bread, often made from unsound flour and only half baked, was usually black, soft and glutinous. The beef was tough and indigestible, not properly cured, and carved from the carcasses of old, emaciated bullocks. Even the wine, though sometimes palatable, was often sour and bad.[21]

Fever and dysentery swept through the Legion in the new year, swelling the death toll from sickness and disease. One hundred soldiers had already died in December, but in the next three and a half months the hospitals were swamped with admissions. Out of approximately 7,000 men quartered in or near Vitoria, 4,706 were admitted to hospital, 819 died, and 787 remained incapacitated when the Legion began its departure on 13th April. Fortunately Evans had enrolled a substantial medical corps: each of the fourteen regiments had a complement of three doctors, and there was a general medical staff of nine senior surgeons and sixteen assistants. But this staff was hopelessly stretched. Some of the regimental doctors had resigned before the Legion reached Vitoria, eight of the general staff were still in the original depot at Santander, tending a sick list of over 300, and another four were at the depot in Briviesca, where 100 to 200 lay sick. Required to tend patients in the officers' quarters, seven general hospitals, and regiments in separate villages, the doctors were soon overwhelmed with cases. Medical supplies were woefully inadequate; indeed, the first medicines, blankets, baths, cooking utensils and general stores did not arrive from Britain until mid-February. From January to April, eleven medical officers died (as well as thirty-four officers) and seventeen doctors were invalided.[22]

Morale sagged as the winter worsened and the sick toll mounted. The arrears of pay only compounded the feelings of discontent. The promises which Juan Mendizábal, the Queen's chief Minister, had made to Colonel Wylde were never honoured.[23] Soldiers were induced to sell items of clothing and kit to buy wine and spirits; some resorted to petty crime and theft, so alienating the people whom they had volunteered to defend. Burials were especially depressing: once officers could no longer afford to buy coffins for their men, bodies were piled into carts and buried *en masse*. As the Spanish still buried their dead with full ceremony, British spirits sank even further. Criticism of General Evans mounted among the officers and other ranks. While some accepted that he must have been deceived by the Spanish authorities, others doubted his concern for the troops. Some men, as Somerville records, believed that Evans neither visited nor inspected the regimental quarters and hospitals.[24] As officers began to resign, Brigadier-General Shaw insisted that 'Evans must think and act for himself': only by such initiative could the Legion's predicament improve.[25] More informed criticism came from Wylde, who had heard Córdoba promise ample supplies and proper lodgings for the Legion on their arrival in Vitoria. He argued, as a consequence, that Evans had shown 'a want of decision and firmness' in his dealings with the Spanish authorities. He claimed, too, that the subsequent neglect of the Legion had contributed, along with a lack of active employment, to the discontent in the officer corps.[26]

Villiers was also appalled by the reports of the Legion and the leadership, or lack of it, shown by Evans. On 13th February he informed Palmerston that the Legion had 'fallen into disorder and disrepute'. He accepted that the government had contributed to the malaise by failing to keep its engagements, but this failure could not excuse the absence of discipline in Vitoria. Villiers described Evans as

mild and indolent – an excellent honourable gentleman and in the field an intrepid officer, but no disciplinarian and wanting the energy – perhaps too the knowledge – necessary for making raw officers do their duty, and keeping in subjection many hundreds of men – not the very cream of society in Westminster.[27]

Over the next few weeks he continued to receive depressing accounts of the Legion and its predicament. He believed that British prestige had suffered on account of the reputation of the force, and that the privileges of the Legion had aroused jealousy within the Queen's army. On the one hand, Evans's high Spanish rank was 'an embarrassment', as he outranked every other general in Navarre but could not speak the language and knew little of the country. On the other hand, the Legion was entitled to higher rates of pay than either the Spanish army or the French legion: 'when this vast expense is coupled with their inefficiency' it caused even more resentment.[28]

Villiers received reports from Colonel de la Saussaye, an Irish officer serving in the Spanish army. He was fiercely critical of the indiscipline within the Legion, which he attributed to the composition of the force, the neglect of the Spanish government, and the 'listlessness' of the commanding officer. Evans, he claimed, had been much too ready to retain the services of unworthy, imprudent and even mutinous officers. His tolerance of incompetence was 'amiable and good hearted but highly subversive of discipline and subordination ...'. The reason, argued de la Saussaye, was Evans's concern with his reputation at home: although interested in the success of the Legion, he was much more concerned with 'the Political Nightmare weighing upon him as to what the Public in England and especially in *Westminster* should think of his use or abuse of authority'.[29]

There was some truth in these criticisms. Evans was worried about his reputation and political base in Westminster; he sent letters to his constituency for publication in the national press, and fretted increasingly, the longer he remained in Spain, about his return to Parliament.[30] He was not a stern disciplinarian in the mould of the Duke of Wellington. Instinctively he disliked recourse to the lash, preferring to retain the support of his men by regular pay and rewards for gallant service, inducements which were lacking during the winter of 1835–36. As discipline deteriorated in several regiments, Evans was not oblivious of the privations and boredom, the basic causes of discontent. He repeatedly demanded pay and provisions from Madrid, pressing the authorities to honour their commitments and to redress the grievances of the Legion. Neither entreaties nor threats of resignation were of any avail. In March 1836 he sent Colonel Wylde and Brigadier-General Duncan MacDougall on another mission to Madrid. Although their presence added weight to the representations of Villiers, a four-hour meeting with Mendizábal yielded nothing for the Legion.[31]

It was not true that Evans lacked the co-operation and assistance of Villiers.[32] The Minister had never had much respect for Evans, whom he viewed, on the basis of his political career, as 'a man of mighty intentions and small performance'. Indeed, his contempt deepened during the course of the Legion's activities in Spain.[33] Nevertheless, he wholeheartedly supported him, praising the Legion in his despatches, acting as intermediary between Evans and Córdoba, and drawing the attention of the Spanish government to the plight and requirements of the Legion. MacDougall, who observed his strenuous representations in Madrid, was impressed by his 'warm and powerful assistance'. Evans echoed this view; he recognised that the Legion, without the support of Villiers, 'in the midst of so many jealousies, and real wants, would be very helpless'.[34]

Even with the assistance of Villiers, however, Evans could not relieve the distress of the troops in Vitoria. The Spanish Treasury was short of funds, and, whenever resources were available, it usually paid Spanish regiments before the auxiliaries. Arrears of pay were a characteristic of Spanish military service. Some Spanish generals, like Córdoba, disapproved of paying their men in full, lest they 'commit lamentable excesses' in consequence. By keeping several months' pay in arrears the authorities could restrain the passions of, and retain a hold over, the rank and file.[35] When confronted with requests for pay, Spanish Ministers either dissembled or retorted that the Legion had never kept any accounts of its income and expenditure and of the supplies and stores which it had received from England. The absence of accounts was corroborated by Robert Grindley, head of the Legion's commissariat, who admitted, in a meeting with Villiers, that the inexperienced company captains had failed to keep proper records of their expenditure.[36] A virtual stalemate ensued, with the Treasury refusing to remit further payments until it was furnished with accounts. As Mendizábal informed Palmerston on 6th March, the Legion's arrears were not 'a very extraordinary occurrence in Spain'; indeed, he surmised that parallels might have occurred in the British army.[37]

Faced with such complacency, Evans could only await supplies from Britain and take what local initiatives he could to ease the immediate problems. He acted decisively when Carlist agents were uncovered among the principal suppliers of the Legion. As the Legion's baker had not only been encouraging men to desert but had also been poisoning the bread, Evans ordered his execution.[38] He pressed, too, for an active rôle for the Legion in the line of blockade, which Córdoba had hoped to establish in a semicircular arc from Bilbao to Pamplona, over a distance of 150 miles. By dispersing his effective units in the various towns and villages, Evans hoped to reduce the congestion, and hence the disease, in Vitoria. He also yearned for 'some excitement' to occupy the minds of his disgruntled men, believing that a successful military action, followed by a plentiful distribution of medals, would stimulate his officers, 'who are peculiarly desirious of these distinctions'. For these reasons he began deploying units along the road to Salvatierra, on 1st January 1836, even before he had received any orders from Córdoba, the general-in-chief.[39]

As the winter worsened, the blockade proved more and more onerous. Some units were effective, especially the three Irish regiments; they were well organised and disciplined in the field, an assessment shared by Evans and his critics.[40] But these forces were extremely stretched: by 15th February some 3,000 or 3,300 infantry were supposed to protect Vitoria, Penacerrada, Trevino, Ariziez, Naclares, La Puebla, Arminion and Miranda. Evans pleaded for reinforcements, aware that any reverse would merely worsen the Legion's reputation in Madrid.[41] He realised that his deployment was rendered even more precarious by the lack of intelligence. As he informed Villiers on 23rd February 1836:

In this kind of war – above all others – it is more than necessary that spies should be paid before any other persons – and *liberally* as well as punctually. The population being generally in favour of the enemy (and when not favourable are treated with such barbarous severity as to be reduced to inaction) it is next to impossible that we can have as good information as them. Their superiority in this respect is worth them a dozen Bat[talion]ns. Tho' we may not destroy, we may diminish this superiority.[42]

Fortunately, in view of its lack of numbers, intelligence and reinforcements, the Legion saw comparatively little action. The largest skirmish occurred at Arlaban on 16th January 1836, where it drove the Carlists out of the village of Mendijur and thereafter occupied part of the Barundia valley beneath the Maturana mountains. The Legion suffered about twenty casualties. In the wake of this action, Córdoba withdrew his troops to Vitoria without giving his subordinate commanders any warning. Evans was livid and felt betrayed, as he had been left in an exposed position by the Spanish general. This reaction was more a symptom of his mounting frustrations than a clear assessment of his tactical position. Córdoba had judged correctly that the Carlists were unlikely to descend from their secure mountainous outposts in a precipitate attack.[43]

Relations between Evans and Córdoba grew strained during the first quarter of 1836. Evans deplored Córdoba's hostility towards the government of Mendizábal. He knew that Córdoba had never been enamoured of the small volunteer legions raised in Britain, France and Portugal by the authorities in Madrid and had always favoured the intervention of a French army. He also believed that Córdoba, in the course of a frustrating winter campaign without adequate reinforcements from the south, had become too preoccupied with political intrigue, too intent on thwarting the policies of Mendizábal.[44] In objecting to this behaviour, Evans was not criticising Córdoba from the stance of an apolitical officer whose sole duty was to serve the government of the day. On the contrary, he criticised Córdoba because he supported Mendizábal, trusting that his Ministry would ensure a constitutional, conciliatory and reforming government. He considered Mendizábal as a 'friend' of the Legion, and, despite a succession of broken promises, still viewed his government as basically well intentioned – 'they would have done better for us if they could'.[45]

Evans feared that Córdoba, in seeking a French army of intervention, had adopted an ultra-cautious strategy, refusing to advance on the enemy from any direction. He contended, too, that Córdoba had compromised his subordinate commanders, Espartero, Espeleta and himself, by delegating command to them in their respective areas. In Evans's view, this was merely an attempt to avoid responsibility and to place 'the blame on other shoulders' in case of disaster. Having lost all confidence in the 'sincerity and common judgement' of Córdoba, Evans chafed at the 'inaction and thraldom' of the blockade. He urged Villiers to press for his return to the northern coast, where the Legion could act in conjunction with the battalion of Royal Marines, under Lord John Hay, which had been ordered to assist the Cristino armies. 'If Espartero were allowed to go with me,' argued Evans, 'we should soon recover all Biscay.'[46]

Even more than Córdoba's political and strategic views, Evans resented his tendency to discredit and disparage the Legion. Córdoba had never concealed his doubts about the Legion's value, especially its ability to bear the privations and hardships of a civil war in Spain. He had complained to the Minister of War about the want of discipline shown by the Legion in Vitoria.[47] Evans felt that the deprecation went much further, involving intrigues at Madrid and the neglect of the Legion's requirements.[48] When the rift was debated in the House of Commons, Córdoba wrote a public letter to Evans denying all charges of neglecting the Legion. To appease Villiers and Wylde, Evans sent a conciliatory reply, and Córdoba promised to publish a letter in *El Espanol*, praising the services of the Legion.[49] This exchange of letters in late March did not soothe Evans's feelings. He was delighted to leave Vitoria for Santander on 15th April:

> We are all full of joy at escaping from this centre of inactivity (to use a mild term) – not of operations.
> The *do-nothing, risk-nothing* principle guides here – in fact it is a diplomatic not military war – intervention not victory being the object – a shallow short-sighted game – in my humble opinion – for a military chief to play. It may partly however be attributable to military incapacity.[50]

Though delighted at the prospect of action, Evans bemoaned his lack of forces. Before leaving Vitoria he had reckoned that his maximum force would number between 7,000 and 8,000 men, far short of the 10,000 troops promised by Córdoba.[51] More soldiers fell sick on the march to Santander, whence the Legion was due to embark for San Sebastian at the end of April. As only two steamships, the *James Watt* and the *Isabel*, were available, it took nearly a fortnight to ferry the Legion to San Sebastian. Evans requested reinforcements. Like Lord John Hay, he was confident of the Legion's success as soon as it numbered at least 10,000 men. Hay even believed that the Legion, at full strength, could clear the province of Carlists within a month, but he doubted that the present force could advance more than five miles from San Sebastian.[52] The invaluable Villiers wrote to Córdoba, urging his immediate compliance with the request for reinforcements.[53]

Without waiting for further troops, or even for his entire Legion to arrive from Santander, Evans resolved to strike an early blow by raising the siege of San Sebastian. Some 4,000 Carlists, under the command of General Segastibelsa, had established three lines of fortifications from the Urumea river – then unfordable – in the east to a deep glen which opened on to the sea two miles westwards. The first line of fortifications was half a mile from San Sebastian. The second and third lines were constructed on the heights above, linking natural defences with barricades, breastworks, and several fortified buildings, and supported by pieces of heavy artillery. As the main road from San Sebastian to Hernani ran through this ground, Evans had to lift the siege before he could begin any active operations.

Evans planned to attack the enemy's lines on 5th May, with about six thousand troops, fourteen hundred of whom were Spanish. He decided to launch his assault in three columns, before daybreak, near the enemy's first line. The Light Brigade, under Brigadier-General

Reid, composed of the Rifles, 3rd, 6th and Chapelgorris (Spanish irregulars), was to attack the right of the enemy lines, towards the river Urumea. The Irish Brigade, consisting of the 7th, 9th and 10th, commanded by Shaw, was to breach the centre. Brigadier-General Chichester's Brigade, which included the 1st, two companies of the 8th (the remainder of the 8th and the 4th had not yet landed), and about 800 Spaniards, was to march along the shore and turn the enemy's left. Conditions did not favour an uphill advance, as a week's rain had left the countryside wet and muddy.

The battle was joined at four o'clock in the morning, with the Light Brigade and the Irish Brigade sweeping over the enemy picquets. The first line of defences fell quickly, but further progress was checked by sustained fire from musketry and artillery. Several frontal attacks failed, notwithstanding the exhortations of Evans, who appeared briefly at the head of his troops in a characteristic display of bravado. Success was only secured by the fortunate arrival of Lord John Hay, with the 4th and 8th regiments, in the *Phoenix* and *Salamander*. Whilst landing the troops to support Chichester's Brigade, which had twice been repulsed in an attack on the fort at Lugariz, the *Phoenix* opened fire with its ten-inch guns, making a breach in the entrenchments. The 4th and 8th regiments poured through the gap, turning the Carlists' line. As the defenders wavered, the other brigades joined the assault, carrying the trenches at bayonet point within ten minutes. By eleven o'clock the whole of the enemy's defences and five pieces of heavy artillery had been taken. The victory had cost the Legion the lives of eleven officers and 120 rank and file, with another 64 officers and 645 men wounded. The Spanish regiments had lost one officer and eleven men killed, with nine officers and eighty-four men wounded.[54] Evans, bespattered in mud, his clothes rent and torn, rode along the lines after the battle. Loudly cheered by his troops, he doffed his hat, saying, 'You have done well, all of you; you have made a noble beginning.'[55]

Evan's tactics aroused controversy within his officer corps both before and after the battle. Prior to launching the attack, Shaw disapproved of pressing the advance until the Legion had mustered in its entirety.[56] Colonel de la Saussaye, though initially astounded by an 'almost miraculous' triumph, was more critical, on reflection, of the costly frontal assaults. He believed that Evans had regretted the attacks on the centre, and, in launching them, had yielded to the advice of MacDougall, 'an old Armadillo [who] likes knocking his head against a wall "chacun à son goût".'⁵⁷ Colonel Wylde was equally grudging in his report to Lord Palmerston. Without 'the opportune arrival of Lord John Hay,' he argued, 'the issue would have been doubtful at least the loss would have been terribly increased.'⁵⁸

Nevertheless, the strategic and diplomatic significance of the victory was manifest. The Legion had proved its mettle, so strengthening the case for reinforcements. Impressed by the gallantry displayed by the legionaries and the leadership of Evans, Lord John Hay was convinced that if Evans had 10,000 men under his command he could 'clear the whole of this part of the Country or break the neck of this war . . .'.⁵⁹ Evans was equally sanguine; he requested more troops to exploit the success and enable the Legion to seize Passages, Fuenterrabia, Irun and eventually Hernani.⁶⁰ Villiers fully endorsed these sentiments, claiming that the Legion, if properly reinforced and able to follow up its victory, could end the war 'before the autumn without French aid'.⁶¹ He felt, too, that the victory would have a profound effect upon Spanish opinion, reviving confidence in the Queen's cause and galvanising Córdoba into action. To sustain that confidence, which he rated as more important than the purely strategic significance of the victory, Villiers hoped that the Legion would honour its promises to protect life and property 'in order that the English may be looked on as conciliators as well as conquerors . . .'.⁶²

Both Palmerston and Villiers acted upon Evans's request, and were partially successful in seeking immediate reinforcements. General Córdoba sent three Spanish battalions, promised a fourth but refused to send any more, as his forces were assuming the offensive on 20th May and moving against the Carlist lines at Arlaban. By 23rd May some 1,600 soldiers, 900 recruits and 500 former convalescents from Vitoria had joined the Legion (the fourth Spanish battalion arrived on 10th June). But Evans could not deploy his entire corps of nearly 9,000 men, because he refused to take recruits into action and left garrisons of 1,000 men in San Sebastian and 450 in Guetaria. He also had to guard his lines of communications, as the Legion rarely had more than two or three days' supplies at a time. Consequently, Evans could only take the field with about 7,000 soldiers, a body marginally larger than the garrison at Hernani, which could be reinforced from the main Carlist army.⁶³ Lack of numbers still bedevilled the Legion, restricting the scope of its operations and reducing the likelihood of any decisive success. Palmerston, ever confident of the Legion's potential, exhorted Villiers to demand additional troops from the new

Spanish government (Mendizábal's Ministry having resigned on 14th May, to be replaced by a government headed by Francisco Javier Istúriz). Villiers did so, but found the Ministry more concerned with diverting troops to meet the main Carlist thrust in Aragon and Valencia.[64]

Evans was not inhibited by the shortage of troops. 'By cautious movements,' he assured Lord Palmerston, 'I shall I trust not have much difficulty in securing ... Passages, Fuenterrabbia[sic] and Irun.'[65] Once the redoubts protecting the bay of San Sebastian had been constructed – a process delayed by the lack of entrenching tools – Evans moved his troops across the Urumea river on 28th May. At six o'clock in the morning he launched his onslaught on the Carlist positions with fire from thirty pieces of artillery. A combined force of Spanish infantry, irregular troops, Chichester's brigade, and a battalion of Royal Marines swept over the retreating enemy. Lancers under Lieutenant-Colonel James Rait charged into Passages, while the nearby castle was shelled by the *Phoenix* and *Salamander*, and soon evacuated by the Carlists. By a swift offensive, with little loss, Evans had captured a vital port and established a foothold on the coast of about nine miles in extent.[66]

Evans now found his corps, already vulnerable to counter-attack, even more exposed by Córdoba's decision to withdraw to Vitoria, after incurring a loss of 600 men at Arlaban. Incensed by the retreat, Evans was even more annoyed by Córdoba's public pronouncement that his army required 'repose'. Uncertain whether this represented 'unheard of duplicity, or selfishness or incapacity', Evans feared that the Carlists would exploit the decision by attacking his own position in strength.[67] Three Carlist attacks were launched on 31st May, 6th and 9th June, but each was repulsed, with a total enemy loss of about 1,400 (the defenders suffered some 500 killed and wounded). Notwithstanding these attacks, and a concentration of over 8,000 troops in the north, the Carlists were more concerned with mounting raids into southern and western Spain. Able to contain Evans within a thin coastal strip, they refrained from further attacks during the summer.

Evans rashly attempted to break the stalemate on 11th July. With a force of 5,000 men, including Royal Marines, he tried to capture the town of Fuenterrabia on the French frontier. Had he taken Fuenterrabia and the neighbouring town of Irun, he would have closed the main Carlist supply route from France. But the attack was beset by difficulties from the outset. Evans himself was extremely ill, and, though present at the battle, was unable to command the operations. In late June he had contracted a bilious complaint and fever, and by 11th July was hardly able to ride a horse in the fierce mid-day sun.[68] Brigadier-General William Reid was effectively the commander of the operations, but he was not responsible for the main oversight in the preparatory planning, namely the failure to include artillery in the line of attack. Evans was entirely to blame: he had accepted intelligence that the Carlists were about to reduce their garrison and withdraw their guns, and so deemed it unnecessary to take artillery. In fact the Carlists had spent the previous two months repairing the walls of Fuentarrabia and strengthening their defences. Hence when several battalions, led by Shaw and Fitzgerald, seized the bridge over the Bidassoa, they found themselves before a rampart about thirty or forty feet high and walls too strong to be breached by mountain guns. As the defences were beyond the range of effective fire from the Marines, the Legion could only withdraw, with about 120 killed, wounded or missing.[69]

Although the troops had proved steady in the advance and retreat, the outcome depressed morale at a peculiarly inappropriate time. In the two months since 5th May the Legion had become preoccupied with its own problems, including the distribution of medals, pay arrears, the contract of service, and relations with the Royal Marines. Evans fully appreciated the importance of decorating officers and men as a means of retaining their services. Having already awarded about forty decorations after the abortive attack on Arlaban, he recommended a lavish distribution of medals after 5th May – the Cross of Isabel II for noncommissioned officers and men, the Cross of San Fernando, first class, for ensigns up to lieutenant-colonels, second class for colonels, and third class for generals. Officers were not mollified, however. Some believed that the distribution had been too lavish, while others, who had not been decorated, threatened to write books about the Legion or appeal to the Horse Guards.[70]

Arguably Evans was the most aggrieved. Already irritated by delays in implementing his recommendations for medals, he was infuriated by the Queen's decision to send his Grand Cross of San Fernando through her general-in-chief, Córdoba. This was customary Spanish practice, but Evans considered it a massive slight on his services. When he received the diploma from Major-General Espartero, a junior ranking general, serving as *locum tenens* for the absent Córdoba, he was even more enraged and returned the award. In a letter to Istúriz, Evans complained that the process was 'in the highest degree offensive to me', and, in letters to Palmerston and Villiers, threatened to resign his command.[71] The controversy raged throughout the month of June, before a letter from the Queen Regent, coupled with the conciliatory correspondence of Villiers, persuaded Evans to accept the award. Although he had cause to feel aggrieved, Evans had wildly overreacted and had never troubled to acquaint himself with Spanish procedure. His vanity and ill-considered response embarrassed Villiers, who had had to defend his conduct in Madrid. By the end of the month, the Minister had found his behaviour tiresome and tedious. Evans, he wrote,

is a man exceedingly *difficile à vivre*, always believing every idle report that it is told him, & surrounded by a set of toadeaters who make his life miserable by representing every thing as a premeditated insult to his dignity.[72]

Evans's resentment was compounded by the recurrence of pay arrears at San Sebastian. By June 1836 the men were again two months in arrears and the officers six months, nearly four months more than the Spanish officers. Evans protested repeatedly over the non-payments, but the arrears of the Legion were not significantly worse than those of other regiments in the Queen's army. Istúriz, prompted by Villiers, managed to raise £12,000 from the Bayonne bankers to cover the pay of the legionaries up to the end of May. Evans dismissed the sum as a trifle, a verdict which Villiers deeply resented in view of the Legion's chaotic accounting. It was extremely difficult to secure any money from the government when the Legion could not show how previous sums had been spent. Even worse, Evans was exercising little or no supervision over the sums requested. The receipt of vastly inflated requests, based on bogus accounts, merely discredited the Legion and made the Treasury even more suspicious of its pay department. As Evans refused to interfere with either the commissariat or the pay department, and was supported in this stance by Palmerston, the difficulties over pay and accounting were bound to persist.[73]

Discontent mounted within the officer corps during the summer. Some officers resented not only their lack of pay but also the attitudes of officers of the Royal Marines. Although the Marines had rendered invaluable service, not least on 6th June, when their accurate fire had rescued three companies of legionaries from being overwhelmed, many of their officers disliked associating with a body which included deserters and drunkards from their own corps. Even more galling was the general appearance of the legionaries and the exalted rank enjoyed by most of their officers. Evans responded to this resentment by issuing an order giving officers of the Royal Marines a superior local rank over those of the Legion. Henceforth a Marine colonel would rank with Legion generals, a captain with colonels, and a subaltern with captains. The order was bitterly disliked by the officers of the Legion, who felt that their services had been devalued. Indeed, legionaries were under more risk than the Marines, as Don Carlos had exempted the latter from the provisions of the Durango Decree. In seeking to mollify the Marines, Evans had merely antagonised his own officers.[74]

Evans suspected that some of his officers were so ambitious and self-opinionated that they could not be satisfied by service in Spain. He feared that malcontents who left Spain would disparage the Legion and his own activities on their return to Britain. Some did, and the conspiracy-conscious Evans warned Palmerston that General Duncan MacDougall might behave in a similar fashion. The Foreign Secretary was astounded to learn of these forebodings. Having interviewed MacDougall, he recalled that the general had highly praised the Legion and had never criticised Evans.[75] Nevertheless, the commander remained anxious, especially of reports in the British press. After Fuenterrabia, he berated Charles Shaw over a report in the *Courier* which had praised him as the only competent officer in the action. Evans believed that Shaw himself had sent the reports to the *Courier*, a charge denied by both Shaw and the editor of the paper.[76] Shaw left Spain in high dudgeon, so depriving the Legion of one of its more enterprising senior officers.

The friction between Evans and some senior officers reflected a more profound malaise within the Legion's officer corps. Dissatisfaction persisted over the conditions of service, the arrears of pay, the lack of action, and the status of the Legion. In early July seven officers claimed the right to terminate their contracts after one year's service. Under the terms of contract, signed by Evans on 22nd June 1835, they had enrolled 'for either one or two years, as may be preferred by the individual engaging to enter Her Majesty's Service'.[77] If these officers succeeded in resigning, Evans feared that others would follow suit, and possibly their men as well. Embarrassed by the requests, he also feared lest the resignations impair the ability of the Legion to take the offensive – the 8th regiment had refused to march on 15th July, demanding pay and final settlement.[78] Istúriz was appalled at the prospect of officers and men leaving Spain, and urged Evans to stand firm. He did so, issuing a general order, on 23rd July, which stated that officers could not resign after one year unless they had specified this intention at the time of entering the service. He exhorted officers to remember that they had volunteered in a struggle to overthrow 'oppression and despotism', and that withdrawal now would leave the task uncompleted, at a critical moment, when their valour had already been proven on the field of battle.[79]

Evans coupled this order with extensive efforts to remove the pay arrears. From his own pay of £5,000 a year as commander he advanced about £1,200 to pay the 7th regiment up to the 30th June. Captain Peyton, the paymaster of the 4th regiment, offered to pay the officers and men of his own regiment up to the same date, and to go on paying them from his own funds until September. Chichester criticised the policy, fearing that concessions would not mollify the discontented.[80] The dissension persisted, especially within the Lancer regiments and the two Scottish regiments, the 6th and 8th. Some seventy Lancers were dismounted lest they defect to the Carlists, who were offering fifty dollars for each horse, and passports to those defectors who wished to return to Britain through France. The bulk of the Scots soldiers, whom Shaw had enrolled without any form of enlistment, remained unappeasable. Some 200 troops of the 6th laid down their arms on 1st August, another 200 did so on 8th August, and about 400 from the 8th threatened to do so as soon as their first year of service expired. Their mutinies occurred at the worst possible moment for Evans. He was still severely ill and unable to leave his room to remonstrate with the mutineers. Fatalistically, he accepted the loss of these Scottish troops; as he assured Lord Palmerston, 'it will be a good riddance. They are accustomed to the organisation of political unions – unnecessarily litigious and decidedly less brave than any other corps.'[81]

Once the mutineers were withdrawn from the front line and due to return to Britain, Evans reported a significant improvement in morale and discipline. Having forecast the possibility of mutiny, he sought to profit from the occurrence by securing a settlement of the outstanding pay arrears. He sent Colonel de Lancey to Madrid, expecting a favourable response in view of the recent change of government, involving the return of Mendizábal in a council headed by José Calatrava.[82] His emissary, however, approached the new government with a large claim for which he lacked the necessary accounts. De Lancey, who arrived in Madrid on 26th August, presented a claim for £60,000, whereas the Spanish Treasury doubted that the sum should exceed £20,000. After nearly a month's negotiation, in which Villiers, according to de Lancey, played a prominent rôle, £25,000 was remitted to the Legion. This paid the claims of the Legion up to 31st August.[83]

By September 1836 the Legion had recovered from the worst of the midsummer dissension. In discipline and appearance the troops seemed markedly improved. Evans had completely recovered from his fever and was no longer talking of his imminent return to Westminster, despite the 'painful irksomeness' of his command. The Legion had fortified its defences, so consolidating its hold on the northern coastline. A shortage of manpower prevented any further offensives; without another three or four thousand troops, wrote Evans, he could not move from his defensive position.[84]

On 1st October 1836 the Carlists launched a determined assault on the Legion's defences. Using heavy artillery brought up from Hernani and Irun, they began shelling the whole line at daylight. Some 10,000 troops attacked along the whole line, but a particularly fierce effort was made to capture the village of Alza on the Legion's left, with the aim of threatening Passages. Several picquets were captured and recaptured, but the defences, composed of fortified houses on hill tops separated by ravines, held firm. By noon the Carlists ceased their attacks, although they continued the artillery bombardment until four o'clock in the afternoon.[85] Evans was constantly to the fore throughout the action, riding from one part of the line to another, in complete disregard for personal safety. He incurred a slight injury from a musket ball through one of his ears, but risked a more severe injury in a remarkable, if somewhat reckless, display of bravery.[86] The Legion and its Spanish allies suffered fewer than 500 casualties, but the Carlist losses were estimated at over 1,200. Evans refrained from counter-attacking for fear of further casualties and a possible reverse, as so many of his Spanish troops were recently recruited and not fully trained. This prudence was applauded by Palmerston and the Spanish government. With his position secure, Evans was ordered on to the defensive by General Rodil. He had to send 2,000 of his best troops to reinforce the reserve and another 340 to strengthen the garrison at Portugalette.[87]

Evans now faced a long period of inactivity, and almost immediately the internal problems of the Legion re-surfaced. He received letters of protest from six senior officers, including four brigadier-generals, and from Don Mateo Llanos, the inspector-general of the Legion's civil department. The letters, written on various dates from 20th to 30th October, drew attention to the arrears of pay of officers and men, the lack of trust of the Spanish government, doubts over pensions for widows and wounded, the personal sacrifices required of individual officers, and the possible recurrence of mutiny unless the arrears were paid and future pay, gratuities, pensions and provisions guaranteed.[88] In his reply, Evans fully sympathised with their complaints, and stressed that justice should be done to them in view of the frequent assurances and broken promises of the Spanish authorities. He also stated that ultimate responsibility rested with the British government, under whose auspices and desire the officers had entered the service of Queen Isabella. He promised to appeal 'in the last resort' to the British government, seeking rectification of past claims, guarantees for the future pay and pensions, and supplies for the coming winter. Having lost all confidence in the Spanish government, he enclosed a copy of his reply in a letter to Lord Palmerston. He emphasised that if Britain could not intervene, then the 'Legion must immediately dissolve'.[89]

As Evans explained to Palmerston, the officers and men feared for their future in Spain. The crews of the steamers under the orders of Commodore Henry were now twelve to fourteen months in arrears. The sailors had refused to weigh anchor and demanded their discharge, complaining that their protests were ignored now that regular British war steamers were operating off the coast of Spain. The Legion anticipated similar treatment when its services were no longer required. Evans insisted, too, that his own retirement was now due, having struggled with 'annoyances until my patience is thoroughly worn out'. He had sacrificed much, including his health, to form without adequate means 'a considerable force of different arms', and had gained 'some successes not without brilliancy'. For these services, he had received scant reward – he was still a brevet lieutenant-colonel in the British army and the commander of an ill-considered force in the Queen's service (in a recent letter Mendizábal had not even mentioned the action of 1st October). Even worse, some officers had threatened to take legal action against him for breach of contract. Apart from his conviction that the Carlist cause was doomed, and that liberal and legal institutions would now take root in Spain, Evans was in a depressed and fatalistic mood, consumed with self-pity.⁹⁰

Colonel Wylde, a perceptive observer, reckoned that the disorder and indiscipline of the previous August would soon recur if more pay was not forthcoming. In a letter to Lord Palmerston, he emphasised that the Spanish authorities could no longer delay payment by claiming that the accounts were not in order. Only the records of the commissariat were still confused; the accounts of the paymaster and the Quartermaster-General were balanced and in order. He believed, moreover, that Evans was determined to resume his seat in Parliament, and that his departure would be disastrous. He doubted that any other officer could keep the Legion together for a single month unless it was paid and fed with 'the strictest punctuality'.⁹¹

These entreaties, coupled with the pleas of General Le Marchant in London and Colonel Godfrey in Madrid, brought scant relief. Palmerston refused any money, and merely exhorted Mendizábal to make the Legion the first and not the last of his priorities.⁹² The Spanish Minister could not oblige. The upsurge of Carlist activity in midsummer had exhausted the more productive provinces and thwarted the raising of revenue. Mendizábal's objections to the accounts of the Legion were now partly a facade; he simply lacked the funds to pay the arrears in full. After strenuous representations, Godfrey and Villiers secured a mere £10,000 for the Legion. Villiers anticipated that this sum would not appease Evans: 'He has now, as he has long had, Westminster and nothing but Westminster in his eye ...'.⁹³

The criticism was less than entirely fair. Evans was worried about his parliamentary seat, and feared the consequences of reneging upon his pledge to return to Westminster. Indeed, he seemed to dwell upon these fears during the long periods of inactivity, when the Spanish authorities were proving unco-operative. Nevertheless, he could be swayed by protestations and flattery, especially by the argument that the Legion would disintegrate without him. This reasoning seemed peculiarly apposite in mid-December when two regiments, the 3rd and 4th, laid down their arms and tried to seduce other corps to join them. As the mutineers were following the example of two lieutenant-colonels, Churchill and Kirby, their actions were even more serious than those of the previous August, which had merely involved the ranks. Within a few days the revolts subsided as the other corps stood fast and the ringleaders were arrested.⁹⁴ The incidents, however, prompted Evans to withdraw his resignation and to seek only a temporary leave of absence to attend the opening of Parliament. He proposed leaving Brigadier-General Chichester in command, as the possibility of offensive operations, which depended upon massive reinforcements, could not be undertaken until the end of February.[95]

Changes of strategy induced Evans to abandon this plan of returning to England. On 25th December the Carlists suffered a severe reverse when their siege of Bilbao was raised by an army of 22,000 men under Espartero, assisted by Lord John Hay. Acting upon his own discretion, Evans refused either to join the relief of Bilbao or to create any diversion by a local offensive. Despite criticism from Madrid, he resolved to keep his distance from the operation in view of his profound distrust of Espartero. Evans was suspicious of this junior-ranking general, who had gained command of the army in September; he feared that Espartero, like General Oraa, was determined to deny him 'the means of taking any prominent part in the war'.[96] But as soon as the siege was lifted, he saw the enormous potential of the army in northern Spain and the possibility of a rapid victory over the Carlist forces. With 8,000 reinforcements, he was sure that he could reach the river Bidassoa and so cut the Carlist supply lines. He was delighted to learn that Villiers endorsed this strategy and would impress it upon the Spanish authorities. He was pleased, too, by the sudden transformation of the Legion's morale as half the pay, raised by Godfrey and Villiers, arrived in San Sebastian on 29th December. As the Legion had sufficient supplies and rations to endure the winter without any recurrence of the scenes witnessed at Vitoria, Evans was convinced that it was in 'better order for fighting' than ever before. The prospect of a renewed and possibly decisive military offensive, approved by the government on 18th January, encouraged him to withdraw the request for a leave of absence.[97] Anticipating this *volte face*, Palmerston wrote to him:

Your constituents will surely see that you are doing more service to the general cause of liberty, and to the real interests of England by remaining at the head of your troops than any man could have the means of effecting in the House of Commons. You have toiled through the ploughing and sowing. It would be unfair upon you that another sh[oul]d step in to reap the harvest.[98]

General Saarsfield, then captain-general of Navarre, had devised the plan for an advance into the heart of Carlist country. He proposed that three columns – his own from Pamplona, Evans's from San Sebastian, and Espartero's from Bilbao – should converge on Oyarzun and thereafter strike at the Carlist positions in the province of Guipúzcoa. The campaign required secure defences of existing positions, especially on the Ebro line, the co-ordinated movement of the three forces, and the reinforcement of Evans. Guarding the Ebro required comparatively few units from Espartero's army, since the river was unfordable in midwinter, but the severe weather rendered co-ordinated movement extremely difficult, as communications were slow and uncertain. It took five days to reach Bayonne from Bilbao by steamer, six to travel from Vitoria to Bilbao, and Pamplona was virtually inaccessible. The mutual suspicion of the generals compounded these problems. Evans's fears of Espartero revived as he awaited the arrival of 6,000 reinforcements from Bilbao. Frustrated by the delay, he sent a stream of letters to Villiers, criticising 'the temper and cunning', the lack of vigour and resolve, and the tactical failings of Espartero. He favoured the appointment of Saarsfield as commander-in-chief or, failing that, a ministerial directive ordering Espartero to send reinforcements.[99]

Villiers, who doubted the military capacity of Espartero and detested his political intrigues, readily obliged. He remonstrated with Calatrava, persuading him to send peremptory orders to his general-in-chief. These orders, combined with the intercession of Colonel Wylde at Bilbao, had the desired effect. On 7th February 5,135 men and 210 officers arrived in San Sebastian, adding, after the deduction of cooks, servants and musicians, some 4,600 bayonets to Evans's force. He could take the field with nearly 9,000 troops, leaving a reserve of about 3,000 men to guard Passages and to support the lines. The mixed force included some 5,000 Spanish troops, 3,300 legionaries, about 450 Royal Marines, and small detachments of Royal Marine artillery and Royal Artillery. Delighted by the quality of his reinforcements, Evans was confident of 'striking a pretty sharp blow'. He forgave Espartero, looked forward to the struggle, and dubbed himself 'the happiest man in Europe'.[100]

Ready to commence operations on 18th February, Evans fumed at the subsequent delays. Saarsfield, having formulated the plan, found more and more reasons for postponing its implementation. He waited initially upon money and provisions. Once these arrived, he sought authorisation to leave the line of Tubiri, and, when it was given, requested reinforcements to replace the disorganised Foreign Legion. On 21st February he wrote to Evans, doubting the wisdom of combined operations, as he had to reinforce his defences before leaving the province. He was reluctant to move until Espartero had taken Durango and Evans had begun his coastal operations.[101] Evans, though appalled by this indecision, was determined to move as quickly as possible. Only the late arrival of a Spanish Marine battalion and the saturated state of the ground, which prevented the movement of field artillery, forestalled his immediate advance. The Carlists, meanwhile, had begun to concentrate in his locality. Don Carlos had moved his headquarters to Andoin, about three miles from Hernani, and had withdrawn his main army from Durango. By 2nd March, Evans reckoned that the Carlists could deploy some 16,000 or 17,000 troops in the northern sector, manning formidable redoubts and defences, and operating on interior lines of communication.[102]

The concentration of Carlists at least facilitated the forward movement of the Cristino columns. On 10th March, Espartero moved out of Bilbao, encountering comparatively little resistance, and entered Durango on the 13th, where he halted to resupply his troops instead of pushing on to Vergara as originally planned. Evans also moved his forces on the 10th, crossing the Urumea and attacking the fortified heights of Ametzagama. Despite heavy losses, the heights were stormed successfully and then held against Carlist counter-attacks. The Spanish brigade, under General Jáuregui, completed a triumphant day by capturing San Marco. Evans had lost nearly a thousand men, killed and wounded, in these frontal assaults, but the results of the 10th had exceeded expectations.

On the evening of the 11th Evans received Saarsfield's letter of the 9th, indicating that he would move within forty-eight hours towards 'the enemy's centre of operation'. Evans was astounded; he assumed that Saarsfield was no longer marching upon Vera and Oyarzun, but through the mountainous passes of Lecumbri towards Hernani. He claimed in letters to Villiers, and in his memoirs, that he now prepared a frontal attack on Hernani to divert Carlist forces from Saarsfield's column. Even if true, this motive hardly warranted the risk of a premature attack, with insufficient forces, against a town so vital to the Carlist cause that it was bound to be heavily defended. Nevertheless, Evans sent three battalions across the Urumea in boats on the 12th to capture the village of Loyola. He secured his communications on the following day by the construction of a pontoon bridge. Although further movement was thwarted by incessant rain, he determined to launch his attack on the 15th, having received further despatches from Saarsfield, which confirmed his departure from Pamplona on the 11th by 'the shortest road to the enemy's lines'.[103] Not until three o'clock in the afternoon of the 16th did Evans learn that Saarsfield had withdrawn his forces to Pamplona, after one day's march, on account of bad weather.

On the morning of the 15th, Evans moved in two columns against the hill fort of Oriamendi and the range of fortified heights which extended from it and covered Hernani. After a fierce resistance, the Carlists were driven from their positions, eventually by use of the bayonet. On the following morning the last entrenchments were cleared, and a bombardment of Hernani began. The prospect of a remarkable victory suddenly vanished with the arrival of Don Sebastian, the Carlist commander-in-chief, at the head of a flying column of reinforcements – some eleven battalions with cavalry and artillery. He counter-attacked on both flanks, passing three battalions into the rear of Evans's left flank near the bridge of Astigarraga. Panicked by the outflanking, the 1st battalion of the Legion, followed by a Castile battalion, broke and fled, spreading disorder and confusion throughout the regiments on the left. Demoralised, these units abandoned their advanced positions and fell back in complete disarray. The right flank, under more severe attack, held firm: although its advanced posts were driven in, a battalion of Royal Marines displayed 'admirable steadiness and firmness' and checked further incursions. By mid-afternoon, Evans still had the option of defending the heights above Hernani, but his forces were outnumbered by nearly two to one, many regiments were totally disorganised, and the prospect of reinforcement vanished with news of Saarsfield's withdrawal. He accepted defeat, ordered the destruction of captured guns and the dismantling of defences at Oriamendi, and retreated to San Sebastian. He had lost nearly 900 men in killed and wounded, not including a company of about 120 men who were surrounded and captured.[104]

Evans was profoundly depressed by the defeat. He attributed the blame to himself, his troops, and Saarsfield. He could excuse neither the panic of some battalions nor the incapacity of Saarsfield; but he also admitted that he had taken a risk in pressing the offensive, and that he had deployed his small force 'on a strong but too extended position', a criticism echoed by Lord John Hay. He accepted, too, that the significance of the defeat lay not in the size of the casualty list, but in the loss of 'prestige and morale of our troops . . .'.[105] Though few self-criticisms would appear in his memoirs, where he reproved Hay for withdrawing the Marines in mid-afternoon,[106] Evans was acutely aware of his own failure in the aftermath of battle. Both Wylde and Villiers tried to console the dejected commander and prevent him from resigning immediately. With his usual hyperbole, Villiers informed Evans that his resignation 'would be the greatest blow the Queen's cause had received for it would be the greatest victory the Carlists had gained'.[107]

Villier's assessment of the reverse underwent a rapid change. Initially, he feared that the 'disaster at Hernani' would embarrass the government in Madrid, revive the spirits of the Carlists, and confirm the expectations of Tories in Britain. He doubted that Evans possessed the qualities of a general, apart from personal bravery, and deplored the delays in launching the assaults on the 15th and 16th March. He also criticised the payment of troops on the 15th, whereupon some had become drunk and disobedient on the following day. Above all, he condemned Evans's *penchant* for publicity, especially the issuing of a despatch to the press on the 16th, which was ill-considered and excessively despondent. As Villiers wrote to his brother,

You know my opinion of that worthy and of the canaille he commands. I have always been prepared therefore for a catastrophe but the blockhead may thank himself for all that will be said in Eng[lan]d about it.[108]

Nevertheless, he accepted that Evans alone could hold the Legion together until June, when its term of service expired. Once more accurate returns of the combatants and casualties reached Madrid, he agreed that the retreat appeared neither so unnecessary nor so disgraceful. He thought that the disaster would soon be forgotten if Evans could recommence effective operations, an option which depended entirely upon the co-operation of Espartero.[109]

The revival of Villier's spirits reflected more positive correspondence from Evans. The general's depression had lasted only a few days while he was unwell and preoccupied with removing officers and consolidating regiments. He was soon convinced that the military consequences of the 16th were not significant, that the enemy had lost more than the Legion by the action, and that a fresh intiative could soon be mounted with reinforcements from Espartero. On 26th March he sent Colonel Wylde to Bilbao to persuade the general-in-chief of the wisdom of concentrating forces in the north for an advance on Hernani. But Evans insisted that he could not possibly remain in Spain beyond the 10th June, when the Legion's contract ended. He doubted that more than 2,000 men could be tempted to re-engage by pay settlements and bounties, and feared that the number might be considerably less.[110]

With only two months' service remaining, Evans was able to bargain more effectively over the arrears of pay. The Spanish government wanted to retain the services of the Legion for an additional six months, and the best men for another year or two. Apart from its military utility, the Legion represented, albeit in limited form, foreign support for the Cristino cause. As Villiers maintained, 'the moral effect of the Legion's departure will be very bad'.[111] Evans, however, could argue plausibly that the re-engagement of the bulk of the Legion was unlikely until the arrears were paid, especially the thirteen months' pay owed to the officers. He sent Mr Llanos, head of the financial department of the Legion, and Mr Black, head of the accounts department, to Madrid to answer all enquiries about the arrears, gratuities and accounts. He warned Villiers, too, that the consequences of non-payment could be dire when the Legion ceased to be Spanish soldiers on 11th June. As everyone would revert to the status of British subject, officers would no longer have any authority over their men.[112] Alarmed at the thought of the legionaries pillaging San Sebastian, he pressed Calatrava to meet the claims of the Legion. A Council of Ministers was convened to discuss the subject, and it authorised Mendizábal to find the necessary funds. Villiers, who should have known better, believed that the promise would be fulfilled. By 13th May he affirmed that sufficient money had been raised, and that the appeals of Evans and Wylde would induce all senior officers to remain, as well as some 2,500 to 3,000 men.[113] Although the men were paid in full at the end of their contract, the officers remained in arrears and a mere 120 extended their service, along with some 120 sergeants and 1,500 men.

While Villiers was lobbying the Spanish government, Evans fretted in San Sebastian. He desperately wanted to accomplish 'something important' before his contract expired, but the Legion was much depleted. Of the original force, about 3,400 noncommissioned officers and men remained in the infantry (or nearly 3,000 fighting men exclusive of servants, etc.), some 240 N.C.O.s and men in the artillery, and about 400 in the cavalry. Another 1,300 men were hospitalised or sick.[114] In these circumstances, he could not undertake any operations without assistance from Espartero, and had sent Wylde to Bilbao to advocate the strategy of concentrating forces for an attack on Hernani and the frontier towns. He deeply resented this rôle, informing Villiers that 'I determined for the first and *last* time to put myself in the false position as a subordinate officer of *proposing* and *urging* a project of campaign . . .'.[115] By 19th April the weather relented, enabling Wylde to return to San Sebastian with the news that Espartero and the Generals Seoane and Escalera had endorsed Evans's plan. Delighted with the information, Evans predicted that the enemy would be driven from their strongholds 'within a month'.[116]

Don Carlos virtually assured the accuracy of this forecast by removing the main body of his army to Estella for a march on Madrid. He left about 14,000 men, including armed peasants, to guard the northern positions. Evans and Espartero would command forces of 10,000 and 14,000 men respectively. As soon as reinforcements of six battalions reached San Sebastian, Evans began moving his force across the Urumea. By 3rd May he had reoccupied Loyola and Aquirre, the positions taken on 14th March, and was ready to commence operations upon the arrival of Espartero. On 9th May, Espartero landed in San Sebastian, having travelled by sea from Bilbao. Within a couple of days the whole of his force had disembarked. Facing overwhelming odds – not the 'nearly equal terms' mentioned in Evans's memoirs[117] – the Carlists withdrew their artillery from Oriamendi, and feinted an expedition into Castile by drawing away a large part of their defending army. Undeceived, the Cristino armies began their attack on 14th May. In wet and stormy weather, Evans led the Legion and a Spanish division in an assault on the heights which overlooked Hernani. The enemy yielded after nominal resistance, so facilitating an immediate attack on the town. While General Guerra covered the left flank, and took Astigarraga, Evans launched his forces on Hernani, carrying not only the town but also the village of Urrieta before nightfall.

Espartero, who had generously allowed Evans to lead the vanguard in these assaults, now established his headquarters at Hernani. Willing to give Evans all the glory, he let him have the sole responsibility of investing Oyarzun, Irun and Fuenterrabia. On 16th May, Evans moved on to the attack with about 10,000 men in fourteen battalions, along with some seamen and Marines under Lord John Hay. The Carlists had left a mere three battalions to defend these places. The two battalions before Oyarzun were quickly scattered, and Irun was invested at noon. The walled defences of the town and the nearby citadel, Fort del Parque, proved extremely resilient, and two twelve-pounders had to be brought up from the fort of Behovia to breach the gates. Even so, it took nearly eighteen hours to reduce the fort by bombardment, followed by scaling the parapets and fighting from house to house in the suburbs. Evans had permitted the women and children to leave Irun and pass into France. He also ordered that the prisoners should be spared. The troops, nonetheless, having taken the town by storm, were not easily controlled. They enjoyed nearly two hours of plunder, desecration and rape (of some women who had never left their homes).[118]

Evans's magnanimity in sparing the Carlist prisoners had its desired effect. On 18th May the garrison at Fuenterrabia requested that two officers be allowed to go to Irun to confirm that the prisoners were still alive. Once they returned, the garrison surrendered immediately. Evans rejoiced that the Legion had 'vindicated itself in the most brilliant manner . . .'.[119] Villiers was equally enthusiastic, praising not only the military triumphs but also the 'humanity after the combat was over'.[120] Lord Palmerston applauded the victories and the concentration of the Cristino armies at San Sebastian in accordance with Evans's advice: these achievements, he wrote, 'have I trust struck a mortal blow to the Carlist cause'.[121] The Spanish government expressed its warm approval, though somewhat tardily (the letter of congratulations to Evans was dated 29th May): it ordered a medal to be struck for the troops who were engaged at Irun, decorated several senior officers, and awarded Evans the Grand Cross of Charles III. Indeed, Calatrava hoped that Evans would now re-engage and continue as commander of the Legion.[122]

But Evans, exhausted by the campaign, was determined to return home. He was extremely worried about his political future, as another general election was likely in view of the imminent death of William IV. He refused to visit Madrid to receive his decoration lest he forfeit the chance of re-election. As he informed Villiers,

from my position and pledges to my constituents of Westminster I could not remain without forfeiting all title to credit as a man of veracity – and in fact without separating myself almost wholly from my country – at least as a public man – Besides which I have suffered too deeply in my feelings and health by the wants I have been exposed to . . . In truth I believe myself to have been cruelly treated.[123]

He had cause for some bitterness and concern. He knew that the activities of the Legion had been hotly debated and often condemned in Britain, without regard for the difficulties encountered. He also feared that the criticism would continue as disgruntled officers returned, bereft of payment for the last fifteen months of service. He resented the manner in which the Spanish government had treated the Legion – its record of broken promises reflecting a lowly estimate of its military value. Indeed, the mere presence of the Legion, symbolising foreign support for the Cristino cause, had seemed almost as important as its military contribution. Yet Evans had always believed that, in spite of its composition and neglect by the Spanish authorities, the Legion could have intervened decisively in the campaign. On the other hand, he never shared the extravagant hopes of Palmerston about the impact of 10,000 British troops, partly because he realised the difference between the legionaries and regular British soldiers and partly because he never commanded a full-strength Legion. Although the sick list oscillated over the two years, reaching a peak during the winter at Vitoria, it was always substantial: of its 10,000 men the Legion lost 1,850 (62 officers and 1,788 other ranks) from disease and another 629 (36 officers and 593 other ranks) from wounds in action.[124] Hence Evans had constantly sought reinforcements, and a concentrated war effort to cut the Carlist supply lines to France. On mature reflection, he accepted that the war in the northern provinces was not decisive in and of itself, and that the services of the Legion were essentially limited. 'This small force,' he wrote, provided 'an honest, gallant, and highly useful auxiliary support'.[125]

Some of Evans's problems as commander derived from the essentially limited rôle and utility of the Legion. On account of his small force and subordinate command, he could never sustain an independent campaign. He had to liaise with his general-in-chief, a task complicated by the jealousies, suspicions and political intrigues within the Spanish high command. He had to co-operate, too, with the commander of the Royal Marines, Lord John Hay, whose views of the Legion varied from extremes of optimism to pessimism. But the difficulties of liaison, always likely in combined operations during a civil war, were complicated by the mistakes of Evans himself. He repeatedly misjudged the Spanish generals, especially Córdoba, Saarsfield and Espartero. His opinion of Córdoba lurched from high praise and gratitude initially, to outright condemnation during the winter in Vitoria. This criticism, which was reasonable in some respects, became increasingly strident as soon as Evans reached San Sebastian. Finding himself isolated from the main theatre of operations, Evans felt frustrated by the lack of action. Under immense psychological strain, albeit partially self-inflicted, he eagerly endorsed the plan of General Saarsfield. He accepted Saarsfield's promises of support and rated him as an extremely talented commander, fit to be general-in-chief. Within a month, however, he was deriding him as virtually mad.[126]

Evans's views of Espartero fluctuated even more wildly. Having served with him at Bilbao in September 1835, he considered him a competent general with whom he could co-operate. He rapidly changed this assessment once Espartero replaced Córdoba as general-in-chief. Thereafter Evans began to harbour suspicions and fears of him, suspecting that he was spiteful and self-seeking – a general who was determined to dominate the war effort. Only in the last few weeks of the campaign would Evans recant completely, recognising Espartero's remarkable generosity during the attacks on Hernani and the frontier towns.[127] Reflected in his earlier forebodings were the resentments derived from inactivity and isolation in San Sebastian, exacerbated by acute anxieties, largely of his own creation.

Throughout the war, Evans detested the prolonged periods of inactivity, enforced by his lack of manpower. Desperate to accomplish 'something important', he had chafed at his own predicament, made even more intolerable by the periodic pleas of Mendizábal to assume the offensive,[128] and by the discontent which recurrently surfaced within his officer corps. He found the frustration particularly galling as he believed fiercely in the imperative necessity of cutting the Carlist supplies. Convinced of this strategic requirement, but short of troops, prone to misjudge his allies, and frustrated in his desire for action, Evans took risks in strategic planning and in tactical initiatives. By endorsing Saarsfield's plan for a triple offensive, and by attacking Hernani precipitately, he made important mistakes.

Nevertheless, Evans possessed real gifts as a commander. He supervised the comparatively rapid transformation of the Legion into a fighting force. He led it, after the ordeal at Vitoria, to a gruelling if somewhat hazardous victory on 5th May 1836. He rallied it after the reverse at Fuenterrabia, the mutinies of August and December, and the defeat at Hernani. Never a stern disciplinarian in the mould of the 'Iron Duke', and so criticised accordingly by some of his officers, Evans could inspire his men both on and off the field. His audacious acts of bravery, coolness under fire, and numerous speeches and tributes appeared to maintain morale and confidence.

Finally, as a British commander fighting in a Spanish civil war, he possessed one vital attribute – a deeply held and sincere belief in his particular cause. He believed that reform, liberalism, and a constitutional government – the issues he endorsed in the British context – would ultimately prevail in Spain. It was indicative that, *en route* to Britain, he should still urge Villiers to preserve the concilitary measures in the Basque Provinces: as he claimed,

for the future security of the new institutions of Spain – I think it of the utmost importance to remove the causes of hostility – amidst this warlike and formidable people.[129]

5
'Count I-run'

In view of the impending general election, De Lacy Evans hurried back to England. He declined an invitation to receive his Cross of Charles III from Queen Isabella in Madrid, and paused only to have an audience with Louis Philippe and the Duke of Orleans in Paris. He was profoundly concerned about his chances of re-election.[1] During his absence, remarkable events had occurred in Westminster. Sir Francis Burdett, having represented the borough for thirty years in the Radical interest, had become estranged from his party over its links with O'Connellism, policies of political reform, and attitudes towards the privileges of the Established Church. Asked by some constituents to resign, he accepted the challenge and was re-elected at a by-election, on 10th May 1837, by 515 votes, becoming the first Tory representative of Westminster in nearly thirty years. Nationally, the Conservative party had also emerged as a more formidable force; it had grown steadily since 1835 and was more organised to contest the elections.[2] Evans, finally, was not returning as a conquering hero. Despite the successes of his final campaign, the Legion had endured two years of caustic comment from some Conservatives in Parliament and from sections of the press. He had to confront his critics and reassure his constituents.

Conservative criticism had erupted even before the Legion set sail for Spain. The Duke of Wellington's assertion that Britain had no title to intervene, even in the limited form of a Legion, was readily accepted by many newspaper editors. This charge was repeated throughout the campaign; indeed, *The Morning Post* was particularly vehement, condemning those who served with the Legion as 'mercenaries', and as 'men belonging to no country or Government ... insolent freebooters, having no right to the usages of civilized warfare'.[3] Editors were also sceptical about the likely impact of 7,000 untrained legionaries upon the balance of military power in northern Spain. The early, though minor, reverses of the Legion only seemed to confirm their foresight.[4]

Doubts, too, were expressed about the ability of Evans to command the Legion. Several London papers reviewed his military career with varying degrees of accuracy. *The Morning Post* questioned whether he had sufficient experience after a relatively brief period of active service at a fairly humble rank. It accepted that he had displayed considerable gallantry and some skill as a quartermaster in the Peninsular War, but doubted that this entitled him to a field command. The paper concluded that Evans had been selected 'more on account of his political opinions than his military science and experience'.[5] Although *The Courier* and *The Morning Chronicle* rallied to his defence,[6] criticism persisted, often focusing on petty, if sensitive, points like the size of his personal staff and the exalted rank which he held in Spain. Editors who viewed the war through this blinkered perspective considered any reverse or defeat as 'proof' of Evans's incapacity and attributed any victories to the bravery of his troops.[7]

Many Conservatives either sympathised with or openly supported the Carlist cause. Several journalists accompanied the Carlist armies, and some individuals, most notably C. F. Henningsen, served under Zumalacárregui. They despatched glowing reports of stubborn and fierce resistance by the supporters of Don Carlos against numerically superior foes – reports which contrasted sharply with the descriptions of the Legion either wintering without adequate provisions in Vitoria or languishing without pay in San Sebastian. In fact British observers of all political persuasions frequently censured the Madrid authorities for their neglect of the Legion, while some feared that the legionaries would become brutalised by their experiences in northern Spain, partly by the flogging which was thought to be extensive within the Legion and partly by the nature of the war itself. In the House of Lords, on 12th February 1836, Lord Londonderry claimed that the killing and butchery of the civil war had become infectious, and that legionaries had murdered 130 Carlist prisoners. After a protest from Evans, Londonderry revealed that his source for this unfounded allegation was an anonymous letter in the Carlist journal, *Gazette de France*.[8] Although the incident reflected little credit on Lord Londonderry, it was not untypical of the way in which the war was described by some parliamentarians and newspaper editors. Throughout the campaign, numerous letters and reports reached Britain containing unflattering accounts of the Legion and its activities: many were from officers, disgruntled over their pay and promotion prospects. Such complaints provided valuable ammunition for those who were willing to believe any ill of the Legion.

Understandably, Evans deeply resented the criticism of the Legion and of himself. Angered by the lies and distortions, he was even more concerned about their impact upon, and possible erosion of, his political base. By accepting command of the Legion, he had broken a pledge to his constituents and had incurred the wrath of those ultra-Radicals who believed that aristocratic repression in Britain was a more pressing concern than its counterpart in Spain.[9] Consequently, Evans chose to reply to his critics by writing open letters to his constituents. In these lengthy epistles he defended his participation in the cause of countering 'despotism and the inquisition', explained his military strategy, and refuted the more extreme charges which had been levelled against him. He noted, correctly, that his main parliamentary criticism had come from the more extreme Conservatives, and that the leader of the Opposition had not traduced the Legion but merely objected to the policy of limited intervention. Seeking to allay fears about the Legion's health, Evans insisted that its proportion of sick and wounded was smaller than that endured by the British army in the Peninsular War. Above all, he emphasised that the Spanish cause was not purely a matter of local succession, but was equally 'an English and European cause', a struggle between freedom and absolutism – 'the great principle which divides the European nations'.[10]

By expressing such sentiments Evans merely infuriated his opponents and kindled the debate in Britain. Ordinarily, condemnation by *The Times* and *The Morning Post* could only have enhanced his standing in Westminster, but these papers did not simply deride him as a partisan Radical. They also deplored the 'bungling' of his generalship and poured scorn on the Legion's achievements. They dubbed him 'a lashing disciplinarian', juxtaposing the flogging of the legionaries with his protestations before the Royal Commission on Military Punishments. They claimed, too, that Evans was ultimately responsible for the privations of his men, and that he should have pressed their case more resolutely before the Spanish authorities. As *The Times* concluded,

The only conceivable excuse for the disastrous blundering of Colonel Evans is, that he was bewildered by the difficulties of the position, for which he was utterly unqualified by previous experience or military talent.[11]

By characterising Evans as an incompetent and a hypocrite, these papers were disparaging his credibility as a public figure, a potentially more damaging charge than any attack on his political views.

Although *The Morning Chronicle* loyally defended him, the attacks persisted, reaching a peak of intensity after the Legion's defeat at Hernani (16th March 1837). On 17th April 1837 Sir Henry Hardinge, the former Secretary at War, raised the Legion as an issue in the House of Commons. He deprecated the despatch of the force, arguing that its 'failings and disasters' had tarnished the national honour. He summarised the military exploits of the Legion, emphasising its previous defeats, its privations at Vitoria, and its cruel neglect by the Spanish authorities: 'had he been in General Evans's place, he would not have trusted to such promises'. Using the correspondence of disappointed officers like Majors Hall and Richardson and Colonel Churchill, he dwelt upon the scenes of mutiny and insubordination at San Sebastian, and on the brutality and slaughter which followed the battles. Finally, he reviewed the action of 16th March, contrasting the performance of the Royal Marines and Royal Artillery with the cowardice of some legionaries, and urged the government to recall the Legion.[12]

Ministers resisted the demand, mustering a majority of thirty-six votes in support of their policy. They were clearly relieved by Evans's victories in late April and May, but the critics were by no means penitent. *The Times* sustained its barrage of censorious editorials, questioning whether anything of substance had been achieved after two years of fighting. Describing Evans as a 'flogging patriot' and a 'Whig-Radical non-representative', it noted that even some Whig papers, notably the *London and Westminster Review*, had joined in the mockery of the returning colonel. The *Review* had compared the Legion's achievements to those of 'the celebrated King of France, who, "with fifty thousand men, marched up the hill, and then marched down again" '.[13] Evans, as a consequence, had to reassure his constituents over his activities in Spain during the forthcoming election campaign.

Almost as worrying for him was the balance of political support within Westminster and the organisation of the rival parties. At the recent by-election the Radicals had suffered an unexpectedly resounding defeat. Burdett had benefited from the high turn-out of voters to carry six parishes, narrowly losing three others, and only suffered a clear defeat in the Radical bailiwick of St Anne. Indeed, he polled 1,223 votes in St George's, more than double his winning tally in 1835. Conservative support had been vital, particularly the organisation spearheaded by the Carlton Club. Moreover, Burdett, after thirty years as M.P. for Westminster, had benefited from a large personal vote.[14] Just how large, no one really knew, as he decided to forsake Westminster at the general election and seek the safer seat of North Wiltshire.

Evans entered the fray, determined to restore Radical fortunes in Westminster and to refute the allegations against him. Campaigning with John Temple Leader, the former Member for Bridgwater, who had challenged Burdett in the by-election, he embarked on a hectic round of meetings. At the outset, he encountered criticism from potential supporters about his conduct over the previous two years. When charged with deserting the constituency, he reminded audiences of the meetings held prior to his departure which had overwhelmingly approved of the venture.[15] To the claim that he had led a foolhardy expedition, he insisted that the Spanish struggle was not a local affair but a battle for 'liberty', in which he had been proud that Britain had participated.[16] To criticism about the neglect of his troops, he insisted that the men had been paid completely, and that he was more in arrears than any other officer. He dismissed the privations endured at Vitoria as simply the normal 'hardships' of war, declaring that, ordinarily, 'the troops were fed better, far better he was sorry to say, than four-fifths of the working poor in England'.[17]

But his main concern was to rebut any suggestion that he had ordered the flogging of men under his command. Had this rumour gained credence, it could have damaged both his reputation and Radical credentials irreparably. To account for the flogging in the Legion, he explained that the force had served under English law, and that regimental courts-martial could inflict flogging as a punishment. As commander-in-chief, however, he had only presided over general courts-martial, where he had invariably commuted corporal punishment to imprisonment. He repeatedly stressed the distinction between regimental and general courts-martial, sometimes reeling off a list of soldiers whom he had sentenced, along with their commuted punishments: the list was usually greeted with loud applause.[18]

Evans defended himself by seizing the offensive. He depicted himself as the victim of malicious and scurrilous attacks by the ultra-Tories. He frequently referred to the calumnies of Lord Londonderry as examples of the irresponsible criticisms which had been levelled against him. The more extreme critics, he argued, were fervent supporters of Don Carlos, and hence any defeat of the Carlist forces had simply compounded their hatred of him.[19] As the campaign developed, the personal attacks on Evans intensified. While Sir George Murray, the Conservative candidate, normally confined himself to denouncing the Radical platform of Evans and Leader,[20] his supporters were much less scrupulous. Conservative canvassers virtually ceased any criticism of Leader, urging the electors to split their votes.[21] Others carried placards through the streets caricaturing Evans in the act of running away and bearing the title 'Count I-run' (a reference to the charge that Evans had not merely deserted Westminster but also had deserted the Legion).[22] Some Conservatives, in the guise of legionaries, attended Evans's meetings with the purpose of heckling him. Evans responded with panache: he demanded that the hecklers should come forward one by one to recount their charges in front of him and name their commanding officers. As none did so, the audience roared its approval, and the hecklers were promptly ejected.[23]

After the first week of the campaign, Evans became increasingly confident. In his hectic round of speaking engagements he addressed large and usually enthusiastic audiences. He still had to answer questions about Spain, but the Tory tactics, particularly the insertion of hecklers, were proving counter-productive. He began to broaden the theme and content of his speeches, reminding voters about his record of fulfilling political pledges and of his continuing commitment to parliamentary and electoral reform. To counter the Conservative challenge, he urged all reformers to sink their differences and unite together. He praised the Liberals and 'many of the wealthy Whigs' who had already endorsed him. He bitterly attacked the Conservatives, jibing at their 'favourite', the Duke of Cumberland, who had become the *bête noire* of the Radicals for his activities as head of the Orange Lodge in Ireland and as King of Hanover, where he had recently annulled the constitution.[24] Scenting victory, Evans rallied many of his own supporters by publicly repudiating 'the indiscriminate and unrestricted sale of spirits' as advocated by the Licensed Victuallers' Protection Society.[25]

At the eve-of-poll hustings, on 25th July, he delivered a long and somewhat rambling defence of his military and political record. Oratorically the performance was poor, and was completely overshadowed by Leader's brief but highly partisan address. Evans, however, admitted that he could never sway voters by the power of his rhetoric. Instead 'he had rendered some service to the great cause of liberty on another soil', and, in a lengthy review of his Spanish service, refuted many of the accusations which had been hurled against him. Indeed, he challenged his accusers to cite any 'Tory Commander' who had managed to restrain his troops in their moment of triumph, as he had managed to do at Irun. In a wildly extravagant claim, he compared his service in Spain with 'what Lafayette had done for America upon the invitation of Washington and Franklin, and what William the Third did for the liberties of his country in 1688'. On domestic issues, he roused his supporters by reiterating his commitment to electoral reform, to the reform of Church temporalities, to the amendment of some clauses in the Poor Law Act, and to equal laws for Ireland. Finally, he proffered his support to 'the young and patriotic Queen' against 'her Tory uncle [the Duke of Cumberland] and his Tory and armed Orange confederates'.[26]

Table 2

Parish	Evans	Leader	Murray
St Margaret's	345	352	177
St John's	315	324	179
Savoy	12	13	17
St Mary-le-Strand	42	42	27
St Paul's	148	147	86
St Anne's	233	248	121
St Clement's	261	259	273
St James's	743	762	473
St Martin's	555	564	356
St George's	1,061	1,082	911
Total	3,715	3,793	2,620

The election results vindicated the three-week campaign which Evans had mounted. Although more Liberals 'plumped' for Leader, the colonel still secured a majority of 1,095 votes over Murray. In another large turn-out, the votes in Table 2 were recorded in each parish.[27] Apart from St Clements and Savoy, the Radicals had trounced their Conservative opponent. Their massive votes in St George's were especially gratifying, testifying, at least partially, to the improvement in organisation which Leader had promised his supporters.[28] The Westminster result was even more impressive in view of the other results in 1837: although there were some Radical gains, seven leading Radicals, including Hume and Roebuck, lost their seats, and Grote came within six votes of defeat in the City.[29] Without Burdett's personal following, which was probably a waning asset, the Conservatives had made little progress in the borough, but they had consolidated their base of support, from which future assaults could be launched on the Radical citadel. In a triumphant editorial *The Morning Chronicle* attributed Evans's success to the actions of the King of Hanover, to the endorsement of Murray by the discredited Burdett, to the failure of Murray to uphold his previous pledges to his constituents at Perth, to the attacks of *The Times*, and to the maladroit and underhand tactics of Murray's committee.[30] Whether these issues were decisive is by no means certain, but the Conservatives' choice of candidate and their style of campaign hardly advanced their cause: 'Count I-run' had returned in triumph.

Re-election, though gratifying, did not assuage Evans's feelings of having been maligned and misunderstood during his period of service in Spain. He pressed Villiers to represent his claims for 'some favour from the Government', especially as he had been 'attacked in so very gross and indecent a manner by the Tories and the Press'. In passing the request on to Palmerston, Villiers added that rewarding Evans might 'please his Constituents and render him a better *Member of Parliament*'.[31] Once Parliament reassembled, Evans asked repeatedly for an opportunity to state his case and to answer his critics.[32] Regarded as the spokesman for the Legion, he still received numerous letters from ex-officers, protesting about the protracted delay in settling their arrears of pay. As the longest arrears were due to him, Evans did not wish to be the sole advocate of their claims in case he appeared to be self-seeking; hence he sanctioned the formation of a committee of ex-officers under the chairmanship of Colonel Wetherall. He urged all claimants to pass their claims through the committee as a means of expediting the duties of the Spanish Royal Commission, and not to complain 'through a medium hitherto conspicuously hostile to us', presumably Conservative M.P.s.[33]

Evans was able to concentrate upon Spanish affairs because he was required neither by his constituents, nor by the business of the Commons, to devote all his attention to measures of reform. After the election, he was no longer the main Radical champion for the borough. In John Temple Leader the Radicals of Westminster had a younger, more eloquent, and equally committed advocate of their various causes. During the Parliament of 1837–41 he campaigned for the ballot, 'The People's Charter', and the reform of the Corn Laws. Constituents tended to ask him to lay their petitions before Parliament, with Evans as merely the seconder.[34] Moreover, the Conservative gains in the general election of 1837 had left the Whigs dependent upon Irish support for their bare majority in the Commons. Radical hopes were blocked by the reinvigorated Conservative Party, the hostile House of Lords, and by Lord Melbourne, who neither appointed Radicals to his Cabinet in 1837–38, nor countenanced further measures of reform. When George Grote tabled his ballot questions in 1838 and 1839, they were treated as 'open' questions by the government, so revealing its own weakness and internal divisions. Evans honoured his pledges on both occasions, but the reformers were swamped by a combination of Conservatives and a minority of government supporters (the votes were lost by 315 to 198 and by 333 to 216).

Evans regularly attended the House and loyally proffered his voting support when required. As Villiers anticipated, his creation as a Knight Commander of the Bath, dutifully acknowledged by Evans in January 1838,[35] may have tempered his rebellious instincts. On several procedural votes he indicated his desire to reform the system of electoral registration, but the government could count on his support for its Irish legislation, the Canada and New Zealand Bills, and in votes of confidence. Evans steadfastly supported O'Connell, voting for him when he was arraigned by the House for a breach of privilege. On 21st February 1838 he took the chair after a dinner in honour of O'Connell at the Crown and Anchor. In his introductory speech, he congratulated the government upon trying 'to remedy the abuses of Ireland', and praised O'Connell for agitating in a peaceful and responsible manner on behalf of his country. Without his guidance, argued Evans, the struggle for freedom in Ireland 'might have steeped the country in blood'. O'Connell had 'never violated any law, but by the force of argument and reason, urged on the march of freedom, and vindicated the great cause of his country'. After a lengthy speech advocating the extension of parliamentary and municipal reform in Ireland, O'Connell reciprocated by thanking 'his personal friend and his fellow countryman'. He extolled the political record and military services of Evans, applauding his recent knighthood. He was delighted that the overwhelming majority of voters in the borough had rewarded him for 'his firmness in the field and his fidelity as a citizen'.[36]

On the following night Evans encountered a much less gratifying reception. He heard, at first hand, the disdain of his military services so keenly felt by some Members of the House. When Sir Henry Hardinge drew attention to the plight of the remaining legionaries at San Sebastian, protesting that they were in a state of 'great misery, destitution, and starvation', Evans interjected to insist that they were not in a worse condition than the troops had been 'under his own command'. The whole House – 'Whigs and all', according to one observer[37] – convulsed with laughter, and the tumult reached new heights when Evans added that those troops had not been in as 'bad a state as the British army was at different periods during the Peninsular war'. The House had hardly recovered its decorum when James Bradshaw, a Conservative, asked Lord Palmerston whether Evans's knighthood had passed through the regular channels, involving due consultation with the Horse Guards. Palmerston admitted that the appointment had been made by Ministers on their own responsibility. He also conceded that Evans had not been appointed as one of the ten foreign officers who were eligible to receive the honour. Incensed by the questions, Evans asked Bradshaw if he had been authorised by Lord Hill, the Commander-in-Chief, to raise the matter. Bradshaw replied that Lord Hill had not made a request, but many officers had sent him letters complaining that it was 'an unjust appointment'.[38]

The debate was continued in the editorial columns, with *The Morning Chronicle* defending Evans against the attacks of *The Times*, *The Standard* and *The Morning Post*.[39] It was resumed in the House of Commons, on 26th March, when Lord Hotham drew attention to the numerous officers who held the second and third-class rank of the Order of the Bath and who had been by-passed by the appointment of Evans. Palmerston stressed that the award had been made for distinguished service and not for length of service. Evans again intervened, foolishly suggesting that his military services stood comparison with those of any other member of the Order. *The Morning Post* could not resist the challenge; it observed that as the Duke of Wellington was a member of the Order 'there cannot be a moment's hesitation about Colonel Evans's fitness for it'.[40] The episode, so petty in substance and spiteful in its presentation, reflected the depth of partisan feeling which reference to the Legion could still engender. By his own infelicitous comments Evans had only exacerbated those feelings.

On 13th March 1838 he delivered his belated account of the

Legion's activities in Spain. To refute the aspersions cast on the Legion, he presented a minutely detailed narrative of its formation, operations and liaison with the Spanish authorities. Into this narrative Evans inserted the various criticisms which had been voiced in Parliament, but he did so in a highly indiscriminate fashion. As a consequence, the speech veered off on a semantic digression about the meaning of a 'mercenary', and lapsed into trivia by discussing the propriety of fighting on a Sunday. Trying to correct the misleading information which had been given on the losses and the sick list of the Legion, he quoted from the official returns, and endeavoured, where possible, to compare the statistics with similar returns from the Peninsular War. He denied any disagreement with the Spanish generals, which was patently untrue, evaded the issue of flogging by his subalterns (by simply repeating that he had always commuted floggings in general courts-martial), and cited the approval of the Legion by the Spanish government. He ascribed the criticisms of the Legion, and of himself, to party rather than personal motives, and regretted that there were persons in the House who did not sympathise with 'the cause of constitutional liberty throughout the world'.[41]

Evans had failed miserably. He appeared nervous and hesitant, possibly in reaction to the uproar occasioned by his award of a K.C.B. He neither roused those supporters who had rallied behind the Legion in April 1837, nor appeased his critics. The Liberal press was terse and perfunctory in comment, while *The Times* and *The Morning Post* gloated over his ineffective performance, which had exuded, in their view, complacency and self-satisfaction. In commenting upon the speech, editors noted that it had been bereft of passion and anger, and that its impact had suffered from a 'disjointed conversational style', a diffident manner, and a 'voice so low as to be uncomfortably indistinct and often quite inaudible'.[42] Members of Parliament had been more courteous and charitable. Those who criticised the Legion focused their wrath on the government for permitting its formation and on the Madrid authorities for neglecting its wants in pay and provisions.

Sir Henry Hardinge, nonetheless, replied to Evans's speech directly. Unwilling to retract any of his previous statements, he continued to buttress his arguments by quoting from various memoirs, including the recently published work by Private Alexander Somerville: he noted, correctly, that Evans had not disputed the veracity of these accounts. In a highly indignant tone, Hardinge repudiated any comparison between the privations of the Legion and those of the

Peninsular army. He stressed that the circumstances were not remotely analogous, in as much as the Peninsular army had had to fight a series of major campaigns, often involving lengthy marches under a burning sun, and usually requiring the soldiers to live under canvas. He denied, too, that any statistical comparison could mitigate the sufferings endured at Vitoria. He criticised the abuse of the provost system of military punishment, by which the power of flogging was delegated to junior officers so 'that the men were constantly flogged at the will and pleasure of the commanding officers'. Finally, he attributed the mutinies and insubordination of the legionaries to the neglect of the Spanish government, and reiterated his opposition to the policy of sending a Legion to Spain.[43]

Evans responded somewhat feebly to this robust critique. Unready to contradict former officers, he simply dismissed their testimony as 'hostile' to him. The riposte was not entirely true,[44] and it failed to answer the specific charges which Hardinge had raised concerning the conditions at Vitoria and the extent of flogging by junior officers. When Evans added that harrowing scenes in military hospitals occurred at all times in war, it merely reinforced the impression of complacency. He also admitted, in a subsequent debate on military flogging, that some abuse of corporal punishment had occurred in the Legion, but claimed that such 'abuses must prevail, more or less, in every army'. His critics would still contend that the degree of abuse could have been mitigated had Evans strictly enforced the British articles of war, whereby a provost-marshal had actually to see an offence before he inflicted summary punishment.[45]

By his apparent complacency and toleration of flogging Evans had enhanced neither his reputation nor his parliamentary standing. Some Radicals were appalled by his reasoning. *The Morning Advertiser*, formerly a staunch supporter, condemned his arguments as 'silly, contemptible, base, and disgusting'. Any 'abuse of flogging' it likened to 'an abuse of thieving, housebreaking, or throat-cutting', arguing that the former was 'as great an outrage on the rights of humanity as any of the crimes referred to are against social order'.[46] For Evans, fortunately, the Legion was no longer a prominent issue of political controversy (as distinct from the fate of the former officers and men, and their arrears of pay, which were still smouldering problems). Also, his personal objections to military flogging were widely known and applauded in Radical circles. Within Westminster, too, he soon gained useful publicity by ostentatiously refusing to attend a meeting at the Crown and Anchor to consider the postponement of the coronation. As Sir Francis Burdett was to have chaired the meeting, Evans dismissed the gathering as Tory-inspired.[47] On 29th May he attended a dinner in honour of Joseph Hume, paying a fulsome tribute to him for his many years of parliamentary service.[48]

Nevertheless, Spanish issues periodically recurred, as ex-officers of the Legion became more and more irritated by their arrears of pay. Some protested to Conservative M.P.s with service connections, who promptly raised their plight in the House. Captains Mathew and Boldero pressed Palmerston to remonstrate with the Spanish government about the tardy payments. During his speech Boldero criticised Evans for failing to advocate these claims, arguing that he should have refused to accept any honours from Madrid until his men were paid. Unmoved, Evans explained that he had been reluctant to press the claims because he was the largest claimant. He was convinced that the arrears had become a party question in Britain, and deplored any attempt to coerce the Spanish authorities. Even so, he agreed that the government should continue to urge the payment of the arrears.[49]

Evans bitterly resented the manner in which he had been treated since his return from Spain. Re-election and a K.C.B. had been his only recompense. He had encountered enduring hostility and derision from his political opponents, and merely lukewarm support, with some notable exceptions, from his parliamentary colleagues. He realised that campaign speeches and parliamentary statements could not restore a reputation sullied and belittled in war. To counter the voluminous criticisms of the Legion which had appeared in print, he too would have to take up his pen and prepare a thoroughly researched reply. He was not simply concerned about reputation for its own sake; he was also desperately anxious to have that reputation suitably rewarded. Almost as soon as the book was published, in January 1840, he would draw the attention of Lord Melbourne to it as evidence of his service to 'the policy & interests of the British Government'. He stressed that in all previous cases bearing any analogy to his own the officers involved were rewarded by the army itself. In view of his political services, however, any promotion was 'completely proscribed by the Head of my own profession', and so he languished after thirty-three years in the army on the half-pay of a captain – £130 a year. Seeking preferment from the Prime Minister, he asked him to consult the two or three members of his Cabinet who had already read the book and could assess 'what foundation there may be for my present supposed claim'.⁵⁰

Evans's *Memoranda of the Contest in Spain* (1840) is divided into three main sections. It begins with a brief history of the Spanish constitutional controversy, followed by a chronological narrative of the Legion's activities, and ends with an assessment of its achievements. Neither in style nor in content does it compare with Alexander Somerville's history of the Legion, and in their accounts of the battles and the living conditions several other memoirs are immeasurably superior. But, in writing, Evans was mainly concerned with self-exculpation: he hoped to answer his critics by explaining the difficulties experienced and overcome by the Legion, by recounting its military achievements, and by stressing the appreciation of those services by the Spanish authorities.

The difficulties the Legion faced are emphasised throughout the book. Recruiting was checked by the opposition of 'high military personages' and by the promulgation of the Durango Decree. Once the corps had reached Spain, it required a long period of initial training and suffered from the precariousness of its supplies during the winter of 1836–37. Even worse was the irregularity of pay which precipitated the mutinies at San Sebastian he had anticipated. The Legion, he averred, was continually hampered by the paucity of its numbers and by the recurrent problems of securing pay and provisions. As commander, he was merely a Spanish general with certain additional responsibilities, but he was not responsible for the payment, food or clothing of the troops, and his disciplinary powers were restricted by the possibility of civil prosecution in England should he order any sentences of capital punishment. Nevertheless, the Legion had surmounted these difficulties, and 'the unceasing unscrupulous hostility of the Conservative opposition', by the zeal, spirit, comradeship and loyalty of the great majority of officers and men. Without these qualities the Legion 'could not have remained embodied for half the period of its duration'.⁵¹

Evans argued that the Legion, boosted by this indomitable spirit, realised some notable achievements in the field and recovered from minor reverses. He listed the Carlist advantages as including a strong central position, protected by natural and man-made defences, interior lines of communication, and often a local superiority of men and artillery. Such strong defences, coupled with the persistent problem of securing accurate intelligence, accounted for the occasional defeats of the Legion. Evans dismissed these incidents as comparatively 'small' affairs, which never warranted the consternation expressed in Britain. He blamed General Saarsfield for failing to inform him of his movements prior to the battle of 16th March 1837, and deplored the invidious comparisons so often made between the Legion and the Royal Marines. He claimed that the Marines, though invaluable, were too small in number to cover any retreat by the Legion. Furthermore the Legion had triumphed in several battles, overcoming formidable defences outside San Sebastian on 5th May 1836, and the desperate resistance of defenders at Irun a year later. By capturing Oyarzun, Irun and Fuentarrabia the Legion, aided by Espartero's forces, had cut the Carlist supply lines, forcing Don Carlos to leave the Basque provinces.[52]

For these achievements, Evans emphasised, the Legion had been praised by the authorities in Madrid. He quoted extensively from ministerial letters of approval, contrasting their sentiments with the aspersions hurled at the Legion by its Tory critics. This defamation he ascribed, at least partially, to personal malice and professional jealousy of his own rôle as commander. Where he believed that the difficulties or defeats of the Legion had been magnified out of all proportion, he compared the incidents with the experiences of the Peninsular army. By such comparisons he tried to undermine the criticism of the Legion's medical record and its periodic failure in the field. Above all, he condemned his critics for failing to deplore those Carlists who murdered British prisoners under the terms of the Durango Decree. He concluded by dismissing 'the ridiculous or disingenous attempts to disparage' the Legion, claiming that they should be treated with contempt and left 'totally unnoticed'.[53]

By writing a tract so polemical and partisan in substance Evans did not enhance his reputation. In the first place, the book was published in January 1840, some three and a half years after the author's return from Spain. By this time interest in the Legion, apart from the on-going saga about pay arrears, had largely dissipated. After the early Chartist meetings and the emergence of an Anti-Corn Law movement, the attention of the press and Parliament had become preoccupied with domestic issues. Indeed, when the vexed issue of the relative contributions of the Royal Marines and the Legion was revived in the wake of Evans's memoirs, the letters from Lord John Hay, Evans and Colonel John Owen were confined to the correspondence columns of *The Morning Chronicle*.[54] Secondly, there was little prospect of Evans securing any preferment from the government, particularly an 'appointment about the Court',[55] while the controversial pay arrears remained unsettled. The officials of the Association of Officers of the late British Auxiliary Legion were now briefing Lord Londonderry and pressing him to harrass the Melbourne government over their claims.[56] As a consequence, Evans travelled alone to Madrid, in April 1840, to remonstrate with the Spanish authorities.

In Madrid he advanced the claims of the Legion and himself for arrears of pay and compensation. He had audiences with the Queen, the Finance Minister, and Perez de Castro, the new Prime Minister, who acknowledged the 'justice and equity' of the claim, but pleaded for time to pay, in view of the penury of the Spanish treasury.[57] These meetings were the culmination of several years of pressure from Palmerston, Villiers (now Lord Clarendon) and Arthur Aston, the new Minister-plenipotentiary in Madrid. On 18th May the Spanish authorities agreed to pay five instalments of £50,000 at half-yearly intervals over the next thirty months, beginning on 1st December 1840. They also deposited 30 million rials as a guarantee of payment, and accepted that Evans should receive £5,000 in compensation.[58] Despite repeated representations, Evans failed to receive his compensation, but the instalments were paid, albeit in a somewhat desultory fashion (part of the fifth instalment was paid only in May 1843).[59] Nevertheless, officers were delighted by the prospect of payment; over two hundred contributed to a plate which Rutherford Alcock, the Legion's former deputy inspector of hospitals, presented to Evans on 15th March 1841. In thanking these officers, Evans paid tribute to their bravery in overcoming obstacles which 'no English regular army' had ever encountered.[60]

By concentrating upon issues pertaining to the Legion, Evans had become less and less prominent as a Radical spokesman for Westminster. Although he regularly attended and voted in the House of Commons, he left the brunt of the public speaking to Leader, his constituency colleague. Evans limited himself to occasional interjections in the army debates, urging, in one instance, the maintenance of very strict discipline in the Military Academy at Woolwich.[61] Outside the House, he was conspicuously absent from the meetings of the Westminster Reform Association, and from the activities of the Metropolitan Anti-Corn Law Association. Apart from attending some dinners (another in honour of Hume on 1st May 1839 and the annual dinner of the Anti-Corn Law League in Manchester, on 13th January 1840),[62] he never displayed the same political commitment as he had shown during his earlier years as a Member of Parliament.

Complacency, even if largely subconscious, was almost certainly a factor. In 1837 Westminster had defied the Conservative trend, returning to its traditional Radical allegiance. Having survived the Conservative smear campaign in the previous general election, Evans had few qualms about contesting another. Faced with the possibility of a ministerial defeat over the sugar, timber and corn duties in May 1841, he addressed parishioners from St Martin's in the Fields at an anniversary dinner celebrating seven years of municipal reform. He urged them to support the government over the current issue of parliamentary concern, claiming that it embraced the whole principle of free trade and not simply the Corn Laws.[63] Although the government survived a defeat in the Committee on Ways and Means, it lost a subsequent vote of confidence by one vote on 5th June. The forthcoming general election would test Evans's confidence about his electoral position.

Imprudent editorials in *The Morning Chronicle* reflected, and possibly compounded, the self-confidence in the liberal camp. Despite the erosion of support for the government over the past four years, as reflected in the series of by-election defeats, *The Morning Chronicle* had few fears about Westminster. It argued that Burdett's success in May 1837 had left a lasting impression upon the local Liberal party, ensuring that it maintained a competent and comprehensive organisation. Within thirty-six hours, it affirmed, the Westminster Liberals could rout even the most formidable of Tory candidates 'by an overwhelming majority', and the present Members would 'walk over the course'.[64] As the local Conservatives struggled to find anyone prepared to contest the seat, *The Morning Chronicle* became even more derisive. When Captain Henry John Rous, a former naval captain and keen sportsman, eventually entered the fray, the paper dismissed him as having 'got upon the wrong scent', and forecast that he would be 'thrown out of the hunt'.[65]

The late entry of a Conservative candidate shortened the campaign to less than a week. Though readopted on 18th June 1841, Evans did not face any opponent until seven days later. At his readoption meeting he had assured the voters of St Margaret's that the ballot and the restricted duration of Parliaments would be 'merely theoretical' issues in the general election. The 'grand question', he declared, was the justice and equality of English law, particularly the government's proposals to alter the duties on corn, timber and sugar.[66] As soon as Rous came forward, Evans focused his campaign upon this issue. He reminded audiences that he had always voted for the abolition of duties which pressed most heavily upon the 'poorer classes'. He commended aspects of the government's record — its modest educational grant, dislike of Church rates, support of liberty overseas, and willingness to amend part of the Poor Law Act. But he still favoured radical change, especially the 'total extinction' of Church rates and the reduction of assessed and indirect taxation (contrary to the government's former proposals). He was fervently opposed to the Conservatives, and, in his last few speeches, compared the Tory record from 1784 to 1830 with the Whig record of the 1830s. While the former had massively increased public expenditure and augmented the national debt by over £500 million, the Whigs had remitted some £15 million in taxation. By firmly denouncing the Conservatives 'and the gold of the Carlton Club', Evans rallied the Radical vote and gained the endorsement of the local Chartists.[67]

Such support proved of little avail. In an election focused upon national issues, the Liberal poll slumped in Westminster while the Conservatives gained 618 votes. Although Leader and Evans increased their votes in the Radical bastions of St Anne's and St John's, they only narrowly held St James's, St Paul's, St Margaret's and St Mary-le-Strand. Rous retained St Clements and the Savoy, barely won St Martin's, but decisively captured St George's. By securing an additional 285 votes in this vital parish, Rous became a totally unexpected victor. It was, wrote *The Times*, 'a glorious day in the annals of the city of Westminster . . .'.[68] The votes by parish are shown in Table 3.[69]

Evans was merely one of many casualties as the Conservatives swept through the English constituencies, carrying the bulk of the counties and smaller boroughs, and making some notable gains in the more wealthy and established urban constituencies. Apart from Westminster, Conservatives were also returned for Hull, Leeds, Bristol, Liverpool and even the City of London.[70] Along with a few victories in the Celtic fringes, they won the election with a majority of seventy-six seats. The sudden conversion of the Whigs to free trade had done them little good; indeed, it had undoubtedly harmed their cause in the rural constituencies. Although there had always been individual free-traders among the Whigs, the party collectively had not pursued such a policy in government. After the onset of an economic depression in 1837, however, the Ministry had endured three years of budget deficits. Faced with mounting insolvency, Baring, the Chancellor of the Exchequer, had adopted the Radical policy of reducing duties in the hope of securing a higher tax yield through increased consumption.

Table 3

Parish	Evans	Leader	Rous
St Margaret's	322	320	294
St John's	329	364	265
Savoy	6	8	11
St Mary-le-Strand	31	29	25
St Paul's	138	140	109
St Anne's	254	265	135
St Clement's	202	211	290
St James's	619	601	543
St Martin's	449	445	470
St George's	908	898	1,196
Total	3,258	3,281	3,338

By proposing a reduction of the duties on timber, sugar and, at Russell's behest, corn, the Whigs ensured that the election would be fought on the issue of free trade versus protection. But the abrupt change of government policy was viewed with widespread suspicion: while free trade may have won votes in some boroughs, doubts were expressed about the Whigs' sincerity (some even voiced by Evans himself),[71] based on the fear that they might not implement their promises. Conversely, the Conservatives, though identified as the party of protection, were not wedded to any particular programme. Peel kept his options open, insisting that he would be guided by his own view of the national interest. Rous, like the two businessmen who were returned for the City of London, followed Peel's pragmatic approach (they would all vote for repeal of the Corn Laws in 1846).[72]

More important than policy was probably the impression of leadership Peel gave during the campaign. His promise of a strong, competent government, conducted in a moderate and empirical spirit, had boosted the Conservative cause in the English boroughs. By contrast, Melbourne's leadership seemed weak and ineffectual. He had failed to arrest the erosion of support for the Whigs over the previous few years. Indeed, his government, since 1837, had lacked any clear objectives or principles; it had left the most pressing issues of the Corn Laws and the ballot open, while stumbling from one expedient to another. This record was a major electoral liability.

Within the borough of Westminster, local factors complemented the national issues. Rous was a much more popular candidate than Murray; he was widely known in London and was respected among the sporting fraternity, and was probably assisted by the corruption and intimidation so common in general elections. During the campaign the Conservatives were reported to have hired nearly two hundred 'herculean fellows', at five shillings each, to attend the nomination hustings at Covent Garden and to assist in maximising the vote on election day.[73] But even these pressures would have come to naught had the Reformers united in common cause. Despite the pleas of Evans, some fifty-nine voters 'plumped' for him and ninety-nine for Leader: had these 'plumpers' split their votes between the Reform candidates, both Reformers would have been returned.[74]

The result was a bitter and unexpected blow for Evans. At the declaration of the result he bravely assured supporters that, as before, he would soon be returned as their representative. He defended the government's record, and urged Liberal voters to support the party whether in office or in opposition. Failing, as on previous occasions, to judge the temper of his audience, he recounted the achievements of the government amid mounting uproar: his speech soon became totally inaudible as he was barracked with shouts of 'Where's the Legion?', 'We've done with you, Count I-run,' and 'Run back to Spain.'[75] Although the product of a well paid and probably well liquored mob, these catcalls were profoundly ironic, as the Legion had not been an issue in the election, despite Evans's preoccupation with the honour of the force and the pay of its former officers. In 1837 he had held his seat after a two-year absence, overcoming a highly personal campaign against him. Four years later he succumbed − a victim of the government's unpopularity and the rising tide of Conservative support.

6
An ageing Radical

Though embarrassed by electoral defeat, Evans was not totally dejected. At the age of fifty-three, he was not about to retire to private life. He still regarded himself as a 'public man', with a duty to speak on the issues of national significance.¹ He waited for the next election, with his personal finances buttressed by the inheritance of £20,000 from the estate of a close admirer, the Hon. R. Otway Cave.² Evans was confident of regaining his seat at the next contest; he regarded the result in 1841 as an aberration – a reflection of over-confidence and disunity among Liberal supporters. Within three months of the election, he urged members of the Middlesex Registration Association to bury their differences and to present a united opposition. 'Co-operation', he declared, 'should be their watchword'; the Liberals should rally together, using public meetings to protest over ministerial policy.³

But Lord John Russell was neither willing nor able to lead a national crusade against the Conservatives. The electoral defeat, followed by the condemnation of the new House of Commons by 360 votes to 269, on 24th August 1841, had precipitated Melbourne's resignation and plunged the Whigs into disarray. During the next four years the Opposition floundered, lacking any coherence in policy or leadership. Lord Melbourne, despite his advancing years, still believed as late as 1844 that he would return to office if only Peel was defeated.⁴ This attitude, coupled with his reluctance to support any radical revision of the Corn Laws, merely compounded the problems of Russell and encouraged the protectionist Whig peers to defy official party policy.⁵ Even worse, the Opposition was overshadowed by the bold and innovative policies of the Peel Ministry. In his budget of 1842 Peel introduced an income tax of sevenpence in the pound on incomes over £150, thereby balancing the budget and securing a handsome surplus in subsequent years. In the same session he modified the sliding scale on corn import duties and reduced the duties on 750 of the 1,200 articles on the customs list. By introducing a liberal economic policy, which he expanded three years later by further tariff reductions, Peel gained a clear ascendancy over Russell. Liberal morale sank;[6] the party mustered dismal turn-outs in the division lobbies and lost several by-elections in succession. Above all, Lord John could not persuade Radicals like Richard Cobden, the newly elected M.P. for Stockport, that their first priority should be helping the Whigs to oust the Tories.

Cobden had more immediate concerns, particularly the repeal of the Corn Laws, a passion shared by the many Radicals in the Anti-Corn Law League. Fervently committed to free trade, they depicted agricultural protection as a burden upon the poor, a barrier to commercial expansion, an obstacle to the interdependence of nations, and hence a barrier to international peace. They attracted support from manufacturers, eager to profit from the absence of State interference; from Dissenters, keen to describe the Established Church, on account of its tithes, as the thief of the poor man's bread; and from those who believed in the intrinsic merits of commerce and resented the traditional privileges of the aristocracy. For many Radicals, especially in the north of England, where the campaign had originated, agitation against the Corn Laws was a means of attacking the political and social control of the aristocratic interests.[7]

The activities of the League flourished during the depression of the late 1830s and early 1840s. The harsh winter of 1841–42 caused a slump in employment, precipitating widespread destitution and providing fresh ammunition for the League. Peel's budget, presented on 11th March 1842, did not relieve the industrial depression immediately: pauper numbers continued to increase, while the high price of corn aggravated the sufferings of the urban poor. The League could only redouble its efforts. As Cobden had forecast, 'whatever pressure is to be put upon the House of Commons must come from *without*'.[8] Evans endorsed this approach. An advocate of free trade, he had lost the last election, in his own view, by favouring its implementation.[9] If an extra-parliamentary campaign could enhance the credibility of the doctrine, he would readily join it. On 4th February 1842 he attended the Anti-Corn Law meeting at the Western Literary Institution, Leicester Square, to demonstrate that electoral defeat had not shaken his commitment.[10]

Evans, however, was not entirely preoccupied with free trade. In

1841 Spanish affairs had acquired a brief notoriety in Britain after a revolt was crushed in Madrid. Two officers were executed with the approval of Espartero, the new regent of Spain, despite the prosecutor's request that they should receive ten years' imprisonment. Daniel O'Connell led the outburst of British indignation: he denounced the judgement and castigated the regent for 'slaughtering his brother officers'. Evans rebutted these charges in a pamphlet which defended his former comrade in arms and absolved the regime from criticism. He emphasised that the court and not the regent had sentenced the officers, that capital punishment was a normal sentence for high treason, and that Espartero, far from being a tyrannical despot, was a popular, generous and respected general. O'Connell, he surmised, had been misinformed, for no Liberal could wish the destruction of representative government in Spain.[11] Though indicative of Evans's lingering sensitivity over Spanish issues, the clash of opinion was not very significant: the feelings provoked by executions in Madrid proved much more transitory than the passions aroused by free trade.

During the winter of 1842–43 Evans became a regular participant in the meetings of the Metropolitan Anti-Corn Law Association. Lacking training in political economy or first-hand knowledge of industry and commerce, he rarely lectured upon the economic advantages of repeal. He preferred to deliver brief morale-boosting speeches, assuring his audiences that their cause was right and their prospects hopeful. At the meeting of the Association on 14th November 1842 he congratulated members upon the 'excellent progress' of the movement, particularly their impact upon the new House of Commons. 'The declarations of the premier', he argued, had advanced the cause despite the palpable resentment of many Conservative Members.[12] In the Theatre of the London Mechanics' Institution he assured a crowded gathering of Westminster free-traders that the volume of cross-party support, coupled with the relative modernity of the Corn Laws, enhanced the likelihood of repeal.[13] As he stressed at subsequent meetings, there had been a massive change of opinion on this subject. 'The aristocracy', he asserted, could not have chosen 'a more unfavourable battlefield than the bread tax'; if they did not yield, the people might begin to question the value of 'primogeniture and hereditary legislation'. He did not favour such action: 'He had no desire to treat the aristocracy in any other way than with respect, provided they acted in a spirit of equity to their fellow subjects'. Only repeal would meet this requirement, so relieving the burden upon 'the poor and working classes'.[14]

Evans earned a notable accolade from this speaking, namely an invitation to address the annual rally of the Anti-Corn Law League in Manchester. As the focal point of the League's activities in each year, this gathering provided an opportunity for collecting more subscriptions and demonstrated the strength of the movement before Parliament reassembled after the Christmas recess. In 1843 the occasion was rendered even more momentous by convening the proceedings in the newly built Free Trade Hall, the first building to bear that name.[15] On 1st February the conference culminated with a splendid banquet for 3,800 people, seated throughout the hall and gallery in surroundings festooned with union jacks and velvet drapery. Evans responded to a rousing toast by the hugely popular Radical, Lieutenant-Colonel Thomas Perronet Thompson. He spoke without the benefit of the 'sound reflector', and delivered a barely audible speech which lacked any substance or coherence. After the customary apology for his lack of oratorical gifts, he began by claiming to have experienced the baleful effects of monopoly at first hand during his Spanish services, gave a *résumé* of the history of the extra parliamentary movements which had preceded and served as a model for the Anti-Corn Law campaign, and finished by predicting the ultimate triumph of the League. Mark Philips, the chairman, immediately apologised for the accoustics, but several guests and reporters were profoundly disappointed by the speech, which was completely overshadowed by the other contributions, especially the eloquent address of Daniel O'Connell.[16] So critical were some notices of the speech that one delegate was moved to defend Evans in an anonymous letter to *The Morning Chronicle*. He complained that Evans had been unfairly traduced, and that his speech, though devoid of passion or rhetoric, had reflected the sound common sense of this 'practical, consistent, and talented politician'.[17]

Evans was not too perturbed by criticism in the press. He even welcomed unfavourable notices from Conservative newspapers like *The Morning Post*, as condemnation from this source, irrespective of its substance, bolstered his Radical credentials in the metropolis.[18] He continued to speak, when invited, on behalf of the free trade movement, so demonstrating his commitment to the main cause of contemporary Radicalism. In 1843 this was particularly important, as the League was trying to transform itself from a sectional movement, based largely in the North-West, into a nationwide crusade. Having moved its headquarters from Newall's Buildings, Manchester, to 67 Fleet Street, the League began to canvass, raise funds, and hold public meetings in London. Since many of the meetings were held on the stage at the Theatre Royal, Drury Lane, or at Covent Garden, Evans gained useful publicity within Westminster by attending and occasionally speaking.[19] He nursed the constituency, periodically reminding the Westminster Reform Society of his pledges and votes in favour of free trade.[20] Evans, in short, benefited from his involvement in the Anti-Corn Law movement; although he contributed little to the agitation, he gained some useful publicity for himself and secured his political base prior to re-entering the political arena.

Sir Robert Peel ensured that this return would come sooner than Evans expected. The Prime Minister, having split his party over the Maynooth Grant in 1845, risked an even more serious split over economic policy in the wake of the Irish potato famine. Convinced that the Corn Laws must now be repealed, he tried unsuccessfully to convert his Cabinet and resigned in December. Lord John Russell, another convert to repeal, endeavoured to form a minority government, but, in view of his party's minority status in the Commons and Lords, and its own internal divisions, declined the Queen's commission. Peel resumed office, determined to repeal the Corn Laws in the national interest. To prepare for repeal, which would be formally proposed in the Commons in late January 1846, Peel reshuffled his Ministry. He appointed Rous, who had become a free-trader two years previously, to the Admiralty, so precipitating a by-election in Westminster. As he subsequently confirmed, Peel had only made the appointment because he was absolutely certain of Rous's re-election.[21]

Evans prudently did not rush into the lists. He waited until the Westminster Reform Society had decided to contest the election, a wise precaution, as some Liberals doubted the propriety of opposing Rous, on account of his free trade views and Russell's failure to form a government. After a prolonged discussion, the Society resolved by a margin of eleven votes to three to fight the election and to support Evans as the Liberal candidate.[22] To maximise his appeal, Evans formed a broadly based election committee, two-thirds of whom were peers or the sons of peers. Several prominent Whigs, including Admiral Dundas, Lord Fitzroy and the Earl of Shelburne, joined the committee, as did some Radical M.P.s, notably Thomas Duncombe, Tennyson D'Eyncourt and Captain Pechell. The committee was chaired by the Hon. Edward Bouverie M.P., the second son of the Earl of Radnor.

The brief campaign was launched at the Crown and Anchor on 13th February 1846. Bouverie chaired the proceedings; he described the election as an opportunity to reverse the disgraceful result of 1841, caused largely by 'over-confidence' in the Liberal ranks. He predicted that complacency would not recur because this election was essentially a clash of personalities between two men, of whom one had changed his views and the other had served Westminster 'honestly and faithfully and zealously'. Howard Elphinstone, M.P., concurred; he introduced Evans as an 'old and tried friend of liberty', who had been a consistent advocate of free trade. Evans came forward to rapturous applause. He stressed that he had not sought the nomination and had only agreed to stand at the behest of the Reform Society. Referring immediately to the doubts still being aired in Liberal circles about the wisdom of contesting the election, he asserted that the government, by calling this election at short notice, had hoped to change 'a free and enlightened constituency into a rotten borough'. The contest, he argued, was still between a Tory and a Liberal: Rous, despite his conversion to free trade, had supported the imposition of an income tax and was now utterly tied to the government, whereas he remained a consistent Liberal.[23]

At subsequent meetings Evans emphasised the differences between Rous and himself, particularly over religious issues, and tried to reassure wavering supporters.[24] But any Liberal doubts or disagreements paled by comparison with those in the Conservative camp. From the outset, many Conservatives pledged to support Evans or threatened to abstain. Their concerns were reflected in the Tory press, where the candidacy of Rous was viewed with unconcealed dismay. *The Morning Post* quoted extensively from Rous's former speeches in favour of protection, bemoaned his *volte face*, and feared lest Westminster became a 'pocket borough' for the Admiralty. Unwilling to support Evans, it still hoped that a protectionist candidate would come forth to provide a real alternative.[25] *The Standard* was less circumspect. Having deplored the change of heart by Rous some two years previously, it now endorsed Evans, since 'he cannot be so unworthy a representative of Westminster as his competitor'.[26]

Given the enormous rift within the Conservative ranks, the result was never in doubt. On 18th February Evans attracted the largest vote of any candidate in Westminster since the Reform Act. He also carried every parish (for the first time by a Radical in over a generation), so turning the deficit of eighty in 1841 into a majority of 937 (Table 4).[27]

Table 4

Parish	Evans	Rous	Majority for Evans
St Anne's	346	158	188
St Clement Dane's	296	227	69
St George's	1,109	1,015	94
St James's	595	480	115
St John's	426	208	218
St Margaret's	381	284	97
St Martin's	481	413	68
St Mary-le-Strand	38	27	11
St Paul's	153	86	67
Savoy	18	8	10
Total	3,843	2,906	937

Evans's triumph was even more decisive than it appeared from the parish returns. The weight of governmental influence, which had assisted him in 1841, had favoured Rous in the by-election. Conservative editors, gloating over the latter's demise, estimated that he had lost despite the votes of three hundred to five hundred government employees who lived in the vicinity of their place of work – either the Royal Household or the forty-one government offices in the constituency.[28] Westminster, moreover, had undergone extensive redevelopment in the early 1840s. Although the electoral roll had increased by over 1,000 to 14,801, many of the poorer houses had been demolished, so diminishing the potential Liberal vote. Whereas Evans had increased his vote by 18 per cent over the 1841 tally, his two worst results occurred in parishes most severely affected by removals, namely St Martin's (+7 per cent) and St James's (−4 per cent).[29] The timing of the by-election should also have favoured the Conservatives. Many of the wealthier classes and the legal profession had not left the metropolis, as they had done in June 1841 either to take their holidays or to participate in other elections. But several hundred Conservatives abstained and some fifty voted for Evans, easily dwarfing the Liberal abstentions.[30] For the Westminster Conservatives the result was an unmitigated disaster. It undermined their steady accretion of support over the past decade, and enabled Evans to regain his parliamentary seat, which he would hold for the next twenty years.

On returning to the House of Commons, Evans embarked upon the most active phase of his political career. He voted in favour of repealing the Corn Laws, the last act accomplished by Peel's government before its fall on 29th June 1846. Five days previously, Evans had introduced his Parliamentary Electors and Freemen Bill, by which electors would have been entitled to vote if they had paid all their rates and taxes within a six-month period instead of the three prescribed by the Reform Act. Sir James Graham, the Home Secretary, strenuously objected to the proposal, which was rejected by ninety-four votes to fifty-three. When reintroduced by Duncombe, in the following session, the measure again fell, but only by sixty-seven votes to seventy-two.[31] The narrowing margin reflected the replacement of Peel's administration by a new government headed by Russell. Party alignments were now disrupted, with the Conservative Party in utter disarray. Evans welcomed this state of affairs, as it boosted the chances of measures which he favoured, like John Fielden's Ten Hours Bill. This Bill, which proposed the reduction of factory hours for young people and adults, had incurred the opposition of Peel and had split the Radical group. Hume, Roebuck and Bright opposed the measure, fearing a reduction of wages and an interference in *laissez-faire* economics. Fielden, however, gained the unenthusiastic support of Russell and his colleagues, as well as some protectionist Tories and the other Radicals, like Evans, Brotherton and Wakley, to pass the measure.

On the other hand, Evans was not so enamoured of the government's education scheme. As presented to the House of Commons on 19th April 1847 the scheme sought to raise the status of the teaching profession by extending governmental inspection and by introducing professional examinations. Teachers who received certificates of merit would receive extra pay and entry into pension schemes, but the proposal would not apply to Roman Catholic schools or to those schools which did not employ the authorised version of the Bible. Although the Wesleyans were largely appeased by these anti-Catholic and anti-secular concessions, the main body of Dissenters deplored the extension of State influence, and feared that Church of England schools would absorb a disproportionate volume of State expenditure. A massive campaign was organised against the scheme.

Some 4,204 petitions signed by 559,978 persons were sent to Parliament, and the Dissenters' objections were raised by several Radicals, including Evans.[32]

Evans, however, never concentrated exclusively upon the main national and Radical issues. During the 1846 and 1847 sessions he was virtually the sole representative for Westminster, as Leader, a somewhat indolent M.P., rarely attended the House and preferred to travel on the Continent. Consequently, Evans had to concern himself with a host of local issues. He attended meetings of the Poor Man's Guardian Society, a locally based pressure group concerned about the administration of the Poor Law. He championed the campaign against the demolition of Westminster bridge, and he joined other Radical M.P.s and metropolitan delegates in pressing the Premier to repeal the window tax immediately. By representing these issues so assiduously, he gained useful publicity in the metropolitan press and proved his willingness to fulfil his constituency duties.[33]

Within the House of Commons, Evans became closely identified with military issues. He spoke more often and more perceptively about the army than about any other issue. On 13th July 1846 he announced that he could no longer adhere to the traditional Radical concern about excessive military expenditure. Alarmed by the growth of military spending and the construction of fortifications in France, he declared 'that he was not now so very anxious for economy in military expenditure ...'.[34] He still insisted that any additional expenditure had to be upon improving the efficiency of the forces at home and overseas. He pressed Ministers to ensure that troops in the colonies were not deprived of allowances enjoyed by the army at home. He applauded the recent improvements in barrack accommodation, the establishment of regimental schools, and the provision of libraries for the ordinary soldier. He urged the government to go further and to reduce the period of enlistment, then nominally for life and effectively for twenty-one years, to an initial period of ten years. 'Such a change,' he argued, 'would purify the service, and do much towards rendering it popular.' Similarly, he advocated an experimental prohibition upon the sale of alcoholic drinks in regimental canteens as a means of improving the image of the army and the health of the soldier.[35] Evans, in short, had associated himself with the demands for army reform which had already emanated from some civilian and military journals.[36]

He was concerned, too, about rewards for army officers. He

exhorted Peel's administration to reward Sir Harry Smith for his victory at Aliwal in the Sikh War. He claimed that Sir Harry, with whom he had served in North America, was at least entitled to some monetary reward, since his rank precluded promotion to Commander-in-Chief.[37] More generally, he believed that army officers had suffered financially from the purchase system and lacked the promotion prospects of their naval colleagues. In raising such issues, Evans was merely reiterating some familiar complaints against the purchase system. As he did not propose any alternative, Lord John Russell could easily reject his views. Captain Pechell, another Radical military Member, applauded Evans's sentiments, but Hume utterly disagreed: he doubted that any other European State 'had to pay so heavy a charge for officers of the army as England'.[38] The seeds of a future split within the Radical group over military policy were already sown.

Evans realised that he could do little, as a back-bench Member of Parliament, to promote army reform. As he informed Sir John Philippart, editor of *The Naval and Military Gazette*, 'At present I can do no more. Intermediately, at least for the moment, the advocacy of the claims of the officers depends altogether on the organ, with which you are so influentially connected.'[39] Pressure from the military and civilian press was a contributory but not decisive influence. Earl Grey, Secretary of State for War and the Colonies (1846–52), was the mainspring of reform, although his impact upon the home army was blunted by the Duke of Wellington, Commander-in-Chief from 1842 to 1852. An advocate of limited service, Grey gained the reluctant acquiescence of the Duke to an Army Service Bill which reduced the term of enlistment to ten years, but only for new recruits (a *caveat* added at the Duke's insistence). Evans heartily approved of the Bill. He doubted that any military success in the past could be attributed to the system of unlimited service, and insisted that the 'character' of the army could only be improved by rendering military service more popular. He also disputed that a representative of a large urban constituency like himself would lose votes by supporting the measure. 'The people,' he argued, 'would approve of the establishment of a national guard.'[40]

But the army did not become a prominent political issue until the 'invasion panics' of the late '40s and early '50s. It aroused little interest or concern during the general election of July and August 1847. Other topics, particularly education and religion, provoked much more controversy in an election which lacked the traditional party rivalry. In many constituencies the Conservative Party, split over Maynooth and free trade, had disintegrated, leaving numerous country divisions uncontested. Within Westminster, the issues were largely parochial and were complicated by the appearance of an independent Liberal candidate. In the previous December the Reform Society had failed to agree upon a suitable candidate to replace Leader. While the Society quarrelled about the qualifications of a candidate, with a minority insisting upon a man of independent means and some 'station in society',[41] Charles Cochrane came forward as an independent Liberal. A brother of the late Earl of Dundonald, Cochrane was a highly charismatic figure who was closely associated with philanthropic and progressive causes in the metropolis. He had campaigned on behalf of the legionaries when they returned from Spain. He had taken a keen interest in metropolitan sanitation, founding the National Philanthropic Association for the Formation of Social and Sanatory Improvements and for the Employment of the Poor. Having spent some three to four thousand pounds upon the Association, he had also formed sanitary societies in the City of London, Westminster and Marylebone, besides establishing the Poor Man's Guardian Society. Immensely wealthy and well-connected, he drew large audiences as he toured the parishes, setting up an independent organisation to contest the election.[42]

Opposed by so formidable a candidate, the Westminster Reform Society composed its differences and nominated Charles Lushington, a former Radical M.P., to campaign alongside Evans. For the next six months, from February to July 1847, Cochrane and Lushington addressed numerous meetings throughout Westminster, each seeking support from Liberal voters. Cochrane's campaign seemed particularly effective: he drew large audiences throughout the constituency, attracted a vast following among the 'wives, daughters, and sisters of the electors', and established a well financed electoral committee.[43] Encouraged by the prospect of a deep division in the Liberal ranks, the Conservatives chose Lord Mandeville, a son of the Duke of Manchester, to carry their colours in a fiercely anti-Catholic campaign.

At the nomination hustings the candidates were greeted by a raucous crowd of six to eight thousand people, many of whom supported Cochrane. Nevertheless, Evans, as the sitting Member, received a favourable hearing. He gained some easy applause by reminding the audience of his vote to repeal the Corn Laws, and by ridiculing the disarray in the Tory party. Determined to retain the support of Dissenters, he promised to seek a redistribution of educational grants upon 'an equal, just, and enlightened footing'. He also pledged to support any revision of taxation which would place the burden 'more equally upon fixed and real property', and assured listeners that he would continue to oppose the appointment of bishops to the House of Lords and to support measures of Church reform.[44]

On the following day, 29th July, Evans and Lushington just managed to win the election. In a desperately close result, Evans topped the poll and won six of the ten parishes. But his by-election vote was scythed, and he polled fewer votes than in any of his last three contests (Table 5).[45] Although the Westminster election was overshadowed by Russell's triumph in the City of London, and so received scant coverage in the metropolitan press, Cochrane seems to have explained his defeat correctly. Embarrassed by the charge of being a 'Tory in disguise', he had refused to split votes with Lord Mandeville and had relied upon plumpers. Some 2,600 voters had plumped for him, but his victory in St George's suggested that even more Conservatives might have been willing to do so. Moreover, his agent and election committee had failed at a critical moment in the contest. Throughout the campaign they had proved adept at organising meetings, canvassing voters, and in distributing placards and pamphlets, but on the morning of the poll they had failed to distribute polling cards to their supporters, so wasting the first three hours of the election in utter confusion. Defeat by twelve votes could almost certainly be attributed to the more experienced organisation of the Westminster Liberals.[46]

Buoyed by his electoral triumph, Evans returned to the Commons with renewed self-confidence. He spoke frequently in the financial debates which dominated the early months of 1848. Unlike many Radicals, he did not object to the raising of taxes to bolster the national defences, but he adamantly opposed the 'unjust and unequal distribution' of taxes, particularly the window tax and the burden of income tax.[47] He welcomed the abrupt withdrawal of the government's proposed increase in the rate of income tax from 7d to 1s in the pound, on account of Conservative and Radical opposition and angry protests from income tax payers. Accepting the promise of a reform of taxation by Lord John Russell, Evans defended the service estimates and deplored the retrenchment proposals of Hume and Cobden. He berated Cobden, who was 'not connected with either service', for implying that he knew 'better what was wanted for the defence of the country ... than the illustrious Chief who was at the head of the army'.[48] Although these sentiments earned warm applause from Conservative benches, they provoked a sarcastic retort from Bright: Evans, he observed,

ought to be as good an authority on military affairs as any in that House; for so fond was he of warfare, that he was prepared to do battle, not only for his own Queen, but even for the queen of another country.[49]

Table 5

Parish	Evans	Lushington	Cochrane	Mandeville
St Anne's	237	216	227	74
St Clement Dane's	246	233	187	149
St George's	825	769	908	797
St James's	583	531	386	341
St John's	314	272	306	114
St Margaret's	332	306	289	170
St Martin's	434	375	338	245
St Mary-le-Strand	30	29	33	21
St Paul's	123	96	140	64
Savoy	15	16	5	10
Total	3,139	2,831	2,819	1,985

Divided by Hume's motion to reduce the army by 13,000 men, only thirty-nine Radicals supported the motion, some abstained, and several, including Lushington, Thomas Headlam, Hugh Adair and Robert Adair, joined Evans in the opposite lobby of 293 MPs.

Such dissension among Radicals was soon overshadowed as Parliament responded to the upsurge of Chartism in the spring of 1848. The economic crises of 1847 and 1848, coupled with the news of revolutions in Italy and France, had revived the Chartist movement. A mass demonstration on Kensington Common and the presentation of a new petition were planned for 10th April. Many M.P.s dreaded the possibility of public disorder, a view echoed by Evans, who testified to the 'extreme alarm and terror' of his constituents about any procession through their locality. A strong supporter of the government's extraordinary policing measures, he applauded the containment of this 'contemptible meeting'. After the peace had been successfully preserved, he declared that 'every friend of order, every person in favour of the maintenance of property ... had reason to thank the government for the result'.[50] But neither the maintenance of public order nor the disintegration of the Chartist movement, amid the derision evoked by the multitude of forged signatures on its petition, satisfied middle-class Radicals. Sympathy for the grievances, if not the tactics, of the Chartists was widespread; it was clearly expressed in a meeting of the Westminster Reform Society on 13th April, where members agreed that political reform was now essential, especially the introduction of the ballot and an extension of the franchise. Reflecting a fairly basic difference within the Radical camp, the members disagreed about whether the suffrage should be universal (as the Chartists desired) or based upon household or educational criteria.[51]

Evans endorsed the need for constitutional change (his perennial Parliamentary Electors Bill passed its second reading on 17th May), and accepted that Chartist sentiments should be appeased to a limited extent. Addressing the parishioners of St Anne's, on 12th June 1848, he backed the objectives of the 'New Reform Movement' – the ballot, household suffrage, triennial Parliaments, and a more equal distribution of constituencies. He also promised to join the parliamentary campaign in favour of these proposals, to be led by Hume, so deflecting criticism, already voiced in Westminster, about his disagreements with other Radical Members of Parliament.[52] Evans amply fulfilled his pledges. On 6th July he voted in favour of a comprehensive reform of the electoral system, as proposed by Hume – a division which was lost by 358 votes to 84. On 8th August he joined in the rejoicing when the Radicals gained an unprecedented victory over the ballot; but the narrow margin of 86 votes to 81 indicated that the victory was largely hollow, more a reflection of temporary government weakness than any decisive shift of parliamentary opinion. Even more galling was the failure to realise Jewish emancipation, which had secured a majority vote in the Commons, but was consistently blocked in the Lords. A keen advocate of religious freedom, Evans favoured the removal of Jewish disabilities, and campaigned actively for Baron Rothschild in his quest to become Member of Parliament for the City of London.[53] Thwarted on this issue, as on all matters of constitutional reform, Evans had found the parliamentary session immensely frustrating.

Nevertheless, he was consoled by Palmerston's adroit handling of foreign affairs during the revolutionary turmoil of 1848. He shared the priorities of the Foreign Secretary, namely to preserve the peace of

Europe and cordial relations with France.⁵⁴ He applauded, too, the public expressions of sympathy by Palmerston for the liberal and nationalist movements in the Austro-Hungarian empire. Although Palmerston accepted that Austria had to be restored to maintain the balance of power, he deplored the way in which her generals had crushed the revolts in Lombardy and Hungary. When Austria and Russia demanded the extradition of Polish generals and Hungarian refugees from Turkey, Palmerston approved of the Turkish refusal to comply and organised the despatch of British and French fleets to the Near East.⁵⁵

On 30th July 1849 Evans attended a large public meeting in Marylebone, where many speeches were delivered by leading Radicals and Russophobes in favour of Hungarian independence. Speaking with passion and fervour, Evans defended the 'just and holy cause' of Hungarian nationalism. He urged the government to move beyond expressions of moral support and recognise the *de facto* government of Hungary. He also condemned the 'barbarous' intervention of the Austrian armies, which merited the 'indignant reprobation of all civilised nations'.⁵⁶ In December he joined a group of eighty-three peers and M.P.s which sent a memorial to Russell and Palmerston, proposing that Britain should press the case for clemency upon the Austrian government.⁵⁷ Both in Parliament and in public meetings, Evans defended the Hungarian cause and denounced policies of repression in Europe, whether by Austrian, Russian or Neapolitan rulers.⁵⁸ On the eve of the visit to England of Louis Kossuth, the Hungarian *émigré* leader, Evans chaired a large meeting in Westminster to adopt an address of welcome. He likened the Hungarian cause to 'the cause in which Englishmen themselves had struggled for many centuries', namely to preserve their national rights and to improve their 'domestic and internal condition'. He commended the reforms which the Hungarian Diet had sought: the emancipation of the serfs, with compensation for the proprietors; a limited extension of the franchise, which showed that the leaders were 'moderate men'; a commutation of tithes; freedom of the press; and trial by jury. He deprecated the Austrian intervention, maintaining that the Austrians had now become 'the revolutionists'. He also praised Kossuth, whom he bracketed with Mazzini and George Washington as a great leader of a noble cause. 'European history,' declared Evans, 'presented no really greater man than Kossuth.'⁵⁹

Advocating liberty abroad only carried conviction if the speaker was identified with similar causes at home. To his profound embarrassment, Evans discovered that many London Radicals no longer shared his views on political reform. The measures which he favoured were still rooted in the rhetoric and priorities of the early 1830s: they did not meet the demands of the Chartists and their sympathisers. When he rose to speak at the Marylebone meeting Evans was heckled severely, and the chairman, Lord Dudley Stuart, had to intervene repeatedly to assure him a hearing. Evans, who had never previously been denounced as insufficiently Radical, was shaken by the jeers, derision, and cries that he was 'no friend to the people'. As *The Inquirer* remarked, he had alienated 'his quondam Radical admirers' by his recent political conduct.[60] On 3rd July he had abstained from voting on O'Connor's motion about the People's Charter, though present in the House and willing to vote in the next division on 'The Sale of Bread'. This order of priorities reflected that Evans was primarily concerned about the interests of the enfranchised voter (many bakers, unlike the majority of Chartists, had the vote in Westminster), and that he favoured a 'gradualist' approach to reform, believing that an extension of the household suffrage was a more feasible objective than universal suffrage.[61] Even more seriously, Evans had attended the House less assiduously than in previous years. He had voted for the motions on the ballot, extending the franchise, and on shortening the duration of Parliament, which passed its first reading by 46 votes to 41. But he missed the second division, where the motion fell by 157 votes to 132, and was absent from 190 of the 219 divisions in 1849. These embarrassing statistics, published by *The Spectator*, revealed Evans as the fourth worst attender of the fifteen metropolitan Members. He could not even plead advancing years as an excuse, since Thomas Perronet Thompson, four years his senior, had the best record in the House, having attended 217 divisions.[62] To remain in politics, Evans could ill afford such publicity or the persistence of doubts about his Radical commitment.

Over the next three parliamentary sessions he devoted himself to domestic politics. He loyally supported the Radical motions on political reform, voting for the ballot, a moderate extension of the household suffrage, and the Parliamentary Voters (Ireland) Bill. He denounced bribery and corruption in electoral politics, and, on two occasions, drew attention to the notorious corruption in the borough of Harwich. He demanded either the disfranchisement of the borough or, at least, a Commission of Inquiry into its politics. In formally proposing the latter, Evans meticulously catalogued the petitions of protest which had followed each Harwich election in the 1840s, the increase of its electorate despite a declining population in the borough, and bribery on a scale which was extraordinary by contemporary standards. Although the government was unmoved, Evans mustered ninety-five votes in favour of his motion, losing by a majority of forty-two.[63]

Evans raised a host of local issues in and out of Parliament. An avowed advocate of self-government and local management, he opposed legislation which threatened to increase the degree of centralised administration. He campaigned vigorously, though ineffectively, against the Metropolitan Internments Bill, the Metropolis Water Bill, and the Poor Law Board. In a Commons motion, he proposed that the powers of the Poor Law Commissioners should be curtailed. He maintained that the parochial boards of the metropolis could 'manage the whole business of poor relief', whereas the Poor Law Board was 'part of that objectionable system of centralisation which of late years has been the policy of almost every Government'.[64] Defeated by ninety-eight votes to twenty-nine, Evans found that he could not stem the tide of State encroachments. Nevertheless, he persevered in raising local issues, repeatedly seeking a reduction of the duty on carriages, a burden resented by many of his constituents.[65]

Few issues aroused more concern in Westminster than assessed taxation, particularly the window tax. In 1850 the Whig government, which had suffered several humiliating rebuffs over its financial proposals since 1846, only saved the tax in a parliamentary division by a majority of three votes. On the eve of the next session, a campaign against the duty was mounted in the metropolis. Evans spoke at various meetings, describing the tax as unfair in principle, as a disproportionate burden upon the capital, and, above all, as a threat to public health. He also opposed the idea of substituting a new house tax for window duty, fearing that it would impose a heavy burden upon many of the three million householders who were exempted from the present tax.[66] But Sir Charles Wood, the Chancellor of the Exchequer, was unwilling forgo the entire revenue of £1,900,000 from the window duty. He resolved to introduce a new tax on houses whose annual value exceeded £20, to be levied at 6*d* in the pound on shops, inns and farmhouses and at 9*d* on all other dwellings. By these measures, especially the exemption rate, which doubled the previous £10 limit,

Wood mollified the majority of his critics. Even Evans, who cavilled about minor details, accepted that the new tax was a 'very great improvement' on its predecessor.[67]

On national issues, Evans voted consistently against the protectionist Tories and approved of some controversial legislation by Lord John Russell's government. On 27th March 1851 he voted in favour of the second reading of the Ecclesiastical Titles Bill, which legitimised the protest, first aired by Russell in his *Durham Letter* of the previous November, against the papal division of England into Catholic bishopric areas. By exploiting Protestant fears of 'papal aggression', the government gained the ratification of its Bill by 438 votes to 95. Whigs, Conservatives and some Radicals like Thompson, D'Eyncourt and Evans, supported the Bill, while the Irish Nationalists, Peelites and leading Radicals like Bright and Hume opposed it. By entering the government lobby Evans had performed 'one of the most painful duties' of his parliamentary career, deviating from 'the principles of religious equality he had always professed'. As he explained to his constituents, he had done so because

a great and important principle was involved, and his guiding motive . . . was the conviction that the agression the measure was intended to repel struck at the root of our national independence and the supremacy and authority of our beloved Sovereign.[68]

Evans also supported the government's reaction to the invasion scare aroused by Louis Napoleon's seizure of power in France in December 1851. By proposing to increase the army by 5,000 men, and to form a local Militia, Russell split the Radicals. Cobden deplored the endorsements proffered by his military colleagues. In a letter to Joseph Sturge, the Quaker philanthropist, he bemoaned those Radicals 'like *Colonel* Thompson and ex Captain Osborne' who derided any opposition to the government's scheme.[69] Evans even admonished the government to go beyond its present proposals and to accept the services of Volunteer rifle corps. Hitherto such clubs, including the Metropolitan Volunteer Rifles, had not been sanctioned, pending the legislative approval of the Militia. Evans argued that the government should harness the patriotic enthusiasm of these clubs, so recognising their value in home defence and confirming that the people could now be trusted in the bearing of arms.[70] The government demurred, preferring to press ahead with its Militia Bill. It faced opposition from Palmerston, who had recently been dismissed from the Cabinet. He advocated a national rather than a local militia, and in his 'tit for tat' with Lord John Russell carried the vote in the Commons.

The government resigned, to be replaced by a Conservative administration, under Lord Derby. It introduced a new Militia Bill, with the support of Palmerston, providing for the embodiment of 80,000 Militiamen, who were to be enlisted voluntarily or, if necessary, chosen by a ballot. Like Cobden and Bright, Evans opposed the Bill, but he presented a more moderate critique of its proposals in his own amendment. He sought to amend the Bill because it required Militiamen to serve in any part of the country and did not encourage the enrolment of Volunteer corps. He insisted that Volunteers would prove much less expensive than the £400,000 earmarked for the new Militia, and favoured withdrawing 15,000 regular troops from the colonies, so saving between £200,000 and £300,000 on the estimates and bolstering the home defences.[71] Cobden deplored this amendment, as it prevented a more wide-ranging debate on the case for a Militia. He advised the Reverend Henry Richard, secretary of the Peace Society, to persuade some Westminster constituents to exert pressure upon Evans. 'In going to De Lacy Evans,' argued Cobden, 'do not let my name or [Milner] Gibson's be mentioned. Your only chance with him is by bringing a constituent or two down upon him. He is a sham Radical, & hates us all most cordially. So expect nothing from his affection for you or your cause.'[72] Evans refused to give way, and his motion, though resoundingly defeated, gained 165 votes, almost double the vote which Cobden subsequently secured for a motion to postpone the Bill. During the committee stage of the Militia Bill, Evans persistently opposed the government, and, in a final amendment, proposed that recourse to the ballot should be limited to time of war or its imminent danger. Although he rallied Radicals behind this amendment, he was again defeated by 178 votes to 82.[73] On 7th June 1852 the Militia Bill passed its third reading – the last major piece of legislation before the general election.

In the forthcoming election Evans faced a serious challenge from an ultra-Radical candidate, William Coningham. For Evans, this was a unique experience, a reflection of the profound dissension within his constituency. The Westminster Reform Society had contributed to the malaise by its process of candidate selection. Having heard of Lushington's intention to retire, it had chosen Sir John Shelley, a wealthy landowner, to contest the election with Evans. The *Morning Advertiser* denounced 'the arrogance and presumption of this little clique of persons – the sole survivors of the Westminster Rump', who 'snugly and quietly meet together, and presume to dictate to the electors what gentleman they should choose as their representative'.[74] Non-electors were also angry about the slow pace of parliamentary reform; they warmly endorsed Coningham, who promised to campaign for manhood suffrage, the ballot, annual elections, equal electoral districts, the abolition of property qualifications, State provision for education, and the separation of Church and State. Non-electors promised to run Coningham's campaign, canvassing voters after working hours.[75] Their candidate was an Irish Radical, who professed to be more inspired by the writings of William Cobbett than by the People's Charter. Nonetheless, he harnessed the lingering Chartist sentiments in Westminster, and sought to exploit the discontent with Evans as the sitting Member. As he toured the constituency, Coningham attacked Evans with increasing vehemence. He described him as a 'liberty-professing general who had flogged more men in the army than any officer of his time'. He criticised Evans's absenteeism and his squabbling with Cobden, when he should have been voting for the reduction of the army, navy and Church expenditure. He deplored the latter's vote for the Ecclesiastical Titles Bill, and declared that Westminster should send 'men of peace, and not men of war, to the House of Commons.'[76]

Coningham's challenge was steeped in irony. Nearly twenty years previously Evans had opposed Sir John Hobhouse, an incumbent whose views no longer chimed with the preferences of the more extreme Radicals in Westminster. Unlike Hobhouse, Evans still espoused his former Radicalism and had never compromised his opinions by seeking a ministerial appointment. But, as an ageing Radical, he was extremely vulnerable. His brand of Radicalism had lost some of its former appeal. His parliamentary record was tarnished by absenteeism, and his voting record hardly endeared him to pacifists and Catholics. Although Coningham was unlikely to win the election, he threatened to syphon off sufficient votes from Evans to let in the Conservative candidate, Lord Maidstone. The *Morning Advertiser*, though critical of the Westminster 'clique', dreaded this possibility, fearing the loss of the constituency 'to the popular cause'. It condemned Coningham for splitting the Radical vote and exhorted its readers to vote for Shelley and Evans.[77]

Evans responded to the challenge with a frantic round of speech-making which belied his sixty-four years. He reminded audiences of his long record of constituency service: while Burdett, Leader and Lushington had concentrated upon national issues, he had always attended to local grievances and had brought them before the House of Commons. He recalled his strenuous opposition to the window tax and his pleas for a modification of the income tax. He denounced charges that he had ordered the flogging of men and women in Spain as utterly false and a distortion of his attitudes to corporal punishment. Stressing his Radical commitment, he insisted that he was not a 'candidate for place, either from Whigs, Tories or Radicals'.[78] Towards the end of the campaign Evans moved increasingly on to the defensive – a sign that Coningham, who was drawing much larger crowds,[79] was proving an effective critic. Forced to discuss the charges of absenteeism, Evans dissembled, disputing the statistics and claiming that they were 'not a test of Parliamentary fitness'. On his abstention from O'Connor's motion in favour of universal suffrage and annual Parliaments, he stated that the time was 'not ripe' for such legislation. On religious issues, he reaffirmed his opposition to all religious grants and endowments and his support for an enquiry into the entry requirements for Oxford and Cambridge. In defence of his military credentials, he asserted that his career had been hindered and not advanced by political involvement, since he had clashed so often with the military authorities.[80]

During the course of the campaign the Liberal election committee had become increasingly worried. While Coningham was attracting large and vociferous crowds in the traditionally Radical parishes, the Conservatives had conducted a discreet and well financed canvass, without any public meetings. As uncertainty mounted about the eventual outcome, Liberal tactics became less and less scrupulous. Hecklers denounced Coningham as a 'Romanist', a charge which was strenuously denied but still extensively reported in the daily press. The Liberal election committee also published a pamphlet describing Coningham as a Socialist, committed to the doctrines of Robert Owen.[81] Whether these tactics proved effective or counter-productive was by no means clear, but they ensured that even more opprobrium was heaped upon Evans. Denounced by *The Patriot* and *The Nonconformist* for conducting a dishonourable campaign,[82] he encountered unprecedented hostility at the nomination hustings. He barely obtained a hearing as he struggled to explain his vote over the Ecclesiastical Titles Bill and to reiterate his commitment to political, fiscal and ecclesiastical reform. In the formal show of hands, several thousand were raised for Shelley and Coningham, leaving Evans and Maidstone to demand a vote.[83]

On 8th July the voters of Westminster went to the polls. Excitement mounted throughout the day as Maidstone held a narrow lead over Evans until late in the afternoon. The eventual result gave Shelley 4,199 votes, Evans 3,756, Maidstone 3,373, and Coningham 1,716. A potentially comfortable Liberal vote had been scythed by Coningham's intervention. More 'plumpers' had favoured Shelley than Evans, and the latter had only just defeated a strong Conservative challenge. At the announcement of the result, Evans was barracked even more viciously than on previous occasions. He ended the proceedings with a barely audible defence of the Westminster 'rump': 'respectable inhabitants . . . who had gratuitously given their time, their labour, and money to the public service for many years past . . .'. He was certainly indebted to them.[84]

To his credit, Evans did not dwell excessively upon his traumatic electoral experience. As soon as Parliament resumed, he brought in another Parliamentary Electors Bill to take account of a ruling in the Court of Common Pleas about the timing of the payment of taxes to qualify for the franchise. Although the House of Lords had approved of Evans's Bill in 1848, extending the period of payment from three months to six, the Lord Chief Justice had since ruled that the law was unclear about the issue of timing. Evans argued that over 100,000 solvent voters had been disfranchised as a consequence of the present state of the law, but Lord Stanley, on behalf of the government, opposed the motion, insisting that only voters who had failed to pay their taxes had been disfranchised. The Bill was defeated by 103 votes to 67.[85] Undaunted, Evans displayed much of his former passion in campaigning against the budget of Benjamin Disraeli. He deplored the Chancellor's desire to increase taxes despite a budgetary surplus, particularly as he proposed to reduce the exemption rate for the house tax from £20 to £10, so making another 42,000 houses eligible for taxation. Addressing his constituents on 13th December 1852, he described the budget as dishonest, onerous, and only of benefit for 'capitalists and agriculturists'. He was heartily cheered by his audience, who promptly agreed to submit a petition of protest to Parliament.[86] On 17th December Evans had the satisfaction of seeing the government defeated over its budget and replaced by a coalition of Whigs and Peelites, headed by Lord Aberdeen.

Evans generally supported this government, which included one

Radical, Sir William Molesworth, in its Cabinet. In the Commons he continued to vote for Radical motions and to raise constituency issues,[87] but he could rarely command the ear of the House or secure the passage of fresh legislation. In these circumstances, it was not too surprising that he should consider resuming his military career. He had never lost his love of soldiering. At Liberal dinners he frequently gave the toast to the army, and in doing so always praised its achievements.[88] He had regularly spoken in the army debates not only in opposing the retrenchment proposals of Hume and Cobden, but also in commending the services of the Kilmainham hospital, the recent improvement in sanitary provisions, and the importance of instituting lectureships in military surgery in London and Dublin.[89] Privately he had also discussed current military issues, especially with Perronet Thompson, another veteran Radical with military connections.[90] Nevertheless, Evans's military career had foundered during the previous fifteen years; he had only been promoted once, by process of seniority, to the rank of Major-General (9th November 1846). Attributing this stagnation to the political conflicts he had had with the Duke of Wellington, he had little hope of an attachment or a field command until the Duke died in September 1852.

Lord Hardinge, a former Secretary at War (1828–30 and 1841–44), succeeded the Duke as Commander-in-Chief. Having been largely responsible for the introduction of the Minié rifle into the British service, Hardinge had come to office with the reputation of being a pragmatic reformer.[91] To embark upon reform he had the assistance of Sidney Herbert, the Secretary at War, and the enthusiastic encouragement of Prince Albert. He promptly established a School of Musketry at Hythe, and adopted the idea, first mooted by Albert in 1847,[92] of testing part of the army in a military camp. Herbert agreed to meet the necessary expenses by a vote in the estimates, and a division, under the command of Lord Seaton, was encamped at Chobham from 14th June to 14th August 1853. Evans was offered a brigade command, being one of the few senior officers with recent field experience who was free from other military commitments. He readily accepted, even missing a vote on the ballot and raising speculation about his imminent return to a military appointment.[93]

Lord Hardinge had hoped that the camp would fulfil several objectives. It would enable a division and its brigades to manoeuvre, so affording officers and men practice in the use of ground and in combined operations between the three arms. It would facilitate the trial of new ammunition waggons and of new items of clothing and equipment. It would also sustain popular interest in the army, already revived by Wellington's funeral and the fears of a French invasion, by welcoming visitors and conducting the main events on Saturdays.[94] Evans, though never entrusted with a divisional command, figured prominently in the first month's exercises (another body of officers and men were tested in the second month). On Saturday 2nd July he manoeuvred his brigade, without any noticeable failing, in the presence of Lord Hardinge and Prince Lucien Bonaparte.[95] In spite of his advancing years, he had acquitted himself successfully, and on 29th August was appointed colonel of the 21st Royal North British Fusiliers.

From a military viewpoint, however, Chobham camp had not been entirely successful. On the one hand, large crowds had come to watch the manoeuvres, and the visitors and soldiers had established a good-natured *rapport*.[96] On the other hand, the training over rough and broken ground had proved more beneficial to the infantry than to the cavalry. The camp lacked realism in several respects: the troops neither performed outpost work nor fired live ammunition, and only the second contingent threw up any fieldworks. Deficiencies were revealed in the staff work, and some manoeuvres were hopelessly confused. Shortcomings were apparent, wrote *The Naval and Military Gazette*, 'in the organisation, training, clothing, equipping, and arming of all branches of the Service'.[97] Although Chobham was supposed to reveal such failings, if they existed, and the purchase of a permanent camp site at Aldershot was supposed to correct them, there was too little time to remedy the evident defects. The rapidly worsening situation in the Near East ensured that the army would be tested in battle before it could be reformed in peace.

The deteriorating relations between Russia and Turkey had been evident throughout 1853. The two countries had found it impossible to compose their differences over the privileges of the Catholic and Orthodox monks in Jerusalem, and over the rights of ten million Orthodox Christians in the Ottoman Empire. After declaring war on Russia in October, Turkey had suffered a devastating naval defeat at Sinope on 30th November. Once the news of Sinope reached Britain, war fever swept the nation. Russophobia, recently kindled by the huge receptions for Kossuth, resurfaced; it found expression in newspaper editorials, particularly those of *The Times*, and in mass meetings throughout the country. Hatred of the Tsar, his despotic rule, and his designs on Constantinople were no longer the preserve of pamphleteers like Evans in the 1820s. Fanned by the speeches of ex-Chartists and several Radicals, popular wrath and indignation were directed at Nicholas I [98] and, not less significantly, at the leaders of the peace movement, Cobden and Bright. The latter were even burned in effigy by the crowds in Manchester. Lord Aberdeen, who presided over a divided Cabinet, had sought a negotiated settlement. Loath to intervene, he reluctantly bowed before the pressure of opinion at home, the worsening turn of events in the Near East, and the fear of independent action by France. In January 1854 Britain and France sent their fleets to the Black Sea.

As the prospect of war became increasingly imminent, the Radicals split assunder. In February the House debated the question of Russia and the Porte. Cobden deplored the possibility of Britain siding with the Mohammedans against the Christian population of Turkey: he saw neither profit nor honour in a war with Russia.[99] Evans, like Hume, totally disagreed. He applauded the press for enlightening the people, and the government for resolving to check 'the aggression and domination of Russia'. He denounced the Tsar's 'long-premeditated policy', which had always threatened the peace. He accepted that war seemed inevitable and had hopes of a successful outcome. Britain, he declared, would enter such a conflict with the advantage of a close alliance with France, a 'splendid and efficient' army and navy, and, above all, 'right and justice' on her side.[100] Five days later, Britain despatched her ultimatum to St Petersburg and after a month had elapsed, on 28th March, declared war on Russia.

7
Crimean hero

Britain despatched an expeditionary force of approximately 27,000 men to the Crimea. It was composed of five infantry divisions and one cavalry division, with complementary units of artillery and engineers. Lord Raglan, a sixty-five-year-old Peninsular veteran, was appointed to command the force, his first independent command. Evans, nearly a year older, was appointed to command the Second Division. He was the oldest and most experienced of the infantry commanders. The Duke of Cambridge, the only commander under sixty years of age, had never seen active service, the Hon. Sir George Cathcart had only recently seen any service in a minor colonial expedition, while Sir George Brown had not held a field command since being wounded at Bladensburg. Sir Richard England had served in several campaigns, especially in India and the 'sixth' Kaffir War, but he had not distinguished himself in the Scinde campaign. After thirty-nine years of peace, the army lacked experience of large-scale regular warfare, a shortcoming which affected not merely the high command but also the staff and Commissariat Department. The capacity of the pre-war army to keep officers and men trained, ready, and equipped for active service against regular troops would be fully tested in the Crimea. Confident of the outcome, *The Times* described the army as 'admirably efficient', able 'to act with a vigour heretofore unknown'.[1]

Evans reacted to his appointment in characteristic fashion. Though gratified by official recognition of his military experience, he was not entirely satisfied. He regarded the appointment as belated and as less than adequate. Still vain and tactless, he wrote to Lord Hardinge and to the Duke of Newcastle, the Secretary of State for War, requesting promotion to a higher class in the Order of the Bath. He enclosed a fifteen-page memorandum, containing a description of his military career, embellished by approbatory comments on his services in the

In the Crimea: a photograph by Roger Fenton

Peninsular War, North America, Waterloo and the Carlist War. 'No other general officer,' he asserted, in similar circumstances, has ever been 'left in a subordinate class of the Order of the Bath.'² Neither Lord Hardinge nor the Duke of Newcastle was much impressed. Hardinge insisted that the Secretary of State had to forward any applications to the Queen, while the Duke refused to make such an application without the previous suggestion of the Commander-in-Chief.³

Undaunted, Evans continued to plead his case during the voyage to the Near East. When his troopship, *City of London*, berthed off Gibraltar, he sent another copy of the memorandum to Lord Aberdeen with an even more tendentious covering letter. Quoting Lord Raglan's observation that all ranks, especially the higher ranks of the army, should receive their 'just requitals', he deplored any deviation from this rule. He feared that it would constitute

some infringement in this instance on the independence of a Parliamentary Representative, – were a proportionate honorary recognition of proved services, – withheld or restricted through any influences of a party character.

He reminded the Prime Minister that the Legion and its commander had suffered an 'unmeasured degree of misstatement and censure' from the 'powerful opposition of that day, under the Duke of Wellington, Sir Robert Peel and your Lordship'. As the passions and concerns of the 1830s had 'long ceased to exist', he sought 'some act of reparative justice'.⁴ Lord Aberdeen ignored the letter. After four months had elapsed, Evans sent another copy of the memorandum to Downing Street, and, one month later, sent Lady Evans to press for a reply in person.⁵ The Premier replied, refusing the request because he could not advise the Queen over the award of a G.C.B. without a recommendation from the Commander-in-Chief.⁶

Fortunately, Evans did not dwell unduly upon his injured sense of self-importance. On 23rd April he reached the Scutari barracks on the Asiatic side of the Bosphorus, where some 5,000 to 6,000 men had already arrived.⁷ During the next seven weeks the whole army assembled at Scutari and Koulali, and in the adjoining camps. Until Lord Raglan arrived in early May, Evans commanded the force at Scutari. He encountered a multitude of problems, not least the lack of accurate information about the state of Russo-Turkish hostilities. He had heard of a Greek insurrection at Salonica, but took comfort from the despatch of two thousand Egyptians 'to attack these rascals'. In the same letter to Sir George Brown he admitted that he knew 'nothing yet of our future destination'.[8] At a more mundane level, he had to organise provisional formations for the regiments which had arrived, so that they could practise their field movements and other duties. Faced with a growing disciplinary problem, largely on account of drunkenness, he convened a district court-martial. On 27th April he confirmed the sentences on two soldiers but commuted corporal punishment in one instance, on account of the youth of the prisoner. On the same day he arranged a review of the British troops for the benefit of the Turkish Minister of War.[9] But his main concern was the lack of accommodation. Although the new barracks at Scutari provided accommodation for 6,000 men, he had to find quarters for more than 12,000.[10] In allocating the facilities, he accorded rank its traditional priority; the Sultan's apartments were set aside for the Queen's cousin, the Duke of Cambridge, and barracks were reserved for the Brigade of Guards. So after accommodating generals, the staff, a hospital, and the commissariat stores in the barracks, there was only room for the brigade of Brigadier-General Adams. All other regiments had to pitch camp, but Evans assured Brown that 'the camping ground is good & convenient'.[11] General Bentinck confirmed this assessment; he preferred to encamp the Brigade of Guards than to leave the battalions divided between the various barracks. Evans used the vacated accommodation to house other battalions.[12]

When Lord Raglan assumed overall command, Evans concentrated his energies upon the Second Division. He commanded six regiments of infantry, two brigades of artillery, and a company of sappers and miners – a force of about 6,200 men. The regiments were divided into two brigades: the 30th, 55th and 95th composed the 1st Brigade under Major-General John L. Pennefather; the 41st, 47th and 49th formed the 2nd Brigade under Brigadier-General Henry W. Adams. All regiments, save the 95th, had recently been quartered in Mediterranean garrisons and were fully acclimatised. Despite the insufferable heat, the troops remained reasonably free from serious ailments. Evans insisted upon the regular practice of drills and field manoeuvres, ensuring that his brigades attained an impressive degree of disciplined movement. On 17th May the Second Division was formally inspected by Lord Raglan; one week later, it took part in the splendid military review to commemorate the Queen's birthday.[13] On 16th June it set sail in twelve vessels bound for Varna on the Bulgarian coast.

After a calm crossing of the Black Sea, the Second Division arrived at Varna on the night of 18th June. It disembarked the following morning and encamped on the outskirts of the town. The French had already reached the town and established themselves on the higher slopes. They had also appropriated the best part of the town, where they had renamed some streets and opened cafés and shops for the sale of cheap champagne and vermouth. Drunkenness soon became prevalent as British, French and Turkish troops swarmed into the town during the day. Although Evans's camp, pitched near a shallow lake, was reasonably healthy, and the men were well fed, there were few amenities on site. Sports and hunting were encouraged to offset the boredom and to discourage excessive drinking.[14] In these circumstances, morale was fragile; it faltered perceptibly when news reached Varna that the Russians had raised the siege of Silistria and retreated northwards. Many soldiers were disappointed, fearing that they had lost their chance 'after coming so far, of having one brush with the Russians'. So pervasive were these fears that Evans tried to reassure his Division with a bombastic speech after church service on 25th June.[15]

Evans, however, knew nothing of the army's ultimate destination. When he was ordered to move camp some three weeks later, it was only to a hill about eighteen miles to the west of Varna. Lacking any information about the place, Evans examined it personally for two or three days prior to moving his troops. Concerned about the inadequate supplies of water and wood near Varna, he chose a site surrounded by a wood and containing a running stream of water. His prudence was warranted, as the cholera which broke out in the French camp on 19th July soon affected the British forces. Like other generals, Evans again moved camp, even dispersing the division into regiments and brigades because he could not find sizeable locations with sufficient water and wood. Even so, the sickness spread; some sixty men died from cholera, and the strength of the Second Division slumped to about 4,500 men, a total which, Evans believed, compared favourably with other British divisions.[16] He himself had already established his reputation 'as one of the first officers' among the divisional commanders and his division was highly regarded.[17] Nevertheless, he was not privy to the planning of Lord Raglan. When the commander-in-chief received his instructions to proceed to the Crimea, he consulted Sir George Brown but not Evans. Indeed, the latter only learnt of an impending expedition from a rumour among his junior

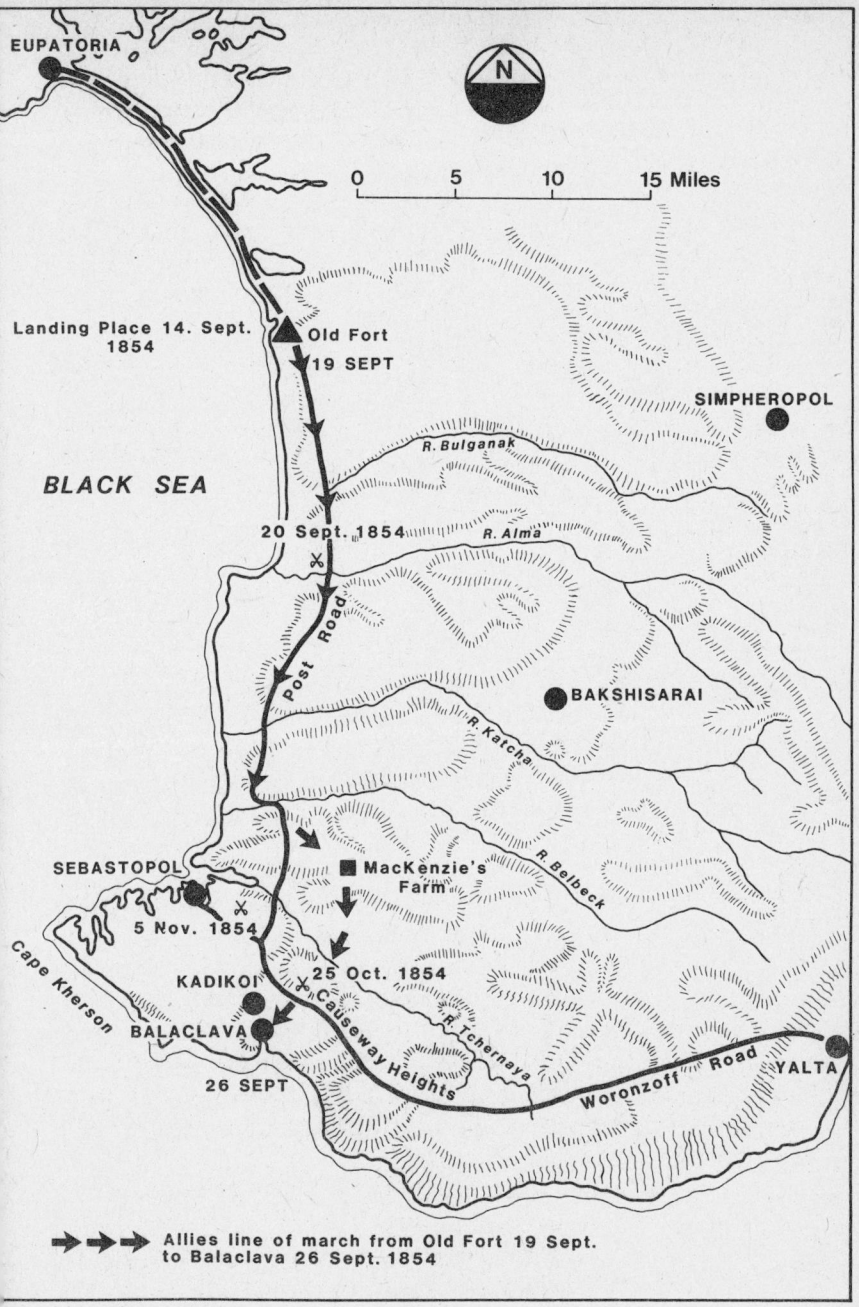

4. The advance on Sebastopol

officers. Even when the Second Division embarked at Varna on 1st September, he knew nothing about the projected destination. Bitterly resenting this treatment, he later informed the Sebastopol Committee that 'I never had the honour of being consulted'.[18]

The Second Division set sail in five steamers, with its ordnance, cannon, artillerymen and sappers carried by several sailing vessels. After twelve days' sailing, it reached the Crimean coastline, anchoring off the town of Eupatoria. Two days later, on 14th September, the division disembarked about ten miles to the south at a place called the Old Fort. Bereft of transport, the soldiers struggled ashore; each carried his rifle, bayonet and fifty rounds of ammunition, along with a greatcoat, blanket, extra clothing, a canteen, and three days' rations. As the Second Division bivouacked on cliffs about three miles south of the fort, disembarkation proved particularly arduous. Given the lack of time and transport, the troops landed without tents and many regiments left their knapsacks on board. Rain began falling in the afternoon and was followed by a thunderstorm at night. Only Evans slept in a tent; all other officers and men endured a miserable evening. Tents were brought ashore during the brief stay at the Old Fort, but, as the army lacked sufficient transport, they had to be returned to the ships when the march to Sebastopol was begun on 19th September.[19]

At nine o'clock in the morning the allies marched southwards, with the French on the right, between the British and the sea. Evans's division, flanked on its left by the Light Division, comprised the British front, supported by the Third and First Divisions respectively. During the march Evans, unlike the majority of generals, happily talked to the press. He had already arranged a berth for William Howard Russell of *The Times* on the *City of London*; he had also assured the editor of *The Daily News* that he would have done the same for his correspondent had he been given adequate warning.[20] But Evans took a particular interest in Russell, a fellow Irishman with a convivial manner. When Russell said that he had not made any arrangements about how he would accompany the army, Evans rebuked him sternly. 'You do not know what you are about. Nor do those who sent you understand what they are doing. Do get attached to something or other. You must go to the Commissary-General, to the Chaplain-in-Chief – to anyone you know. Get attached to something. Go at once.'[21]

After five hours' marching beneath a fiercely hot sun, the armies reached the Bulganak river. As Cossacks were espied on rising ground nearly a mile off, Lord Raglan ordered Lord Cardigan, with four squadrons of light cavalry, to reconnoitre the southern bank. In doing so, the cavalry drew the fire of the Russians and prompted an immediate deployment of the Light and Second Divisions across the river. Lord Raglan then detected much larger Russian forces behind their cavalry and withdrew his advance guard. The Russians responded by withdrawing to their formidable defences above the river Alma and leaving the allies to bivouac for the night in order of battle.

Evans waited restlessly to receive instructions for his division, which was deployed in the centre of the allies' front, flanked by the Light Division on the left and Prince Napoleon's division on the right. Shortly after daybreak, Prince Napoleon and General Canrobert visited Evans in his tent to confer about the co-operation of Evans's and the Prince's forces in the ensuing conflict. Finding Evans impatient to receive his marching orders,[22] they informed him that a plan had already been agreed between Marshal St Arnaud and Lord Raglan. This was not correct. The Marshal had presented a plan for a classical pincer operation, involving a combined attack on the Russian front and flanks, but Lord Raglan had been reluctant to commit himself until the allies had discovered the full extent of the Russian position. Though reticent, he had offered bland assurances of co-operation, which were, quite reasonably, interpreted as consent to the plan.[23] Unaware of this discussion, Evans heartily endorsed the plan and assured the French of his co-operation in the frontal attack. He immediately requested permission from Lord Raglan to muster his troops in battle formation. Three hours elapsed before the orders to advance were issued, largely occasioned by the realignment of those British forces which had guarded the eastern front at night and by the tortuous movement of the baggage train bringing reserve ammunition into the line of march. Before moving off, Lord Raglan contacted Evans and expressed his reservations about the French plan. He also reproved Evans for taking orders from the French, suggesting that the latter were trying to appropriate his division. Understandably annoyed, Evans suggested that his lordship might care to inform the French on these matters and possibly appoint Major Claremont, a British commissioner with the French army, as a channel of communication.[24]

At about one o'clock the advance was sounded and the Second Division moved off with Pennefather's brigade on the left and Adams's on the right. It was flanked by the Light Division, which was not sufficiently extended to its left and was also advancing at an oblique

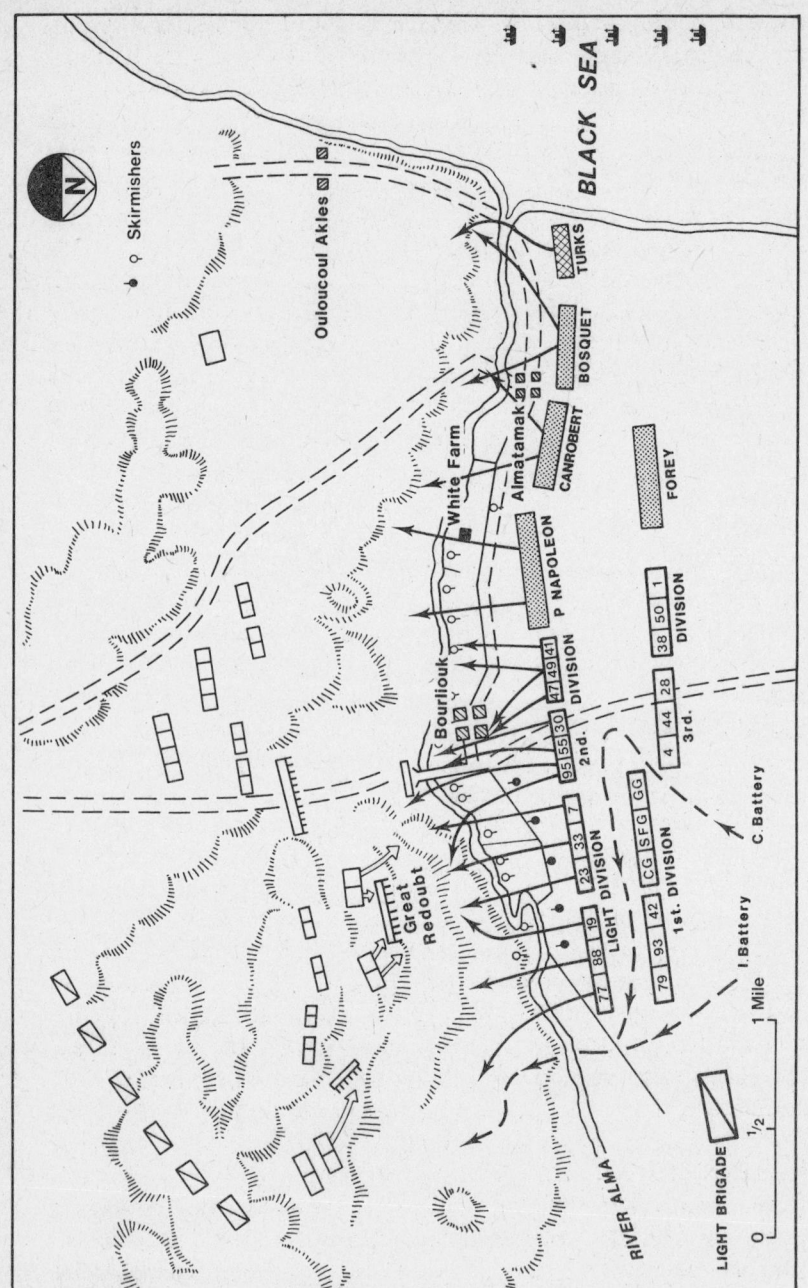

5. The battle of the Alma

angle to the rest of the army. Soon the men of its right-hand regiment, the 7th Foot, became inextricably muddled with those of the 95th. To avoid a similar mistake, the Duke of Cambridge deployed the First Division in the rear of the Second Division. Consequently, Lord Raglan withdrew the Third Division, which should have supported the Second from that part of the field, and placed it in reserve. Compared with the closely compacted French and Turkish forces, the British troops presented a far from impressive spectacle.

After about three miles the armies halted within range of the Russian guns. As the soldiers lay down under heavy fire, the village of Bourliuk in front of the Second Division suddenly burst into flames. The choking fumes and intense heat made the village impenetrable, so further cramping the advance of Evans's troops. News then reached him from Major Claremont that the French army had already engaged the enemy, and that they would be compromised unless the Russians were drawn away by a frontal attack. Evans passed this information on to Lord Raglan through Lieutenant-Colonel the Hon. Percy Herbert. As Lord Raglan had already received similar reports, he approved an attack. He despatched Captain Nolan with the formal orders to advance, which Major Daniel Lysons, the Assistant Adjutant-General to the Second Division, carried to his general and brigadiers.[25]

Evans faced a formidable task in pressing his assault on either side of the burning village. He divided his force, despatching General Adams to his right with the 41st and 49th regiments, supported by Captain Turner's field artillery. Adams had to drive away some Russian skirmishers and march down to the ford which divided the French and British armies. Evans himself, with the First Brigade, the 47th regiment, and Major James W. Fitzmayer's battery of field artillery, had to move along the unsheltered line of the Great Causeway in a narrow and crowded front. Prince Mentschikoff had massed artillery to cover the pass and the great road. As Evans's troops scrambled forward, they were pounded by the sixteen guns of the causeway batteries and by eight other guns planted near by; their left flank was enfiladed by shelling from the heavy artillery in the Great Redoubt, and their approach at ground level was covered by the fire of Russian infantry screened by the conflagration.[26]

The advance had perforce to be slow, as the soldiers stole forward in groups from one sheltering spot to another in full view of the Russian gunners. The troops were supported by fire from eighteen guns

(Fitzmayer's battery and two additional batteries from the First and Light Divisions, whose services had been offered by their battery commanders, Lieutenant-Colonel Dacres and Captain Anderson respectively).[27] Nevertheless, the infantry advanced gradually under a hail of grape, canister and musket balls, finding some shelter in the walls and isolated buildings. When the enemy shattered these walls with round shot, many men were crushed or suffocated in the ruins. Evans observed the advance from a hillock just clear of the smoke of the village opposite the Russian batteries. Concerned about the fate of Adams's brigade, he despatched Lysons to reassemble its scattered forces.[28] Meanwhile, Pennefather's brigade and the 47th pressed forward, eventually crossing the river and re-forming under the cover of the steep bank on the Russian side. The losses had been severe. Evans was wounded in the right shoulder, almost all his staff had been struck and Pennefather's brigade had lost nearly a quarter of its strength in killed and wounded. Moreover, some companies of the 95th had become detached, joining General Codrington's brigade in its assault on the Great Redoubt.[29]

Evans ordered his shattered regiments to hold their ground and engage the guns in front with their Minié rifles. Waiting for an opportunity to advance, he heard the sound of a British nine-pounder shelling the enemy position. Captain Turner had reached Lord Raglan's forward knoll with two guns, from which he had begun to enfilade the artillery astride the main road. As the shelling was soon followed by the limbering up and retreat of the Russian batteries, Evans seized the initiative. He mustered his three regiments, the 47th, 30th and 55th, for an advance and annexed artillery to provide support. To his own battery he added the two batteries apparently neglected by the commanders of the Light and First Divisions, and two more batteries proffered by Sir Richard England from the Third Division. With about thirty guns at his disposal (a few were lost in the river crossing), Evans advanced into the pass. While the 55th, under Colonel Warren, moved up the valley to support the Royal Fusiliers in firing on the left flank of the Russian position, Evans established his guns near the site of the batteries which had just been withdrawn by the Russians.[30]

Whether Evans's action merits the accolade 'a Napoleonic stroke'[31] is debatable, but it certainly revealed an understanding of the battle and the value of concentrated artillery fire. In sustaining the momentum of the frontal assault he displayed more enterprise than Sir

Richard England, whose units remained in reserve for most of the battle and only latterly supported the Second Division. Evans also ensured that the momentum was maintained despite the feckless behaviour of the Duke of Cambridge. About half-way up the hill, Evans 'saw in profile the swift disordered advance of Codrington's Brigade', and feared that one of his regiments might be driven back to the Alma. He saw, too, that the First Division was still stationary on the northern side of the river. Consequently, he sent Colonel Steele, the Military Secretary, to the hesitant Duke, informing him 'that he was the bearer of orders from the Commander of the Forces', and that the First Division 'should forthwith pass the river and proceed as rapidly as possible to support the troops under Sir G. Brown'.[32] Evans assumed full responsibility for this action, which prompted the Duke to resume his advance.

Once the Alma heights had been secured, Evans formally reported to Lord Raglan. He praised the ability and gallantry of his two brigadiers, and paid tribute to the 'capital service' of Captain Turner's battery, whose fire from Lord Raglan's knoll had facilitated his advance. He recognised the assistance of battery commanders from other divisions, and lamented the loss of 540 men of all ranks, including thirty-six officers. In commending several members of his staff, he emphasised that the assault had been extremely arduous. The Second Division, he claimed, had been 'the first engaged' with the Russians and had never seen any troops in front of it 'except those of the Enemy . . .'.[33]

For two days the army buried its dead and transferred the wounded to hospital ships. On the morning of the 23rd September, the allies marched down from the heights above the Alma into the valley of the Katcha river. After bivouacking for the night on the left bank of the river, they crossed the river Belbeck the following day, camping that night on the opposite heights. Cholera was still taking its toll,[34] but morale was reasonably high, as the camp was within sight of Sebastopol. During one of the halts, Evans addressed the division, praising the army in general and the Second Division in particular for their conduct at the battle of the Alma.[35] From the river Belbeck, the troops were ordered to embark on a flank march around Sebastopol, with a view to mounting an attack against the city's imperfectly constructed southern defences. At eight o'clock in the morning the infantry began its march south-south-east by the compass, leaving the only road to the artillery and cavalry. Moving in fours, the soldiers stumbled through the thick brushwood of a dense oak forest in a long and extremely laborious march. The Second Division did not reach its bivouac on the banks of the Tchernaya river until about 10.30 p.m., and even then was unable to rest for the night until all the artillery had crossed the river some two hours later. Although the men had suffered severely from a lack of water *en route*, relatively few, at least of the 95th, had fallen out.[36]

On 26th September the army moved south towards Balaclava; but during the attack upon, and capture of, the town, the Second Division remained in reserve on the plain of Kadikoi. On the following day, the division moved to about a mile and a half west of Balaclava and assisted in the reconnaissance of the Sebastopol fortress. While Lord Raglan and his staff assessed the defences, Evans insisted upon his troops maintaining ranks. Appalled by the news that some commanders had allowed their men to fall out and enter the nearby vineyards, he ordered a company of the 95th to drive them back into their corps.[37] Evans kept his troops on the alert for a couple of days before allowing them to relax, wash, and make themselves comfortable in their newly arrived tents. During late September and early October the weather was generally warm and sunny; it contributed, along with abundant supplies of ripened fruit, poultry, water and firewood, to an improvement in the health of the rank and file.

By 30th September the British and French commands had agreed a strategy. Lord Raglan had proposed an immediate assault on the Russian defences, but the French, and some of his own advisers, counselled caution, preferring to conduct a siege. As he was unable to act without the French, Raglan conceded and deployed his forces accordingly. He ordered the Second Division to guard the extreme right of the British position and so occupy the heights of Mount Inkerman – the seaward flank, vulnerable to attack from the Russian field army and from the garrison. Evans, however, lacked sufficient troops to defend the whole ridge; he now commanded about 3,000 men, having incurred heavy losses at the Alma and from cholera. He also had to provide working parties to dig trenches, carry ammunition, and make approaches for the siege guns. Concerned about this exposed position, he chose to concentrate his forces and to protect his line of communications with the rest of the army. Consequently, he refrained from guarding the highest point of the ridge, known as 'Shell Hill', which could not be easily supported. He posted picquets along the ridge and placed his camp some 1,300 yards to the south-east beyond a smaller crest, 'Home Ridge', where he could maintain contact by the post road with the nearby Guards' camp.

Having occupied this position on 4th October, Evans frequently warned Lord Raglan of its precariousness. He tried to fortify the camp by entrenchments, but picquet duties and working parties consumed large numbers of men and prevented the construction of extensive earthworks. By late October, only a small breastwork had been erected on either side of the road and two small walls built for the picquets on the ridge.[38] Meanwhile Evans, whose health was rapidly deteriorating, attended a briefing of divisional commanders on 7th October, to learn of another change of plan from Lord Raglan. To avoid wasting time in digging approaches, the commander-in-chief had decided to deploy his siege guns as close to Sebastopol as possible. If the siege guns could be moved forward with infantry support, as Sir John Burgoyne had advised, the engineers could reconnoitre more effectively and ensure prompt support for their working parties. The generals unanimously opposed this proposal; they insisted that an advanced position could not be maintained without artillery cover.[39] Thwarted again, Lord Raglan authorised the construction of long-range gunnery emplacements, a task which was not completed until 16th October.

Evans had only managed to attend the meeting by taking ammonia and other stimulants. He was suffering from a 'chronic complaint' and from diabetes, whose effects worsened during the bitterly cold nights. Whenever northerly winds swept through the camp he remained in his tent, sometimes for up to twenty-four hours. He gave and accepted orders through his unopened tent doors, and received members of Lord Raglan's staff while lying in bed or huddled in blankets on the ground.[40] Though enfeebled, he could still discern and deflect incompetence. On 23rd October, Colonel the Hon. Alexander Gordon, Deputy Quartermaster-General to the army, brought fresh orders from Lord Raglan. The Second Division, supported by the First, was to move down into the valley of the Tchernaya with the aim of intercepting a Russian convoy. These orders 'astonished' Evans. Neither he nor his staff had observed such a convoy, and any move into the valley in full view of twenty Russian guns could have proved disastrous. He protested that 'somebody must be mistaken' and sent Gordon back to Lord Raglan. Gordon duly returned with the same order, but added that Evans could use his own 'discretion in the matter'. Accordingly, Evans sent Gordon and Colonel Herbert to discover whether a convoy existed; he also despatched Captain Nolan with another staff officer to examine the position. On his return, Nolan admitted that had troops been moved into the valley they could have been utterly compromised. But Gordon, despite failing to locate the convoy, still insisted that the 1,000 carriages had 'probably halted in some corner of the road'. Appalled by this observation, Evans sent a letter to Lord Raglan deploring Gordon's stubborn and self-opinionated behaviour.[41]

While Evans languished in his tent, the bombardment of Sebastopol, which had begun on 17th October, continued daily. The Russians returned fire and mounted counter-attacks. On 25th October, General's Liprandi's army of 25,000 men attacked the token force of Turks, Marines and Highlanders guarding the allies' base at Balaclava. From the ensuing battle the Russians gained the Causeway Heights, carrying the Worontzoff Road, the one good road across the Plain of Balaclava leading to the allied camps and siege works. Heartened by reports of this success, the Russians launched a sortie from Sebastopol. At mid-day on the 26th, while Liprandi still threatened Balaclava, Colonel Federoff led six battalions of infantry and four pieces of light artillery (a force of nearly 5,000 men) in an assault on the Inkerman ridge. Having ordered some troops to carry entrenching tools, Federoff was not simply intent on a diversionary move; he seemed determined to occupy and hold at least part of the Inkerman heights.[42]

Despite overwhelming odds, the picquets of the 30th and 49th regiments resisted with remarkable tenacity. Instead of retiring after an initial volley they fought on, following Major Champion's exhortation to 'slate 'em, slate 'em my boys!'. Evans resisted the temptation to reinforce the picquets; he sent only two companies in support, and when his staff pleaded for the despatch of a battalion he replied, 'Not a man!' Preferring to fight the battle on ground of his own choosing, Evans used the time provided by his picquets to assemble eighteen guns on Home Ridge (his own two batteries and another proffered by the Duke of Cambridge). He also secured his flank by deploying the Brigade of Guards, which the Duke had promptly brought up, on his right. Thereupon, when the picquets withdrew, continually outflanked by three columns of Russian infantry, and positioned themselves behind the rudimentary walls on the ridge, Evans ordered his guns to fire. They crushed the artillery on Shell Hill and then concentrated on the infantry columns in succession. Each broke in turn, Colonel Federoff was seriously wounded, and within minutes the whole force was in retreat, closely pursued by the picquets and the bulk of the Second Division. During an engagement lasting about half an hour the Russians had lost, by their own estimates, about 270 men either killed or wounded. Evans reckoned that their loss could scarcely have been 'less than 600', with another eighty taken prisoner. His own losses were twelve killed and seventy-seven wounded.[43]

Known as 'little Inkerman', this action had revealed many of Evans's qualities as a field commander. Having carefully chosen his ground, he had calmly assessed the situation, methodically concentrated his forces, protected his flank, and then launched a devastating counter-attack. With an 'easy and masterful grace' he had inspired his troops and earned accolades throughout the army.[44] Unfortunately, he never commanded his troops again. After the battle he was compelled to remain in bed for several days, debilitated by a bout of diarrhoea. When he resumed his duties on 30th October he was still extremely weak. He fell from his horse, landed on his head, and suffered further injury when the horse partly rolled over him. Now utterly prostrated, he was removed from the front and hospitalised on board ship at Balaclava.[45]

Within six days, on the 5th November, the Russians launched their major attack on the British position at Inkerman. Upon hearing the sound of gunfire in the morning, Evans rose from his sick berth, took mercury as a stimulant, and rode to the battle. Feeling neither justified nor fit to command the division, he left General Pennefather in charge and never presumed to advise him on his tactical direction. Nevertheless, his appearance heartened the troops,[46] as he remained 'cool and intrepid' till the close of the battle. Captain E. B. Hamley was speaking to him when 'a shell, crashing through some obstacle close by, rose from the ground, passed a foot or two above our heads, and dropping amid a group a few yards behind us, exploded there, wounding some of them – but Sir De Lacy did not turn his head'.[47]

To hold Inkerman ridge, the allies fought a fierce, bloody but indecisive battle. The Russians eventually withdrew, with losses of approximately 20,000 men (as estimated by Lord Raglan). The British had lost 2,573 men, of whom 635 were killed; the French had lost 1,800, of whom 175 were killed.[48] Evans was appalled by these casualties and by the evidence of the enemy's strength. Now distraught, ill, and suffering from a severe sprain, his judgement had lost some of its former acuity. He approached Lord Raglan and urged him to raise the siege, embark the troops, and evacuate the Crimea.

Barely suppressing his indignation, Lord Raglan rejected this counsel, arguing that he could neither abandon his allies nor leave his siege train and material to the enemy.[49] Profoundly depressed, Evans left his commander-in-chief and unburdened himself to William Howard Russell. He bemoaned the failure to heed his warnings about the undefended state of the Second Division's flank. He feared, too, that the Russians would launch another attack before the allies had recuperated: 'I tell you, sir – but you are not to put this in your letter – we cannot remain here, even if we could trust the French or the Turks. I trust neither.'[50]

Evans himself could not remain any longer in the Crimea. As his health was deteriorating with the onset of winter, he wrote to Lord Raglan on 11th November, explaining that he was 'totally incapable of duty' and asking to be relieved of his command.[51] Lord Raglan promptly granted his request. Despite their recent conversation, he felt genuinely sad about Evans's ill health and the loss of his services. Writing to the Duke of Newcastle, he expressed the hope that Evans's actions on 26th October would be 'appreciated by all and will no doubt be honoured by the approbation of Her Majesty'.[52] With characteristic generosity, Evans distributed 30s to each of his servants before leaving Balaclava,[53] and then travelled home via Malta and France. The Duke of Newcastle, who had publicly commended Evans's 'truest heroism and finest chivalry',[54] asked him to elicit information about French planning and troop movements when he met the Emperor and Marshal Vaillant in Paris.[55]

Indebted to the Duke, Evans briefed him on his return from Paris and described conditions in the Crimea. He advised him that the fatigues of the soldiers, particularly the digging of trenches, should be reduced, and recommended that the troops should be provided with roasted coffee beans instead of green beans as hitherto. He passed on letters from the Crimea, testifying to the hardships of the winter and the 'demoralisation' in some divisions. Privately, he evaluated his former colleagues, characterising Major-General George Buller as 'capital in a barrack yard. *But that is all.*'[56] Evans baulked, however, when the Duke invited him to assist in organising a foreign legion which the government was trying to raise. He reminded the Duke of his previous association with the Auxiliary Legion in Spain and of the manner in which he had been traduced in Parliament, not least by the present Prime Minister, the Earl of Aberdeen. He was not willing 'to overlook direct discourtesy, unfeelingness, and refusal to repair or even acknowledge a proved undeniable wrong to the reputation of an officer of high rank in Her Majesty's Army . . .'.[57]

Though prepared to correspond with the War Department, Evans's main concern was convalescence. During the first six weeks of his return to England he recuperated at the Pavilion Hotel, Folkestone, in the care of his wife. Rest, fresh air, regular living, and no medicine other than 'steel drops' were the basis of his gradual recovery.[58] His morale was undoubtedly boosted by the effusion of glowing tributes which greeted his return. In a fulsome editorial *The Naval and Military Gazette* praised his 'skill, tactics, energy, and chivalrous bearing'.[59] *The Times* lauded him as 'one of the best officers in the army', adding, at a time when the paper was becoming increasingly critical of the high command, that he 'was no creature of Horse Guards favour, he was not the protégé of a high connexion, nor pushed forward by unfair influence. He fitted himself for command by constant service in the field.'[60] Even *The Morning Herald* and *Reynolds's Newspaper*, papers which had formerly attacked him from opposite ends of the political spectrum, now extolled his services and commended his gallantry.[61]

On 22nd January some citizens of Hythe, Folkestone and Sandgate, headed by the local M.P., Edward D. Brockman, presented Evans with a sword worth 150 guineas to commemorate his achievements. In receiving it, Evans made his first speech about the army, a highly sensitive undertaking, as *The Times* had already exposed the hospital conditions at Scutari and the sufferings of the ranks during the siege of Sebastopol. Russell had despatched harrowing accounts of fever, dysentery and diarrhoea sweeping through the camps, of mounting sick lists, of men ill clothed and ill housed, and of gross mismanagement by the commissariat in failing to distribute the greatcoats and huts which had landed on the quayside at Balaclava. Evans advised his audience to read these reports with a sense of perspective. 'England,' he argued, 'was not a military power'; she had been at peace for forty years and could not expect a 'perfect war establishment'. The 'many mistakes in details' which had 'certainly occurred' he attributed to 'inexperience'. Nevertheless, he remained confident that the army, in alliance with the armies of France, would ultimately prevail.[62]

Evans could not speak too openly of the army's current predicament. As he informed the Duke of Newcastle, he could not comment with authority upon the military operations, because 'I was never consulted on them & never had the slightest information given to me on the Subject'.[63] Nor could he refute allegations about conditions in the encampments, since he had been hospitalised early in November and left the Crimea before the conditions had rapidly deteriorated. Moreover his correspondence from the front tended to corroborate some of the press accounts. On the other hand, he could hardly criticise officers with whom he had recently served, not least because the Queen intended to honour him with the Grand Cross of the Bath.[64] As a veteran of many winter campaigns, he also accepted, with a degree of resignation bordering on fatalism, that a high mortality rate was inevitable. In mid-January he wrote to Sir John Philippart, expressing the hope

> that before now, the sufferings of my poor comrades, will have been to a great extent diminished — by the arrival of the materials for hutting — warm clothing — improvements of communications etc. ... A winter campaign however never did take place without sickness & severe losses.[65]

In private correspondence he defended the government from charges of mismanagement and tried to reassure the Duke of Newcastle, who had become one of the prime targets of newspaper criticism. If the government, wrote Evans, could prove that it had sent adequate supplies to Balaclava and had placed them 'within the British lines', it could not be blamed. 'If the Commanders,' he added, 'cannot manage to bring the Govt. stores from some part of the lines to another — it is certainly not the fault of the Government.'[66] Though appreciated, this was scant consolation for the Duke. When the Commons reassembled on 23rd January, J. A. Roebuck, an independent M.P., gave notice of a motion for a committee of inquiry into the conduct of the war. Six days later, his motion was carried by an overwhelming vote of 305 to 148. Aberdeen's coalition government fell, to be replaced by another coalition, headed by Lord Palmerston, but lacking Aberdeen, Newcastle and Russell. Writing to the Duke of Cambridge, who had also retired from the war, Evans doubted that any advantage would accrue from a 'change of administration', although 'I am not an admirer of either Lord Aberd[ee]n or Lord John Russell'. He accepted, none the less, that 'we must be very guarded in passing comments on the War'.[67]

Returning to London at the end of January, Evans was immediately greeted with more tributes and accolades. On 1st February a delegation of his constituents, accompanied by Sir John Shelley, visited him at his house in Bryanston Square. Thomas Prout read an address chronicling his achievements in the Crimea and extolling his military services. He also confirmed that they wished him to continue as their Member of Parliament. Evans thanked his old friend profusely. Still physically weak, he replied with an emotional speech, recalling his association with the constituency over the previous quarter of a century. He stressed how much he had valued the support of Westminster, particularly after his previous return from foreign service. He remembered 'the triumphant majority of 1,100' (in the 1837 election) as a 'proud test of your approval of my conduct ...'. Referring to the present war, he paid tribute to officers and men of the Second Division and applauded the upsurge of patriotism throughout the country. Making only a passing comment upon the 'distresses' endured and the losses sustained, he described the struggle as an historic defence of 'liberty, national independence, and the progress of human society'. Whatever the sacrifice, he concluded, the struggle must be pursued 'to a victorious end'.[68]

On the following afternoon, he received a remarkable award from the House of Commons. At twenty minutes past four he entered the chamber, accompanied by Shelley and Colonel W. L. Freestun, his former aide-de-camp in Spain. Dressed in full military uniform and wearing the insignia of his orders and decorations, he was greeted with loud cheering as all Members rose and remained standing until the veteran had taken his seat. After the cheering had subsided, the Speaker informed Evans that the House had resolved unanimously on 15th December to confer its highest honour upon him, namely a vote of thanks for his 'zeal, intrepidity and distinguished exertions ...'. He referred especially to Evans's 'undaunted courage and chivalrous generosity' on the heights of Inkerman. Commending his spirit in leaving his sickbed 'to assist with your counsel and experience' Major-General Pennefather, he applauded Evans's refusal 'to withhold from him the honours, whilst you shared with him the dangers' of the battle. Evans responded in characteristic manner. He compared this vote with the failure of the House to recognise his military services in Spain, an allusion which Cobden regarded as in very 'bad taste'.[69] But he disarmed his critics by attributing the vote 'almost exclusively' to the noble conduct and devotion to duty of the Second Division, especially its achievements at the Alma and the two battles of Inkerman. He resumed his seat amid renewed cheering, and his speech was widely praised in the press, even by *The Morning Post*.[70]

During the next few months Evans continued to receive tributes and honours. He was offered the lieutenant-governorship of Chelsea Hospital but declined, preferring to maintain his independence as a Member of Parliament.[71] He received addresses from local parishioners in St Marylebone, from noncommissioned officers and soldiers who had served with the Legion, and in May from the former officers of the Legion. Embarrassed by this effusion of goodwill, Evans even dissuaded his constituents in early April from raising a public subscription to present him with another testimonial.[72] When the government offered him the governorship of Gibraltar in June, he promptly declined it. 'Since my return from the Crimea,' he explained, 'the Public have done me that justice which had been officially withheld from me – and I am quite satisfied.'[73] In fact, official recognition was neither meagre nor tardy. Awarded Crimean medals by Britain and Turkey, Evans was made a G.C.B. in July. Appointed grand officer of the Legion of Honour in 1856, he also received an honorary D.C.L. from Oxford University and the Turkish Order of Mejidie. Evans could no longer complain that his military services were insufficiently recognised and respected.

Politically, he was extremely inactive. Still weak and prone to protracted illness, he rarely attended the House unless the army or the war were under discussion. On 1st March he supported Viscount Goderich's motion condemning the effects of the purchase system, particularly the lack of promotion opportunities for noncommissioned officers. Describing the system of purchase as a 'corruption', he asserted that it was riddled with favouritism, benefiting 'the wealthy and well-connected'. Even some officers from the gentry, like himself, were hindered in their careers. 'We are beaten by time. We are kept back until we are worn out. Those who have more friends get up to the higher ranks of the army ...'. More promotion from the ranks, he insisted, would encourage more educated and responsible people to enlist, and might diminish 'the inefficiency' of the officer corps.[74] Although Goderich and Evans denied that their views were couched in a levelling or an anti-aristocratic spirit, such fears gripped the Commons. Ministers did not deny that purchase was an anachronism, even 'an evil' in theory. They argued, nonetheless, that NCOs had been promoted (219 in the past five years and ninety in the Crimea), that promotion based on merit would prove unworkable and prone to jobbery, and that abolishing purchase would be extremely expensive. By 158 votes to 114 the Commons backed the government.

The newspapers either regarded this vote as temporary or the debate as irrelevant. *The Daily News* suspected that the Commons had tried to 'burke' the issue of army reform, but prophesied that it would have to bow before public pressure within six months: the nation 'will have no more buying and selling of commissions, no more trafficking in commands as if they were so many bales of cotton'.[75] *The Times* was less convinced. Disconcerted by the levelling tone of the debate, it suggested that army reform 'should proceed from less suspected hands and should be considered as a whole'.[76] Several M.P.s and businessmen, like Samuel Morley, the wealthy hosiery manufacturer, shared this opinion. Using the information compiled by Sir Charles Trevelyan and Sir Stafford Northcote in their *Report on the Organization of the Civil Service*, they began to champion the cause of administrative reform in the military and civil service. They established Administrative Reform Associations throughout the country and organised mass rallies in the Theatre Royal, Drury Lane.

Meanwhile the Sebastopol Committee, chaired by Roebuck, had begun taking evidence in open sessions. Its meetings were always well attended and the evidence was extensively reported in the daily press. On 5th and 6th March, Evans appeared before the committee and answered over 500 questions. He described the food, clothing and living conditions of the troops, the state of the transport and medical services, and the work-load of soldiers on picquet duty or in the trenches. He was extremely critical of the commissariat, presenting a detailed account of its failings at Malta, Scutari and Varna. He attributed the blame not to individuals, but to Treasury regulations and 'the spirit of the Treasury authorities of the Cabinet'. The department, he averred, would be much improved if it was 'a military department and not a civil one'.[77]

During the hearings Evans seemed to be extremely nervous. He spoke in low, almost inaudible tones, and hurried through his evidence at a frantic rate.[78] He carefully refrained from any criticism of individuals or of Lord Raglan's command and staff. When pressed to give his opinion on the Quartermaster-General's department or the inadequacy of clothing and equipment, he merely dissembled. He deflected the criticism of Henry Layard, a Radical M.P., arguing that the public had entertained unreasonable expectations of officers after forty years of peace. Under cross-examination, Evans accepted that the army might have benefited from waterproof clothing, sheeting, and other innovations, but added, dismissively, 'that there are very few institutions which might not be more improved than they have been, and I dare say armies amongst them'.[79]

Evans was widely acclaimed for his evidence and for his response to cross-examination. By providing an immensely detailed account of the Second Division's activities he had offered testimony of much more value than that of the previous witness, George Dundas, an M.P. who had spent only a fortnight in the Crimea.[80] Evans had been forthright, and occasionally critical, without lapsing into personal invective or endorsing the more extreme opinions held by some committee members. Newspaper editors were particularly appreciative; they used his evidence, or aspects of it, to vindicate their own views on the war. *The Naval and Military Gazette* approved his defence of Lord Raglan and his staff, *The Times* claimed that he had substantiated all its criticisms of the camp and the commissariat arrangements, and *The Standard* insisted that all responsibility for the miseries of the winter campaign should now be attributed to the government of Lord Aberdeen.[81] Evans welcomed favourable reporting, but regarded the opinion of some papers much more highly than others. As he believed that *The Times*, by exposing conditions in the Crimea, had largely saved the army, he lauded its achievements in Parliament. He also advised John T. Delane, the editor, even supplying him with private correspondence from the Second Division.[82]

Although the news from the Crimea had been improving since the middle of February (once the track from Balaclava was opened, supplies, huts and food began to reach the soldiers in vast quantities), Evans was still worried about the course of the war. He repeatedly urged the government to reinforce the army and to send remounts for the cavalry. By substituting native for British troops in India and the colonies, and by sending more Militia units to the Mediterranean to free the remaining regular battalions, he reckoned that another 20,000 men could be sent to the Crimea within three months. Lord Palmerston demurred; he accepted that the government must give 'the deepest consideration' to any proposal from Evans on the conduct of the war, but was unwilling to make a precipitate commitment.[83] Unimpressed by the response of the Cabinet and War Department, which he considered 'sadly slack & lazy', Evans sent his information on the Indian army to *The Naval and Military Gazette*. He doubted, however, that the press could agitate successfully over this issue, not least because 'the state of things in the Crimea is evidently improving'.[84]

Throughout the spring and summer, the reports from the Crimea had been steadily encouraging. By diluting the indignation which had erupted earlier in the year, such reports eroded the interest in army reform. The Administrative Reform Movement proved to be little more than a loose coalition, motivated largely by revulsion over the mismanagement of the army. It lacked effective leadership and never produced an agreed programme of reform. Derided in the House, it suffered crushing defeats in the Commons in June and July. Army reform now excited little interest in Parliament: when Henry Rich launched another attack on the purchase system on 3rd July the House was counted out, as fewer than forty Members were present.[85] Even the Sebastopol Committee, which issued its final report on 18th June 1855, found that Lord Raglan and the Aberdeen government had been unfairly blamed. It attributed the causes of the mismanagement to the administration of the pre-war army, and, to some extent, the whole structure of government. Only upon the insistence of Roebuck did the committee indict the government for authorising an expedition without sufficient information about the defences of Sebastopol. This failure, it concluded, 'was the first and chief cause of the calamities which befel our army'.[86]

Determined to act upon his report, whose publication coincided with a major allied reverse in their assault on Redan, Roebuck moved a vote of censure. In a highly vindictive speech, he demanded a retrospective indictment of Lord Aberdeen's government and the punishment of everyone 'who deserves it'. Like many Members, Evans deplored the 'sweeping' denunciations of Roebuck, and regretted the terms of his motion: had it been carried, several members of Palmerston's government would have had to resign. Evans argued that the army's sufferings had been somewhat exaggerated, and that the 'check' of Redan had been 'magnified into a great disaster'. Should the allies persevere, he was convinced that 'a total break-up of the vast Russian empire may be effected'. Palmerston was even more persuasive. He criticised Roebuck for moving a vote of censure against the government on account of the action of a previous administration. Deprecating the timing of the debate, he declared that the nation should be more concerned with prosecuting the war until victory was won. 'The army,' he assured the House, 'is in a fine a condition as any army which ever existed on the face of the earth.' Roebuck's motion, though not formally defeated, was shelved. General Peel moved that 'the previous question' be put, carrying the House by 284 votes to

182.⁸⁷

In dismissing the abortive assault on Redan as a mere 'check', Evans was not being totally disingenuous. Just as he had described his own defeat at Hernani (1837) as a temporary affair, he regarded this action as tactically indecisive. Although he accepted that the British losses of some 1,500 killed and wounded had been severe, he was confident that Sebastopol could be taken (as it was after a French assault on 8th September 1855). Desperately concerned to sustain the war effort, Evans defended his former military colleagues from unfair criticism (notably General Dacres and later Lord Raglan after his death).[88] He pressed the government to send reinforcements and to authorise a loan to Turkey.[89] Almost as important, he reckoned, was the task of countering those parliamentarians whom he dubbed the 'Russian faction'. During the censure debate, he had delivered his bombastic speech immediately after Bright's condemnation of the 'unspeakable madness of invading Russia'.[90] On the last day of session, Evans even thwarted Cobden, who had come to protest about the naval war, specifically 'the atrocities in the Sea of Azov'. Once the Speaker had seated himself, Evans promptly rose and began speaking at inordinate length upon the case for reinforcements. By leaving five minutes for a reply from Palmerston before Parliament was prorogued, he effectively stymied Cobden.[91]

Evans's parliamentary attendances, though fitful, had taken their toll of his health. In August he suffered a relapse, cancelled a public appearance on behalf of the campaign for Polish independence, and returned to Folkestone.[92] He still kept in touch with his friends in Fleet Street, either approving of their editorials or offering his opinion about any controversial news from the front. He fully endorsed the contentious appointment of Colonel Percy Herbert as Quartermaster-General. In a letter to *The Times*, he contradicted the innuendoes and suspicions expressed in correspondence about the appointment from several staff officers.[93] On the other hand, he shared the widespread concern about the competence of Sir James Simpson, Lord Raglan's successor. After Simpson had approved another, even more disastrous assault on Redan on 8th September, Evans assured Delane that he agreed with 'all that *The Times* so admirably advanced respecting that creature Simpson . . . . But I think you have not so deep a contempt for him, or for those who, knowing him personally, could have entrusted to him our Army, – as I have.' Evans doubted that his successor would be an improvement, so long as his selection remained 'a Palace appointment'. Sharing the fears of Delane about the Prince Consort's influence over military matters, he could not see any possibility of countering it 'except by public opinion'. 'Perhaps,' he wrote, 'broad warning hints in the Press to those Ministers & officials, suspected of pandering to his influence, may be amongst the means of checking it.'[94]

Evans was even more alarmed about the possibility of a premature peace settlement with Russia. By January 1856 Palmerston could no longer resist the pressure from France to open negotiations, and the government's willingness to enter the talks was confirmed in the Queen's Speech. In the debate which followed, Evans doggedly insisted that Britain had not fully deployed her military resources, and that she must not give the impression of seeking peace from any want of power. He feared that the terms offered by the Tsar barely constituted a 'guarantee for a secure peace'. Since British prestige in Asia had suffered from the war, he insisted that territorial advantages should be sought at the peace conference. Should France settle too hastily for peace, he maintained, Britain possessed ample naval and military resources to sustain the contest and so realise a 'final success' and a 'great advantage to civilization'.[95] Such advice was wholly unpractical. Without France, Britain could not continue the struggle, and the government readily signed the peace treaty in Paris (30th March) with only a few modifications of the Bessarabian frontier.

From the Crimean War Evans emerged as one of the few senior commanders with his reputation enhanced. He was rightly praised by Parliament and the press for the disposition of his troops in Bulgaria, for his tactical flair at the Alma and on the 26th October, especially the shrewd use of concentrated artillery fire, and for his chivalry and courage at Inkerman. Even *The Morning Post*, formerly an arch critic of his political and military services, dubbed him 'a Crimean hero of the first rank'.[96] Not only had Evans commanded the Second Division in a thoroughly commendable fashion, but he had also contained his personal feelings and avoided tarnishing his image. Periodically moody, introspective, and prone to bouts of depression, he harboured bitter resentments about his own status and the conduct of the war. He felt deeply his lack of a G.C.B., the disdainful treatment of him by Lord Raglan and his staff, and the incapacity of some of his fellow commanders. But he kept his feelings private or confided them to a relatively small coterie of friends, including Russell, upon whose discretion he could rely.[97] Unlike the majority of generals, Evans never resented the intrusions of war correspondents and so ensured a comprehensive coverage of his military activities.

Compared with his reception in 1837, he had returned in triumph. On a purely personal level, the contrast was all too vivid. Although his constituents had rallied around him in the general election of 1837, he neither forgot nor forgave the obloquy which had been hurled at the Legion and himself. Acutely sensitive, he believed that his military service had been thwarted ever since by the deep-rooted animosity of the Duke of Wellington. Admittedly Lord Hardinge, formerly a trenchant critic of the Legion, had acknowledged Evans's experience as a field commander by appointing him to a brigade command at Chobham, a regimental colonelcy, and a divisional command in the Crimea; but only wartime service had enhanced his reputation. To be welcomed so heartily in 1855 was profoundly satisfying, not least because it involved a belated recognition of his professional competence.

The war had also stiffened his resolve, at sixty-eight, to remain in politics. As a widely acclaimed public figure he could expect the continuing support of his constituents at least for the immediate future. He could anticipate, too, an attentive and respectful audience whenever he spoke on military issues, even if his views were not likely to be accepted on more contentious topics. He expected, moreover, that army reform would arouse acrimonious debate in the wake of the war. Already, in January 1856, a commission, headed by Sir John McNeill and Colonel Alexander Tulloch, had issued its report on the failure of the supply system in the Crimea. As the report criticised specific officers and individuals who had served in the commissariat, the army would again become the focus of press and parliamentary concern. Evans would play a prominent rôle in the ensuing controversy.

8
Army reformer

Evans eagerly championed the cause of army reform. During the previous two decades, he had already established his credentials as a military reformer. He had periodically advocated the abolition of purchase, an improvement in military education, and the transformation of the living conditions of the rank and file. Although willing to acknowledge that limited improvements had been accomplished by pre-war administrations, he believed that more extensive reforms could now be sought in view of the greater interest in military matters on the part of the press and Parliament.[1] As a Member of Parliament, he felt entitled to concentrate upon such issues. Having been allowed by his constituents to devote three of the last twenty years to his professional duties, he described himself as 'their military as well as their political representative'.[2] He recognised, too, that his distinguished reputation would assist him in the House of Commons. Unlike some civilian reformers, notably Layard, his opinions could not be discounted by War Office Ministers on account of inexperience or ignorance of military detail.[3] After the Crimean War, Evans was assured of a hearing, as well as the respect of the House.

The report of the McNeill and Tulloch Commission had fomented fresh controversy over the army in the Crimea. It recorded that 35 per cent of the men and 42 per cent of the horses had died from 1st October 1854 to 30th April 1855. Attributing this mortality to overwork, exposure to wet and cold, unsuitable food, and inadequate shelter, it argued that such factors could have been alleviated, at least partially. More horses, it implied, would have survived had Lords Lucan and Cardigan, two senior cavalry officers, taken more care over the provision of temporary shelter and sufficient forage. It was even more critical of the Quartermaster-General's department for the tardy distribution of rugs, blankets and greatcoats, the non-issue of palliases, the shortage of tents and hutting, and the non-delivery of knapsacks at Balaclava. The report compared the evidence of Colonel the Hon. A. Gordon, Deputy Quartermaster-General, with that of other officers, and found it wanting in several respects. It also censured the Commissary-General, Mr Filder, over the quality and quantity of the rations, inefficient transport arrangements, and a lack of flexibility in his organisational procedures.[4]

A storm of indignation erupted over the report. Lords Lucan and Cardigan protested vehemently in the House of Lords. On 15th February 1856 they formally replied to the charges against them in submissions laid upon the table of the House of Commons. Many Members of Parliament were outraged by the report; Roebuck likened it to 'an indictment from a grand jury' and demanded the trial of 'the persons accused'.[5] Lord Panmure, the Secretary of State for War, found himself criticised from all sides, not least by the Crown. Queen Victoria deplored the prospect of officers replying to accusations from a parliamentary commission. She rebuked Lord Palmerston accordingly:

It is quite evident if matters are left so, and military officers of the Queen's Army are to be judged as to the manner in which they have discharged their military duties before an enemy by a Committee of the House of Commons, the command of the Army is at once transferred from the Crown to that Assembly.[6]

To mollify the Queen and defuse the controversy, the Cabinet decided to constitute a commission of inquiry, composed of seven senior officers, assisted by the Judge Advocate-General. Initially, the Cabinet wished to include Evans on the commission, but the Queen vetoed the suggestion because he was a Crimean officer and might be called as a witness[7] (he never was summoned). On 29th February Frederick Peel, the Under-Secretary of State for War, informed the House of the government's decision. In explaining the proposal, he emphasised that the Crimean Commission had been essentially a closed commission. Witnesses had given their evidence in private without knowledge of other testimony or of subsequent charges against them. Some evidence had been contradictory, particularly over the non-issue of knapsacks at Balaclava. The commissioners had regarded this topic as extremely important; they had found that soldiers, lacking their knapsacks, had had to remain in the same clothes, occasionally wet and often soiled from trench work, for more than six weeks, so aggravating their discomfort and increasing their susceptibility to disease. The commissioners had been informed by Colonel Gordon that all generals of division, save the Duke of Cambridge, had refused to receive knapsacks. On returning to England, McNeill and Tulloch took evidence from the surviving generals (General Sir George Cathcart had died at Inkerman). Evans denied that any such offer had been made; Sir Richard England could not recollect an offer, although he admitted that one might have been made; while Sir George Brown was not available for questioning. In these circumstances, argued Peel, officers like Gordon, who had been censured, must have an opportunity of hearing the charges and of replying to them[8]

Evans was livid. He felt that his veracity had been questioned and his honour impugned. He feared, too, that the officers would be absolved by a board of inquiry because they were favourites of the court. Casting discretion aside, he delivered the most intemperate speech of his parliamentary career. Colonel Gordon, he observed, had made in his evidence a 'judicious and courtier-like exception in favour of the Royal Duke'. But, queried Evans, was it likely that the Duke of Cambridge, who had 'never' seen an enemy before, would have been more perceptive in this respect than 'four older generals, of greater experience'? He challenged Peel to adduce proof that the four older generals had refused to receive their divisional knapsacks. Moreover, he noted that the Duke, whatever his intentions, had informed the Sebastopol Committee that he had been unable to collect the knapsacks at Balaclava. Nor had the brigadier-generals of the Second Division been any more successful, 'notwithstanding the wonderful alacrity of Colonel Gordon'. Consumed with anger, Evans disparaged Gordon's credibility as a witness and his competence as a military officer. He condemned his failure to anticipate the consequences of withholding knapsacks, deprecated his *penchant* for shifting the blame onto others, and recounted his blundering over the purported convoy from Sebastopol.[9]

Evans resolutely defended the commissioners and applauded their report. He took issue with the War Department, whose Ministers had selected and appointed the commissioners but were now disputing their findings and deferring to the Crown. Such behaviour he characterised as 'ungrateful and unjust' but only to be expected from Ministers so prone to dispensing patronage and nepotism themselves.

Evans reminded the House that Lord Panmure had recommended the appointment of General Simpson as commander of the forces in the Crimea. Although 'this poor general officer', in Evans's opinion, 'did not wish to have the command', Lord Panmure had insisted upon it and had urged him, once appointed as the new commander, to 'Take care of Dowb' (Captain, later Major, Dowbiggin, a relative of the Secretary of State). Having thus criticised the Crown, Lord Panmure, General Simpson and Colonel Gordon, Evans concluded by praising the work of the commissioners and by accusing the government of a 'gross blunder, injustice, and inconsistency in its handling of the report'.[10]

To make a speech so sweeping in content and vituperative in tone was a serious mistake. Evans had enraged several Members of Parliament, so distracting attention from the government's policy. Arthur Gordon and Lord Claud Hamilton defended their relative, Colonel Gordon. Hamilton even counter-attacked by revealing that Evans had advised Lord Raglan to withdraw the army after the battle of Inkerman. Gladstone and Palmerston also criticised Evans, especially his unflattering reference to Sir James Simpson and his level of personal abuse.[11] John Bright enjoyed the furore. 'Evans,' he wrote, 'is a wonderful fellow for a hero'; the whole incident revealed 'the squabbles & jealousies & selfishness of the military patriots'.[12] The press was more sympathetic. *The Naval and Military Gazette*, fearing a ministerial attempt to discredit the Crimean report, praised Evans for his 'manly and fearless reply'. *The Times* and *The Morning Advertiser* also applauded his speech, but *The Morning Post* published a fiercely critical letter, emphasising that Evans had spent three-quarters of his professional career as a half-pay officer, so that allusions to his military 'experience' were somewhat exaggerated.[13]

Evans soon realised his error. In a letter to Sir George Brown he admitted that he had gone 'much too far' in his reply to Peel. 'One cannot be always prudent,' he added.[14] On 3rd March he recanted in abject fashion before the House of Commons, apologising to Major Dowbiggin, who had recently been promoted for distinguished service in the field, General Simpson, the Duke of Cambridge and Colonel Gordon. Cobden rejoiced. He wrote to Leiutenant-Colonel Fitzmayer, who had served under Evans in the Crimea, claiming that Evans had exhibited himself 'in a worse aspect than I could have expected even from him. One day throwing dirt on his old comrades & the next eating all the dirt himself!'[15] Fitzmayer was not amused. He defended his 'old chief', whom he regarded as a 'brave & capable' general. He still endorsed his advice after the battle of Inkerman – 'a desperate remedy to a desperate state of things' – and bitterly regretted his grovelling apology. 'I despair of everything,' Fitzmayer concluded. 'First Mr Layard takes up a strong cause & breaks down, & now Sir De Lacy, who could have done so much at least in military reform, brings himself into disrepute.'[16]

Evans, though embarrassed, was still suspicious of the board. He informed Delane that the seven officers

> ... are not without sons or relatives dependent on the H[orse] G[uar]ds for their whole professional advancement.
> It is a peculiar affair already. The H. Gds. & Palace have completely identified themselves with the impugned Staff off[ice]rs. The H. Gds are in fact on trial, as much as anyone else. And The H. Gds selects the judges – who would not be sure of acquittal, if possessed of the power of selecting the judges?[17]

Such cynicism was not confined to Evans. Even before the board of inquiry assembled, *The United Service Gazette* predicted its outcome. The approach of the board, it claimed, 'will be to make all smooth', by establishing that 'Lord Lucan was right, and Lord Cardigan was right, and that the Crimean Commissioners were right too . . .'.[18] At the end of July the board duly reported and exonerated all concerned. Lord Palmerston endorsed these findings and those of the Crimean Commission. Lord Panmure assured the Queen that further action would not be taken in respect of the statements contained in the report of McNeill and Tulloch. Although protests were aired in public meetings, newspaper editorials, and the House of Commons, the government contained the controversy. It made only one concession, by accepting the suggestion of Sidney Herbert that Her Majesty should honour the Crimean Commissioners. In March 1857 Colonel Tulloch was created a K.C.B. and Sir John McNeill a Privy Councillor. Such belated recognition hardly compensated for a report which was permanently shelved.

Meanwhile Evans seized the first opportunity to revive the parliamentary debate on the purchase system. On 4th March 1856 he introduced a motion, proposing the appointment of a select committee to consider the abolition of purchase. He insisted that there was a feasible alternative to the existing system: officers could be promoted by selection, and such officers would be loyal to the authorities. The abolition of purchase, he contended, was a practical proposition; it need not involve any confiscation of property nor massive expenditure by the State. Purchase could be allowed to wither away by banning its use for future commissions while providing retirement allowances for purchase officers. At any rate, Evans declared, the existing system had to be abolished; it had permitted incompetent officers to rise to the head of the army, caused 'misery and distress of mind' to meritorious officers bereft of money or interest, and remained 'a dishonour to the English army'.[19] Viscount Goderich, Lord Stanley, and several Radical M.P.s supported the motion.

The government was confident of defeating the proposal. Lord Panmure assured the Queen 'that the feeling in the House of Commons will enable the Government to resist Sir De Lacy Evans' motion . . .'.[20] Although Frederick Peel, backed by Liberal and Conservative M.P.s, opposed reform, the debate lacked the acrimony of previous occasions. Sidney Herbert suggested that it might be possible to modify the extent of purchase within the army, and several Members urged that the system should at least be the subject of an inquiry. Lord Palmerston quickly accepted this compromise; he proposed that a Royal Commission should be appointed to inquire into the system of purchase, an initiative welcomed by Evans.[21] Having anticipated this outcome, Lord Panmure advised the Queen that a commission of inquiry 'will prevent so important a question being dealt with in a manner at all trenching upon Your Majesty's authority'.[22]

The establishment of a Royal Commission was widely approved. *The Daily News*, a staunch supporter of Evans's gradualist approach to reform, praised his flexibility in debate, while *The Naval and Military Gazette*, an advocate of purchase, congratulated him for compelling the government to accept this 'long-demanded enquiry'.[23] But *Reynolds's Newspaper*, an ultra-Radical paper, was critical; it condemned 'the crafty old Premier . . . for burking unpleasant matters by referring them to a committee of his own appointment'.[24] *Reynolds* had perceived the government's intention. As Lord Panmure explained, in a letter to the Queen, the commission would be composed of men in whom the Commons had confidence and in whose hands 'the system of purchase is safe'. Edward Ellice and Sidney Herbert, two former Secretaries at War, had to be included, but only one of them had shown any interest in modifying the system. George Carr Glyn, the banker and M.P. for Kendal, was chosen as a representative of the class whose 'only hope of entry into and promotion in the Army rests upon the maintenance of the present system'. Four senior officers were selected, representing the Guards, line, and non-purchase corps. To give a semblance of balance, two critics of the system were added: Lord Stanley had expressed some 'though not entirely' adverse opinions upon purchase, and Evans, the only avowed reformer, had to be included as 'a matter of necessity rather than of choice'. Aware of the Queen's preference for the arch-reactionary Sir George Brown, Panmure argued that Evans's omission from the Com[missio]n w[oul]d do much harm, while his presence on it can do none'.[25]

Evans, though closely identified with the abolition of purchase, was not preoccupied with the issue. A regular participant in the army debates, he championed other reforms and ameliorative proposals. He favoured augmenting the number of army chaplains from the eleven who served with an army of 200,000 men. He urged that their terms of service should be improved, their pay increased, and their wartime contribution publicly recognised. Palmerston and Herbert readily acknowledged the services of chaplains in the Crimea.[26] Evans pressed, too, for further improvements in military education, especially a revision of the syllabuses at Sandhurst and Woolwich. He protested, unsuccessfully, over a government warrant which excluded relatives of officers who had died from disease in the Crimea from the remuneration entitled to relatives of officers who had died in the field. He deplored the niggardly treatment of the Militia who had been stationed in the Mediterranean during the war, and derided the sum of £40,000 which the government had earmarked for barrack improvements. Unless the War Department radically improved barrack conditions, he argued, 'a great prejudice' against entering the army would persist and only 'the lowest class of men' would enter the service.[27] Whenever he raised such issues, however, Evans left his exhortations in the form of isolated parliamentary statements. He never presented a coherent framework of reform, with priorities listed and expenditure costed. Inevitably, he met with little success.

On 26th May 1856 the Royal Commission on the purchase system began its deliberations. Initially, it questioned witnesses who could explain how promotion operated by purchase and non-purchase methods. Later, it sampled the opinions of senior officers and Cabinet Ministers about the merits of the various systems. Evans, who attended all nineteen meetings spread over two years (only two other commissioners did so), soon established himself as an acute and incisive questioner. From the early witnesses he sought evidence of the abuses and disadvantages of the purchase system, as well as the practical benefits and feasibility of other methods. He extracted several concessions from Major-General Sir Charles Yorke, the Military Secretary. Officers, Yorke admitted, could be mortified at being passed over for a vacancy by a junior who was able to pay the appropriate price. Senior officers might also be deterred from claiming their right to a vacancy at the regulation price in case they blocked promotion within the regiment if the seller insisted upon additional payments. From Charles Hammersley, an army agent, Evans uncovered the huge scale of over-regulation payments (£14,000 for a lieutenant-colonelcy of the cavalry, compared with a regulation price of £6,175) and the inordinate expenses of mess life in the purchase corps (most infantry officers required additional allowances of £100 to £150 per annum, and cavalry officers about £300 per annum). Evans also established that artillery officers preferred to retain their system of promotion by seniority, and that Indian Army officers could live on their pay, frequently continuing their professional study during military service.[28]

In interviewing the more senior officers and politicians, Evans adopted several different approaches. He sought to maximise the impact of testimony from sympathetic witnesses, like Sir Duncan MacDougall, Colonel Lord West, Sir James Scarlett, Colonel Thomas Franks, Sir Colin Campbell and Brigadier-General the Hon. A. Spencer. Asking short, simple questions, he let them expand upon the deleterious effects of the purchase system. He elicited some passionately felt and eminently quotable observations. MacDougall described the feelings of officers who had been purchased over, referring to the 'very iron' going into their souls. West opined that 'one of the great evils of the system is that it leads to a sordid and degrading traffic in commissions in the higher grade . . .'. Franks had 'not the slightest doubt that we have got, generally speaking, in the army, indifferently educated men . . .', a consequence of a system in which merit was not sufficiently rewarded.[29] But Evans was less successful in trying to secure agreement on an alternative system: some favoured selection, others seniority, and others a combination of purchase to the rank of captain followed by selection thereafter.

To limit the damage from this lack of agreement, Evans had to blunt the criticism from the advocates of purchase. He sought to reduce the credibility of their testimony by pressing witnesses, like Sir George

Brown and the Duke of Cambridge, into increasingly extreme pronouncements. Under such questioning, Brown denounced selection in peacetime, doubted that over-regulation payments concerned the public, and suggested that the Horse Guards should 'encourage' exchanges between regiments because the officers involved were obviously 'quick and clever' fellows. The Duke, though less obtuse, was equally obdurate: the present system had 'hitherto worked satisfactorily, and unless I see a system that is likely to work as satisfactorily, I should be very sorry to see that system changed'.[30] Evans struggled, nonetheless, to offset the more pragmatic testimony of Lord Panmure and Earl Grey. Both politicians seized the initiative from their questioners. They defended the practical advantages of purchase (accelerated promotion and keeping the officer corps young), deplored the cost of abolition, and derided the feasibility of any alternative, suggesting that selection would always be attributed to favouritism. Evans failed to deflect them. When he argued that if a bank could operate selection so could the army, Grey replied that an army at peace was like a machine 'at rest', whereas a bank was a fully operational machine, ever able to assess the qualities of its personnel.[31]

Evans's hopes were raised by the evidence of the last witness, Sir Charles Trevelyan, an Assistant Secretary to the Treasury. He appeared before the commission with a comprehensive plan to replace the purchase system. During the last two sessions Trevelyan elaborated upon his critique of purchase and explained his detailed proposal. Prompted by Evans, he described the abuses of the existing system, its baleful effects upon individuals, and its incompatibility with professional requirements. He recommended that officers should enter the army through a process of nominations coupled with competitive examination. Successful candidates would be trained for two years in a military college, promoted by seniority and selection to the rank of lieutenant, examined for the rank of captain, and promoted thereafter by selection.[32]

Despite Evans's protestations, which were appended in a separate statement, the Royal Commission rejected the abolition of purchase. Although it recognised defects in the system, the commission perceived even more difficulties in relying upon seniority or selection. Promotion, it feared, would stagnate if the army depended upon seniority entirely, and few officers would welcome selection, ever fearful of its possible misuse. The commission also rejected abolishing the purchase of the lowest commissioned rank, unless the government was prepared to compensate purchase officers who would otherwise lose all their investment on retirement. But six commissioners, a bare majority, accepted that 'practical evils have resulted from the purchase system'. They disliked the scale of over-regulation payments, in which the largest amounts were paid for lieutenant-colonelcies, and the possibility of incompetent officers attaining regimental command. Hence they proposed that purchase of the rank of lieutenant-colonel should be abolished and replaced by selection from the list of majors. They also maintained that purchase could be reconciled with improvements in professional training. Promotion to the staff, they suggested, could become a means of stimulating military education, rewarding meritorious officers, and alleviating some of the hardships suffered by less wealthy officers under the purchase system.[33]

Evans signed the report, as it represented a movement towards his ultimate objectives. From his own point of view, the enquiry had proved successful. The commission had confounded those sceptics who had thought it incapable of displaying any independence or impartiality. It had enabled some officers to air their grievances against the existing system, so exposing the abuses and shortcomings of purchase as a means of promotion. The report had compared, fully and fairly, the arguments for and against the system and had recommended a modest reform. For Evans the report was a useful beginning and an invaluable work of reference. He endorsed its findings, convinced that the evidence demonstrated that purchase should be terminated sooner than his colleagues envisaged.[34]

Newspaper editors welcomed the report of the Purchase Commission. Though deeply divided over the wisdom of its recommendations, they applauded the publication of such detailed evidence about the system. Some Conservative and military papers still defended purchase or, at least, cautioned against reform without the full support of the officer corps.[35] Several critics of purchase, spanning the political spectrum from *The Standard* to *Reynolds's Newspaper*, deplored the 'feeble and unsatisfactory' proposals of the commission. Quoting extensively from the evidence of MacDougall, Campbell and Trevelyan, they denounced the abuses of purchase and urged its abolition.[36] But *The Times* modified its abolitionist fervour on account of the report. It accepted that practical difficulties could bedevil the process of abolition and so approved the selection of lieutenant-colonels as a useful innovation as well as a basis for future reform.[37]

Evans, who was now recognised as a leader of the abolitionist cause, neither mounted a parliamentary campaign nor utilised the press to promote reform. He let two and a half years elapse before seeking the modification of the purchase system in a Commons' debate. He has been criticised for these dilatory tactics,[38] although such criticism should allow for the problems with which he was confronted. In the first place, the revelation of disagreements within the Purchase Commission undermined the credibility of the report. Three of the four dissenters, headed by Edward Ellice, produced a minority report. They prudently refrained from a defence of purchase in principle, but still accepted the expediency of leaving the system untouched. The selection of lieutenant-colonels, they argued, would neither remove the objections to purchase in principle nor arrest its attendant evils. If implemented, the recommendation would dilute the commitment of junior officers, damage regimental *esprit de corps*, and arouse fears of favouritism and jobbery in the process of selection. Incompetent appointments, they claimed, could be prevented by more rigorous use of the Commander-in-Chief's power of veto, while more professionalism could be inculcated by greater stringency in examinations.[39] Prince Albert welcomed this report as a 'wholesome antidote' to the 'hostile one of Sir De Lacy Evans'; he only regretted that the reports had not been issued simultaneously, since the majority report 'has had time, aided by the "Times" to work upon public opinion ....'.[40]

The timing of the publication of the Purchase Commission's report also limited the prospects of reform. By August 1857 memories of the Crimean campaign had faded, as had interest in the purchase question. Parliament and the press were much more concerned about the course of the China War (1856–60), especially the bombardment of Canton. In March 1857 Palmerston's government had fallen on account of its Chinese policy. During the ensuing election campaign, Evans was never questioned about purchase. Criticised for his absenteeism from the House, particularly for his failure to vote in the Chinese debate, Evans routed his Liberal critics by steadfastly defending Palmerston and his policies.[41] So popular was Palmerston that Evans triumphed without an electoral struggle. Discontented Radicals failed to raise sufficient funds for a campaign by Charles Westerton, the churchwarden of St Pauls, while the local Conservatives chose not to contest the seat.[42] In returning to the House of Commons on the flood tide of Palmerstonian popularity,

Evans realised the complete lack of public interest in the issue of purchase.

Yet there was interest in army reform, at least in the reform of military education. During the Crimean War a select committee had issued a report upon the Royal Military College, Sandhurst. Its findings, coupled with the opinions recorded in the minutes of evidence, endorsed the case for reform. Lieutenant-Colonel W. H. Adams, Professor of Military Science at the Royal Military College, urged the formation of a proper military staff, with all staff officers required to receive a 'high professional education' at a staff school. Currently, he declared, 'military education is but little valued by the greater part of the high military authorities'.[43] Lord Panmure had then established a three-man committee to report on the reorganisation of training for officers in the *scientific* corps (the Royal Artillery and Royal Engineers). Reporting in January 1857, the committee found that foreign armies attached more importance to scientific training than did the British army. It advocated changes in the admission requirements and courses at the Royal Military Academy, Woolwich; general examinations for regimental officers; a complete revision of the senior department at Sandhurst; and, above all, the creation of a Board of Education, headed by the Secretary of State, to draft regulations on discipline and instructions, supervise textbook changes and the examination of candidates, and make annual reports.[44]

The government, prompted by the press, Parliament, and the Prince Consort, accepted the need for educational reform. By April 1857 a Council of Military Education had been established, but, in deference to the Queen's wishes,[45] was placed under the presidency of the Duke of Cambridge, the recently appointed Commander-in-Chief. The Duke, though interested in military education, favoured relatively modest reforms. On 9th April 1857 he listed the qualifications which would be required of all staff officers from 1st January 1858. These were essentially practical, based upon an ability to ride well and write legibly, requiring proficiency in military history, geography, trigonometry and sketching, the knowledge of at least one foreign language, an understanding of the principles of fortification, an ability to judge ground and its occupation by all arms.[46] These proposals disappointed the educational reformers in the Commons. On 28th July, Evans launched another parliamentary debate in support of higher standards of professional instruction 'for the Commissioned

Ranks of the Army, but especially for the Staff'. Quoting from the two reports, he reminded the House of the superior systems of military education in Austria, Prussia, France, and even the United States. All officers should have to pass competitive examinations before qualifying for the staff, and a council of military and civilian members should supervise the process.[47]

Although several military Members questioned the value of examinations, Evans gained the influential support of Herbert and a sympathetic response from Palmerston. As the government approved of competitive examinations for the staff (and within three months the Council of Military Education drafted an examination syllabus), the debate was rightly applauded as an important success for educational reform. Evans earned appropriate accolades from the military and civilian press. Having redeemed his previous vow to bring the issue before Parliament, he had done so in a temperate and non-partisan spirit. He had also secured a highly satisfactory statement of ministerial intentions.[48] In prompting the government to pursue educational reform, however, Evans had blunted the prospects of modifying purchase. Both Lord Panmure and his successor at the War Office, General Jonathan Peel, could use educational reform to demonstrate their interest in raising the professional status of the officer corps, while conveniently ignoring the work of the Purchase Commission.[49]

Nevertheless, the report of the Purchase Commission was bound to be shelved, if only on account of the Indian Mutiny. The revolt of the Bengal sepoys had shattered British complacency and riveted attention upon the subcontinent. Evans fully accepted that crushing the mutiny was a task of paramount importance. On 11th August 1857 he admonished the government, urging it to send more reinforcements to India and so compensate for the raw recruits as well as the losses through sickness and injury from the 28,000 already despatched. Additional men, he claimed, could be found by increasing the recruiting bounty and by using the Militia to replace regular troops in colonial garrisons. He sought, too, some commendation for the heroic exploits of British officers and severe punishment for the mutineers. Evans trusted

that these mutinous assassins would be punished with condign severity, and that no mistaken lenity or false humanity would stand in the way of the well-deserved retribution which ought to fall upon them.[50]

Unperturbed by any hint of criticism, Palmerston reassured the House about the military situation. He used the occasion to applaud the 'energy and heroic courage' of the British officers and to beat the patriotic drum. 'Every Englishmen,' he stated, 'must feel proud of his country, when he sees how a few Englishmen, scattered over a vast country, in many cases acting singly and with the smallest possible support, have proved themselves equal to the emergency ...'.[51] Although Palmerston gained the support of the House and *The Times*, which still praised Evans for raising the issue,[52] Evans was not entirely convinced. In September he complained to Sir John Philippart about the indifference of Lord Panmure. It was 'intolerable', wrote Evans, that Panmure should be grouse shooting in Scotland 'while daily & hourly important military arrangements for our unfortunate comrades in the East have no one to attend them much higher than clerks!'[53]

Yet the course of the mutiny had a profound impact upon army reform. The press, apart from some ultra-Radical papers, extolled and magnified the British successes. Several middle-class generals, like Sir Henry Havelock, Sir Colin Campbell and Brigadier-Generals Neill and Nicholson, earned paeans of praise for their tactical initiatives in command of relatively small bodies of men. Unflattering comparisons were made with their aristocratic predecessors in the Crimea as the press fostered the image of an all-conquering army, overcoming formidable odds. The invaluable services of loyal Indian troops and auxiliaries received scant recognition. Examples of incompetence, indecision and indiscipline were largely ignored, as were the woeful deficiencies of the medical and supply services. Unlike the Crimean War, this distant campaign which produced a rapid and decisive triumph never received close and critical scrutiny from the London-based press. On the contrary, the unreformed army emerged from the campaign with its reputation enhanced. Reforms promoted in the wake of the Crimean War were delayed: from 1st September 1857 officers were accepted for commissions without examination. Apart from the opening of the Staff College in 1858, few institutional changes were accomplished. Interest in reform waned, as the army had proved its mettle in preserving the jewel of the Empire.

Tacitly recognising this shift of mood and opinion, Evans refrained from any campaign in favour of modifying purchase. Instead, he praised the achievements of the army in India and sought from the government a more generous distribution of awards as well as posthumous recognition of military service.⁵⁴ In February 1858 he began his duties as chairman of a select committee appointed to enquire into the despatch of reinforcements during the mutiny. During the next five months he chaired every meeting of the committee, taking evidence from twenty-one witnesses and preparing a lengthy draft report, a task which consumed nearly all his time and energy.⁵⁵ Evans proposed that, henceforth, all reliefs for the eastern army should be sent overland from Britain, Gibraltar and Malta, and that two steamers, in addition to the four monthly mail vessels, should be able to transfer the troops from Suez to Aden. However, this statement, which implicitly criticised the reliance upon sailing ships and the Cape route during the mutiny, was rejected by the Liberal majority on the committee. They preferred a report, prepared by Lord Goderich, which recognised the theoretical advantages of steamers and the overland route, but accepted that both suffered from practical difficulties and could not have been used during the emergency. Once slightly modified, this report was approved. It applauded the authorities, particularly the directors of the East India Company, for their response during the crisis, which had ensured the flow of reinforcements to India.⁵⁶

Evans deeply resented the rejection of his own report and the endorsement of the reinforcement procedures. He distributed a pamphlet among his parliamentary colleagues, explaining his objections to the reinforcement process and suggesting that the majority had reached their verdict out of 'an amiable desire to favour their political friends'. Understandably, his fellow committee members deplored this behaviour. On their behalf, Viscount Goderich formally protested in the House of Commons, whereupon Evans apologised, disclaiming any intention of impugning their motives.⁵⁷ He had again damaged his own credibility; he had spoilt his criticism of official policy by lapsing into personal abuse and so distracting attention from the core of his complaint.

Though embarrassed by the blunder, frustrated over army reform, and prone to periodic bouts of illness, Evans determined to remain in politics. He was still willing to champion constituency issues, protesting to Lord Palmerston and to his successor, the Conservative Prime Minister, Lord Derby, over the imposition of tolls on pedestrians crossing the new Chelsea bridge.⁵⁸ He allayed fears of his waning political commitment by regularly voting in favour of the ballot and of abolishing Church rates. He also vigorously opposed the

Reform Bill of the Conservative government, which would have reduced the size of his constituency by disfranchising the 40s freeholder. Addressing a large meeting in St Martin's Hall on 9th March 1859, he denounced the Bill as a partisan and restrictive measure. He pledged his support for John Bright's Bill, which proposed extending the franchise to another million and a half voters. To barrackers chanting in favour of 'manhood suffrage' he replied that manhood suffrage was not universal suffrage, and that, in theory, they could not deny the vote to independent women (a point greeted with cheers and laughter). He preferred, personally, a gradualist approach but did not fear any extension of the franchise, 'however large'. Reform, he insisted, was necessary to restore popular confidence after the class-based and divisive legislation of the Tory government. It would also secure British institutions at a time when French foreign policy seemed peculiarly threatening.[59]

Fear of a French invasion, the 'Third Panic', as Cobden dubbed it, became widespread in the early months of 1859. Anglo-French relations had already deteriorated over the suspicions aroused by the development of the port of Cherbourg and the creation of a French ironclad fleet, armed with breech-loading rifled cannon. The press in Britain had expressed alarm about reports of French hysteria, following the discovery that the bomb thrown by Orsini at Napoleon III had been made in England. Concern about the trend of Napoleon's foreign policy reached a climax in April 1859, when France intervened in the Austro-Sardinian war. Volunteer enthusiasts, headed by Sir Charles Napier, Sir Duncan MacDougall and A. B. Richards, gathered in St Martin's Hall on 16th April. Their speeches, along with a letter from Evans, expressing concern about the state of the nation's defences and the need for Volunteer enrolment, received extensive coverage in the press.[60] As the government had been defeated over its Reform Bill, and had promptly dissolved Parliament, a general election was fought in a highly charged atmosphere. In Westminster, Evans benefited from the recent Reform Bill agitation as well as the mounting invasion panic: he was re-elected without a contest. At the nomination hustings, he deprecated the Tory Reform Bill and criticised the government's foreign policy. Nevertheless, he promised to refrain from facetious opposition, as national unity had to take precedence in a time of crisis.[61]

Although the Conservatives regained some county seats in the election, the government could not survive a vote of no confidence on

19th June 1859. Palmerston regained the premiership, determined to retain office by avoiding contentious domestic legislation. For the remainder of the Parliament, Evans could devote himself to military issues. He shared the general suspicion of French foreign policy, despite the Peace of Villafranca, signed on 12th July 1859. He regarded Napoleon III as a militaristic adventurer in view of France's unchecked naval spending programme and her offer of military aid against China. Consequently, Evans requested the establishment of a Royal Commission to enquire into the state of the nation's defences, a plea heeded by Sidney Herbert, the new Secretary of State for War. When the commission reported in favour of fortifying several south-coast ports, Cork, Pembroke, Chatham, Woolwich and the Medway, the government insisted that it could not meet the expense involved. Evans approved of the government's more modest scheme of fortifications, but pressed repeatedly for the inclusion of Woolwich in these proposals.[62]

He also supported the burgeoning Volunteer movement. In the wake of the invasion scare, Volunteers enrolled in massive numbers, forming local corps throughout England and Scotland. Evans described this phenomenon as a 'noble demonstration of patriotic feeling'. He chaired the first Volunteer meeting in Middlesex, became an honorary member of the St George's Volunteer Rifle Corps, and donated £50 to the London battalion of the Royal National Rifle Brigade.[63] In the House of Commons, he demanded more generous treatment of the Volunteers by government, and, over the next four years, sought an extension of the Volunteer system to Ireland. He denounced the banning of the formation of Volunteer corps in Ireland as a disgraceful 'insult' to the Irish people. Although he insisted that the existence of sectarian divisions could not justify this want of confidence, the government remained adamant: indeed, its fears of the Volunteers becoming involved in sectarian clashes gained credibility when such an event occurred in Liverpool.[64]

Despite his proclivity for expressing heretical opinions, Evans could not be ignored in either the debates or the discussion of military issues. From March 1859 to July 1860 he served on a select committee, chaired by Sir James Graham, to review the reforms of military organisation effected in 1855. The committee found that the reforms had left many administrative ills untouched and had failed to clarify the responsibilities of the Secretary of State. The committee took evidence from many witnesses but principally from the Duke of

Cambridge and Sidney Herbert. Whereas the former opposed further reform, the latter stressed the anomalies of the existing system and proposed an extensive reorganisation. He recommended that the Secretary of State should be advised by a council of senior officers and War Office officials, and that unison between the Horse Guards and War Office should be promoted, possibly by housing them in one building. The committee endorsed these proposals, only insisting that the traditional division of authority should be preserved. It accepted, in short, that the Duke of Cambridge, formally General Commanding-in-Chief, should retain his authority, derived from the Crown as the ultimate Commander-in-Chief, over command and discipline in the army. The committee declared that appointments, promotion and discipline in the army should remain 'independent of political pressure'.[65]

Evans was not a prominent questioner during the preliminary hearings. He knew little about military administration, having served in neither the War Office nor the Horse Guards. For penetrating questions the committee relied upon its former War Office Ministers – Ellice, Peel and Herbert (who served on the committee as well as giving evidence to it). Nevertheless, Evans remained suspicious of royal influence upon the administration of the army; he feared that the Queen's cousin would try to block any reform which the committee proposed. In the drafting of the report, Evans voted against amendments which commended aspects of the existing system (for example, a vote to include Lord Panmure's observation that a Secretary of State should 'trust to the Commander-in-Chief the chief administration of the army, and, except under very peculiar circumstances, not to interfere . . .'). He also supported Sir James Graham in suggesting that the committee draw attention to the Duke's indifferent attitude towards the practice of over-regulation payments ('officially he knew nothing of it' and 'does not see his way out of it . . .'). He even opposed Herbert's *caveat* that a Secretary of State should be reminded by regulation of 'the necessity of not invading the province of the officer who has military command of the army . . .'. In each instance, Evans found himself in a minority.[66] His suspicions were not groundless. The Queen had expressed fears about the formation of the committee, which Palmerston tried to allay. He observed that Lord Panmure's evidence had 'vexed and disappointed' those who wished 'to make great changes in the existing arrangements'. Although the Queen signed a memorandum in 1861, refining the relationship between the Secretary of State and the Commander-in-Chief, dual control of the army persisted in practice. The subordination of the Commander-in-Chief was not formally declared until 1870, whereupon the Duke was given rooms in the War Office.[67]

Notwithstanding anticipated opposition from the Crown, Evans revived the issue of abolishing purchase. By 1860 he had cause for optimism. Herbert and the Duke of Somerset, the new First Lord of the Admiralty, had been signatories to the majority report of the Purchase Commission. The new Under-Secretary of State for War was Earl de Grey, formerly Viscount Goderich, one of the earliest critics of purchase. Herbert still favoured reform, albeit limited in scope and cautiously approached. Initially, he proposed modifying the existing system to curb the abuse of over-regulation payments, without introducing selection. He suggested that regimental commands should not be held for longer than seven or ten years, and that the purchaser of a lieutenant-colonelcy should not come from the same regiment as the retiring officer.[68] The Duke of Cambridge firmly rejected both proposals, fearing a vast increase in the number of half-pay officers and a disruption of regimental *esprit de corps*. He preferred 'to leave matters as they are'.[69]

Although Herbert heeded these objections and withdrew his plans, he faced a dilemma. Evans, his former co-commissioner, had given notice of a motion which he would introduce in March 1860, calling for a gradual abolition of purchase. Challenged by Evans, and possibly prompted by Earl de Grey,[70] Herbert resolved to implement the commission's recommendation and abolish the sale of the rank of lieutenant-colonel. The Queen and the Prince Consort were appalled: they sent letters of protest to Palmerston and Herbert, and insisted upon the Duke of Cambridge's presence whenever the Cabinet discussed the plan.[71] Herbert, nonetheless, carried his colleagues; he insisted that he could not speak against his recorded opinions in Parliament, a view accepted by Palmerston.[72]

When Evans moved his motion on 6th March he was easily outflanked. In barely audible tones, he deplored the abuses of purchase and its baleful effects upon the efficiency of the army. Given the persistent threat from France, he exhorted the House to begin reform by abolishing the purchase of the ranks of majors and lieutenant-colonels. Herbert replied on behalf of the government with complete consistency. Reiterating his opposition to the entire abolition of purchase, he declared his support, in principle, for the selection of lieutenant-colonels. He had effectively thwarted Evans, for without ministerial backing the motion was doomed. Ellice, Captain Vernon and other military Members opposed seniority or selection as a means of promotion. Captain Jervis added perceptively that, unless the House was 'prepared for a large pension list and increased pay, the resolution of the gallant General would mean nothing at all'. Only fifty-nine Members voted in favour of abolition while 213 voted against – a crushing majority of 154.[73]

The Times, hitherto a staunch supporter of Evans, conceded that 'the advocates of established usage had it all their own way', and that the 'debate was entirely one-sided'. Clearly disappointed with Evans's performance, the paper repeated the familiar criticisms of purchase and its abuses.[74] Several other papers were much less despondent; *The Daily News* and *The Globe* welcomed Herbert's commitment to gradual reform, and even *The Naval and Military Gazette* had 'little objection' to the proposed limitation.[75] But the prospects for reform remained bleak. In the first place, the supporters of purchase were solidly entrenched in the House of Commons. Secondly, the Duke of Cambridge made it abundantly clear that he did not wish to implement the proposal of the Purchase Commission. In the House of Lords, on 23rd March 1860, he stated that 'it shall be my earnest and anxious endeavour – difficult as it may be, and, as I may consider it, impossible – to carry out that decision in such a manner as to promote the best interest of the army . . .'.[76] Thirdly, Herbert, who was overburdened with other work, did not consider purchase reform a priority. He was preoccupied with the war in China, the deliberations of the Graham Committee, the amalgamation of the Queen's and Indian armies, and the completion of the medical and sanitary reforms demanded by Florence Nightingale and her fellow reformers. Suffering from an incurable disease, he never formulated a detailed reform of the purchase system. Transferred to the House of Lords in January 1861, he resigned from the War Office the following June and died on 2nd August 1861.

As Sir George Lewis, the new Secretary of State for War, lacked his predecessor's interest in reform, even modest changes were now unlikely. Evans remained undaunted. In November 1861 he addressed a long letter to his constituents, deploring the 'leapfrog system' of purchase whereby juniors, however incompetent, could supersede veterans like Havelock. In the army, he wrote, 'a long purse is a good substitute for military competency'.[77] He gained wide publicity for this letter, and in the next parliamentary session tabled another moderate abolitionist motion. On this occasion, he merely sought the abolition of purchase for the rank of lieutenant-colonel and found eloquent support from Lord Stanley, a fellow commissioner. Lewis refused to countenance this proposal; he insisted that it must be considered as part of the larger question of abolishing purchase, a reform which could cost in excess of £7 million. Mere mention of this sum ensured that the motion would founder, defeated by a majority of 185 votes.[78]

Abolitionist newspapers were profoundly depressed. *The Globe* accepted that selection was not likely to be implemented 'for many years to come', while *The Daily News* reckoned that the Duke of Cambridge, 'the great obstacle', had blocked reform.[79] Evans incurred criticism for his inept tactics and shortcomings as a parliamentary spokesman. He had failed to compensate for his inaudibility by circularising a summary of his speech to the press. He had presented his proposal without any costings, so enabling Lewis to reject the motion on purely pragmatic grounds (Evans's subsequent letter to *The Times*, challenging the War Office statistics, merely underlined this oversight).[80] He had also persisted with a gradualist approach to reform, which critics dubbed 'an unworthy way of dealing with an important organic question'.[81] Apart from the last argument, which reflected the special pleading of purchase advocates who knew that the chances of reform would be much diminished if purchase was debated in its entirety, these criticisms were fair. But Evans alone cannot be blamed for the failure of reform. Even if he had displayed more tactical finesse, he faced a hostile Commons and a defiant Duke without any semblance of ministerial support. As *The Times* recognised,

> the tide, which ran strongly towards reform in the days after the Crimea, has now turned. Until further experience be gained or some unforeseen calamity causes a new agitation the long-threatened anomaly will plainly continue an institution of the country.[82]

Though primarily concerned with purchase, Evans also championed the cause of the local European forces in India. Even before the passage of the Government of India Act (1858), transferring responsibility for the subcontinent from the East India Company to the Crown, the future rôle, if any, of the company's locally raised regiments was passionately debated. Advocates of a local army, headed by Lord Canning, the Governor-General, maintained that it would serve as a check upon the precipitate withdrawal of European troops from India. Its personnel would possess an intimate knowledge of India's customs and languages, while its officers would be willing to serve on staff secondments for the Governor-General and the Governors of the several presidencies. Opposing these views were the advocates of a line army, including Lord Panmure, Lord Elphinstone, the Governor of Bombay, and several senior officers who had recently served in India – Sir Colin Campbell, Sir William Mansfield and Sir Hugh Rose. Maintaining a double army, they feared, would excite professional jealousies and impair recruiting; it would deprive the line army of valuable service in India, while debarring the Crown from using local forces in India. Above all, they believed that a local force would suffer from the same debilitating influences which had undermined the company's army. After prolonged service in India, regiments would lapse into undisciplined ways, even, in Mansfield's opinion, into 'sloth and debauchery'.[83] A Royal Commission, including four officers from each of the line and local armies, heard such evidence and were unable to agree. Reporting in March 1859, the commission recorded majority and minority viewpoints, with a bare majority favouring amalgamation.[84]

Lacking any clear recommendation from the commission, Lord Derby's Cabinet split, with Lord Stanley, the Secretary of State for India, opposing General Peel, the Secretary of State for War. The Queen, concerned about her prerogative as titular head of the army, insisted upon amalgamation, while the Indian Council lobbied in favour of a local army. Just before it left office, the Conservative government agreed a compromise by which two-fifths of the minimum European army might consist of local forces. Although the Queen acquiesced, the Indian Council remained intransigent, insisting upon local forces comprising two-thirds of the infantry and three-quarters of the cavalry.[85] For Palmerston's Cabinet, events in India resolved the controversy. Ever since the Queen's proclamation of November 1858, converting former company troops into servants of the Crown, there had been protests in the English-language press. Objecting to a switch of allegiances without prior consent, critics claimed that their rights as freeborn Englishmen had been infringed. Some argued that they should have been discharged from the company's service and offered a bounty to re-enlist with the Queen. Faced with rumours of discontent and even of mutinous behaviour (at Barrackpur the men of the 5th European Regiment refused 'to do any duty', but were quickly crushed without bloodshed), the new government acted quickly. It permitted N.C.O.s and men to take their discharge and return to Britain at the State's expense. Described as the 'white mutiny', the affair had dashed the prospects of raising a local army. Following so closely upon the sepoy mutiny, it had further damaged the reputation of Indian forces. As preserving the existing local forces was no longer an option (about two-thirds of the company's men had taken their discharge), the Cabinet resolved, in May 1860, to discontinue a separate European army.[86]

Evans was appalled. He bitterly contested the European Forces (India) Bill through its various stages in the House of Commons. Critical of the policy of successive governments, he denounced the composition of the Royal Commission, especially the inclusion of the Duke of Cambridge and General Peel to ensure a bare majority for amalgamation. Company troops, he argued, had been treated parsimoniously by the Treasury and unfairly criticised. Although they might not look so smart on parade, they had nobly served their country, not least during the mutiny of 1857. Local knowledge, Evans claimed, was indispensbale for Indian warfare; it rendered locally raised forces under their own officers marginally more efficient than Royal regiments. Amalgamation, finally, had a fatal flaw: it vastly augmented the patronage at the disposal of the Horse Guards. Should another 5,000 commissions be added to the Horse Guards list, Evans feared even more 'misplaced appointments' by the military authorities.[87]

Once again Evans had cast himself in the rôle of an independent back-bencher, challenging the policies of successive governments as well as the influence of the Crown. He was doomed to defeat. Both front benches supported the Bill. The debates excited little parliamentary interest; indeed, the chamber had to be counted repeatedly during the protracted committee stage. Few metropolitan papers championed the cause of a local Indian army; even *The Times*, which had favoured a bounty, could not support a force which had resorted to mutiny. It denounced the obstinate opponents of the Bill for wasting parliamentary time and for making 'so sad an exhibition, both in authority, talent, and numbers'.[88] Moreover, Evans's argument was extremely weak. Members doubted that the local army, which had largely disintegrated, could be revived and then vastly increased to meet the new levels required by the Royal Commission. Without disclosing any reason, the majority report had recommended that 80,000 European troops should be retained in India. Evans scorned this 'preposterous' total; he suggested that a moderate increase would have been amply sufficient', but the mutiny was too recent a memory for such reasoning to carry conviction. On 2nd July 1860 Evans's amendment was crushed by a majority of 229 votes.[89]

Thwarted over various military issues, Evans achieved relatively little as an army reformer. For several years he had actively campaigned in the House of Commons, a considerable achievement for a seventy-year-old Member who suffered from recurrent illness. Professionally, he enjoyed further distinctions, being promoted to the rank of general on 19th March 1861. He also received favourable coverage from A. W. Kinglake in his controversial history of the Crimean War. As Kinglake criticised the Duke of Cambridge's rôle in the battle of the Alma, the Duke was predictably enraged and sought Evans's support. He found him unforthcoming. Evans refused several requests for a 'frank friendly' interview with the Duke. 'H.R.H.,' he wrote, 'thinks he has a facility for cajolery & I am not sure that he has not . . . . But this fine quality is unluckily wasted & lost upon me'.[90] Instead Evans sent him a long letter, chronicling his observations during the battle and explaining how he had acted, through Colonel Steele, to prompt an initiative from the Duke. As Evans informed Delane, the difference between the Duke and himself was fundamental. While the Duke considered his comments on the battle 'to be purely of *private & confidential* character', Evans regarded them 'as of a public and historical character'.[91]

On 4th February 1865 Evans informed his constituents of his retirement from public life. He reviewed his political service over the previous thirty-five years:

On becoming a member of the Legislature, I united myself heart and soul with the (then) Liberal party. This was not very advantageous to me as a professional man. From that period, however, followed a series of improvements in the laws and prosperity of this country, unequalled during any similar interval in the long course of our national history . . . . I allow myself to look back with, I trust, pardonable complacency to my honest, if not adroit, support of the great and salutary measures which lead to those results.[92]

Despite tributes in some papers and a testimonial from constituency supporters,[93] Evans incurred criticism even in resignation. He had not been active as an M.P. in his final years, and had failed to heal the divisions among Westminster Liberals. Ever since 1852 the local

Liberals had been split, with the disagreements obscured by the patriotic fervour of the late '50s. Some Liberals 'hailed with pleasure the resignation of Sir De Lacy Evans', seeking an 'advanced Liberal' as his replacement, namely John Stuart Mill.[94]

To leave the Westminster Liberals so deeply divided was profoundly ironic. Evans had always attended to his constituency duties. He had strenuously endeavoured to honour election pledges, reflect his supporters' concerns, and remain independent of ministerial patronage. Yet he had virtually ignored the issues of potential controversy within his constituency, preferring to immerse himself in military debates. He could choose to do so because Palmerston had little desire to split his administration over constitutional questions. Had Evans exploited this opportunity to realise a lasting measure of army reform, his choice would have been more easily defended.

As an army reformer, however, he was largely a failure. His experience and status as a military commander never compensated for his lack of political skill. Unable to inspire the House with oratory, he frequently offended its proprieties by lapsing into personal malice. He also failed to organise his priorities, wasting time and credibility over the defence of a local army in India. These shortcomings, though real and substantial, paled by comparison with the difficulties he encountered. Few back-benchers, irrespective of their ability, could have overcome the indifference of their colleagues, the influence of the Crown, the waning interest of the press, and the opposition of several Secretaries of the State (excepting Herbert). Circumstances had also changed; reform lost much of its former appeal once the army had proved itself in crushing the mutiny. Evans, nevertheless, had displayed remarkable tenacity. He had kept reform before the attention of Parliament. He had also secured the appointment of a Royal Commission, whose report and evidence would be of use for future reformers. When he died on 9th January 1870, aged eighty-two, he had set an example as a reformer, campaigning vigorously, if not always skilfully, but with commendable determination.

9
An assessment

George de Lacy Evans had a remarkable career in public life. As a military officer, he saw campaign service in India, Mauritius, Spain (on two separate occasions), North America, Belgium and the Crimea over a period of forty-seven years. As a Member of Parliament, he represented the constituents of Rye and Westminster for some twenty-eight years. He wrote three books, several pamphlets, and numerous letters to the press. He campaigned tenaciously, if not always adroitly, for various causes, challenging the established wisdom in the military and political realms. Although he never lost his interest in the army – his chosen profession and first concern – he had eagerly sought and zealously pursued his political duties. He was, quintessentially, a soldier-politician.

Regular officers had traditionally formed a prominent group in the House of Commons. In the eighteenth century, membership of the Commons was a recognised avenue of professional advancement. From 1734 to 1832 the military provided about one in six of the Members of the House, the largest single occupational group.[1] This dual rôle persisted beyond the Reform Act of 1832: sixty-seven officers or ex-officers were elected to the Commons in 1832, seventy-one were elected in 1852.[2] Yet the military was neither a powerful nor a cohesive group in Parliament. By the mid-nineteenth century, many of the officers who entered politics had retired or sold out to embark upon a second career (only twenty of the seventy-one officers in 1852 were still on the Active List). Service Members of Parliament were not predisposed towards one party but were fairly evenly split between Whigs and Conservatives, leaving a small rump of Radical eccentrics. Many appear to have entered politics with the aim of protecting or of advancing individual and family interests.[3] Only a few senior officers, like the Duke of Wellington or Sir Henry Hardinge, attained high political appointments. Almost as rare were officers who exuded a fervent political commitment, but undoubtedly the Radical officers, such as Thomas Perronet Thompson and George de Lacy Evans, would be numbered among them.

Evans, though intelligent, was not an intellectual. He never displayed an interest in political theory nor referred, save on rare occasions, to the ideas and values which had inspired his political involvement. Many of his views probably derived from the politics of his family background, especially the Protestant 'Patriots' of eighteenth-century Ireland. He still professed support for several of their causes. He staunchly endorsed the revolution of the American colonists, opposed commercial restrictions and repressive legislation, and championed the political rights of religious minorities. Like the 'Patriots', and to some extent the American colonists, he justified these attitudes as upholding the traditional rights of Englishmen, enshrined in the Glorious Revolution of 1689.[4] He believed that these rights had been subverted by those who had abused the privileges of rank and wealth in society. He inveighed against the aristocracy and its political representatives – the Tories invariably, and the Whigs less often, but, if feeling betrayed by the Whigs in office, he reproached them with even more vehemence. Opposed to the increasing centralisation of government, Evans deprecated the concentration of power and the concomitant growth of taxation. He condemned corrupt electoral practices, repressive legislation, and the prevalence of patronage, sinecures and nepotism in public office. An unswerving advocate of civil rights, he protested over the maltreatment of Mr and Mrs Deacles in 1831, and deplored slavery and flogging as brutal and inhumane. Offended by any semblance of religious discrimination, he criticised the privileges of the Established Church and upheld the civil and political rights of all religious groups. Within his own profession, too, he desperately resented the purchase system; he believed that it had thwarted the careers of meritorious, though poor, officers like himself, while rewarding those with money and influence.

To restore English rights and liberties, Evans favoured extensive measures of political, fiscal and administrative reform. He consistently supported the introduction of the ballot, triennial Parliaments and household suffrage, with the aim of sustaining the progress which had only begun with the Reform Act of 1832. In campaigning for the abolition of the Corn Laws, Church rates and assessed taxation, he sought to redress the balance between the various classes and religions and to relieve the burdens upon the underprivileged. To curb the growth of government, he proposed more local involvement in administering the Poor Law and a locally based as distinct from a national Militia. Though considered an 'advanced reformer' in the 1830s, he was never a revolutionary. When Charles Greville described him as 'a Republican',[5] he revealed more personal animus than perception. Although Evans believed that Parliament could be swayed by popular pressure, he never proposed the overthrow of the monarchy or recourse to violence. He castigated the aims and tactics of the more militant wing of the Chartist movement, faithfully reflecting the fears within his constituency about violence in the metropolis.

His priorities in foreign policy mirrored his domestic concerns. He acclaimed liberal movements abroad, especially those which opposed the autocratic rule of the Russians and Austrians. In praising the nationalist movements of Poland, Hungary and Sardinia, he asserted that Britain should support these causes. During the general election of 1857, he assured constituents 'that if Austria dared to crush or interfere with the nascent liberties of Sardinia, the people would compel Lord Palmerston, whether he pleased or not, to throw the aegis of this mighty empire over that small state'.[6] Where a nationalist movement, like the Carlists, was profoundly anti-liberal, Evans backed the constitutional forces in Madrid. When French foreign policy swung from its seemingly liberal stance in the 1830s to the more militaristic and interventionist policies of Napoleon III, Evans abandoned his former support of France. He became increasingly concerned about the possibility of a French invasion and made several bombastic speeches about the state of the nation's defences. Nevertheless, he generally approved of Palmerston's conduct of foreign policy, accepting that compromises had to be made to preserve British interests. Greek nationalism, therefore, received scant support from Evans, as the Ottoman Empire had to be preserved as a buffer against Russian expansion.

Evans attained more success as a polemicist and an electoral campaigner than as a parliamentarian. Although his Russophobic writings lacked either literary or historical merit – their style was stilted, the logic tendentious, and the evidence based upon selective quotation without careful analysis – the books attracted widespread attention. Their impact reflected the salience and importance of the subject matter. Publication coincided with Russian moves in the Balkans and raised latent fears of Tsarist ambitions. The books alarmed Lord Ellenborough, prompted an official inquiry into the state of British defences on the North West Frontier, and contributed to a significant shift in the editorial policy of *The Times*. The furore proved short-lived; the findings of the inquiry, coupled with the evidence of Russian military weakness, doused the fears which Evans had raised. The controversy, however, testified to the immediate impact of his writing, no mean feat for a half-pay lieutenant-colonel who had not yet entered politics.

As an electoral campaigner, Evans won ten out of thirteen contests, to serve as a Member of Parliament for nearly thirty years. In Rye his victories marked a watershed in the pre-Reform politics of the borough. Local reformers had always possessed the organisation and legal skills to contest the seat, but, until Evans appeared, had lacked a suitable candidate. He proved to be an inspirational leader by his canvassing, extensive (if not eloquent) speech-making, and fierce commitment to political reform. Known as 'the idol of the Cinque Ports', he mobilised local support for the first Reform Bill and worked resolutely to win and then regain the seat at Rye. He proved fastidious in his constituency duties and only lost the seat after boundary changes.

The sprawling urban borough of Westminster, then a Radical citadel, offered a different but still demanding challenge. Initially, Evans won the seat by campaigning as an 'advanced Reformer', so exploiting local dissatisfaction with the sitting Member Sir John Cam Hobhouse. Thereafter he endeavoured to fulfil his electoral pledges. Unlike John Temple Leader, a potentially more capable and articulate fellow Member for Westminster, Evans attended to his constituency and parliamentary duties. He faithfully reflected the concerns of his constituency supporters about taxation, the Poor Law, and religious issues. He remained passionately anti-Tory and independent of the main parties, always stressing that he was not a candidate for public office. Faced with an increasingly well organised and heavily financed Conservative challenge, he became increasingly pragmatic on the hustings: he combined with the Whigs whenever a common platform could be devised. Despite a defeat in 1841, Evans regained the seat five years later when the Conservatives split over the Maynooth and Corn Law issues. Henceforth, he was more perturbed by divisions among Westminster Radicals and by mounting criticism from ex-Chartists and their sympathisers. He managed to deflect such opposition largely by exploiting the patriotic fervour which erupted in the wake of the

Crimean War, the Indian Mutiny, and the invasion scare of 1859. Dubbed a hero for his services in the Crimea, and a zealous supporter of Palmerston, Evans confounded his Conservative and ultra-Radical opponents, winning his last two elections without a contest.

In the House of Commons, Evans made relatively little impact. Bereft of oratorical skills, he usually supported rather than instigated debates. He never mastered the procedures of the House and blundered badly in his handling of the Deacles' case. Blunt and self-opinionated, he all too often cast discretion aside in raising an issue or questioning a Minister. In speeches, he occasionally digressed to describe real or imagined slights against himself and, periodically, lapsed into personal abuse. Friends soon realised that his interventions on their behalf could prove counterproductive. Sir George Brown advised Major Norcott, who was seeking a medal for services in the Crimea, to say 'nothing' to Evans in case he raised the issue in the House.[7] Thomas Perronet Thompson was equally reluctant to let Evans draw attention to his own non-promotion. As he shrewdly observed,

Appealing to the House of Commons for anything, but particularly against the military authorities, is the last seal of reprobation. It never succeeds; and when it has failed, it makes a good reason for making a *set* against a man for ever afterwards. On these grounds, I opposed it when General Evans proposed to bring it [his non-promotion] forward in the House.[8]

Sir William Mansfield was even more critical of Evans for his speech during the purchase debate of March 1855. Evans had digressed to complain about the non-promotion of Sergeant Sullivan, whom he had personally recommended for a commission. Evans, reckoned Mansfield, had looked like a 'buffoon', mixing up 'his own personal vanity with a great question. He spoilt a really effective address by all the trash about Sergt. Sullivan.'[9]

Evans never fully compensated for his shortcomings as a public speaker. Although he had some close friends on the back benches, notably Thompson and Colonel Freestun, he was not particularly sociable. Prone to bouts of moody introspection, he harboured suspicions of several parliamentary colleagues and neither forgot nor forgave the criticisms of his command in Spain. He even alluded to these criticisms in accepting the vote of thanks of the House for his services in the Crimea. Lieutenant-Colonel Fitzmayer sensed the depth of his commander's bitterness. Evans, he wrote, was a good deal influenced by personal pique and perhaps by professional disappointment. I never in my life met any one so morbidly sensitive to any newspaper comment or notice of his conduct.[10]

Evans also believed that his experience in politics warranted more respect and deference than some younger Radicals were prepared to accord it. In the late '40s, he repeatedly chided Cobden and Bright. When opposing advocates of military retrenchment, Evans simply agreed to disagree with Hume, a veteran campaigner against the service estimates, but he ridiculed the pretensions of younger critics. Cobden, he scoffed, had returned from Europe with a 'military character', having developed a 'thorough' mastery 'of this very difficult subject'. Evans derided 'Gentlemen who were not connected with either service' setting 'themselves up to reform both . . .'.[11] Using such rhetoric, he incurred the enmity and suspicion of several Radical Members.

A somewhat solitary figure on the back benches, he had even less influence at ministerial level. He had few personal contacts with government Ministers and chose his ministerial support unwisely. In seeking endorsement for his claims to a higher order of the Bath, he suggested that the Prime Minister should turn to Lord Clarendon for advice.[12] Clarendon was one of the few Ministers who knew much about Evans's command in Spain. He had also praised him in public despatches. Privately, however, he had always been contemptuous of Evans's political and military services and had regularly criticised him in letters to Lord Palmerston. He had feared that Evans's 'fault of undertaking more than he can execute which had been displayed in the House of Commons would be equally manifest in Navarre – and so it has turned out'.[13] Palmerston, admittedly, never lost confidence in Evans's command of the Legion, while Lord Aberdeen and the Duke of Newcastle duly applauded his services in the Crimea. But Ministers had scant regard for his political judgement. Evans was never a candidate for public office and never diluted his Radicalism, save over military and foreign policy issues. Moreover, his views were not simply Radical but were often utterly unpractical and uncosted (for example, his advocacy of British intervention on behalf of the Polish nationalists in the 1830s, and his wish to continue the war against Russia in 1856 without the assistance of France). In speaking upon national questions, including army reform, he rarely tempered his views to take account of what seemed feasible or within the realm of practical politics.

Personal failings cannot entirely explain Evans's lack of impact in national politics. As a Radical M.P., he was not a member of a cohesive political group. His colleagues were highly individualistic; they eschewed party organisation and discipline, viewing such concepts as the derivatives of aristocratic faction, place, and patronage. They sought to achieve their objectives by persuasion and demonstration.[14] As Perronet Thompson noted,

Most of the Radical members are sent to parliament by constituencies, who have a high, and in some cases an overweening opinion, of what is to be expected from the exertions of their particular representative. Hence these members are much more in the situation of chiefs of clans, than of the leaders of a regular army, bound together by well-digested discipline and habitual co-operation . . . .[15]

Radicals were divided among themselves. By the 1850s there were social Radicals whose priorities derived from the Chartist movement, militant nationalistic Radicals, and middle-class Radicals of the Manchester school. Although they coalesed over some issues, they frequently quarrelled with each other.[16]

Evans was increasingly, but never exclusively, identified with the nationalistic Radicals. During the Crimean War he refrained from endorsing the protestations of Roebuck, disputing his criticisms of the government and the army.[17] In the '40s and '50s he adhered to many different causes, endorsing the Anti-Corn Law agitation and supporting Fielden's factory legislation. He remained consistently in favour of political reform, especially the ballot, triennial Parliaments, household suffrage, and a more equal distribution of seats. He voted for motions in favour of such proposals, whether introduced by Grote, Hume or Bright. In these debates Evans provided voting rather than vocal support, a reflection of his limited oratory, influence and expertise. Only in military debates, particularly those concerned with army reform, did he attain some prominence in the House, a status which reflected his military experience as much as the causes he chose to promote.

In a military career spanning nearly half a century, Evans's experience was strikingly diverse. He served with nine different armies in three continents. He was a subaltern in infantry and cavalry regiments and volunteered for duties with the engineers and navy. Within eight years of entering the army he was appointed to the Quartermaster-General's staff, acting as a staff officer in the

Peninsular, North American and Waterloo campaigns. Ambitious and eager for active service, he proved audacious on the field of battle. He was commended in ten despatches, reports or gazettes for his services in America and at Waterloo. Throughout his whole career, he participated in some fifty operations, sieges and battles, incurring five wounds and losing seven horses shot or sabred from under him. As a senior officer, he commanded an allied army corps in Spain and a division in the Crimea.[18]

Evans always suspected that his military career had suffered on account of his political involvement.[19] Nevertheless, he still rose to the peak of his profession, albeit in a slow and desultory manner. As an officer, he possessed many attributes which transcended his political eccentricities. Although born into a family of modest means, he came from gentry stock and from a family with a distinguished military tradition. He knew how to behave as an officer and a gentleman, and, if unable to purchase his promotion, could earn it by daring acts of bravery. This instinctive aptitude was reflected by his commendations as a subaltern and a staff officer. He also gained invaluable experience in the handling of a large formation of troops against a European adversary when he commanded an army corps in Spain. Such recent experience was unrivalled among the senior officers who were fit and available to serve on the eve of the Crimean expedition. After his performance in the Crimea, he was generally acclaimed as a respected general and suitably awarded.

No aspect of Evans's career was fraught with more peculiar and demanding problems than his command of the British Auxiliary Legion. Hastily organised in 1835, the Legion was composed of largely untrained men. It suffered from appalling living conditions in the winter of 1835–36 and remained permanently under strength. Evans struggled to retain the loyalty of officers and men despite the lowly status of the force, disputes over the contract of employment, and the lack of rewards and payment from Madrid. Although mutinies occurred, and some units panicked at Hernani, Evans rallied his officers and men and generally maintained discipline. Unable to undertake independent tactical initiatives, save on a comparatively small scale, he relied upon allied support. He had to liaise with Spanish generals, some of whom had scant respect for the Legion's military potential, and with the Marines and naval forces under the command of Lord John Hay. Even with such backing, which was intermittently and fitfully provided, Evans faced a tenacious and resourceful enemy, who was fighting on his own mountainous terrain and enjoyed a large measure of local support.

Politically, Evans carried the burden of the inordinate hopes of Palmerston and the British government. Ministerial spokesmen repeatedly asserted that the Legion could prove decisive in the conflict and ensure the triumph of the Constitutional cause.[20] Several Conservatives, however, deplored the intervention of Britain, even in the limited form of the Legion. Some openly sympathised with the Carlists, others dismissed the legionaries as mercenaries lacking in discipline or military value. Lord Aberdeen described the British contribution as 'most disgraceful and most dangerous in principle ...'.[21] The Duke of Wellington was even more scathing. 'Evans' position at St Sebastian,' he wrote, 'was not a military but a political stock jobbing position. He was placed there in order that the British fleet might do something; that is to say co-operate with Evans in making a Noise; but in reality nothing else.' The Spanish authorities, he added, had sacrificed the strategic advantages of combining their army corps to ensure a conspicuous British support, so gaining some 'movement on the Stock Exchange'.[22]

Evans deeply resented the vilification of his Spanish command. He felt, quite reasonably, that many of the accusations by returning officers, journalists and politicians were unfair and ill-informed, especially the glib comparisons between the Legion and the Peninsular army. He feared, too, that his future career in the army would be blocked, following his condemnation by senior military officers, particularly the Duke of Wellington. Although he could never substantiate this charge, and the Duke always denied that he ever interfered with the appointments of the Commander-in-Chief,[23] Evans's career stagnated over the next sixteen years. What rankled was the realisation that much of the criticism of his Spanish service had been politically motivated, a reflection of the profound division between Whigs and Tories over the conduct of foreign policy. A fervent ideologue himself, he had consistently advocated British military intervention on behalf of liberal causes or against autocratic regimes. In Spain, Evans had never been merely an officer undertaking a professional duty, he had always been an officer passionately committed to a particular cause. The Legion, he maintained, reflected British participation in a European struggle between autocratic and constitutional values.[24]

Partisan criticism, however, could not detract from the minor military success which Evans had achieved. By persuading Espartero to adopt his strategy, Evans mounted an attack in strength upon the Carlist positions which guarded the northern route to France. In a mere four days, the allied corps captured the towns of Hernani, Irun and Fuenterrabia, and overwhelmed the garrisons of Oyarzun and Fort del Parque. Carlist supply lines to France were cut, and the honour of the Legion was largely restored. As important as the victory itself was the manner in which it was achieved. Realising the importance of popular support in a guerrilla war, Evans spared not only the women and children at Irun but also the lives of the garrison which surrendered. He thereby ensured the immediate capitulation of Fuenterrabia (one hundred officers, one thousand men and thirty pieces of cannon), and scored a propaganda triumph over the Carlists. The sixty-six officers who surrendered at Irun sent a public letter to the Pretender, acknowledging the humanity of the Legion and asking him to rescind the infamous Durango Decree.[25] Under Evans's command, the Legion had vindicated its rôle in Spain. Primarily a symbol of Britain's commitment to the Constitutional cause, it had also bolstered the northern armies, enabling them to achieve a localised triumph in the Basque provinces (if not the 'mortal blow' envisaged by Palmerston).[26]

During his long career Evans became increasingly shrewd and flexible as a military tactician. In his early years he was somewhat reckless, prone to advise or order rash frontal assaults. Personally intrepid, he yearned to assume the offensive, an approach which met with mixed results at Baltimore and later in Spain. When supported by naval fire-power, the Legion's offensive succeeded at San Sebastian, but, without support and in one case with faulty intelligence, foundered in the battles of Fuenterrabia and Hernani. From his Spanish experience Evans learned the value of combined arms operations and the utility of concentrated artillery fire. Such tactics would prove invaluable in the Crimea. At the battle of the Alma, he employed artillery batteries, neglected by other commanders, to breech the Russian defences and facilitate the advance of the Second Division. At the battle of little Inkerman, he held his defensive position against a formidable Russian attack. Having calmly chosen his ground and protected his flanks, Evans used his guns to pound the enemy and disrupt their formations, before launching a decisive counter-attack. Impressed by the standard of gunnery in the Crimea, he rated the artillery as first 'in point of efficiency' above the other two arms.[27]

In the Crimean campaign, Evans distinguished himself as a divisional commander. He was always concerned about the comforts and morale of his men. When the army languished in Bulgaria prior to the war, he took inordinate care over the choice of camp sites, so minimising his division's losses from cholera. By authorising regimental sports and recreation, he tried to relieve the boredom and sustain *esprit de corps*. At the Alma, he not only led his troops with his customary flair, and broke through the Russian defences, but he also maintained the offensive by prompting the feckless Duke of Cambridge to provide support. Lieutenant-Colonel Fitzmayer was profoundly impressed. His 'old chief' had proved 'as brave as a Lion, always clear in his orders, and thoroughly at home with troops when near the enemy'.[28] Though wounded at the Alma and progressively weakened by illness, Evans remained a perceptive commander. He urged Lord Raglan to fortify the Inkerman heights, managed with other commanders to dissuade Raglan from a precipitate attack on Sebastopol, and overruled Colonel Gordon's order to launch a diversionary attack on a mythical Russian convoy. Hospitalised after a fall from a horse, he returned to his division during the main battle of Inkerman. Displaying impressive courage and resilience, he inspired both officers and men, while proffering advice but not usurping the command of Major-General Pennefather. Debilitated by his exertions, he retired prematurely from the war to return as a national hero.

Within three months of his return, Evans appeared before the select committee appointed to enquire into the conduct of the war. In his detailed and highly informative evidence, he refused to endorse the more extreme criticisms of the state of the pre-war army, the planning of the campaign, and the predicament of the army before Sebastopol. In this testimony he evinced more discretion than candour. Admittedly, he could not comment upon several issues, having been excluded from the innermost counsels of Lord Raglan and having left the Crimea before the onset of winter. Nevertheless, he had received letters from the front which had convinced him that Russell's reports on the conditions in the camp were largely correct. His reluctance to voice such fears publicly reflected a lack of respect for many of the wartime critics and their priorities. As in the aftermath of the Spanish campaign, Evans resented any criticism of the army from politicians who had no experience of war. Unlike many civilians, he was not shocked by the casualty returns of a winter campaign. Remembering the winter of 1835–36, he accepted fatalities with a grim sense of inevitability. He refused to join the widespread condemnation of the government, accepting that it could not be held responsible for administrative blunders at Balaclava. Above all, he believed that Parliament should concentrate upon supporting the war effort, and so continued to defend the army during the course of the war. He bitterly deprecated the cessation of hostilities in January 1856, regarding it as premature and unnecessary.[29]

Despite his staunch defence of the army, Evans remained passionately committed to its reform. In the pre-war parliamentary debates he had advocated the abolition of the purchase system, the abolition of flogging in the peacetime army, and improvements in pay, conditions and terms of service for the rank and file. He had approved the modest reforms of Earl Grey, especially the Army Service Bill of 1847, only wishing that the Earl had managed to gain Horse Guards support for an immediate introduction of limited enlistment.[30] Evans also applauded the improvements in several overseas stations effected during Grey's term of office, but realised that much more needed to be done to ameliorate the living conditions of the ranks and the appeal of a military career. Concerned about the health of the soldier, he deplored the state of barrack accommodation in the United Kingdom. He drew attention to the appalling conditions in some metropolitan barracks, particularly the overcrowding and lack of married quarters, and sought improvements in the status of the army medical staff. To broaden the appeal of the service, he favoured a radical revision of recruiting methods, including the abolition of a bounty on enlistment 'which has the effect of deceiving the men who enlist'. By increasing pay, enhancing living conditions, and removing the element of dishonesty from the recruiting process, Evans believed that the government could transform the image of military service and so induce a better class of man to enlist.[31]

For personal as well as professional reasons, Evans was profoundly concerned about the command structure within the army. Unlike Grey, Ellice and Panmure, he believed that the reform of the purchase system was of pivotal importance for the future of the army. He maintained that the abuses of the system far outweighed any possible benefits, and that the difficulties of reform hardly excused inaction. As a battle-scarred officer, he deplored the ease with which young, affluent aristocrats obtained their military commands. He criticised the appointment of Lord Brudenell (later the seventh Earl of Cardigan) to command the 15th Hussars over the heads of 'many older and more experienced and very able officers . . .'.[32] He also looked askance at the meteoric career of the Queen's cousin, the Duke of Cambridge. A major-general at the age of twenty-six, the Duke was subsequently offered a divisional command in the Chobham exercise of 1853 and was appointed commander of the First Division in the Crimea without any active service experience. At the Alma, Evans deplored the Duke's lack of initiative and fear of committing himself, traits which were even more apparent at the battle of Inkerman. Despite this incompetence in the field,[33] the Duke was duly appointed as General Commanding-in-Chief.

Promoting army reform became Evans's prime concern during his last ten years in Parliament. On account of his recent military service, he could no longer be ignored by governments and the House of Commons. He was appointed to several Royal Commissions and select committees. Despite ill health and advancing years, he still spoke in army debates, tabled motions in the House, and wrote letters to the press. He repeatedly pressed the Commons to approve the abolition, in part or in whole, of the purchase system. In this cause he proved a doughty champion, declaring that purchase had produced 'the greatest abuses which existed in the army of any civilized country in the world'.[34] Even Cobden, who regarded Evans as 'a shabby' or 'very shifty' politician, applauded his advocacy of purchase reform. On this issue, he wrote, Evans 'displayed a heart & an earnestness which I had not given him credit for'.[35]

Yet Evans's protestations came to naught. His dismal oratory, laced all too often with personal invective, failed to impress the House. He dissipated his energies in the forlorn cause of the East India Company's army and never co-ordinated his supporters in a campaign against the purchase system. In fact, the prospects for reform were never as bright as they had appeared in the winter months of 1854–55. Once the Crimean War was over, governments were no longer primarily concerned about army reform. Sidney Herbert, the only reformer who was appointed Secretary of State for War, was burdened by overwork and ill health; he proffered only token support for purchase reform. Vested interests resisted stubbornly. Many service MPs defended the virtues of the existing system and carried the majority of their colleagues by stressing the financial costs of reform. Royal opposition was also apparent. Prince Albert and the Duke of Cambridge, though prepared to approve and encourage educational reform in the army, vigorously opposed the abolition of purchase. Evans periodically tried to rally his friends in Fleet Street, but their interest had waned after the triumphs of the army in India. In these circumstances, reform was doomed; Evans had contributed to the failure, but his shortcomings were a fairly minor factor compared with the erosion of press and parliamentary interest and the lack of ministerial initiative.

Evans's public career had hardly been a failure. His military services had been remarkable in their scope and diversity. He had overcome a formidable array of problems in his Spanish command, and later returned from the Crimea as one of the few divisional commanders with an enhanced reputation. A staunch advocate of political reform, he won remarkable victories in Rye and represented Westminster for nearly thirty years. Even as an army reformer, a rôle in which he achieved relatively little, he at least ensured that the Royal Commission would provide a fund of valuable information about the abuses of the purchase system. By his abortive campaigns, he also demonstrated that a successful assault could not be launched from the back benches, and that a ministerial initiative was essential. Finally, he sustained and promoted many political and military causes which would eventually be realised, though not in his lifetime. Evans may have lacked the tactical finesse and influence to realise these causes, but he bequeathed a testimony and a commitment of lasting value.

Notes and references

Preface

1. A. P. C. Bruce, *An Annotated Bibliography of the British Army 1660–1914* (Garland Publishing, New York, 1975), p. 135.
2. G. Harries-Jenkins, *The Army in Victorian Society* (Routledge & Kegan Paul, London, 1977), pp. 220–1.
3. The best general account of Russophobia is J. H. Gleason, *The Genesis of Russophobia in Great Britain* (Harvard University Press, Cambridge, Mass., 1950).
4. These population changes merely continued changes already evident in earlier decades. See R. E. Zegger, *John Cam Hobhouse: A Political Life, 1819–1852* (University of Missouri Press, Columbia, 1973), pp. 13–14.

Chapter 1

1. An Irish division of land.
2. Several standard reference works, including the *Dictionary of National Biography*, Vol. 18, p. 62, are inaccurate in their details of Evans's parentage. See deed No. 227572, Registry of Deeds, Dublin, Book 340, p. 113, and 'Pedigree of De Lacy Evans', Genealogical Office, Dublin Castle, Mss. 176 and 177.
3. Deed No. 278632, Registry of Deeds, Book 427, p. 224.
4. Deed No. 469420, Registry of Deeds, Book 682, p. 269.
5. J. O'Hart, *Irish Landed Gentry* (Dublin, 1887), p. 625.
6. J. Begley, *The Diocese of Limerick From 1691 to the Present Time* (Browne & Nolan, Dublin, 1938), p. 29, and De Lacy-Bellingari, *The Roll of the House of Lacy* (Waverly Press, Baltimore, Md., 1928), p. 250.
7. De Lacy-Bellingari, *op. cit.*, pp. 238 and 250.
8. E. MacLysaght, *Irish families: their names, arms and origins* (Hodges Figgis & Co., Dublin, 1957), p. 205, and M. Lenihan, *Limerick, its history and antiquities* (Hodges Smith & Co., Dublin, 1866), pp. 332–5.
9. De Lacy-Bellingari, *op. cit.*, p. 254.
10. J. H. Leslie, 'Reminiscences of a Woolwich Cadet of 1802 by the late Capt. Frederick Robertson, R.A.', *Journal of the Society of Army Historical Research*, Vol. 5, No. 19 (January–March 1926), pp. 6–7. See also Col. W. D. Jones, *Records of the Royal Military Academy*,

1741–1850 (Woolwich, 1851), pp. 66–7.
11 Sir G. de Lacy Evans, 'Memorandum to His Grace the Duke of Newcastle', Aberdeen Mss., B[ritish] L[ibrary] Add. Mss. 43,252, f. 333, p. 1.
12 (Q. 573) Evidence before *His Majesty's Commissioners for inquiring into the System of Military Punishments in the Army*, C. 59 (1836), XXII, p. 39.
13 Sir G. de Lacy Evans, *op. cit.*, p. 1.
14 *Ibid.* See also G. Ryan, *Our Heroes of the Crimea* (Routledge, London, 1855), pp. 14–15.
15 Sir G. de Lacy Evans, *op. cit.*, p. 1.
16 Lt. W. Bragge to his father, 24 June 1813, *Peninsular Portrait 1811–14. The Letters of Capt. William Bragge*, ed. S. A. C. Cassels (Oxford University Press, London, 1963), p. 102. C. Oman, *A History of the Peninsular War*, 7 vols. (Oxford University Press, London, 1902–30), Vol. 6, p. 440.
17 Sir G. de Lacy Evans, *op. cit.*, and G. Ryan, *op. cit.*, p. 14.
18 A. Brett-James, 'Wellington's army', *History of the British Army*, ed. Brigadier Peter Young and Lt.-Col. J. P. Lawford (A. Barker, London, 1970), p. 128.
19 Lt. W. Bragge to his father, 18 October, 26 November 1812 and 22 July 1813, *Peninsular Portrait*, pp. 78, 83, 108.
20 The medals of Sir George de Lacy Evans are retained by the Queen's Own Hussars Museum, Warwick. See also S. G. P. Ward, 'The Quartermaster-General's Department in the Peninsula, 1809–1814', *Journal of the Society for Army Historical Research*, Vol. 24 (winter 1946), p. 151.
21 Lt.-Gen. Dalhousie to Maj.-Gen. Ross, 29 May 1814, *Supplementary Despatches, Correspondence and Memoranda of Field-Marshal Arthur, Duke of Wellington*, ed. by his son, the Duke of Wellington, 11 vols. (John Murray, London, 1858–72), Vol. 9, p. 117.
22 J. W. Croker to Admiral Sir A. Cochrane, 19 May 1814, P[ublic] R[ecord] O[ffice], Adm[iralty], 2/1380, p. 144.
23 Lt.-Gen. Dalhousie to Sir G. Murray, 27 May 1814, *Supplementary Despatches*, Vol. 9, pp. 118–19. R. Reilly, *The British at the Gates* (G. Putnam, New York, 1974), pp. 150 and 153.
24 *The Autobiography of Lieutenant-General Sir Harry Smith*, ed. G. C. Moore Smith, 2 vols. (J. Murray, London, 1901), Vol. 1, pp. 193 and 195, Vol. 2, p. 203. Sir Duncan MacDougall served under Evans as Quartermaster-General in the British Auxiliary Legion, and remained a friend of Evans. See Evans to Sir D. MacDougall, 13 May 1862, N[ational] L[ibrary of] I[reland], Evans, Ms. 15,756.
25 R. Reilly, *op. cit.*, pp. 152–3; R. Horsman, *The War of 1812* (A. A. Knopf, New York, 1969), pp. 196–7; and Lt.-Col. G. de Lacy Evans, *Facts relating to the capture of Washington in reply to some statements contained in the memoirs of Admiral Sir G. Cockburn* (W. Clowes, London, 1829), pp. 7–8.
26 Lt.-Col. G. de Lacy Evans, *Facts relating to the capture of Washington*,

p. 8.
27 Lt. G. de Lacy Evans to Col. W. Thornton, 17 August 1814, Maryland Historical Society, Baltimore, Ms. 1,846.
28 Maj.-Gen. Ross to Earl Bathurst, 30 August 1814, P.R.O., W[ar] O[ffice] 1/141, p. 32.
29 *Ibid*, pp. 31–4, 45, and R. Horsman, *op. cit.*, p. 200.
30 Sir G. de Lacy Evans, 'Memorandum to His Grace the Duke of Newcastle', p. 1, and G. Ryan, *op. cit.*, p. 15.
31 Maj.-Gen. Ross to Earl Bathurst, 30 August 1814, P.R.O., W.O. 1/141, p. 34–5.
32 R. F. A. Fabel, 'The laws of war in the 1812 conflict', *Journal of American Studies*, Vol. 14, No. 2 (August 1980), pp. 210–13, and R. Horsman, *op. cit.*, 201–2.
33 Maj.-Gen. Ross to Earl Bathurst, 30 August 1814, P.R.O., W.O. 1/141, p. 37, and Sir G. de Lacy Evans, 'Memorandum to His Grace the Duke of Newcastle', p. 2.
34 G. C. Moore Smith, *op. cit.*, Vol. 1, pp. 206–7, and Sir A. Cochrane to Earl Bathurst, 28 August 1814, P.R.O., W.O. 1/141, pp. 27–30.
35 Sir A. Cochrane to J. W. Croker, 17 September 1814, P.R.O., Adm. 1/507, p. 171.
36 R. Horsman, *op. cit.*, pp. 206–7.
37 Col. A. Brooke to Earl Bathurst, 17 September 1814, P.R.O., W.O. 1/141, pp. 75–84 and 91–8, and Rear Admiral G. Cockburn to Cochrane, 15 September 1814, P.R.O., Adm. 1/507, pp. 185–95 and 241–2.
38 Col. A. Brooke to Earl Bathurst, 17 September 1814, P.R.O., W.O. 1/141, p. 88.
39 Col. A. Brooke to Earl Bathurst, 9 October 1814; Lt. G. de Lacy Evans, 'Memorandum', 1 October 1814; report by Lt. Evans and Capt. J. Barney, 7 October 1814, P.R.O., W.O. 1/141, pp. 105, 113–14 and 121.
40 Earl Bathurst to Maj.-Gen. Ross, 6 September 1814, P.R.O., W.O. 1/142, pp. 495–501.
41 Admiral Cochrane to J. W. Croker, 28 December 1814, and Capt. Lockyer to Cochrane, 16 December 1814, P.R.O., Adm. 1/508, pp. 268–70 and 364–7.
42 R. Reilly, *op. cit.*, p.240.
43 Maj.-Gen. J. Keane to Maj.-Gen. Sir E. Pakenham, 26 December 1814, and 'Return of Casualties in the Army . . . on the 23rd December 1814', P.R.O., W.O. 1/141, pp. 149–56 and 179–81.
44 (Q. 794) *Evidence before the Select Committee on the Army Before Sebastopol: with proceedings of the committee*, C. 86 (1854–55), IX, p. 48. Sir A. S. MacNalty, *The British Medical Dictionary* (Caxton, London, 1961), p. 603.
45 Maj.-Gen. J. Lambert to Earl Bathurst, 10 January 1815, and 'Return of Casualties in the Army . . . on 8th January 1815', P.R.O., W.O. 1/141, pp. 137–46 and 220.
46 Maj.-Gen. J. Lambert to Earl Bathurst, 28 January 1815, P.R.O., W.O. 1/141, pp. 196–9.

Notes and references

47 Maj.-Gen. J. Lambert to Earl Bathurst, 14 February 1815, P.R.O., W.O. 1/141, pp. 259–63 and 267–8.
48 Compare De-Lacy Bellingari, *op. cit.*, p. 259, with A. Brett-James, *op. cit.*, p. 128. See also J. Philippart, *The Royal Military Calendar*, 5 vols. (Valpy, London, 1820), Vol. 5, p. 111.
49 *The Dispatches of Field-Marshal the Duke of Wellington*, ed. Lt.-Col. J. Gurwood, 8 vols. (John Murray, London, 1852), Vol. 8, pp. 142–3.
50 *Ibid.*, p. 144.
51 Col. Sir G. de Lacy Evans to Capt. H. T. Siborne, 14 October 1843, Waterloo Mss., B.L. Add. Mss. 34,708, f. 130.
52 *Ibid.*, ff. 130–1.
53 Col. Evans to Siborne, 1 September 1839, Waterloo Mss., B.L. Add. Mss. 34,707, f. 119.
54 Col. Evans to Siborne, n.d., Waterloo Mss., B.L. Add. Mss. 34,707, f. 124.
55 Col. Evans to Siborne, 1 September 1839, Waterloo Mss., B.L. Add. Mss. 34,707, f. 120.
56 Lt. Col. G. de Lacy Evans, *The reappearance of Buonaparte on the shores of France* (private, London, 1818), p. 11.
57 Col. Evans to Siborne, 1 September 1839, Waterloo Mss., B.L. Add. Mss. 34,707, f. 121.
58 Col. Evans to Siborne, 23 August 1842, Waterloo Mss., B.L. Add. Mss. 34,707, f. 392.
59 Sir G. de Lacy Evans, 'Memorandum to His Grace the Duke of Newcastle', p. 2.
60 *Ibid*.
61 J. H. Lehmann, *Remember you are an Englishman* (J. Cape, London, 1977), p. 126.
62 Sir G. de Lacy Evans, 'Memorandum to His Grace the Duke of Newcastle', p. 3.
63 *Ibid*, p. 2.
64 *The Daily News*, 6 July 1852, p. 5.

Chapter 2

1 On 20 October 1819 Evans transferred the £500 and the various farms and lands he had inherited from his father to Eliza Evans. Deed No. 507261, Registry of Deeds, Book 745, p. 326.
2 D. Le Marchant, diary, 9 December 1832, *Three Early Nineteenth Century Diaries*, ed. A. Aspinall (Williams & Norgate, London, 1952), p. 285.
3 Sir R. Wilson, *Sketch of the Military and Political Power of Russia in the Year 1817* (James Ridgway, London, 1817), p. vii, and J. H. Gleason, *The Genesis of Russophobia in Great Britain* (Harvard University Press, Cambridge, Mass., 1950), pp. 26–9 and 50–6.
4 C. K. Webster, *The Foreign Policy of Castlereagh*, 2 vols. (G. Bell, London, 1925), Vol. 2, pp. 237–40.

5   M. Anderson, 'Russia and the Eastern Question, 1821–41', *Europe's Balance of Power 1815–1848*, ed. A. Sked (Macmillan, London, 1979), pp. 80–5.
6   Lt.-Col. G. de Lacy Evans, *On the Designs of Russia* (John Murray, London, 1828), pp. 7–19.
7   *Ibid.*, p. 93.
8   *Ibid.*, p. 69. See also pp. 48, 51–2, 104, 115–18.
9   *Ibid.*, p. 175. See also pp. 151–3, 168–74, 240–4.
10 *Ibid.*, pp. 147–9, 199–206.
11 *Ibid.*, p. 165.
12 *The Times*, 22 August 1828, p. 2.
13 *The Times*, 23 August 1828, p. 2, and 11 September 1829, p. 2.
14 J. H. Gleason, *op. cit.*, p. 102.
15 *The Standard*, 25 August 1828, p. 2, and *The Globe*, 25 August 1828, p. 2.
16 *The Morning Chronicle*, 23 August 1828, p. 2, and 25 August 1828, p. 2.
17 *The Examiner*, 7 September 1828, p. 582.
18 *The Quarterly Review*, Vol. XXXIX, No. LXXVIII (January 1829), pp. 29–38.
19 *Dictionary of Anonymous and Pseudonymous English Literature*, ed. J. Kennedy, W. A. Smith and A. F. Johnson, 6 vols. (Oliver & Boyd, Edinburgh, 1926–32), Vol. 2, p. 284.
20 'A Non Alarmist', *A Few Words on our Relations with Russia including some remarks on a recent publication by Colonel De Lacy Evans* (Baldwin & Cradock, London, 1828), pp. 18–20.
21 *Ibid.*, p. 30.
22 *Ibid.*, p. 58. See also pp. 44–5 and 56–8.
23 Lt.-Col. G. de Lacy Evans, *On the Practicability of an Invasion of British India: and on the commercial and financial prospects and resources of the Empire* (J. M. Richardson, London, 1829), pp. xlix–1.
24 *Ibid.*, p. iii.
25 *Ibid.*, pp. 1–3.
26 *Ibid.*, pp. 12–16, 22, 25–36, 40–1, 45, 53–64, 70–2, 85–6.
27 *Ibid.*, pp. 86–101.
28 *A Political Diary 1828–1830 by Edward Law Lord Ellenborough*, ed. Lord Colchester, 2 vols. (R. Bentley, London, 1881), Vol. 2, p. 92.
29 *Ibid.*, Vol. 2, pp. 122 and 149–50.
30 *Ibid.*, Vol. 2, p. 150.
31 Lord Aberdeen to Lord Heytesbury, 23 December 1829, enclosing a questionnaire from the India Board, 18 December 1829, P.R.O., F[oreign] O[ffice] 181/79, No. 33, and Lord Heytesbury to Lord Aberdeen, 28 February and 11 March 1830, P.R.O., F.O. 65/185, Nos. 26 and 33.
32 Lord Colchester, *op. cit.*, Vol. 2, pp. 153 and 157.
33 Col. Sir J. McDonald, 'Remarks on Lieutenant Colonel Evans' late work on the Invasion of India', 11 March 1830, 'Memoranda on the North-West Frontier of British India and On the importance of the River Indus as connected with its Defence', B.L. Add. Mss. 21,178, ff. 34–5, 37,

49–51, 53. Colonel Kinneir remained on the Indian Army List under his middle name of McDonald; *Dictionary of National Biography*, Vol. 31, p. 192.
34 Col. Sir J. McDonald, *op. cit.*, ff. 35–6, 38, 54–9.
35 *Ibid.*, f. 59.
36 *Ibid.*, f. 61.
37 Sir J. Malcolm, 'Notes on the Invasion of India by Russia', 4 July 1830, B.L. Add. Mss. 21,178, ff. 71 and 73.
38 *Ibid.*, ff. 72–7.
39 T. Grzebieniowski, 'The Polish cause in England a century ago', *Slavonic Review*, Vol. 11 (1932–33), pp. 81–2.
40 *The Morning Post*, 1 January 1831, p. 2, and *The Standard*, 4 January 1831, p. 2.
41 *The Times*, 20 July 1831, p. 3, and 20 September 1831, p. 3.
42 Sir C. K. Webster, *The Foreign Policy of Palmerston, 1830–1841*, 2 vols. (G. Bell, London, 1951), Vol. 1, pp. 181–2.
43 Lord Palmerston to Lord Heytesbury, 21 March, 26 August 1831, enclosing a copy of a letter to Prince de Talleyrand, 22 July and 23 November 1831, P.R.O., F.O. 181/84, No. 11, /86, No. 40, and /87, No. 52.
44 See Chapter 3.
45 *The Morning Chronicle*, 7 March 1831, p. 1, and 10 March 1831, p. 1. See also Chapter 3.
46 *Parl[iamentary] Deb[ates]*, Third Ser[ies], Vol. V (8 August 1831), col. 932.
47 *Parl. Deb.*, Third Ser., Vol. VI (16 August 1831), cols. 101–10.
48 *Ibid.*, col. 101.
49 *Parl. Deb.*, Third Ser., Vol. VI (7 September 1831), cols. 1,216–18.
50 *Parl. Deb.*, Third Ser., Vol. VIII (13 October 1831), cols. 696–7.
51 Tadeusz Kosciusko (1746–1817) was the Polish army officer who led the national revolt against the Russians in 1794.
52 T. Grzebieniowski, *op. cit.*, pp. 82–3; *Memoirs of Prince Adam Czartoryski*, ed. A. Gielgud, 2 vols. (Remington, London, 1888), Vol. 2, p. 334; J. H. Gleason, *op. cit.*, p. 120.
53 T. Campbell to W. Gray, 7 March 1832, quoted in W. Beattie, *Life and Letters of Thomas Campbell*, 3 vols. (Hall Virtue & Co., London, 1850), Vol 3, p. 111.
54 *Parl. Deb.*, Third Ser., Vol. XIII (28 June 1832), cols. 1,138–9.
55 *Parl. Deb.*, Third Ser., Vol. XIV (7 August 1832), cols. 1,209–14.
56 Sir C. K. Webster, *The Foreign Policy of Palmerston, 1830–1841*, Vol. 1, pp. 150–1.
57 *Parl. Deb.*, Third Ser., Vol. XIV (7 August 1832), cols. 1,209–30.
58 *Parl. Deb.*, Third Ser., Vol. XIX (9 July 1833), cols. 394–465, and J. H. Gleason, *op. cit.*, pp. 125–9.
59 *Parl. Deb.*, Third Ser., Vol. XIV (7 August 1832), col. 1,213. For the pertinence of this supposition, at least in its timing, see Sir C. K. Webster, *The Foreign Policy of Palmerston 1830–1841*, Vol. 1, p. 189.
60 *Parl. Deb.*, Third Ser., Vol. XXII (25 March 1834), cols. 651–3.

61 C. Bartlett, 'Britain and the European balance, 1815–48' in A. Sked, *op. cit.*, pp. 153–5.
62 *Parl. Deb.*, Third Ser., Vol. XX (24 August 1833), col. 873.
63 *Parl. Deb.*, Third Ser., Vol. XIX (11 July 1833), cols. 582–3.
64 *The Morning Herald*, 21 August 1833, p. 5.
65 *Parl. Deb.*, Third Ser., Vol. XX (24 August 1833), cols. 872–6.
66 *Parl. Deb.*, Third Ser., Vol. XX (29 August 1833), col. 903.
67 *The Morning Herald*, 16 October 1833, p. 3.
68 M. Anderson, 'Russia and the Eastern Question, 1821–41', in A. Sked, *op. cit.*, p. 91.
69 *Parl. Deb.*, Third Ser., Vol. XXI (4 February 1834), col. 57.
70 *Parl. Deb.*, Third Ser., Vol. XXII (17 March 1834), cols. 307–32.
71 Lord Palmerston to Earl Granville, 3 December 1833, B[roadlands] P[apers] GC/GR/1500/2.
72 J. H. Gleason, *op. cit.*, pp. 153–271; G. Robinson, *David Urquhart* (Blackwell, Oxford, 1920); G. H. Bolsover, 'David Urquhart and the Eastern Question, 1833–37: a study in publicity and diplomacy', *Journal of Modern History*, Vol. VIII, No. 4 (December 1936), pp. 444–67.

Chapter 3

1 *Parl. Deb.*, Third Ser., Vol. XXII (26th March 1834), col. 725.
2 *The Hastings and Cinque Ports Iris*, 23 October 1830, p. 2.
3 *Brighton Guardian and Lewes Free Press*, 23 June 1830, p. 4.
4 *The Hastings and Cinque Ports Iris*, 23 October 1830, p. 2.
5 *The Times*, 4 March 1830, p. 5.
6 *Brighton Guardian and Lewes Free Press*, 23 June 1830, pp. 3–4.
7 *Brighton Guardian and Lewes Free Press*, 11 August 1830, pp. 2–4.
8 M. R. Brock, *The Great Reform Act* (Hutchinson, London, 1973), pp. 86–9, 98–100, 103–5.
9 *Brighton Guardian and Lewes Free Press*, 29 September 1830, p. 3.
10 *The Hastings and Cinque Ports Iris*, 23 October 1830, p. 2.
11 *The Hastings and Cinque Ports Iris*, 13 November 1830, p. 1, and 1 January 1831, p. 1.
12 *The Hastings and Cinque Ports Iris*, 1 January 1831, p. 3.
13 *The Hastings and Cinque Ports Iris*, 29 January 1831, p. 3.
14 *The Hastings and Cinque Ports Iris*, 5 February 1831, p. 3.
15 *The Hastings and Cinque Ports Iris*, 23 October 1830, p. 2, and 5 February 1831, p. 3.
16 M. R. Brock, *op. cit.*, pp. 136–52.
17 *The Hastings and Cinque Ports Iris*, 5 March 1831, p. 4.
18 *Ibid.*, p. 3.
19 *Morning Advertiser*, 5 March 1831, p. 4.
20 *The Hastings and Cinque Ports Iris*, 12 March 1831, p. 4.
21 F. Place to Sir J. C. Hobhouse, 24 April and 7 May 1831, Broughton Mss., B.L. Add. Mss. 36,466, ff. 317 and 333.

22 W. Holloway, *The History and Antiquities of the Ancient Town and Port of Rye, in the county of Sussex* (John Russell Smith, London, 1847), p. 265.
23 *The Hastings and Cinque Ports Iris*, 21 May 1831, p. 3. See also *Brighton Guardian and Lewes Free Press*, 4 May 1831, p. 3, and *The Hastings and Cinque Ports Iris*, 30 April 1831, p. 3, and 7 May 1831, p. 3.
24 *Brighton Guardian and Lewes Free Press*, 18 May 1831, p. 3.
25 *Brighton Guardian and Lewes Free Press*, 16 November 1831, p. 4.
26 *Brighton Guardian and Lewes Free Press*, 14 September 1831, p. 3. See also 7 March 1832, p. 3, and 5 September 1832, p. 4.
27 *Parl. Deb.*, Third Ser., Vol. VI (22 August 1831), col. 383; Vol. VIII (13 October 1831), cols. 696–7.
28 *Parl. Deb.*, Third Ser., Vol. XX (29 July 1833), col. 76.
29 *Parl. Deb.*, Third Ser., Vol. IV (27 June 1831), col. 395, and Vol. VII (3 October 1831), cols. 1,027–8.
30 *Parl. Deb.*, Third Ser., Vol. VIII (10 October 1831), cols. 449–50. See also Vol. VII (4 October 1831), cols. 1,209–11.
31 E. J. Hobsbawm and G. Rudé, *Captain Swing* (Lawrence & Wishart, London, 1969), p. 116.
32 *The Times*, 16 July 1831, pp. 2–3, and *The Examiner*, 24 July 1831, p. 465. See also A. M. Colson, 'The Revolt of the Hampshire Agricultural Labourers and its Causes 1812–1831', unpublished M.A. thesis (University of London, 1937), pp. 250–1.
33 *Parl. Deb.*, Third Ser., Vol. V (21 July 1831), cols. 146–60.
34 T. Deacle to the editor, *The Morning Chronicle*, 22 September 1831, p. 1.
35 *Parl. Deb.*, Third Ser., Vol. VII (27 September 1831), cols. 687–701.
36 *Parl. Deb.*, Third Ser., Vol. V (21 July 1831), col. 164.
37 *Ibid.*, cols. 146–7.
38 *Parl. Deb.*, Third Ser., Vol. VI (22 August 1831), col. 380.
39 *The Morning Chronicle*, 22 September 1831, p. 4. Like many others, Evans simply assumed that William IV favoured Reform, an assumption which had little foundation. M. R. Brock, *op. cit.*, p. 202.
40 *The Morning Herald*, 11 October 1831, p. 4, and the *Morning Advertiser*, 1 November 1831, p. 2. See also Lt.-Col. George de Lacy Evans, *A Letter to the Electors of Westminster* (Dalton, London, 1833), p. 22.
41 *The Morning Chronicle*, 8 November 1831, p. 2.
42 *Brighton Guardian and Lewes Free Press*, 2 December 1831, p. 3.
43 *Parl. Deb.*, Third Ser., Vol. XIV (26 July 1832), col. 779. See also Vol. XI (28 March 1832), col. 1,039, and Vol. XIII (19 June 1832), col. 894.
44 *Parl. Deb.*, Third Ser., Vol. XIV (2 August 1832), cols. 1,059–60. See also R. Bullen, 'Party politics and foreign policy: Whigs, Tories and Iberian affairs, 1830–6', *Bulletin of the Institute of Historical Research*, Vol. LI, No. 123 (May 1978), pp. 38–9.
45 *The Morning Chronicle*, 12 May 1832, p. 3.
46 *Parl. Deb.*, Third Ser., Vol. XII (23 May 1832), col. 1,411.

47 *Parl. Deb.*, Third Ser., Vol. XIV (9 and 11 August 1832), cols. 1,291–3 and 1,330.
48 N. Gash, *Politics in the Age of Peel* (Longman, London 1953), pp. 218 and 432; W. Holloway, *op. cit.*, p. 269.
49 *Brighton Guardian and Lewes Free Press*, 19 December 1832, p. 4. See also *Parl. Deb.*, Third Ser., Vol. XXII (26 March 1834), col. 725, and W. Holloway, *op. cit.*, p. 270.
50 R. E. Zegger, *John Cam Hobhouse: a political life, 1819–1852* (University of Missouri Press, Columbia, 1973), pp. 199–201.
51 *The Times*, 20 November 1832, p. 3.
52 *Morning Advertiser*, 21 November 1832, p. 2.
53 *The Morning Chronicle*, 23 November 1832, p. 3.
54 *An Authentic Report of Proceedings at a meeting of the electors of the parishes of St. Paul, Covent Garden, St. Clement Danes, and St. Mary-le-Strand, held at the Crown & Anchor Tavern, Strand, on Monday, December 3, 1832, to hear Colonel Evans state his political opinions, and the course he would pursue as a Member of Parliament, if returned for Westminster* (W. Barnes, London, 1832), pp. 19 and 31. See also *Morning Advertiser*, 28 November 1832, p. 3.
55 Sir D. Le Marchant, diary, 9 December 1832, *Three Early Nineteenth Century Diaries*, ed. A. Aspinall, p. 284.
56 *Ibid.*, and *Recollections of a Long Life by Lord Broughton*, ed. Lady Dorchester, 6 vols. (John Murray, London, 1909–11), Vol. 4, pp. 263–4.
57 Lt.-Col. G. de Lacy Evans, *A Letter to the Electors of Westminster*, pp. 32–3.
58 *The Morning Chronicle*, 4 May 1833, p. 1.
59 Lady Dorchester, *op. cit.*, vol. 4, p. 310.
60 *Ibid.*, and *The Morning Chronicle*, 8 May 1833, p. 2.
61 *The Morning Chronicle*, 13 May 1833, p. 3.
62 R. E. Zegger, *op. cit.*, p. 208.
63 *Morning Advertiser*, 10 May 1833, p. 2, and *The Freeman's Journal*, 13 May 1833, p. 2.
64 *The Morning Chronicle*, 13 May 1833, p. 3.
65 *The Morning Chronicle*, 30 May 1833, p. 2.
66 *Parl. Deb.*, Third Ser., Vol. XVIII (20 June 1833), cols. 1,020–1. See also S. Dowell, *A History of Taxation and Taxes in England*, 4 vols. (Longman, London, 1888), Vol. 2, pp. 303–4, and S. Buxton, *Finance and Politics*, 2 vols. (John Murray, London, 1888), Vol. 1, pp. 96–7.
67 F. Place to Lt.-Col. Evans, 24th July 1832, Place Mss., B.L. Add. Mss. 35,149, f. 135.
68 *Parl. Deb.*, Third Ser., Vol. XVIII (21 May 1833), cols. 24–5.
69 *Parl. Deb.*, Third Ser., Vol. XVIII (20 June 1833), col. 1,020.
70 *Parl. Deb.*, Third Ser., Vol. XIX (3 July 1833), col. 70; Vol. XXI (13 February 1834), col. 269; *The Morning Chronicle*, 25 February 1834, p. 2.
71 *The Times*, 29 October 1833, p. 3 and *The Morning Chronicle*, 29 October 1833, p. 3, and 25 February 1834, p. 2.

72 *The Morning Chronicle*, 8 February 1834, p. 2.
73 *Parl. Deb.*, Third Ser., Vol. XVIII (24 May 1833), col. 94; Vol. XIX (23 July 1833), col. 1,139; Vol. XXIV (19 June 1834), col. 562.
74 *Parl. Deb.*, Third Ser., Vol. XVIII (27 June 1833), col. 1,261.
75 *Parl. Deb.*, Third Ser., Vol. XX (22 August 1833), col. 836.
76 *The Manchester and Salford Advertiser*, 16 November 1833, p. 4.
77 *The Manchester and Salford Advertiser*, 30 November 1833, p. 3, and *The Poor Man's Guardian*, 30 November 1833, p. 386.
78 *The Morning Chronicle*, 19 April 1834, p. 1.
79 *Parl. Deb.*, Third Ser., Vol. XXIII (28 April 1834), cols. 121 and 126; *The Globe*, 29 April 1834, p. 4.
80 *Parl. Deb.*, Third Ser., Vol. XXII (11 March 1834), col. 7, and Vol. XXIII (6 May 1834), col. 619.
81 *Parl. Deb.*, Third Ser., Vol. XXII (14 March 1834), col. 253; Vol. XXV (21 July 1834), cols. 283–4, and (8 August 1834), col. 1,102.
82 *Parl. Deb.*, Third Ser., Vol. XXIII (9 May 1834), cols. 805–7.
83 *The Morning Chronicle*, 16 May 1834, p. 3.
84 *The Morning Chronicle*, 3 December 1834, p. 3.
85 *The Morning Chronicle*, 25 December 1834, p. 3.
86 *The Morning Chronicle*, 7 January 1835, pp. 1–2.
87 *Morning Advertiser*, 12 January 1835, p. 3.
88 N. Gash, *Sir Robert Peel* (Longman, London, 1972), p. 101.
89 *Parl. Deb.*, Third Ser., Vol. XXVII (6 April 1835), cols. 834–5.
90 *Morning Advertiser*, 16 February 1835, p. 3.
91 *The Morning Chronicle*, 23 April 1835, p. 3.
92 (Qq 565–660, esp. q. 597) *Evidence Before His Majesty's Commissioners for inquiring into the System of Military Punishments in the Army*, C. 59 (1836), XXII.
93 G. Villiers to Lord Palmerston, 7 and 22 June 1835, B[roadlands] P[apers] GC/CL/190 and 193, and Col. J. Gurwood to Lord Fitzroy, 15 April 1835, quoted in Lord St Germans, *Papers Relating to Lord Eliot's Mission to Spain* (private, London, 1871), pp. 110–12.
94 Lord Palmerston to Villiers, 11 February 1834, B.P., GC/CL/1219.
95 R. Bullen, *op. cit.*, pp. 48 and 55–6.
96 *Parl. Deb.*, Third Ser., Vol. XXVIII (24 June 1835), cols. 1,137–8.
97 Lord Palmerston to G. Villiers, 16 June 1835, B.P., GC/CL/1240. See also P. F. Janke, 'Mendizábal and the Development of Liberalism in the Iberian Peninsula 1833–1843', unpublished D.Phil thesis (University of Oxford, 1972), p. 180.
98 *Parl. Deb.*, Third Ser., Vol. XVIII (6 June 1833), col. 441, and Vol. XXI (4 February 1834), col. 56.
99 *The Morning Chronicle*, 7 January 1835, pp. 1–2.
100 *Gentleman's Magazine*, New Series, 2 (1834), p. 208. For details of Josette Arbuthnot's wealth, see her will in *The Illustrated London News*, 22 June 1861, p. 577.
101 *Parl. Deb.*, Third Ser., Vol. XXVIII (24 June 1835), cols. 1152–3, and Col. Sir George de Lacy Evans, *Memoranda of the Contest in Spain* (J. Ridgway, London, 1840), p. 23.

Chapter 4

1. A. Somerville, *History of the British Legion, and War in Spain* (James Pattie, London, 1839), p. 276.
2. R. Alcock, *Notes on the Medical History and Statistics of the British Legion in Spain* (John Churchill, London, 1838), pp. 6–7.
3. *Parl. Deb.*, Third Ser., Vol. XXVIII (15 June 1835), col. 780, and G. Villiers to Earl Granville, 13 July 1835, B.P., GC/CL/197.
4. A. Somerville, *op. cit.*, p. 6.
5. R. Alcock, *op. cit.*, p. 4.
6. Col. Evans, *Memoranda*, p. 26.
7. Lord Palmerston to Villiers, 9 July 1835, B.P., GC/CL/1242.
8. Villiers to Lord Palmerston, 9 August 1835, B.P., GC/CL/200.
9. C. F. Henningsen, *The Most Striking Events of a Twelvemonth's Campaign with Zumalacarregui in Navarre & the Basque Provinces*, 2 vols. (John Murray, London, 1836), Vol. 2, p. 287.
10. Villiers to Lord Palmerston, 3 November 1835, B.P., GC/CL/218.
11. Villiers to Lord Palmerston, 1 August 1835, B.P., GC/CL/199.
12. Villiers to Lord Palmerston, 22 August 1835, B.P., GC/CL/202.
13. Evans to Villiers, 23 August 1835, Clarendon Mss., Bodleian Library, Oxford, C-460.
14. Evans to Lord Palmerston, 9 September, 1835, P.R.O., F.O. 72/446.
15. Evans to Villiers, 24 September 1835, Clarendon Mss., C-460.
16. Evans to Lord Palmerston, 30 September 1835, B.P., GC/EV/2/1.
17. Evans to Villiers, 9 November 1835, Clarendon Mss., C-460. See also J. F. Bacon, *Six Years in Biscay* (Smith Elder & Co., London, 1838), pp. 287–93.
18. Evans to Villiers, 9 November 1835, Clarendon Mss., C-460.
19. Evans to Villiers, 9 and 11 November 1835, Clarendon Mss., C-460, and Villiers to Lord Palmerston, 16 November 1835, B.P., GC/CL/223.
20. Evans to Villiers, 6 December 1835, Clarendon Mss., C-460. See also Villiers to Lord Palmerston, 13 December 1835, Clarendon Mss., C-442.
21. Evans to Villiers, 2 January 1836, Clarendon Mss., C-460. See also R. Alcock, *op. cit.*, pp. 13–15, and *A Concise Account of the British Auxiliary Legion by a Volunteer in the Queen's Service* (Ainsworth, London, 1837), pp. 7–9.
22. R. Alcock, *op. cit.*, pp. 16–28.
23. Col. W. Wylde to Lord Palmerston, 13 January 1836, No. 55, P.R.O., F.O. 72/464.
24. A. Somerville, *op. cit.*, p. 304.
25. Col. C. Shaw to T. G. Shaw, 30 January 1835, in Col. C. Shaw, *Personal Memoirs and Correspondence*, 2 vols. (Colburn, London, 1837), Vol. 2, p. 491.
26. Col. Wylde to Lord Palmerston, 9 and 28 February 1836, Nos. 58 and 59, P.R.O., F.O. 72/464.
27. Villiers to Lord Palmerston, 13 February 1836, B.P., GC/CL/241.

28 Villiers to Lord Palmerston, 27 February 1836, B.P., GC/CL/244.
29 Col. de la Saussaye to Villiers, 1 April 1836, Clarendon Mss., C-463.
30 *The Times*, 22 April 1836, p. 6. See also Evans to Lord Palmerston, 19 December 1836, B.P., GC/EV/22/1.
31 Villiers to Lord Palmerston, 7 March 1836, Clarendon Mss., C-443.
32 Maj.-Gen. G. N. Wood, 'Evans and the British Legion in Spain', *Army Quarterly and Defence Journal*, Vol. 14, No. 2 (January 1974), p. 219.
33 Villiers to Lord Palmerston, 12 March 1836, B.P., GC/CL/246, and Villiers to E. Villiers, 1 April 1837, Clarendon Mss., C-467.
34 Evans to Villiers, 19 March 1836, Clarendon Mss., C-460. See also Col. Evans, *Memoranda*, pp. 41–2.
35 General F. F. de Córdoba, *Mis memorias intimas*, 3 vols. (Madrid, 1886), Vol. 2, p. 295. See also E. Christiansen, *The Origins of Military Power in Spain 1800–1854* (Oxford University Press, Oxford, 1967), p. 75.
36 Villiers to Lord Palmerston, 12 March 1836, B.P., GC/CL/246.
37 J. Mendizábal to Lord Palmerston, 6 March 1836, B.P., GC/ME/581.
38 Evans to Villiers, 25 March 1836, Clarendon Mss., C-460.
39 Evans to Villiers, 2 and 13 January 1836, Clarendon Mss., C-460.
40 Evans to Villiers, 20 February, 25 and 31 March 1836, Clarendon Mss., C-460; Col. C. Shaw, *op. cit.*, Vol. 2, p. 508; Col. de la Saussaye to Villiers, 1 April 1836, Clarendon Mss., C-463.
41 Evans to Villiers, 15 and 20 February 1836, Clarendon Mss., C-460.
42 Evans to Villiers, 23 February 1836, Clarendon Mss., C-460.
43 Evans to Villiers, 19 January 1836, Clarendon Mss., C-460; Wylde to Villiers, 6 March 1836, enclosed in Villiers to Lord Palmerston, 7 March 1836, No. 53, P.R.O., F.O. 72/458.
44 Evans to Villiers, 26 and 31 January 1836, Clarendon Mss., C-460, and Evans to Lord Palmerston, 6 May 1836, B.P., GC/EV/4/1.
45 Evans to Villiers, 19 September and 11 December 1835, and 20 March 1836, Clarendon Mss., C-460.
46 Evans to Villiers, 16 February, 25 March and 19 April 1836, Clarendon Mss., C-460.
47 Villiers to Lord Palmerston, 27 February 1836, B.P., GC/CL/244, and Evans to Villiers, 26 January 1836, Clarendon Mss., C-460.
48 Evans to Villiers, 20 March 1836, Clarendon Mss., C-460.
49 Gen. Córdoba to Evans, 21 March 1836, Evans to Córdoba, 28 March 1836, and Evans to Villiers, 31 March 1836, Clarendon Mss., C-460.
50 Evans to Villiers, 15 April 1836, B.P., GC/CL/256.
51 Evans to Villiers, 11 April 1836, Clarendon Mss., C-460.
52 Lord John Hay to Villiers, 27 April 1836, Clarendon Mss., C-459. See also Evans to Villiers, 11 April 1836, Clarendon Mss., C-460.
53 Villiers to Lord Palmerston, 23 April 1836, No. 100, Clarendon Mss., C-443.
54 Evans to Count Almodovar, 5 May 1836, and Col. Wylde to Lord Palmerston, 6 and 12 May 1836, Nos. 66 and 68, P.R.O., F.O. 72/464.
55 A. Somerville, *op. cit.*, p. 30.

56 Col. Shaw to T. G. Shaw, 3 May 1836 cited in Col. Shaw, *op. cit.*, Vol. 2, pp. 556–7.
57 Col. de la Saussaye to Villiers, 7 and 16 May 1836, B.P., GC/CL/260, and Clarendon Mss., C-463.
58 Col. Wylde to Lord Palmerston, 6 May 1836, No. 66, P.R.O., F.O. 72/464.
59 Lord John Hay to Villiers, 5 May 1836, Clarendon Mss., C-459.
60 Evans to Villiers, 5 and 10 May 1836, Clarendon Mss., C-460.
61 Villiers to Lord Palmerston, 15 May 1836, B.P., GC/CL/260.
62 Villiers to Lord Palmerston, 4 June 1836, B.P., GC/CL/266. See also his letters to Lord Palmerston, 15 and 29 May 1836, B.P., GC/CL/260 and /264.
63 Evans to Lord Palmerston, 23 May 1836, B.P., GC/EV/6/1.
64 Lord Palmerston to Villiers, 11 May and 2 June 1836, and Villiers to Lord Palmerston, 18 June 1836, B.P., GC/CL/1261, /1262 and /268.
65 Evans to Lord Palmerston, 26 May 1836, B.P., GC/EV/7.
66 Evans to the Minister at War, 28 May 1836, Clarendon Mss., C-460.
67 Evans to Lord Palmerston, 14 June 1836, B.P., GC/EV/9, and Evans to Villiers, 13 June 1836, Clarendon Mss., C-461.
68 Col. Wylde to Lord Palmerston, 30 June 1836, No. 76, P.R.O., F.O. 72/464, and Evans to Lord Palmerston, 17 July 1836, B.P., GC/EV/13.
69 Evans to General Córdoba, 12 July 1836, and Col. Wylde to Lord Palmerston, 13 July 1836, No. 79, P.R.O., F.O. 72/464.
70 Evans to Lord Palmerston, 14 June 1836, B.P., GC/EV/9; A. Somerville, *op. cit.*, p. 38; and Col. C. Field, *Britain's Sea Soldiers*, 2 vols. (Lyceum Press, London, 1924), Vol. 2, p. 34.
71 Evans to Villiers, 30 May, 19 and 22 June 1836, Clarendon Mss., C-460; Evans to Lord Palmerston, 14 June 1836, and to Istúriz, 12 June 1836, B.P., GC/EV/9 and GC/EV/9/enc. 3.
72 Villiers to Lord Palmerston, 29 June 1836, B.P., GC/CL/272.
73 Villiers to Lord Palmerston, 18 and 23 June and 16 July 1836, B.P., GC/CL/268, /270 and /276. See also P. F. Janke, *op. cit.*, pp. 181–3.
74 A. Somerville, *op. cit.*, pp. 109–10.
75 See the marginalia of 'P' on Evans to Lord Palmerston, 14 June 1836, B.P., GC/EV/9.
76 Col. Shaw, *op. cit.*, Vol. 2, pp. 613–14 and 626–7.
77 *Army List of the British Legion in Spain* (May 1836), p. 29.
78 Evans to Villiers, 4 July 1836, Clarendon Mss., C-461, and Evans to Lord Palmerston, 4 July 1836, B.P., GC/EV/12.
79 General Order, 23 July 1836, Clarendon Mss., 461. See also Villiers to Lord Palmerston, 12 and 16 July 1836, B.P., GC/CL/275, and Clarendon Mss., C-444.
80 Evans to Villiers, 24 July 1836, Clarendon Mss., C-461. See also C. Chichester, diary, 22 August 1836, Chichester Mss., University of Hull.
81 Evans to Lord Palmerston, 10 August 1836, B.P., GC/EV/14. See also A. Somerville, *op. cit.*, pp. 141–9. Evans to Villiers, 28 July, 30 July

and 'July' 1836, Clarendon Mss., C-461; Wylde to Lord Palmerston, 28 July and 8 August 1836, Nos. 81 and 82, P.R.O., F.O. 72/464.
82 Evans to Lord Palmerston, 30 August 1836, B.P., GC/EV/18.
83 Villiers to Lord Palmerston, 31 August and 21 September 1836, Clarendon Mss., C-444. See also Evans to Villiers, 27 September 1836, Clarendon Mss., C-461.
84 Evans to Villiers, 5 September 1836, Clarendon Mss., C-461. See also Evans to Lord Palmerston, 9 September 1836, B.P., GC/EV/19, and Wylde to Lord Palmerston, 18 September 1836, No. 86, P.R.O., F.O. 72/464.
85 Wylde to Lord Palmerston, 1 October 1836, No. 88, P.R.O., F.O. 72/464.
86 A. Somerville, *op. cit.*, pp. 167–8.
87 Evans to Lord Palmerston, 5 October 1836, and Lord Palmerston to Evans, 13 October 1836, B.P., GC/EV/20 and /53. Villiers to Lord Palmerston, 15 October 1836, Clarendon Mss., C-444. Col. Evans, *Memoranda*, pp. 50–1. See also Evans to Lord Palmerston, 5 November 1836, P.R.O., F.O. 72/468.
88 Letters to Evans from Brigadier-Generals Chichester, Le Marchant, Godfrey and Fitzgerald, Colonels Jochmus and de Lancey, and Don Mateo Llanos, P.R.O., F.O. 72/464.
89 Evans to his senior officers, 31 October 1836, and to Lord Palmerston, 1 November 1836, P.R.O., F.O. 72/464.
90 Evans to Lord Palmerston, 1 November 1836, P.R.O., F.O. 72/464, and to Villiers, 3 November 1836, Clarendon Mss., C-461.
91 Wylde to Lord Palmerston, 6 November 1836, No. 91, P.R.O., F.O. 72/464.
92 Lord Palmerston to Evans, 17 November and 12 December 1836, B.P., GC/EV/54 and /57, and Evans to Villiers, 24 November 1836, Clarendon Mss., C-461.
93 Villiers to Lord Palmerston, 19 and 26 November and 3 December 1836, B.P., GC/CL/305, /306 and /307.
94 Evans to Lord Palmerston, 14 and 19 December 1836, B.P., GC/EV/21 and /22. See also Lord John Hay to Villiers, 6 January 1837, Clarendon Mss., C-459.
95 Evans to Villiers, 13 December 1836, Clarendon Mss., C-461.
96 Evans to Villiers, 23 December 1836 and 28 January 1837, Clarendon Mss., C-461.
97 Evans to Villiers, 1 and 20 January 1837, Clarendon Mss., C-461, and Evans to Lord Palmerston, 3 and 10 January 1837, B.P., GC/EV/25 and /26.
98 Lord Palmerston to Evans, 18 January 1837, B.P., GC/EV/59.
99 Evans to Villiers, 28 January 1837, Clarendon Mss., C-461, and Villiers to Lord Palmerston, 28 January 1837, No. 33, Clarendon Mss., C-445.
100 Evans to Villiers, 9 February 1837, Clarendon Mss., C-461, and Evans to Lord Palmerston, 15 February 1837, B.P., GC/EV/28.
101 General Saarsfield to Evans, 21 February 1837, Clarendon Mss., C-

102 461.
102 Evans to Lord Palmerston, 2 March 1837, B.P., GC/EV/29.
103 Col. Evans, *Memoranda*, pp. 76–7.
104 Evans to the Minister at War, 16 March 1837, Clarendon Mss., C-461.
105 Evans to Lord Palmerston, 21 March 1837, B.P., GC/EV/30, and Lord John Hay to Villiers, 20 March 1837, Clarendon Mss., C-459.
106 Col. Evans, *Memoranda*, pp. 80–1.
107 Villiers to Lord Palmerston, 25 March 1837, B.P., GC/CL/324.
108 Villiers to E. Villiers, 1 April 1837, Clarendon Mss., C-467, f. 129.
109 Villiers to Lord Palmerston, 25 March and 1 April 1837, Clarendon Mss., C-445.
110 Evans to Villiers, 25 and 30 March, 5 April 1837, Clarendon Mss., C-461.
111 Villiers to Lord Palmerston, 8 April 1837, B.P., GC/CL/327.
112 Evans to Villiers, 5 and 10 April 1837, Clarendon Mss., C-461.
113 Villiers to E. Villiers, 13 May 1837, Clarendon Mss., C-467, f. 151, and Villiers to Lord Palmerston, 22 April 1837, Clarendon Mss., C-445.
114 Evans to Villiers, 30 March and 2 April 1837, Clarendon Mss., C-461.
115 Evans to Villiers, 18 April 1837, Clarendon Mss., C-461.
116 Evans to Lord Palmerston, 20 April 1837, B.P., GC/EV/31.
117 Col. Evans, *Memoranda*, p. 97.
118 A. Somerville, *op. cit.*, p. 107. *A Concise Account*, *op. cit.*, pp. 44–7.
119 Evans to Villiers, 18 May 1837, Clarendon Mss., C-461.
120 Villiers to Lord Palmerston, 28 May 1837, No. 138, Clarendon Mss., C-445.
121 Lord Palmerston to Evans, 16 June 1837, B.P., GC/EV/62.
122 Villiers to Lord Palmerston, 18 June 1837, B.P., GC/CL/338.
123 Evans to Villiers, 9 June 1837. See also Evans to Villiers, 5 and 18 June and 11 July 1837, Clarendon Mss., C-461.
124 R. Alcock, *op. cit.*, p. 9.
125 Col. Evans, *Memoranda*, p. 135.
126 Evans to Villiers, 25 March 1837, Clarendon Mss., C-461.
127 Evans to Villiers, 23 May 1837, Clarendon Mss., C-461.
128 Evans to Villiers, 18 April 1837, Clarendon Mss., C-461.
129 Evans to Villiers, 18 June 1837, Clarendon Mss., C-461.

Chapter 5

1 Evans to Villiers, 18 June and 11 July 1837, Clarendon Mss., C-461.
2 N. Gash, *Reaction and Reconstruction in English Politics 1832–1852* (Oxford University Press, Oxford, 1965), pp. 142–3.
3 *The Morning Post*, 13 June 1835, p. 4.
4 *Ibid.*, and *The Morning Post*, 23 September 1835, p. 2.
5 *The Morning Post*, 24 September 1835, p. 2, and 25 September 1835, p. 2.
6 'General Evans' [from *The Courier*], *The Morning Chronicle*, 25

September 1835, p. 2.
7 *The Morning Post*, 28 October 1835, p. 2; *The Times*, 12 May 1836, p. 2, and 14 May 1836, p. 5.
8 *Parl. Deb.*, Third Ser., Vol. XXXI (12 February 1836), col. 316, and Vol. XXXIII (22 April 1836), cols. 114–16; *The Morning Chronicle*, 25 April 1836, p. 5.
9 See Chapter 3, and *The Poor Man's Guardian*, 27 June 1835, pp. 575–8.
10 *The Times*, 22 April 1836, p. 6.
11 *The Times*, 30 April 1836, p. 4. See also *The Times*, 22 April 1836, p. 5, 25 April 1836, p. 4, 11 November 1836, p. 3, 10 February 1837, p. 4, and *The Morning Post*, 22 April 1836, p. 3.
12 *Parl. Deb.*, Third Ser., Vol. XXXVII (17 April 1837), cols. 1,329–53.
13 *The Times*, 3 July 1837, p. 4.
14 M. W. Patterson, *Sir Francis Burdett and his Times 1770–1844*, 2 vols. (Macmillan, London, 1931), Vol. 2, pp. 648–9.
15 *Morning Advertiser*, 4 July 1837, p. 3, and 6 July 1837, p. 3.
16 *Morning Advertiser*, 6 July 1837, p. 3, and *The Morning Chronicle*, 18 July 1837, p. 3.
17 *The Morning Chronicle*, 13 July 1837, p. 3.
18 *Ibid.*, *Morning Advertiser*, 4 July 1837, p. 3, and 19 July 1837, p. 3. These disclaimers may not have been entirely true. Chichester records that Evans ordered him to flog some soldiers who looted on the march to Vitoria. C. Chichester, diary, 7 November 1835, Chichester Mss.
19 *Morning Advertiser*, 4 July 1837, p. 3, and 12 July 1837, p. 3.
20 *The Morning Post*, 19 July 1837, pp. 1–2.
21 *Morning Advertiser*, 12 July 1837, p. 3, and *The Morning Chronicle*, 20 July 1837, p. 1.
22 *The Morning Chronicle*, 13 July 1837, p. 3, and 20 July 1837, p. 1; *Morning Advertiser*, 19 July 1837, p. 3.
23 *The Morning Chronicle*, 14 July 1837, p. 3, 18 July 1837, p. 3, 22 July 1837, p. 1.
24 *Morning Advertiser*, 12 July 1837, p. 3, and 19 July 1837, p. 3; *The Morning Chronicle*, 14 July 1837, p. 3, and 22 July 1837, p. 1.
25 *The Morning Chronicle*, 25 July 1837, p. 2.
26 *Morning Advertiser*, 26 July 1837, pp. 1–2.
27 'Abstract of the Poll in the various parishes at the late Westminster Elections', *Westminster Election: a Poll* (J. Oliver, London, 1841).
28 *Morning Advertiser*, 4 July 1837, p. 3.
29 N. Gash, *Reaction and Reconstruction in English Politics 1832–1852*, pp. 172–3, and G. K. Clark, *Peel and the Conservative Party: a study in party politics 1832–1841* (F. Cass, London, 1964), p. 363.
30 *The Morning Chronicle*, 29 July 1837, p. 3.
31 Villiers to Lord Palmerston, 28 October 1837, B.P., GC/CL/362.
32 *Parl. Deb.*, Third Ser., Vol. XXXIX (21 November 1837), cols. 113–14, and (12 December 1837), cols. 1,003–4.
33 *The Morning Chronicle*, 30 December 1837, pp. 2 and 3.
34 *The Morning Chronicle*, 21 December 1837, p. 3, and 15 June 1839, p. 6.

35 Evans to Lord Palmerston, 29 January 1838, B.P., GC/EV/35/1.
36 *Morning Advertiser*, 22 February 1838, pp. 2–3.
37 *The Times*, 24 February 1838, p. 4.
38 *Parl. Deb.*, Third Ser., Vol. XLI (23 February 1838), cols. 53–8.
39 *The Morning Chronicle*, 24 February, 1838, p. 3, *The Times*, 24 February 1838, p. 4, *The Standard*, 24 February 1838, p. 2, and *The Morning Post*, 24 February 1838, p. 3.
40 *The Morning Post*, 27 March 1838, p. 3, and *Parl. Deb.*, Third Ser., Vol. XLI (26 March 1838), cols. 1,282–9.
41 *Parl. Deb.*, Third Ser., Vol. XLI (13 March 1838), cols. 823–44.
42 Compare *The Times*, 14 March 1838, p. 5, and *The Morning Post*, 14 March 1838, p. 3, with *Morning Advertiser*, 14 March 1838, p. 3, and *The Morning Chronicle*, 14 March 1838, p. 4.
43 *Parl. Deb.*, Third Ser., Vol. XLI (13 March 1838), cols. 844–62.
44 Alexander Somerville, in particular, wrote a fairly dispassionate account of the Legion which praised Evans for many of his actions.
45 *Parl. Deb.*, Third Ser., Vol. XLI (13 March 1838), cols. 872–4, and (26 March 1838), cols. 1,266–76.
46 *Morning Advertiser*, 28 March 1838, p. 3.
47 *The Morning Chronicle*, 22 May 1838, p. 3.
48 *The Morning Chronicle*, 30 May 1838, p. 3.
49 *Parl. Deb.*, Third Ser., Vol. XLIII (26 June 1838), cols. 1,139–42.
50 Evans to Lord Melbourne, 26 January 1840, Melbourne Mss., R[oyal] A[rchives], Box 53/79.
51 Col. Sir G. de Lacy Evans, *Memoranda of the Contest in Spain*, p. 133. See also pp. 26–7, 38, 47, 56–7, 59, 123 and 125–8.
52 *Ibid.*, pp. 32, 45, 50, 71, 75–86, 99 and 104.
53 *Ibid.*, p. 135. See also pp. 40–1, 89–92, 111, 123, 129 and 153–5.
54 *The Morning Chronicle*, 28 March 1840, p. 4, 1 April 1840, p. 3, 6 April 1840, p. 2, 8 April 1840, p. 4, and 11 April 1840, p. 3.
55 Evans to Lord Palmerston, 7 February 1840, B.P., GC/EV/43/1.
56 J. B. Meagher to Lord Londonderry, 4 May 1840, Londonderry Mss., Durham County Archives, D/LO/C131(2). For earlier correspondence on the pay arrears see *Papers relative to The War in Spain*, C. 192 (1839), L, pp. 5–60.
57 Evans to Lord Clarendon, 2 May 1840, Clarendon Mss., C-461, and A. Aston to Lord Palmerston, 2 May 1840, P.R.O., F.O. 355/3.
58 Aston to de Castro, 15 May 1840; to Lord Palmerston, 23 May, 13 June and 25 July 1840, P.R.O., F.O. 355/3.
59 Aston to Lord Palmerston, 4 May, 13 June and 31 July 1841, and Aston to Lord Aberdeen, 18 May 1843, P.R.O., F.O. 355/4 and /5.
60 *The Morning Chronicle*, 25 March 1841, p. 3.
61 *Parl. Deb.*, Third Ser., Vol. LII (20 March 1840), cols. 1,287–8.
62 *The Morning Chronicle*, 18 September 1838, p. 3; 14 December 1838, p. 3; 18 March 1839, p. 3; 2 May 1839, p. 3; 15 January 1840, p. 3; 25 February 1840, p. 3; and 1 April 1841, p. 3. See also Evans to G. M. Wilson, 26 December 1839, G. M. Wilson Mss., Manchester Central Reference Library.

Notes and references

63 *The Morning Chronicle*, 12 May 1841, p. 6.
64 *The Morning Chronicle*, 21 June 1841, p. 2.
65 *The Morning Chronicle*, 26 June 1841, p. 4.
66 *The Morning Chronicle*, 19 June 1841, p. 3.
67 *The Morning Chronicle*, 26 June 1841, p. 4, 29 June 1841, p. 6, and 30 June 1841, p. 2.
68 *The Times*, 1 July 1841, p. 2.
69 'Abstract of the poll . . .', *op. cit.*
70 Where the Conservatives gained two of the four seats after an unbroken run of defeats at every election since the Reform Act, and Lord John Russell only narrowly won the fourth seat.
71 *The Morning Chronicle*, 19 June 1841, p. 3.
72 D. Southgate, *The Passing of the Whigs 1832–1886* (Macmillan, London, 1962), p. 122.
73 *The Morning Chronicle*, 29 June 1841, p. 6.
74 J. Diprose, *Some Account of the Parish of Saint Clement Danes (Westminster) Past and Present* (Diprose & Bateman, London, 1868), p. 66.
75 *The Times*, 2 July 1841, p. 3.

Chapter 6

1 *The Morning Chronicle*, 16 February 1846, p. 2.
2 *The Times*, 4 March 1845, p. 4.
3 *The Morning Chronicle*, 9 September 1841, p. 3.
4 *Lord Melbourne's Papers*, ed. L. C. Sanders, 3 vols. (Longman, London, 1889), Vol. 3, p. 527.
5 As 200 peers did when they voted against party policy in the House of Lords on 14 March 1843. D. Southgate, *op. cit.*, p. 125. See also P. Ziegler, *Melbourne* (Collins, London, 1976), pp. 352–3, and J. Prest, *Lord John Russell* (Macmillan, London, 1972), p. 189.
6 *Life of John, Lord Campbell*, ed. Hon. Mrs Hardcastle, 2 vols. (John Murray, London, 1881) Vol. 2, pp. 62 and 184.
7 N. McCord, *The Anti-Corn Law League 1838–1846* (Allen & Unwin, London, 1958), pp. 22–33.
8 R. Cobden to G. M. Wilson, 24 February 1842, Wilson Mss., Manchester Central Reference Library.
9 *The Times*, 18 February 1846, p. 6.
10 *The Morning Chronicle*, 5 February 1842, p. 3.
11 Sir G. de Lacy Evans, *Sir De Lacy Evans' Reply to Mr O'Connell's Attacks on the Regent etc. of Spain* (Torran, London, 1842), pp. 3–15.
12 *The Morning Chronicle*, 15 November 1842, p. 3.
13 *The Morning Chronicle*, 2 December 1842, p. 3.
14 *The Morning Chronicle*, 22 December 1842, p. 3, and *Morning Advertiser*, 6 January 1843, p. 3.
15 N. McCord, *op. cit.*, p. 139.

16 *The Manchester Guardian*, 4 February 1843, p. 3.
17 *The Morning Chronicle*, 17 February 1843, p. 4.
18 *The Morning Post*, 6 February 1843, p. 4, and 7 February 1843, p. 6.
19 *Morning Advertiser*, 9 February 1844, p. 3.
20 *The Morning Chronicle*, 28 March 1843, p. 3.
21 Sir R. Peel to Capt. Rous, 19 February 1846, quoted in *Sir Robert Peel from his private papers*, ed. C. S. Parker, 3 vols. (John Murray, London, 1889), Vol. 3, p. 334.
22 *The Morning Chronicle*, 12 February 1846, p. 4.
23 *The Morning Chronicle*, 14 February 1846, pp. 5–6.
24 *The Morning Chronicle*, 16 February 1846, p. 2, and 17 February 1846, p. 7; *The Morning Herald*, 18 February 1846, p. 11.
25 *The Morning Post*, 16 February 1846, p. 4.
26 *The Standard*, 14 February 1846, p. 4.
27 *The Times*, 20 February 1846, p. 6.
28 *The Morning Herald*, 19 February 1846, p. 4; *The Standard*, 19 February 1846, p. 2.
29 *Morning Advertiser*, 19 February 1846, p. 2.
30 *The Times*, 20 February, 1846, p. 6.
31 *Parl. Deb.*, Third Ser., Vol. LXXXVII (24 June 1846), cols. 909–17, and Vol. XCIV (7 July 1847), cols. 8–11.
32 *Parl. Deb.*, Third Ser., Vol. XCIII (25 June 1846), cols. 919–21. See also S. Maccoby, *English Radicalism 1832–1852* (Allen & Unwin, London, 1935), pp. 272–3.
33 *Morning Advertiser*, 2 May 1846, p. 3; 15 December 1846, p. 3; 12 January 1847, p. 3; 30 January 1847, p. 3.
34 *Parl. Deb.*, Third Ser., Vol. LXXXVII (13 July 1846), col. 1,101.
35 *Parl. Deb.*, Third Ser., Vol. LXXXVIII (3 August 1846), cols. 306–8; Vol. LXXXVII (17 July 1846), col. 1,231; and Vol. XC (5 March 1847), col. 962.
36 For an expert analysis of the military press in this period see H. F. A. Strachan, 'The Pre-Crimean Origins of Reform in the British Army', unpublished Ph.D. thesis (University of Cambridge, 1976), pp. 31–49.
37 *Parl. Deb.*, Third Ser., Vol. LXXXVI (4 May 1846), col. 30.
38 *Parl. Deb.*, Third Ser., Vol. LXXXVIII (19 August 1846), cols. 879–91. See also Vol. XC (1 March 1847), cols. 635–8.
39 Sir G. de Lacy Evans to Sir J. Philippart, August 1846, Evans Mss., quoted by courtesy of Mr P. Metcalfe.
40 *Parl. Deb.*, Third Ser., Vol. XCI (22 March 1847), col. 295.
41 *Morning Advertiser*, 10 December 1846, p. 2; 19 December 1846, p. 2; and 22 December 1846, p. 3.
42 *Morning Advertiser*, 17 December 1846, p. 1; 18 December 1846, p. 3; 23 December 1846, p. 3; 21 January 1847, p. 3; 28 January 1847, p. 3.
43 *The Daily News*, 26 July 1847, p. 2.
44 *The Daily News*, 29 July 1847, p. 4, and *The Sun*, 28 July 1847, p. 3.
45 *The Sun*, 30 July 1847, p. 2.
46 *Morning Advertiser*, 31 July 1847, p. 2.
47 *Parl. Deb.*, Third Ser., Vol. XCVI (24 February 1848), cols. 1,270–1,

and Vol. XCVII (20 March 1848), cols. 771–2.
48. *Parl. Deb.*, Third Ser., Vol. XCVII (31 March 1848), col. 1,182.
49. *Parl. Deb.*, Third Ser., Vol. XCVII (31 March 1848), col. 1,183.
50. *Parl. Deb.*, Third Ser., Vol. XCVIII (7 and 11 April 1848), cols. 17–18 and 164–5.
51. *Morning Advertiser*, 14 April 1848, p. 3.
52. *Morning Advertiser*, 13 June 1848, p. 1.
53. *Morning Advertiser*, 1 February 1848, p. 1, and 29 June 1849, p. 3.
54. *Parl. Deb.*, Third Ser., Vol. CII (2 February 1849), cols. 192–3.
55. S. Maccoby, *op. cit.*, p. 373.
56. *Morning Advertiser*, 31 July 1849, p. 3.
57. *Morning Advertiser*, 5 December 1849, p. 2.
58. *Parl. Deb.*, Third Ser., Vol. CVIII (7 February 1850), cols. 515–16, and Vol. CXVIII (7 August 1851), cols. 1,947–8.
59. *The Patriot*, 23 October 1851, p. 686.
60. *Morning Advertiser*, 31 July 1849, p. 3, and *The Inquirer*, 4 August 1849, p. 491.
61. *Parl. Deb.*, Third Ser., Vol. CVI (3 July 1849), cols. 1,304–10, and Vol. CXII (9 July 1850), cols. 1,149–51.
62. *The Spectator*, 13 October 1849, p. 960.
63. *Parl. Deb.*, Third Ser., Vol. CXX (1 April 1852), cols. 526–42. See also Vol. CIX (27 February 1852), cols. 916–17.
64. *Parl. Deb.*, Third Ser., Vol. CXXII (21 June 1852), cols. 1,067–9. See also Vol. CXI (3 June 1850), cols. 682–3, and Vol. CXVII (5 July 1851), cols. 509–10. *Morning Advertiser*, 24 May 1850, p. 4.
65. *Parl. Deb.*, Third Ser., Vol. CXVIII (1 July 1851), col. 102, and Vol. CXIX (17 February 1852), cols. 687–9.
66. *Morning Advertiser*, 9 January 1851, p. 3; 21 January 1851, p. 3; 20 February 1851, p. 3; and *The Daily News*, 17 January 1851, p. 5.
67. S. Buxton, *op. cit.*, Vol. 1, pp. 95–6; S. Dowell, *op. cit.*, Vol. 2, pp. 315–17; *Parl. Deb.*, Third Ser., Vol. CXV (4 April 1851), cols. 1,091–2.
68. *The Daily News*, 8 July 1852, p. 5.
69. R. Cobden to J. Sturge, 17 February 1852, Cobden Mss., B.L. Add. Mss., 43,656, f. 249.
70. *Parl. Deb.*, Third Ser., Vol. CXIX (22 March 1852), cols. 1,413–4.
71. *Parl. Deb.*, Third Ser., Vol. CXX (23 April 1852), cols. 1,035–42.
72. R. Cobden to Rev. H. Richard, 23 April 1852, Cobden Mss., B.L. Add. Mss., 43,657, ff. 132–3.
73. *Parl. Deb.*, Third Ser., Vol. CXXII (7 June 1852), cols. 185–6. See also Vol. CXXI (4 May 1852), cols. 207–13, (14 May 1852), col. 659, and (21 May 1852), col. 919.
74. *Morning Advertiser*, 24 June 1852, p. 4.
75. *The Times*, 26 June 1852, p. 4.
76. *Ibid.*, *Morning Advertiser*, 26 June 1852, p. 3; *The Times*, 29 June 1852, p. 5, and 3 July 1852, p. 5.
77. *Morning Advertiser*, 24 June 1852, p. 4, and 8 July 1852, p. 4.
78. *The Times*, 3 July 1852, p. 5. See also *Morning Advertiser*, 2 July

1852, p. 3.
79 *The Times*, 3 July 1852, p. 5.
80 *The Daily News*, 6 July 1852, p. 5.
81 *The Sun*, 5 July 1852, p. 1.
82 *The Patriot*, 5 July 1852, p. 433, and *The Nonconformist*, 7 July 1852, p. 527.
83 *The Daily News*, 8 July 1852, p. 5.
84 *The Daily News*, 10 July 1852, p. 2.
85 *Parl. Deb.*, Third Ser., Vol. CXXIII (8 December 1852), cols. 1,144–51.
86 *Morning Advertiser*, 14 December 1852, p. 6.
87 *Parl. Deb.*, Third Ser., Vol. CXXV (12 April 1853), cols. 1,034–41; *Morning Advertiser*, 10 December 1853, p. 3.
88 *Morning Advertiser*, 22 July 1850, p. 3.
89 *Parl. Deb.*, Third Ser., Vol. CXV (28 March 1851), col. 738, and (31 March 1851), col. 814; Vol. CXXIV (25 February 1853), cols. 686–7.
90 T. P. Thompson to Capt. C. W. Thompson, 19 June 1850, Thompson Mss., Hull University Library, DTH 4/13.
91 H. F. A. Strachan, *op. cit.*, pp. 70–1 and 79. See also P. D. Jones 'The British Army in the Age of Reform', unpublished Ph.D. thesis (Duke University, 1968), pp. 203–6.
92 Prince Albert to the Duke of Wellington, 4 November 1847, Queen Victoria's Mss., R.A., E42/3.
93 *Morning Advertiser*, 16 June 1853, p. 4, and *The Naval and Military Gazette*, 18 June 1853, p. 393.
94 Lord Hardinge to Lord Seaton, 4 and 18 June 1853, Queen Victoria's Mss., R.A., E2/87 and E2/97.
95 *The Naval and Military Gazette*, 9 July 1853, p. 442.
96 *The United Service Gazette*, 14 July 1853, p. 4.
97 *The Naval and Military Gazette*, 20 August 1853, p. 536. See also C. Macfarlane, *The Camp of 1853* (Bosworth, London, 1853), pp. 48, 51, and H. F. A. Strachan, *op. cit.*, pp. 259–62.
98 A. Briggs, *The Age of Improvement* (Longman, London, 1959), p. 380.
99 *Parl. Deb.*, Third Ser., Vol. CXXX (20 February 1854), cols. 934–44.
100 *Parl. Deb.*, Third Ser., Vol. CXXX (22 February 1854), cols. 1,118–19.

Chapter 7

1 *The Times*, 14 February 1854, pp. 6–7.
2 Sir G. de Lacy Evans to the Duke of Newcastle, 28 and 30 March 1854, Newcastle Mss., Nottingham University Library, NeC 10,472a, 10,472b, 10,473a and 10,473b.
3 The Duke of Newcastle to Evans, 4 April 1854, Newcastle Mss., NeC 10,780.
4 Evans to Lord Aberdeen, 12 April 1854, Aberdeen Mss., B.L. Add. Mss. 43,252, ff. 331–2.
5 Evans to Lord Aberdeen, 10 August 1854, and Lady Evans to J. H. Cole, 20 September 1854, Aberdeen Mss., B.L. Add. Mss. 43,254, ff. 112–14.

6   Lord Aberdeen to Evans, 30 September 1854, Aberdeen Mss., B.L. Add. Mss. 43,254, ff. 135–6.
7   W. H. Russell, *The War: from the landing at Gallipoli to the death of Lord Raglan* (Routledge, London, 1855), p. 49.
8   Evans to Sir George Brown, 25 April 1854, Brown Mss., N[ational] L[ibrary of] S[cotland], Ms. 1,849, f. 91.
9   *Ibid.*, and Evans to Brown, 28 April 1854, Brown Mss., N.L.S., Ms. 1,849, ff. 93–4.
10 (Q. 386) *Evidence before the Select Committee on the Army before Sebastopol: with the proceedings of the committee*, hereafter referred to as the Sebastopol Committee, C. 86 (1854–55), IX.
11 Evans to Brown, 25 April 1854, Brown Mss., N.L.S., Ms. 1,849, f. 90.
12 Evans to Brown, 28 April 1854, Brown Mss., N.L.S., Ms. 1,849, f. 94.
13 W. H. Russell, *op. cit.*, pp. 73–4; J. R. Hume, *Reminiscences of the Crimean Campaign With The 55th Regiment* (Unwin Bros, London, 1894), pp. 8–9; Gen. Sir C. P. Beauchamp Walker, *Days of a Soldier's Life* (Chapman & Hall, London, 1894), p. 17.
14 J. R. Hume, *op. cit.*, pp. 16–17; (qq. 395–6) Evidence before the Sebastopol Committee, C. 86 (1854–55), IX; *The War in the Crimea. Letters from Headquarters, By a Staff Officer* (John Murray, London, 1858), p. 19; W. H. Russell, *op. cit.*, p. 120.
15 W. H. Russell, *op. cit.*, p. 101, and *A Sketch of the Life of Lt. Col. Champion, of the 95th Regiment, with Extracts from his Correspondence* (Bradbury & Evans, London, n.d.), p. 21.
16 (Qq. 397–406 and 749–50) Evidence before the Sebastopol Committee, C. 86 (1854–55), IX; W. H. Russell, *op. cit.*, p. 144.
17 J. A. Lloyd to Gen. C. Grey, 29 June 1854, Gen. C. Grey Mss., Department of Palaeography and Diplomatic, University of Durham, IX/10(c).
18 (Qq. 399–401) Evidence before the Sebastopol Committee, C. 86 (1854–55), IX.
19 (Qq. 414–24) Evidence before the Sebastopol Committee, C. 86 (1854–55), IX.
20 Evans to Knight Hunt, 8 September 1854, Crimean Letters, N[ational] A[rmy] M[useum], Acc. 6,804/3/22.
21 J. B. Atkins, *The Life of Sir William Howard Russell*, 2 vols. (John Murray, London, 1911), Vol. 1, p. 156.
22 G. Bapst, *Le maréchal Canrobert*, 6 vols. (Plon-Nourrit, Paris, 1902), Vol. 2, p. 201.
23 A. W. Kinglake, *The Invasion of the Crimea*, 9 vols., sixth edition (Blackwood, Edinburgh, 1877–78), Vol. 3, pp. 22–7.
24 Letter from Evans in *The Times*, 2 July 1855, p. 12.
25 *Ibid.*, A. W. Kinglake, *op. cit.*, Vol. 3, p. 84; Sir Daniel Lysons, *The Crimean War from first to last* (John Murray, London, 1895), p. 96.
26 A. W. Kinglake, *op. cit.*, Vol. 3, pp. 85–7.
27 Evans to Lord Raglan, 22 September 1854, Raglan Mss., N.A.M., Acc. 6,807/228/1.
28 Sir D. Lysons, *op. cit.*, p. 99.

29 Evans to Lord Raglan, 22 September 1854, Raglan Mss., N.A.M., Acc. 6,807/228/1; A. W. Kinglake, *op. cit.*, Vol. 3, pp. 88–90.
30 A. W. Kinglake, *op. cit.*, Vol. 3, pp. 196–200; C. Hibbert, *The Destruction of Lord Raglan* (Penguin, London, 1961), pp. 106–7.
31 Maj.-Gen. G. N. Wood, 'Evans in the Crimea', *Army Quarterly and Defence Journal*, Vol. 102, No. 3 (April 1972), p. 347.
32 Evans to the Duke of Cambridge, 7 February 1863, Cambridge Mss., R.A., Add. E1/3,861; A. W. Kinglake, *op. cit.*, Vol. 3, p. 137.
33 Evans to Lord Raglan, 22 September 1854, Raglan Mss., N.A.M., Acc. 6,807/228/1.
34 Major H. C. Wylly, *The 95th (The Derbyshire) Regiment in the Crimea* (Swan Sonnenschein, London, 1899), p. 20.
35 J. R. Hume, *op. cit.*, pp. 45–6.
36 Major H. C. Wylly, *op. cit.*, p. 20; J. R. Hume, *op. cit.*, pp. 46–7; Sir D. Lysons, *op. cit.*, pp. 108–9.
37 Major H. C. Wylly, *op. cit.*, p. 21.
38 Evans to Lord Raglan, 11 November 1854, Newcastle Mss., NeC 9,909b; Major H. C. Wylly, *op. cit.*, pp. 33–4.
39 Lord Raglan to the Duke of Newcastle, 8 October 1854, Raglan Mss., N.A.M., Acc. 6,807/284/1, and A. W. Kinglake, *op. cit.*, Vol. 4, pp. 247–8.
40 Evans to Lord Raglan, 11 November 1854, Newcastle Mss., NeC 9,909b, and Evans to the Duke of Cambridge, 22 November 1854, Cambridge Mss., R.A., Add. E1/203.
41 *Parl. Deb.*, Third Ser., Vol. CXL (29 February 1856), cols. 1,637–40.
42 A. W. Kinglake, *op. cit.*, Vol. 5, pp. 368–9 and 372.
43 A. W. Kinglake, *op. cit.*, Vol. 5, pp. 372–88; Evans to Lord Raglan, 27 October 1854, reproduced in G. Ryan, *op. cit.*, p. 24–6.
44 A. W. Kinglake, *op. cit.*, Vol. 5, p. 386; Gen. Sir C. P. Beauchamp Walker, *op. cit.*, p. 133; *A Sketch of the Life of Lt. Col. Champion*, p. 53; *A Diary of the Crimea by George Palmer Evelyn*, ed. C. Falls (Duckworth, London, 1954), p. 98; Lord Raglan to the Duke of Newcastle, 13 November 1854, Newcastle Mss., NeC 9,909a.
45 Lord Raglan to the Duke of Newcastle, 3 November 1854, Newcastle Mss., NeC 9,900.
46 Lt.-Gen. Sir J. L. Pennefather to Major the Hon. Somerset Calthorpe, 15 February 1857, *The War in the Crimea. Letters from Headquarters, By a Staff Officer*, p. 159.
47 Lt.-Col. E. B. Hamley, *The Story of The Campaign of Sebastopol* (Blackwood, Edinburgh, 1855), p. 104.
48 A. W. Kinglake, *op. cit.*, Vol. 6, p. 466.
49 *The War in the Crimea. Letters from Headquarters, By a Staff Officer*, pp. 163–4.
50 J. B. Atkins, *op. cit.*, Vol. 1, p. 171.
51 Evans to Lord Raglan, 11 November 1854, Newcastle Mss., NeC 9,909b.
52 Lord Raglan to the Duke of Newcastle, 13 November 1854, Newcastle Mss., NeC 9,909a.

53 *The Examiner*, 30 December 1854, p. 839.
54 *The Times*, 12 December 1854, p. 11.
55 Duke of Newcastle to Evans, 23 December 1854, Newcastle Mss., NeC 10,827.
56 Evans to the Duke of Newcastle, 27 December 1854, 7 and 25 January 1855, Newcastle Mss., NeC 10,475, 10,478 and 10,482.
57 Evans to the Duke of Newcastle, 20 January 1855; see also the Duke of Newcastle to Evans, 17 and 31 January 1855, Newcastle Mss., NeC 10,481a, 10,840 and 10,850.
58 Evans to Sir J. Philippart, 14 January 1855, Evans Mss.; Evans to the Duke of Cambridge, February 1855, Cambridge Mss., R.A., Add. E1/219a.
59 *The Naval and Military Gazette*, 30 December 1854, p. 839.
60 *The Times*, 2 January 1855, p. 6.
61 *The Morning Herald*, 2 January 1855, p. 4, and *Reynolds's Newspaper*, 7 January 1855, p. 3.
62 *The Times*, 23 January 1855, p. 10.
63 Evans to the Duke of Newcastle, n.d., Newcastle Mss., NeC 10,480.
64 *The Naval and Military Gazette*, 27 January 1855, p. 57.
65 Evans to Sir John Philippart, 14 January 1855, Evans Mss.
66 Evans to the Duke of Newcastle, n.d., Newcastle Mss., NeC 10,480.
67 Evans to the Duke of Cambridge, n.d., Cambridge Mss., R.A., Add. E1/219a.
68 *The Times*, 2 February 1855, p. 8.
69 R. Cobden to Maj. J. W. Fitzmayer, 10 March 1855, Cobden Mss., B.L. Add. Mss. 43,665, f. 11.
70 *Parl. Deb.*, Third Ser., Vol. CXXXVI (2 February 1855), cols. 1,263–7; *The Morning Post*, 3 February 1855, p. 4; *The Patriot*, 5 February 1855, p. 84; *The Globe*, 2 February 1855, p. 2.
71 *The Times*, 5 February 1855, p. 6.
72 *Reynolds's Newspaper*, 18 February 1855, p. 16; *The Times*, 1 March 1855, p. 12; *The Morning Advertiser*, 7 May 1855, p. 3; and *The Times*, 6 April 1855, p. 6.
73 Evans to Lord Panmure, 6 June 1855, Dalhousie Muniments, S[cottish] R[ecord] O[ffice], GD45/8/253, cited by permission of the Earl of Dalhousie, Brechin Castle, Angus.
74 *Parl. Deb.*, Third Ser., Vol. CXXXVI (1 March 1855), cols. 2,137–56.
75 *The Daily News*, 15 March 1855, p. 4.
76 *The Times*, 2 March 1855, p. 7. Goderich accepted this criticism. See Viscount Goderich to T. Hughes, 8 March 1855, Ripon Mss., B.L. Add. Mss. 43,547, f. 159.
77 (Qq. 380–949, especially q. 669) Evidence before the Sebastopol Committee, C. 86 (1854–55), IX.
78 *Reynolds's Newspaper*, 11 March 1855, p. 9.
79 (Qq. 710 and 889–98) Evidence before the Sebastopol Committee, C. 86 (1854–55), IX.
80 *The Morning Chronicle*, 6 March 1855, p. 4.
81 *The Naval and Military Gazette*, 10 March 1855, p. 153; *The Times*, 7

March 1855, p. 8; and *The Standard*, 8 March 1855, p. 2.
82 Evans to J. T. Delane, n.d., Delane Mss., *The Times* Archive, Vol. 6/20. See also *Parl. Deb.*, Third Ser., Vol. CXXXIX (19 July 1855), col. 1,119.
83 *Parl. Deb.*, Third Ser., Vol. CXXXIX (14 August 1855), cols. 2,148–54. See also Vol. CXXXVII (30 March 1855), cols. 1,406–9, and Vol. CXXXIX (22 June 1855), cols. 57–9.
84 Evans to Sir J. Philippart, 30 August 1855, Evans Mss.
85 *Parl. Deb.*, Third Ser., Vol. CXXXIX (3 July 1855), cols. 429–30.
86 *Fifth Report of the Sebastopol Committee*, C. 318 (1854–55), IX, p. 23.
87 *Parl. Deb.*, Third Ser., Vol. CXXXIX (19 July 1855), cols. 1,116–26 and 1,172–4.
88 *Parl. Deb.*, Third Ser., Vol. CXXXIX (22 June 1855), cols. 13–14 and (3 July 1855), cols. 420–2.
89 *Parl. Deb.*, Third Ser., Vol. CXXXIX (20 July 1855), cols. 1,246–7, and (23 July 1855), cols. 1,296–7.
90 Evans to Sir G. Brown, 24 July 1855, Brown Mss., N.L.S., Ms. 1,851, f. 20. See also *Parl. Deb.*, Third Ser., Vol. CXXXIX (19 July 1855), col. 1,106.
91 R. Cobden to J. Sturge, 15 August 1855, Cobden Mss., B.L. Add. Mss. 43,656, ff. 354–5.
92 *Morning Advertiser*, 2 August 1855, p. 4, and Evans to Sir G. Brown, 24 July 1855, Brown Mss., N.L.S., Ms. 1851, f. 20.
93 *The Times*, 27 November 1855, p. 6.
94 Evans to J. T. Delane, 28 November 1855, Delane Mss., Vol. 6/78. See also Evans to Sir J. Philippart, 27 November 1855, Evans Mss.
95 *Parl. Deb.*, Third Ser., Vol. CXL (31 January 1856), cols. 83–6.
96 *The Morning Post*, 9 March 1857, p. 2.
97 J. B. Atkins, *op. cit.*, Vol. 1, p. 171.

Chapter 8

1 *Parl. Deb.*, Third Ser., Vol. CXXXVII (9 March 1855), col. 372.
2 *The Morning Advertiser*, 27 March 1857, p. 2.
3 *Parl. Deb.*, Third Ser., Vol. CXXXVIII (18 June 1855), cols. 2,163–78.
4 *Report of the Commission of Enquiry into the Supplies of the British Army in the Crimea*, hereafter referred to as the McNeill and Tulloch Report, C. 2,007 (1856), XX, pp. 3–37.
5 *Parl. Deb.*, Third Ser., Vol. CXL (29 February 1856), col. 1,585.
6 Queen Victoria to Lord Palmerston, 16 February 1856, *The Letters of Queen Victoria 1837–1861*, ed. A. C. Benson and Viscount Esher, 3 vols. (John Murray, London, 1907), Vol. 3, p. 222.
7 Lord Panmure to Queen Victoria, 17 February 1856, and Queen Victoria to Lord Panmure, 17 February 1856, Dalhousie Muniments, S[cottish] R[ecord] O[ffice], GD45/8/144/1/46 and GD45/8/142/2/125.
8 *Parl. Deb.*, Third Ser., Vol. CXL (29 February 1856), cols. 1,601–13. See also the McNeill and Tulloch report, p. 24.

9   See Chapter 7.
10 *Parl. Deb.*, Third Ser., Vol. CXL (29 February 1856), cols. 1,628–46.
11 *Parl. Deb.*, Third Ser., Vol. CXL (29 February 1856), cols. 1,646–50, 1,659 and 1,670.
12 J. Bright to R. Cobden, 6 March 1856, Bright Mss., B.L. Add. Mss. 43,384, f. 55.
13 *The Naval and Military Gazette*, 8 March 1856, pp. 152–3; *The Times*, 1 March 1856, p. 9; *The Morning Advertiser*, 1 March 1856, p. 4; *The Morning Post*, 4 March 1856, p. 5.
14 Evans to Sir G. Brown, 17 March 1856, Brown Mss., N.L.S., Ms. 1,852, f. 113.
15 *Parl. Deb.*, Third Ser., Vol. CXL (3 March 1856), cols. 1,702–6, and R. Cobden to Col. J. W. Fitzmayer, 7 March 1856, Cobden Mss., B.L., Add. Mss. 43,665, f. 20.
16 Col. J. W. Fitzmayer to Cobden, 9 March 1856, Cobden Mss., B.L. Add. Mss. 43,665, ff. 22–4.
17 Evans to J. T. Delane, 25 March (1856?), Delane Mss., *The Times* Archive, Vol. 6/20.
18 *The United Service Gazette*, 1 March 1856, p. 4.
19 *Parl. Deb.*, Third Ser., Vol. CXL (4 March 1856), cols. 1,791–4.
20 Lord Panmure to Queen Victoria, 4 March 1856, Dalhousie Muniments, S.R.O., GD45/8/144/1/54.
21 *Parl. Deb.*, Third Ser., Vol. CXL (4 March 1856), cols. 1,848–50.
22 Lord Panmure to Queen Victoria, 4 March 1856, Dalhousie Muniments, S.R.O., GD45/8/144/1/54.
23 *The Daily News*, 5 March 1856, p. 4, and *The Naval and Military Gazette*, 8 March 1856, p. 154.
24 *Reynolds's Newspaper*, 9 March 1856, p. 9.
25 Lord Panmure to Queen Victoria, 20 April 1856, and Queen Victoria to Lord Panmure, 20 April 1856, Dalhousie Muniments, S.R.O., GD45/8/144/1/57 and GD45/8/142/2/146.
26 *Parl. Deb.*, Third Ser., Vol. CXLI (11 April 1856), cols. 878–81.
27 *Parl. Deb.*, Third Ser., Vol. CXLII (5 June 1856), cols. 1,011–13; (16 June 1856), cols. 1,518–19 and 1,537–41; (19 June 1856), cols. 1,712–13.
28 (Qq. 165, 196–7, 931, 1,206, 874 and 705) *Evidence before the Commissioners appointed to inquire into the System of Purchase and Sale of Commissions in the Army*, hereafter referred to as the Purchase Commission, C. 2,267 (1857 – Sess. 2), XVII.
29 (Qq. 2,275, 2,628 3,287 and 3,302) Evidence before the Purchase Commission, C. 2,267 (1857 – Sess. 2), XVIII.
30 (Qq. 1,808–9, 1,888 and 4,279) Evidence before the Purchase Commission, C. 2,267 (1857 – Sess. 2), XVIII.
31 (Q. 4,094) Evidence before the Purchase Commission, C. 2,267 (1857 – Sess. 2), XVIII.
32 (Qq. 4,348–840) Evidence before the Purchase Commission, C. 2,267 (1857 – Sess. 2), XVIII.
33 Report of the Purchase Commission, C. 2,267 (1857 – Sess. 2), XVIII,

pp. xxx–xxxiv.
34 'Statement of Lieutenant-General Sir De Lacy Evans', annexed to the Report of the Purchase Commission, C. 2,267 (1857 – Sess. 2), XVIII, p. xxxvi.
35 *The Morning Post*, 24 August 1857, p. 4; *The Morning Herald*, 26 August 1857, p. 4; *The United Service Gazette*, 22 August 1857, p. 4.
36 *The Standard*, 21 August 1857, p. 4; *Reynolds's Newspaper*, 30 August 1857, p. 1; *The Daily News*, 20 August 1857, p. 4.
37 *The Times*, 20 August 1857, p. 8.
38 A. Bruce *The Purchase System in the British Army, 1660–1871* (Royal Historical Society, London, 1980), p. 113.
39 *Report of the Right Hon. Edward Ellice M.P., Lieut-General Edward Buckley Wynyard, C.B., and Major-General Sir Henry John Bentinck, K.C.B.*, C. 2,292 (1857–58), XIX.
40 Prince Albert to Lord Panmure, 20 October 1857, Dalhousie Muniments, S.R.O., GD45/8/146/80.
41 *The Morning Advertiser*, 20 March 1857, p. 6, and 27 March 1857, p. 2.
42 *The Morning Advertiser*, 14 March 1857, p. 3.
43 (Q. 1,277) Evidence before the *Select Committee on Sandhurst Royal Military College*, C. 317 (1854–55), XII.
44 *Report of the Commissioners appointed to consider the best mode of re-organizing the system for Training Officers and for the scientific corps*, C. 52 (1857 – Sess. 1), VI, pp. xix–xl.
45 Queen Victoria to Lord Panmure, 17 February 1857, Dalhousie Muniments, S.R.O., GD45/8/142/2/192.
46 General Order No. 685, cited in Brevet Major A. R. Godwin-Austen, *The Staff and the Staff College* (Constable, London, 1927), pp. 97–9.
47 *Parl. Deb.*, Third Ser., Vol. CXLVII (28 July 1857), cols. 569–78.
48 *The Morning Advertiser*, 31 July 1857, p. 4; *The United Service Gazette*, 1 August 1857, p. 4; *The Naval and Military Gazette*, 1 August 1857, pp. 489–90.
49 J. Wheaton, 'The Effect of the Administrative Reform Movement upon the Army in the Mid-Victorian Period', unpublished Ph.D. thesis (University of Manchester, 1968), pp. 351–2.
50 *Parl. Deb.*, Third Ser., Vol., CXLVII (11 August 1857), col. 1,400.
51 *Parl. Deb.*, Third Ser., Vol. CXLVII (11 August 1857), col. 1,406.
52 *The Times*, 12 August 1857, p. 9.
53 Evans to Sir J. Philippart, September 1857, Evans Mss.
54 *Parl. Deb.*, Third Ser., Vol. CXLVIII (8 February 1858), cols. 920–2.
55 Evans to the Duke of Cambridge, 26 June 1858, Cambridge Mss., R.A., Add. E1/1,069.
56 *Report from the Select Committee on East India (Transport of Troops); together with the proceedings of the Committee, Minutes of Evidence, Appendix and Index*, C. 382 (1857–58), X, pp. iii–iv, viii–xxviii.
57 *Parl. Deb.*, Third Ser., Vol. CLI (21 July 1858), cols. 1,878–2,042.
58 *The Morning Advertiser*, 17 August 1857, p. 3, and 23 March 1858, p. 6.
59 *The Daily News*, 10 March 1859, p. 6.
60 *The Morning Advertiser*, 18 April 1859, p. 6, and 20 April 1859, p. 4.

61 *The Daily News*, 29 April 1859, p. 2.
62 *Parl. Deb.*, Third Ser., Vol. CLV (25 July 1859), cols. 399–400. See also Vol. CLVII (16 March 1860), col. 769; Vol. CLXVIII (10 July 1862), cols. 185–6; Vol. CLXXII (9 July 1863), cols. 449–50; and *The Times* 21 January 1861, p. 9.
63 *The Morning Advertiser*, 8 December 1859, p. 6; *The Times*, 21 September 1860, p. 10; *Parl. Deb.*, Third Ser., Vol. CLX (17 August 1860), cols. 1,486–8.
64 *The Atlas*, 23 November 1861, p. 3; *Parl. Deb.*, Third Ser., Vol. CLX (17 August 1860), cols. 1,486–8 and Vol. CLXXI (4 June 1863), cols. 335–7.
65 *Report from the Select Committee on Military Organization*, C. 441 (1860), VII, pp. xxi–xxii.
66 *Proceedings of the Select Committee on Military Organization*, C. 441 (1860), VII, pp. xxv, 1, lii, lvi–lvii.
67 Queen Victoria to Lord Palmerston, 5 July 1859, and Lord Palmerston to Queen Victoria, 5 July 1859, *Letters of Queen Victoria 1837–1861*, Vol. 3, pp. 448–9. See also H. Gordon, *The War Office* (Putnam, London, 1935), pp. 54 and 58.
68 S. Herbert to the Duke of Cambridge, 7 December 1859, Cambridge Mss., R.A., Add. Mss. E1/2,454.
69 Duke of Cambridge to S. Herbert, 10 December 1859, Cambridge Mss., R.A., Add. Mss. El/2,462.
70 A. P. C. Bruce, 'The system of purchase and sale of commissions in the British Army and the campaign for its abolition 1660–1871', unpublished Ph.D. thesis (University of Manchester, 1973), p. 329.
71 Queen Victoria to Lord Palmerston, 4 and 5 March 1860, B.P., RC/F/941 and 943; Prince Albert to Herbert, 3 February 1860, Herbert Mss., Wilton House, Wilton (reference by permission of Lord Pembroke and Dr James Provan, who is currently writing a biography of Sidney Herbert).
72 S. Herbert to Lord Palmerston, 5 March 1860, B.P., GC/HE/62.
73 *Parl. Deb.*, Third Ser., Vol. CLVII (6 March 1860), cols. 17–68.
74 *The Times*, 8 March 1860, pp. 8 and 9. See also *The Times*, 6 March 1860, p. 9.
75 *The Daily News*, 7 March 1860, p. 4; *The Globe*, 7 March 1860, p. 2; *The Naval and Military Gazette*, 10 March 1860, p. 152.
76 *Parl. Deb.*, Third Ser., Vol. CLVII (23 March 1860), cols. 1,140–1.
77 *The Times*, 14 November 1861, p. 6. See also *The Naval and Military Gazette*, 16 November 1861, p. 731, and *The Daily News*, 22 November 1861, p. 4.
78 *Parl. Deb.*, Third Ser., Vol. CLXVII (30 May 1862), cols. 196–221.
79 *The Globe*, 31 May 1862, p. 2; *The Daily News*, 31 May 1862, p. 4.
80 *The Times*, 2 June 1862, p. 5.
81 *The United Service Gazette*, 7 June 1862, p. 4.
82 *The Times*, 31 May 1862, p. 11.
83 Maj.-Gen. Sir W. Mansfield to the Duke of Cambridge, 20 October 1857, Cambridge Mss., R.A., E1/775.

84 *Report of the Commissioners appointed to inquire into the Organization of the Indian Army*, C. 2,515 (1859), V, pp. x–xii.
85 Queen Victoria to Lord Derby, 5 and 7 February 1859, and to Gen. Peel, 13 February 1859, *Letters of Queen Victoria 1837–1861*, Vol. 3, pp. 404, 407 and 410; R. J. Moore, *Sir Charles Wood's Indian Policy 1853–66* (Manchester University Press, 1966), pp. 208–10; *Report of the Political and Military Committee of the Council of India, the 30th June 1859*, C. 330 (1860), L, p. 7.
86 R. J. Moore, *op. cit.*, pp. 214–16.
87 *Parl. Deb.*, Third Ser., Vol. CLIX (21 June 1860), cols. 806–13. See also Vol. CLIX (2 July 1860), cols. 1,262–72, and Vol. CLX (26 July 1860), cols. 238–40.
88 *The Times*, 3 July 1860, p. 9.
89 *Parl. Deb.*, Third Ser., Vol. CLIX (2 July 1860), cols. 1,262–309.
90 Evans to J. T. Delane, n.d., Delane Mss., *The Times* Archive, Vol. 11/4.
91 Evans to J. T. Delane, 'Wednesday night', Delane Mss., *The Times* Archive, Vol. 11/4. See also Evans to the Duke of Cambridge, 7 February 1863, Cambridge Mss., R.A. Add. E1/3,861.
92 *The Times*, 7 February 1865, p. 5.
93 *The Examiner*, 11 February 1865, p. 83; J. Diprose, *op. cit.*, pp. 67–8.
94 *The Morning Advertiser*, 14 February 1865, p. 2.

Chapter 9

1 G. P. Judd, *Members of Parliament 1734–1832* (Yale University Press, New Haven, 1955), p. 49, and L. Namier, *The Structure of Politics at the Accession of George III* (Macmillan, London, 1960), pp. 24–8.
2 G. Harries-Jenkins, *The Army in Victorian Society* (Routledge & Kegan Paul, London, 1977), pp. 220–1.
3 G. Harries-Jenkins, *op. cit.*, pp. 225–36.
4 R. Kee, *The Green Flag*, 3 vols. (Quartet, London, 1976), Vol. 1, pp. 28–38; B. Bailyn, *The Ideological Origins of the American Revolution* (Belknap Press, Cambridge, Mass., 1967), pp. 46, 81, 132, 201; *The Hastings and Cinque Ports Iris*, 13 November 1830, p. 1, and 5 February 1831, p. 3.
5 *The Greville Memoirs 1814–1860*, ed. L. Strachey and R. Fulford, 8 vols. (Macmillan, London, 1938), Vol. 3, p. 209.
6 *The Morning Advertiser*, 27 March 1857, p. 2.
7 Maj. Norcott to W. H. Russell, 14 March 1856(?), Russell Mss., *The Times* Archive, Vol. 1, No. 284.
8 T. P. Thompson to Capt. C. W. Thompson, 2 July 1853, Thompson Mss., DTH 4/14.
9 Sir W. Mansfield to Viscount Goderich, 5 March 1855(?), Ripon Mss., B.L. Add. Mss. 43,619, f. 1.
10 Col. J. W. Fitzmayer to Cobden, 28 January 1857, Cobden Mss., B.L. Add. Mss. 43,665, ff. 58–9. See also Evans to the Duke of Newcastle, 20 January 1855, Newcastle Mss., NeC 10,481a.

11 *Parl. Deb.*, Third Ser., Vol. XCVII (31 March 1848), cols. 1,182 and 1,187.
12 Evans to Lord Aberdeen, 12 April 1854, Aberdeen Mss., B.L. Add. Mss. 43,252, f. 332.
13 G. Villiers to Lord Palmerston, 12 March 1836, B.P., GC/CL/246(3).
14 W. Thomas, *The Philosophic Radicals: Nine Studies in Theory and Practice 1817–1841* (Oxford University Press, 1979), p. 234.
15 T. P. Thompson, 'Letter of a Representative', 4 February 1837, quoted in *Exercises, political and others*, 6 vols. (Effingham Wilson, London, 1842), Vol. 4, p. 199.
16 A. Briggs, *op. cit.*, p. 430.
17 *Parl. Deb.*, Third Ser., Vol. CXXXIX (19 July 1855), cols. 1,116–17.
18 Though based upon Evans's own data for his pre-Crimean services, the statistics also include his experiences in the Crimea. Evans, 'Memorandum to His Grace the Duke of Newcastle', Aberdeen Mss., B.L. Add. Mss. 43,252, f. 333, p. 13.
19 *The Daily News*, 6 July 1852, p. 5.
20 See Chapter 4.
21 Lord Aberdeen to the Duke of Wellington, 13 January 1836, Wellington Mss., 37/103.
22 Duke of Wellington to Lord Aberdeen, 21 March 1837, Wellington Mss., 45/43.
23 Duke of Wellington to Sir W. Peacocke, 23 November 1836, Wellington Mss., 43/52. But the Duke made an exception to this rule in the case of his son. See Lord Hill to the Duke of Wellington, 6 June 1837, Wellington Mss., 46/37.
24 *The Morning Advertiser*, 6 July 1837, p. 3.
25 Evans, 'Memorandum to His Grace the Duke of Newcastle', p.11.
26 *Ibid.*, p. 12.
27 *The Naval and Military Gazette*, 17 March 1860, p. 167.
28 Col. J. W. Fitzmayer to Cobden, 28 January 1857, Cobden Mss., B.L. Add. Mss. 43,665, f. 58.
29 *The Morning Advertiser*, 31 January 1856, p. 3.
30 *Parl. Deb.*, Third Ser., Vol. XCI (22 March 1847), col. 294.
31 *Parl. Deb.*, Third Ser., Vol. CVI (21 June 1849), cols. 640–4; Vol. CXXXVII (9 March 1855), cols. 370–4; and Vol. CXXXIX (19 July 1855), col. 1,122.
32 *Parl. Deb.*, Third Ser., Vol. XI (28 March 1832), col. 1,039.
33 This incompetence is even confirmed by a sympathetic biographer of the Duke. See G. St Aubyn, *The Royal George* (Constable, London, 1963), pp. 72 and 92.
34 *Parl. Deb.*, Third Ser., Vol. CLVII (6 March 1860), col. 17.
35 R. Cobden to Maj. J. W. Fitzmayer, 10 March 1855; see also the letters of 7 March and 22 March 1856, Cobden Mss., B.L. Add. Mss. 43,665, ff. 11, 20, 31.

Select bibliography

As material for this book has been drawn from a wide variety of sources, only the more important items are listed here. For a full list of sources used, and for references to *Parliamentary Debates*, to *Parliamentary Papers*, and to articles or speeches reported in the national or provincial press, readers should consult the notes.

1 Primary sources. Official papers consulted in the preparation of this book included Admiralty, War Office and Foreign Office records retained in the Public Record Office. The manuscript collections consulted were:

Bodleian Library, Oxford
Clarendon Papers (by permission of the Earl of Clarendon)

British Library
Aberdeen Papers (Add. Mss. 43,252–4)
Bright Papers (Add. Mss. 43,384)
Broughton Papers (Add. Mss. 36,466)
Cobden Papers (Add. Mss. 43,656–7; 43,665)
Memoranda on the North-West Frontier of British India and On the importance of the River Indus as connected with its Defence (Add. Mss. 21,178)
Place Papers (Add. Mss. 35,149; 35,151; 37,949)
Ripon Papers (Add. Mss. 43,547; 43,619)
Waterloo Papers (Add. Mss. 34,707–8)

Department of Palaeography and Diplomatic, University of Durham
3rd Earl Grey Papers
General C. Grey Papers

Durham County Archives
Londonderry Papers

Genealogical Office, Dublin Castle
Pedigree of De Lacy Evans (Mss. 176 and 177)

Hull University Library
Chichester Papers
Thompson Papers

Manchester Central Reference Library
Wilson Papers

Maryland Historical Society, Baltimore
Evans letter (Ms. 1,846)

National Army Museum
Crimean Letters
Raglan Papers

National Library of Ireland
Evans Papers (Ms. 15,756)

National Library of Scotland
Brown Papers (Mss. 1,849–52)
Cochrane Papers (Ms. 2,330)
Gleig Papers (Ms. 3,869)

Nottingham University Library
Newcastle Papers (by permission of the Trustees of the Estate of the 7th Duke of Newcastle deceased)

Registry of Deeds, Dublin
Books 340, 342, 427, 682, 745

Royal Archives
Cambridge Papers
Melbourne Papers
Queen Victoria's Papers

Royal Commission on Historical Manuscripts
Broadlands Papers
Wellington Papers (transferred in March 1983 to Southampton University Library)

Scottish Record Office
Dalhousie Muniments (by permission of the Earl of Dalhousie)

The Times Archive
Delane Papers
Russell Papers

Wilton House, Wilton
Herbert Papers (by permission of Lord Pembroke and Dr James Provan, who is currently writing a biography of Sidney Herbert)

Private possession
Evans Letters (by permission of Mr P. C. Metcalfe)

2 Published diaries, journals and correspondence

Aspinall, A. (ed.). *Three Early Nineteenth Century Diaries*. Williams & Norgate, London, 1952.

Benson, A. C., and Esher, Viscount (eds.). *The Letters of Queen Victoria 1837–1861*. 3 vols. John Murray, London, 1907.
Campbell, Lt.-Col. C. F. *Letters from Camp to his relations during the Siege of Sebastopol 1854–5*. R. Bentley & Sons, London, 1894.
Cassels, S. A. C. (ed.). *Peninsular Portrait 1811–14. The Letters of Capt. William Bragge*. Oxford University Press, London, 1963.
Colchester, Lord (ed.). *A Political Diary 1828–1830 by Edward Law Lord Ellenborough*. 2 vols. R. Bentley, London, 1881.
Dorchester, Lady (ed.). *Recollections of a Long Life by Lord Broughton (John Cam Hobhouse) with additional extracts from his private papers*. 6 vols. John Murray, London, 1909–11.
Douglas, Sir G., and Ramsay, Sir G. D. (eds.). *The Panmure Papers*. 2 vols. Hodder & Stoughton, London, 1908.
Duncombe, T. H. (ed.). *The Life and Correspondence of Thomas Slingsby Duncombe*. 2 vols. Hurst & Blackett, London, 1868.
Falls, C. (ed.). *A Diary of the Crimea by George Palmer Evelyn*. Duckworth, London, 1954.
Fitzherbert, C. *Henry Clifford V.C.: his letters and sketches from the Crimea*. Michael Joseph, London, 1956.
Gurwood, Lt.-Col. J. *The Dispatches of Field-Marshal the Duke of Wellington*. 8 vols. John Murray, London, 1852.
Maxwell, Sir H. *The Life and Letters of George William Frederick fourth Earl of Clarendon, K.G., G.C.B.* 2 vols. E. Arnold, London, 1913.
O'Connell, M. R. (ed.). *The Correspondence of Daniel O'Connell*. 6 vols. Irish University Press, Dublin, 1972–80.
Pakenham, T. (ed.). *Pakenham Letters 1800–1815*. J. & E. Bumpus, London, 1914.
Parker, C. S. (ed.). *Sir Robert Peel from his private papers*. 3 vols. John Murray, London, 1891.
Pearse, Maj. H. *The Crimean Diary and Letters of Lieut.-General Sir Charles Ash Windham*. Kegan Paul, London, 1897.
Sanders, L. C. (ed.). *Lord Melbourne's Papers*. 3 vols. Longman, London, 1889.
Siborne, Maj.-Gen. H. T. *Waterloo Letters*. Cassell, London, 1891.
Wellington, Duke of (ed.). *Supplementary Despatches, Correspondence and Memoranda of Field-Marshal Arthur, Duke of Wellington*. 11 vols. John Murray, London, 1858–72.

3 Books, letters and published speeches of Sir G. de Lacy Evans

An authentic Report of Proceedings at a meeting of the electors of the parishes of St Paul, Covent Garden, St Clement Danes, and St Mary-le-Strand, held at the Crown & Anchor Tavern, Strand on Monday, December 3, 1832, to hear Colonel Evans state his political opinions, and the course he would pursue as a Member of Parliament, if returned for Westminster. W. Barnes, London, 1832.
A Letter to the Electors of Westminster. Dalton, London, 1833.
Facts relating to the capture of Washington in reply to some statements

contained in the memoirs of Admiral Sir G. Cockburn. W. Clowes, London, 1829.
Memoranda of the Contest in Spain. J. Ridgway, London, 1840.
On the Designs of Russia. John Murray, London, 1828.
On the Practicability of an Invasion of British India: and on the commercial and financial prospects and resources of the Empire. J. M. Richardson, London, 1829.
Sir De Lacy Evans' Reply to Mr O'Connell's Attacks on the Regent etc. of Spain. Torran, London, 1842.
The reappearance of Buonaparte on the shores of France. Published privately, London, 1818.

4 Contemporary works

Alcock, R. *Notes on the Medical History and Statistics of the British Legion in Spain*. John Churchill, London, 1838.
A Non Alarmist. *A Few Words on our Relations with Russia including some remarks on a recent publication by Colonel De Lacy Evans*. Baldwin & Cradock, London, 1828.
A Staff Officer. *The War in the Crimea. Letters from Headquarters*. John Murray, London, 1858.
'A Volunteer in the Queen's Service'. *A Concise Account of the British Auxiliary Legion*. Ainsworth, London, 1837.
Bacon, J. F. *Six Years in Biscay*. Smith Elder & Co., London, 1838.
Diprose, J. *Some Account of the Parish of Saint Clement Danes (Westminster) Past and Present*. Diprose & Bateman, London, 1868.
Gleig, C. R. *Campaigns of the British Army at Washington and New Orleans*. John Murray, London, 1826.
Gruneisen, C. L. *Sketches of Spain and the Spaniards during the Carlist War*. R. Hardwicke, London, 1874.
Hamley, Lt.-Col. E. B. *The Story of the Campaign of Sebastopol*. Blackwood, Edinburgh, 1855.
Henningsen, C. F. *The Most Striking Events of a Twelvemonth's Campaign with Zumalacarregui in Navarre & the Basque Provinces*. 2 vols. John Murray, London, 1836.
Holloway, W. *The History and Antiquities of the Ancient Town and Port of Rye, in the county of Sussex*. John Russell Smith, London, 1847.
Macfarlane, C. *The Camp of 1853*. Bosworth, London, 1853.
Russell, W. H. *The War: from the landing at Gallipoli to the death of Lord Raglan*. Routledge, London, 1855.
Somerville, A. *History of the British Legion, and War in Spain*. James Pattie, London, 1839.
Thompson, T. P. *Exercises, political and others*. 6 vols. Effingham Wilson, London, 1842.
Wilson, Sir R. *Sketch of the Military and Political Power of Russia in the Year 1817*. James Ridgway, London, 1817.

5 Newspapers and periodicals

Annual Register
The Army and Navy Gazette
The Atlas
Brighton Guardian and Lewes Free Press
The Daily News
The Examiner
The Freeman's Journal
Gentleman's Magazine
The Globe
The Hastings and Cinque Ports Iris
The Illustrated London News
The Inquirer
The Manchester Guardian
The Manchester and Salford Advertiser
Morning Advertiser
The Morning Chronicle
The Morning Herald
The Morning Post
The Naval and Military Gazette
The Nonconformist
The Patriot
The Poor Man's Guardian
The Quarterly Review
Reynolds's Newspaper
The Spectator
The Standard
The Sun
The Times
The United Service Gazette
The Westminster Review

6 Memoirs and biographies

A Sketch of the Life of Lt. Col. Champion, of the 95th Regiment, with extracts from his correspondence. Bradbury & Evans, London, n.d.
Atkins, J. B. *The Life of Sir William Howard Russell*. 2 vols. John Murray, London, 1911.
Bapst, G. *Le Maréchal Canrobert*. 6 vols. Plon-Nouritt, Paris, 1902.
Beattie, W. *Life and Letters of Thomas Campbell*. 3 vols. Hall Virtue & Co., London, 1850.
Córdoba, Gen. F. F. de. *Mis memorias intimas*. 3 vols. Madrid, 1886.
Fawcett, Mrs. *Life of the Right Hon. Sir William Molesworth*. Macmillan, London, 1901.
Gash, N. *Sir Robert Peel*. Longman, London, 1972.
Gielgud, A. (ed.). *Memoirs of Prince Adam Czartoryski*. 2 vols. Remington, London, 1888.

Grote, Mrs. *The Personal Life of George Grote.* John Murray, London, 1873.
Hardcastle, The Hon. Mrs. (ed.). *Life of John, Lord Campbell.* 2 vols. John Murray, London, 1881.
Hume, J. R. *Reminiscences of the Crimean Campaign with the 55th Regiment.* Unwin Brothers, London, 1894.
Lehmann, J. H. *Remember You are an Englishman.* J. Cape, London, 1977.
Lysons, Sir D. *The Crimean War from first to last.* John Murray, London, 1895.
Myatt, F. *Peninsular General. Sir Thomas Picton 1758–1815.* David & Charles, Newton Abbot, 1980.
Patterson, M. W. *Sir Francis Burdett and his Times 1770–1844.* 2 vols. Macmillan, London, 1931.
Prest, J. *Lord John Russell.* Macmillan, London, 1972.
Ridley, J. *Lord Palmerston.* Constable, London, 1970.
Robbins, K. *John Bright.* Routledge & Kegan Paul, London, 1979.
Robinson, G. *David Urquhart.* Oxford University Press, Oxford, 1920.
Shaw, Col. C. *Personal Memoirs and Correspondence.* 2 vols. Colburn, London, 1837.
Stanmore, Lord. *Sidney Herbert; Lord Herbert of Lea: a Memoir.* 2 vols. John Murray, London, 1906.
St. Aubyn, G. R. *The Royal George.* Constable, London, 1963.
Smith, G. C. Moore (ed.). *The Autobiography of Lieutenant-General Sir Harry Smith.* 2 vols. John Murray, London, 1901.
Walker, Gen. Sir C. P. Beauchamp. *Days of a Soldier's Life.* Chapman & Hall, London, 1894.
Zegger, R. E. *John Cam Hobhouse: a political life, 1819–1852.* University of Missouri Press, Columbia, 1973.
Ziegler, P. *Melbourne.* Collins, London, 1976.

7 Secondary sources

Anderson, Maj.-Gen. W. H. *The History of the Twenty-second Cheshire Regiment 1689–1849.* Hugh Rees, London, 1920.
Bailyn, B. *The Ideological Origins of the American Revolution.* Belknap Press, Cambridge, Mass., 1967.
Beckett, I. F. W., and Gooch, J. (eds.). *Politicians and Defence.* Manchester University Press, 1981.
Begley, J. *The Diocese of Limerick from 1691 to the Present Time.* Browne & Nolan, Dublin, 1938.
Best, G. *Mid-Victorian Britain, 1851–1875.* Shocken, New York, 1972.
Bolitho, H. *The Galloping Third.* John Murray, London, 1963.
Briggs, A. *The Age of Improvement.* Longman, London, 1959.
Brock, M. R. *The Great Reform Act.* Hutchinson, London, 1973.
Bruce, A. *The Purchase System in the British Army, 1660–1871.* Royal Historical Society, London, 1980.
Buxton, S. *Finance and Politics.* 2 vols. John Murray, London, 1888.
Chalfont, Lord (ed.). *Waterloo: Battle of Three Armies.* Sidgwick & Jackson, London, 1979.

Christiansen, E. *The Origins of Military Power in Spain 1800–1854*. Oxford University Press, London, 1967.
Clark, G. K. *Peel and the Conservative Party: a study in party politics 1832–1841*. F. Cass, London, 1964.
Clarke-Kennedy, A. E. *Attack the Colour! The Royal Dragoons in the Peninsula and at Waterloo*. Fudge & Co., London, 1975.
Cunningham, H. *The Volunteer Force*. Croom Helm, London, 1975.
De Lacy-Bellingari. *The Roll of the House of Lacy*. Waverly Press, Baltimore, Md., 1928.
Dowell, S. *A History of Taxation and Taxes in England*. 4 vols. Longman, London, 1888.
Duncan, Maj. F. *The English in Spain*. John Murray, London, 1877.
Field, Col. C. *Britain's Sea Soldiers*. 2 vols. Lyceum Press, London, 1924.
Gash, N. *Politics in the Age of Peel*. Longman, London, 1953.
—. *Reaction and Reconstruction in English Politics 1832–1852*. Oxford University Press, London, 1965.
Germans, Lord St. *Papers Relating to Lord Eliot's Mission to Spain*. Published privately, London, 1871.
Gleason, J. H. *The Genesis of Russophobia in Great Britain*. Harvard University Press, Cambridge, Mass., 1950.
Godwin-Austen, Brevet Maj. A. R. *The Staff and Staff College*. Constable, London, 1927.
Gordon, H. *The War Office*. Putnam, London, 1935.
Harries-Jenkins, G. *The Army in Victorian Society*. Routledge & Kegan Paul, London, 1977.
Hibbert, C. *The Destruction of Lord Raglan*. Penguin, London, 1961.
Hobsbawm, E. J., and Rudé, G. *Captain Swing*. Lawrence & Wishart, London, 1969.
Holt, E. *The Carlist Wars in Spain*. Putnam, London, 1967.
Horsman, R. *The War of 1812*. A. A. Knopf, New York, 1969.
Jones, Col. W. D. *Records of the Royal Military Academy, 1741–1850*. Woolwich, 1851.
Judd, G. P. *Members of Parliament 1734–1832*. Yale University Press, New Haven, 1955.
Kauntze, G. E. F. *Historical Record of the Third or King's Own Regiment of Light Dragoons*. Cousins, London, 1857.
Kee, R. *The Green Flag*. 3 vols. Quartet, London, 1976.
Kinglake, A. W. *The Invasion of the Crimea*. 9 vols. Sixth edition. Blackwood, Edinburgh, 1877–78.
Leniham, M. *Limerick, its history and antiquities*. Hodges Smith & Co., Dublin, 1866.
Maccoby, S. *English Radicalism 1832–1852*. Allen & Unwin, London, 1935.
McCord, N. *The Anti-Corn Law League 1838–1846*. Allen & Unwin, London, 1958.
MacLysaght, E. *Irish families: their names, arms and origins*. Hodges Figgis & Co., Dublin, 1957.
Moore, R. J. *Sir Charles Wood's Indian Policy 1853–66*. Manchester University Press, 1966.

Namier, L. *The Structure of Politics at the Accession of George III*. Macmillan, London, 1960.
Oman, C. *A History of the Peninsular War*. 7 vols. Oxford University Press, London, 1902–30.
Pemberton, W. Baring. *Battles of the Crimean War*. Batsford, London, 1962.
Reilly, R. *The British at the Gates*. Putnam, New York, 1974.
Ryan, G. *Our Heroes of the Crimea*. Routledge, London, 1855.
Sked, A. (ed.). *Europe's Balance of Power 1815–1848*. Macmillan, London, 1979.
Southgate, D. *The Passing of the Whigs 1832–1886*. Macmillan, London, 1962.
Thomas, W. *The Philosophic Radicals: Nine Studies in Theory and Practice 1817–1841*. Oxford University Press, Oxford, 1979.
Webster, C. K. *The Foreign Policy of Castlereagh*. 2 vols. G. Bell, London, 1925.
—. *The Foreign Policy of Palmerston, 1830–1841*. 2 vols. G. Bell, London, 1951.
Wylly, Maj. H. C. *The 95th (The Derbyshire) Regiment in the Crimea*. Swan Sonnenschein, London, 1899.
Young, Brig. P., and Lawford, Lt.-Col. J. P. (eds.). *History of the British Army*. A. Barker, London, 1970.

8 Articles

Bond, B. J. 'Prelude to the Cardwell reforms 1856–1868'. *Journal of the Royal United Services Institution*. Vol. 106. May 1961.
Bullen, R. 'Party politics and foreign policy: Whigs, Tories and Iberian affairs, 1830–6'. *Bulletin of the Institute of Historical Research*. Vol. LI, No. 123. May 1978.
Bolsover, G. H. 'David Urquhart and the Eastern Question, 1833–37: a study in publicity and diplomacy'. *Journal of Modern History*. Vol. VIII, No. 4. December 1936.
Cullum, Gen. G. W. 'The attack on Washington City in 1814'. *American Historical Association Papers*. Vol. 2. 1887.
Fabel, R. F. A. 'The laws of war in the 1812 conflict'. *Journal of American Studies*. Vol. 14, No. 2. August 1980.
Grzebieniowski, T. 'The Polish cause in England a century ago'. *Slavonic Review*. Vol. II. 1932–33.
Leslie, J. H. 'Reminiscences of a Woolwich Cadet of 1802 by the late Capt. Frederick Robertson, R. A.'. *Journal of the Society of Army Historical Research*. Vol. 5, No. 19. January–March 1926.
Main, J. M. 'Radical Westminster, 1807–1820'. *Historical Studies*. Vol. 12, No. 46. April 1966.
Synott, N. J. 'Notes on the family of De Lacy in Ireland'. *Journal of the Royal Society of Antiquaries in Ireland*. Vol. XLIX, part 2. 1919.
Ward, S. G. P. 'The Quartermaster-General's Department in the Peninsula, 1809–1814'. *Journal of the Society for Army Historical Research*. Vol. 24. Winter 1946.

— (ed.). 'The Hawley letters: the letters of Captain R. B. Hawley, 89th, from the Crimea, December 1854 to August 1856'. *Journal of the Society for Army Historical Research*. Special publication No. 10. 1970.

Wood, Maj.-Gen. G. N. 'Evans in the Crimea'. *Army Quarterly and Defence Journal*. Vol. 102, No. 3. April 1972.

—. 'Evans and the British Legion in Spain'. *Army Quarterly and Defence Journal*. Vol. 104, No. 2. January 1974.

—. 'Burning Washington: the lighter side of warfare'. *Army Quarterly and Defence Journal*. Vol. 104, No. 3. April 1974.

—. 'The Union Brigade at Waterloo'. *Army Quarterly and Defence Journal*. Vol. 106, No. 1. January 1976.

9 Unpublished theses

Beckett, I. F. W. 'The English Rifle Volunteer Movement, 1859–1908'. Ph.D. dissertation. University of London, 1974.

Bruce, A. P. C. 'The system of purchase and sale of commissions in the British army and the campaign for its abolition 1660–1871'. Ph.D. dissertation. University of Manchester, 1973.

Colson, A. M. 'The Revolt of the Hampshire Agricultural Labourers and its Causes 1812–1831'. M.A. dissertation. University of London, 1937.

Janke, P. F. 'Mendizábal and the Development of Liberalism in the Iberian Peninsula 1833–1843'. D. Phil. dissertation. Oxford University, 1972.

Jones, P. D. 'The British Army in the Age of Reform'. Ph.D. dissertation. Duke University, 1968.

Strachan, H. F. A. 'The Pre-Crimean Origins of Reform in the British Army'. Ph.D. dissertation. Cambridge University, 1976.

Wheaton, J. 'The Effect of the Administrative Reform Movement upon the Army in the Mid-Victorian Period'. Ph.D. dissertation. University of Manchester, 1968.

Wilson, H. S. 'The British army and public opinion from 1854 to the end of 1873'. B.Litt. dissertation. Oxford University, 1954.

Index

Abercromby, James, 62
Abercromby, Maj.-Gen. the Hon. John, 3
Aberdeen, Earl of, 148, 162, 164, 203, 206; government of, 142, 145, 164, 168–9
Adair, Hugh, 133
Adair, Robert, 133
Adams, Brig.-Gen. Henry W., 149, 153, 155–6
Adams, Lt.-Col. W. H., 184
Additional Articles to the Alliance (1834), 64
Administrative reform movement, 167, 169
Admiralty, 125–6
Adrianople, capture of (1829), 22, 24–5, 36
Afghanistan, 28
Ahumada, Duke of, 69
Akkerman, Convention of (1826), 19
Alava, Gen. Miguel de, 64–5, 69–70
Albert, Prince Consort, 143, 171, 183–4, 191, 210
Alcock, Rutherford, 67, 116
Aldershot, 144
Alexander I, Tsar, 19
Aliwal, battle of (1846), 130
Alma, battle of (1854), 153, 155–8, 165, 196, 207–8
Althorp, Lord, 31, 51–2, 56, 60
Amir Khan, 3
Anderson, Capt. John R., 156
Anglesey, Lord, 14
Anglo-Turkish Treaty (1809), 37
Anti-Corn Law League, 115–16, 122, 124
anti-slavery, 34, 51, 199
Aragon, 66, 72, 82

Arbuthnott, Josette (later Lady Evans), 65, 148, 221n
Arlaban, 81–2; battle of (1836), 77, 83
army, 16, 55, 65, 69, 148, 198, 204; in Peninsular War, 4, 103, 110, 112, 115, 206; in War of 1812, 6, 8–11; at Waterloo, 13; promotion in, 5, 16, 113, 166, 178–81, 192; and public order, 46; reduction of, 49, 51, 133, 140, 203; terms of service in, 129–30, 209; at Chobham camp, 143–4; in the Crimean War, 146, 161, 163, 167–70, 172–4, 208–9; losses from cholera, 150, 157–8; and the press, 152; chaplains, 179; administration of, 189–92
army reform, 129–30, 167, 184, 204, 209; failure of, 169, 183, 193, 203, 210; promoted after Crimean War, 172–3, 179; delayed by Indian Mutiny, 186, 197
Army Service Bill, 130, 209
Artillery, Royal, in War of 1812, 5, 8, 11–13; at Waterloo, 14; in Spain, 91–2, 104; in the Crimean War, 146, 149, 155–60, 171, 207; officers of, 180, 184
Association of Officers of the late British Auxiliary Legion, 116
Aston, Arthur, 116
Attwood, Thomas, 35
Austria, 2, 13, 30, 38, 135, 200; army of, 2, 135, 185
Austro-Sardinian War (1859), 188

Badajoz, battle of (1811), 5
Baillie, Col. H. D., 42
Balaclava, 158, 160–1, 163–4, 168, 174–5, 209

Balkans, 19–20, 22, 24–5, 29, 200
Balkh, 28
ballot, 44, 46, 51, 56, 109, 117, 120, 134, 136, 140, 187, 199, 204
Baltimore, 8; attack on (1814), 9–10, 17
Baring, Alexander, 32
Baring, Francis, 47
Baring, Sir Francis T., 119
Baring, Henry Bingham, 47–8
Barney, Capt. J., 6, 8, 10
barracks, army, 63; improvement of sought, 129, 179, 209
Bayonne, 4, 84, 91
Bedford, Duke of, 61
Behovia, fort of, 97
Belbeck, river, 157
Belgium, 13, 35, 198; army of 13; revolution (1830), 33, 42
Benedict, 6, 8–9
Bentinck, Maj.-Gen. C. A. F., 149
Bidassoa, river, 83, 90
Bilbao, 67, 69, 76, 91–2, 94–6; battle of (1835), 70, 99; siege of (1836), 90
Birmingham, 34, 56
Black, C., 95
Black Sea, 22, 145, 150
Bladensburg, battle of (1814), 8, 10, 146
Blücher, Field-Marshal von, 16
Bokhara, 20, 26–8
Boldero, Capt. H. G., 113
Bonaparte, Prince Lucien, 144
Bonham, Francis R., 42
Bonham, Henry, 40
Borgne, Lake, 11
Bouverie, Hon. Edward, 126
Bowyer, Fort, 13
Bradshaw, James, 110
Bragge, Lt. William, 5
Brigade, Light (1813), 8; Household (1815), 14–15; Union (1815), 14–15; of Guards (Crimea), 149–60
Brotherton, Joseph, 57, 128
Bright, John, 128, 138–9, 188, 203, 204; on Evans, 133, 176; on Crimean War, 145, 170
Brighton Guardian, 45
Bristol, 68, 118
Brockman, Edward D., 163
Brooke, Col. Arthur, 10, 13
Brookes's Club, 44
Brown, Lt.-Gen. Sir George, 179; in the Crimea, 146, 149–50, 157, 175; and Evans, 176, 180–1, 202

Browne, General Count George de Lacy, 2
Browne, Field-Marshal Ulysses Maximilian, 2
Browne, Count Ulysses, 2
Brudenell, Lord (later 7th Earl of Cardigan), 152, 173–4, 177, 209
Bulganak, river, 152
Buller, Maj.-Gen. George, 162
Bulwer, Henry Lytton, 36
Burdett, Sir Francis, 30–1, 48, 51–2, 60–1, 108, 141; as a Tory, 101, 104–5, 113, 117
Burgos, 69; retreat from (1812), 4
Burgoyne, Sir John, 159

Calatrava, José, 86, 95, 97
Cambridge, Duke of, 164, 189–90, 195; in the Crimea, 146, 149, 160, 175, 210; at the Alma, 157, 196, 208, 210; and Evans, 176, 196; and purchase, 181, 191–3, 210–11; and military education, 184, 210–11
Campbell, Lt.-Gen. Sir Colin, 180, 182, 186, 194
Campbell, Thomas, 32
Canada, 5, 9, 16
Canning, George, 19
Canning, Lord, 193
Canningites, 43
Canrobert, Gen., 153
'Captain Swing' movement, 46
Cardigan, Earl of, see Lord Brudenell
Carlist army, 64, 69–70, 79, 81–2, 91; advantages of, 66, 68, 70, 77, 92, 114; at siege of San Sebastian, 79–80; artillery of, 79–80, 87, 96; supply route, 82, 90, 98–9, 115, 207; at Fuenterrabia, 83; attack the Legion, 87; at battle of Hernani, 92–4; surrender frontier towns, 96–7
Carlist War, 63, 66, 68, 148
Carlos, Don, 63–4, 92, 96, 106, 115; Carlism, 66–7, 102, 200; and Durango Decree, 67, 85, 207
Carlton Club, 105, 118
Carolina, 12
Carrick, Earl of, 1
Caspian Sea, 25, 27
Castlereagh, Lord, 18–19
Castro, Perez de, 116
Catalonia, 66
Cathcart, Maj.-Gen. Hon. Sir George,

Index

146, 175
Catherine II, Tsarina, 22
cavalry, 3, 17, 49, 144, 204; in
  Peninsular War, 4–5; at Waterloo,
  14–16; in the Crimean War, 146, 153,
  157, 168, 173; officers, 180
Cave, Hon. R. Otway, 121
Champion, Maj. John, 160
Charles XII, King, 22
Chartism, 109, 115, 118, 133–4, 136,
  140, 200
Chesapeake Bay, 6
Chichester, Brig.-Gen. Charles, 68, 80,
  82, 86, 90, 227n
China War (1856–60), 183, 192
Chobham camp (1853), 143–44, 172,
  210
Churchill, Lt.-Col. C. H., 89, 104
City of London, 148, 152
Claremont, Major Edward S., 153, 155
Clifton, Gen. Sir A., 15
Cobbett, William, 57, 140
Cobden, Richard, 122, 132, 143, 188,
  203; on the Militia, 138–9; on Evans,
  139, 165, 176, 210; on the Crimean
  War, 145, 170
Cochrane, Sir Alexander, 5–6, 9–11, 13
Cochrane, Charles, 131–3
Cochrane, Sir Thomas, 61
Cockburn, Rear-Admiral George, 6,
  8–10
Codrington, Maj.-Gen. William J.,
  156–7
Coningham, William, 139–42
Conservatives, 121, 138, 198; revival
  under Peel, 61–2, 101; in election of
  1837, 109; in election of 1841,
  118–19; on free trade, 119, 123; split
  by Peel, 128, 131, 201; in election of
  1859, 188
Constantinople, 19–20, 22–4, 36–7, 145
Córdoba, Gen. Fernando F. de, 76, 81,
  83; tactics of, 70, 73, 76–7, 82; and
  Evans, 72, 76–8, 98; and Legion, 72,
  74, 78–9; political intrigues of, 78;
  reinforces Evans, 81
Corn Laws, 51, 54, 56, 117, 120, 201;
  campaign to repeal, 123–5, 199, 204;
  repeal of 58, 109, 122, 125, 128
Council of Military Education, 184–5
Crimean War (1854–6), 146, 171, 173,
  184, 186, 202, 204, 210; history of,
  196

Cristina, Maria (Queen Regent of
  Spain), 66–7, 84
Cristino armies, 66, 70, 72, 78, 92, 96–7
Cumberland, Duke of, 106–8
Curteis, Capt. Edward Barrett, 50
Czartoryski, Prince, 29

Dacres, Lt.-Col. (later Brig.-Gen.)
  Richard J., 156, 170
Deacle, Mr and Mrs T., 46–8, 199, 202
Deccan, 3
De Lacy, Count Francis Anthony, 2
De Lacy, Francis Maurice, 2
De Lacy of Grodno, Gen. Maurice, 2
De Lancey, Sir William, 13
Delane, John T., 168, 170–1, 196
Derby, Lord, 139, 187; government of,
  142, 188, 194
De Vear, Thomas, 52, 61
D'Eyncourt, Charles Tennyson, 125,
  138
Disraeli, Benjamin, 142
Divisions, 5th Division (Waterloo), 14,
  16; Second Division (Crimea), 146,
  149–50, 152–3, 155, 157–9, 161–2,
  165, 168, 175; Light Division
  (Crimea), 152, 153, 156; Third
  Division (Crimea), 152, 155–6; First
  Division (Crimea), 152, 155–7, 159
Dodgson, Rev. William, 40
Dowbiggin, Capt. 176
Duncombe, Thomas S., 125, 128
Dundas, Admiral, 125
Dundas, George, 168
Durango, 70, 92; Decree, 67, 69, 85,
  114–15, 207
Durham, Lord, 35
Dyas, Ensign Joseph, 5

Eastern Question, 35
East India Company, 3, 26, 57, 68, 187,
  193, 210; board of, 26–7, 29
Ebrington, Viscount, 32, 34
Ebro, river, 91
Ecclesiastical Titles Bill, 138, 140–1
Edwards, Thomas, 41
Egremont, Earl of, 49
Egypt, 19, 35, 38, 148
Eliot, Viscount (later Earl of St
  Germans), 63; Convention of, 63, 67
Elizabeth I, Queen, 1
Ellenborough, Lord, 26–7, 201
Elley, Sir John, 14

Ellice, Edward, 178, 183, 190, 192, 209
Elphinstone, Lord, 25, 194
Elphinstone, Howard, 126
Engineers, Royal, 5, 17, 204; in the Crimean War, 146, 149; officers of, 184
England, Maj.-Gen. Sir Richard, 146, 156–7, 175
English Boundary Act (1832), 50
Escalera, Gen. Ceballos, 96
Escott, Bickham, 52, 54
Espartero, Maj.-Gen. Joaquin, 70, 78, 83, 92, 98–9, 123; army of, 90–1; reinforces Evans, 91; co-operates with Evans, 95–6, 99, 115, 207
Espeleta, Gen., 70, 78
European Forces (India) Bill, 195
Evans, Sir George de Lacy, family background of, 1–3; as a subaltern, 3–4, 204–5; bravery of, 3–4, 17, 87, 94, 99, 102, 205; on flogging, 3, 17, 49, 51, 59–60, 62–3, 141, 149, 199, 209; in Peninsular War, 4–5, 102, 148, 205; resents slow promotion, 5, 16, 88, 113, 143, 196, 205–6; on Legion's pay arrears, 72, 75, 83–4, 86, 95, 98, 113, 116, 120; and privations, 73, 76, 103, 110, 112; and officers, 74, 77, 83, 85–6, 88, 94, 99, 108, 112; no disciplinarian, 74–5, 86, 89, 99; on Spanish reinforcements, 77, 79, 81, 91, 94, 98; at battle of San Sebastian, 79–81, 207; at battle of Fuenterrabia, 82–3, 99, 207; at battle of Hernani, 92–4, 99, 205, 207; strategy of, 95–9, 207; on criticism of Legion, 101–8, 110–15, 202; on educational reform, 128–9, 132; on French foreign policy, 129, 138, 188–9, 191, 200, 203; on army reform, 129–30, 173, 179, 184–5, 187, 196–7, 203–4, 209–11; on the Militia, 138–9; criticised by Radicals, 133, 136, 139, 165, 176, 203; at Chobham camp, 143–4; commands Second Division, 146, 149–50, 152–3, 157–9, 161–2, 171–2, 207–8; and the press, 152, 163, 168, 170–2, 177, 183, 193; at the battle of the Alma, 153, 155–7, 171, 207–8; at the battles of Inkerman, 160–1, 165, 171, 207; a Crimean hero, 162–6, 171–2, 196, 202, 205, 208, 211; on criticism of the Crimean army, 163–4, 167–71, 174–6, 204, 208–9; on Indian on abolition of purchase, 5, 49, 130, 166, 173, 177–84, 186, 191–3, 199, 209–11; medals of, 5, 11, 83–4, 97, 101, 109–11, 113, 146, 148, 164, 166, 171, 203, 213n; in War of 1812, 5–6, 8–13, 17, 148, 205, 207; at Waterloo, 13–16, 148, 205; leadership qualities of, 16–17, 66, 81, 94, 99, finances of, 18, 44, 53, 62, 65, 120, 215n; Radicalism of, 16, 18, 32, 50, 52, 54, 62, 105, 199–200, 203; on Russian foreign policy, 18–20, 22, 38, 145, 200–1; and press criticism, 23–4, 102–4, 108, 110–11, 124; on defence of India, 24–6, 38; as a polemicist, 29, 38, 200–1; on Poland, 30–5, 38, 40, 46, 51, 203; on liberalism, 31, 38, 64–6, 88, 100, 103, 105, 135, 200, 206; poor speeches of, 31–2, 46, 52, 62, 107, 111, 124, 191, 197, 202, 211; on Treaty of Unkiar-Skelessi, 36–8; command of the Legion, 38, 63–5, 98–100, 102–4, 114, 203, 205–7, 211; in Rye elections (1830), 40–2; (1831), 43–5; on electoral reform, 44, 46, 48–51, 56–7, 107, 109, 128, 134, 136–7, 141–2, 199, 204, 211; as a parliamentarian, 46, 136, 193, 200, 202–3; on public order, 46, 48–9, 133–4, 200; and the Deacles, 46–8; on the Volunteers, 49, 138–9, 188–9; on military economies, 49, 51, 54–5, 129, 132–3, 203; in Westminster elections (1832), 50–2; (1833), 52–4; (1835), 60–2; (1837), 101, 104–8; (1841), 117–20; (1846), 125–8; (1847), 131–3; (1852), 139–42; (1857), 183; (1859), 188; on taxation, 51, 53–6, 118, 132, 137–8, 141–2, 199; on ecclesiastical reform, 51, 57, 59, 62, 107, 118, 132, 138, 141, 199; on slavery, 51, 54, 199; on the Corn Laws, 51, 54, 56–8, 122–5, 128, 131; on local issues, 51, 129, 137, 141, 187–8, 197, 201; on the Metropolitan Police, 51, 57; on Ireland, 51, 57–8, 107, 109; on trade unions, 58–9; on the Poor Law, 60, 107; raising the Legion, 68–70, 99; pledges return to Westminster, 65, 75, 87, 89–90, 97, 103; and Spanish generals, 72, 77–9, 82, 90–3, 98–9, 111, 115, 123;

Index

Mutiny, 185–7; on army administration, 190; on Indian Army, 193, 195–7, 210–11; resignation of, 196–7
Evans, John, 1
Evans, Mary Ann, 1

Factory Act (1833), 57
Federoff, Col., 160
Ferdinand VII, King, 18
Fergusson, Robert Cutlar, 32, 34, 37
Fielden, John, 128, 204
Filder, James, 174
Fitzgerald, Brig.-Gen. C. L., 83
Fitzmeyer, Maj. James W., 155–6; on Evans, 176–7, 202–3, 208
Fitzroy, Lord, 125
Foreign Enlistment Act, 64
Foreign Office, 27, 64
Fox, Charles James, 54
Forrest, Maj., 11
France, 5–6, 86, 98, 207; army of, 4, 13–16, 35, 153, 155, 158, 162, 170–1; and Evans, 19–20, 33, 38; foreign policy of, 30–1, 35–6, 63–4, 135; revolution of 1830, 30, 42, 57; intervention in Spain sought, 67, 78; Legion of, 75, 78; revolution of 1848, 133; and the Crimean War, 145, 150, 152, 155, 158, 162, 170–1; navy of, 188
Franklin, Benjamin, 107
Franks, Col. Thomas, 180
Fraser, J. B., 27
Fraser, William, 43
Freestun, Col. W. L., 165, 202
Fuenterrabia, 81–2, 207; battle of (1836), 82–3, 85, 99; garrison surrenders, 97, 115

Gazette de France, 102
general elections, of 1830, 41–2; of 1831, 30, 44; of 1832, 50; of 1834–5, 60; of 1837, 97, 101, 172; of 1841, 117–20; of 1847, 130–1; of 1852, 139; of 1857, 183, 200; of 1859, 188
George IV, King, 41
Ghent, peace treaty of (1814), 13
Gibbs, Maj.-Gen. Sir Samuel, 12
Gibraltar, 20, 148, 166, 187
Gibson, Thomas Milner, 139
Gladstone, W. E., 176
Glasgow, 16, 67; Polish Association of, 34
Glyn, George Carr, 178
Goderich, Viscount (later Earl de Grey), 166, 178, 187, 191
Godfrey, Col. E. L., 89–90
Gómez, Gen. Miguel, 69
Gordon, Col. the Hon. Alexander, 159–60, 174–6, 208
Gordon, Arthur, 176
Government of India Act (1858), 193
Graham, Sir James, 128, 189–90
Granville, Earl, 38
Greece, 20, 22, 36, 45, 68, 148, 200; revolt in 1821, 19
Greville, Charles, 200
Grey, Charles 2nd earl, 30, 43–4, 50–1; government of, 56, 58–9, 61
Grey, Henry 3rd earl, 130, 181, 209
Grindley, Robert, 76
Grosvenor, Lord Robert (later 1st Marquis of Westminster), 34, 61
Grote, George, 108–9, 204
Guards, Foot, 49
Guerra, Gen. Manuel, 96
Gurwood, Col. J., 63

Hall, Maj., 104
Hamilton, Lord Claud, 176
Hamley, Capt. E. B., 161
Hammersley, Charles, 180
Hardinge, Sir Henry (later Lord), 146, 148, 198; on Legion, 104, 110–12, 172; his reforms, 143–4
Harrowby, 1st Earl of, 32
Harvey, Daniel Whittle, 53
Hastings, 44
Havelock, Maj.-Gen. Sir Henry, 186, 192
Hay, Lord John, 78–90, 115, 205; on Legion, 79, 98; in battle of San Sebastian, 80–1; on Evans, 81, 93
Headlam, Thomas, 133
Henningsen, Capt. C. F., 68, 102
Henry, Commodore, 88
Herbert, Lt.-Col. Hon. Percy E., 155, 159, 170
Herbert, Sidney, 179, 189; and army reform, 143, 185, 190, 197, 210; on the Crimean Commission, 177; and purchase, 178, 191–2
Hernani, 69, 79, 81, 87, 92, 95; battle of (1837), 92–4, 99, 104, 115, 170, 205; capture of, 96, 99, 207

Heytesbury, Lord, 27
Hill, Lord, 68, 110
Hobhouse, Sir John Cam, 44, 50–4, 60–1, 140, 201
Hodges, Col., 53
Holland, 33, 35–6; army of 13
Holloway, William, 40–1, 45
Horse Guards, and Evans, 9–10, 16, 49, 110, 163, 195; on flogging, 63; and the Legion, 83; and the Crimean Commission, 177; and purchase, 181; liaison with War Office, 190–1
Hotham, Lord, 110
Houghton, Lord, 32
Hume, Joseph, 48, 108, 128, 138; on Poland, 30, 34; and Evans, 116, 134, 145, 203–4; on military retrenchment, 130, 132–3, 203
Hungary, 135, 200
Hunt, Henry, 30, 44
Hythe, 43

India, 3, 16, 146, 198; and Russian threat, 19–20, 23–4, 26–7, 29; army in, 24, 28, 168, 180, 186, 192–7, 210–11; defence of, 28, 37; Mutiny in, 185–7, 195–7, 201; Council of, 194
Indus, river, 25–6
infantry, 3, 17, 144, 204; at Waterloo, 14–15; in the Crimean War, 146, 149, 157; officers, 180
Inglis, Sir Robert, 32, 34, 37
Inkerman, 158, 208; battle of 'little' (1854), 160–1, 165, 207; battle of (1854), 161, 165, 175–7, 208, 210
invasion 'panics', 130, 138, 188, 202
Ireland, 1–2, 20, 51, 58, 109, 189; M.P.s of, 32–4, 62, 109, 138; agitation in, 46; Irish Coercion Act, 57–8; potato famine in, 125; Protestant 'patriots' of, 199
Irun, 81–2, 87; capture of, 96–7, 115, 207
Isabel, 79
Isabella, Queen, 63, 74, 81, 83, 88, 101, 116
Istúriz, Francisco Javier, 82, 84–5
Italy, 60; revolution in (1848), 133

Jackson, Maj.-Gen. Andrew, 12, 20
James Watt, 79
Jáuregui, Gen. Gaspar, 69, 92
Jervis, Capt. H. J.-W., 192

Jews, emanicpation of, 54, 57, 134

Kabul, 26
Kaffir War, 146
Kashmir, 26
Katcha, river, 157
Keane, Maj.-Gen. John, 11–12
Kempt, Sir James, 15
Khiva, 20, 26, 28
Khokand, 26
Kinglake, A. W., 196
Kinneir, Lt.-Col. Sir John MacDonald, 25–6; criticises Evans, 27–8
Kirby, Lt.-Col. H. R., 89
Kosciusko, Tadeusz, 32, 217n
Kossuth, Louis, 135, 144

Lacy, Edmond, 2
Lacy, Elizabeth, 1
Lacy, Pierce Edmond, 2
Lacy, Reverend Hugh, 1
Lacy, Colonel John, 2
Lacy of Bruff, Pierce, 2
Lafayette, Marquis de, 107
Lahore, 26
Lalor, Patrick, 54
Lamb, Rev. Dr. George, 40–2, 44–5, 50
Lambert, Maj.-Gen. John, 12–13
Lancey, Lt.-Col. O. de, 86–7
Layard, Austen Henry, 167, 173, 177
Leader, John Temple, 105–9, 116, 118–20, 131, 141; neglects Westminster, 129, 201
Leeds, 56, 118
Legion, British Auxiliary, 38, 64–5, 162, 166, 203; recruitment of, 67; fitness of other ranks in, 67–8; medical staff of, 67, 73; officers of, 68–9, 74–5, 84–6, 88, 95, 98, 103, 108, 112, 116, 205; expectations of, 68–70, 72, 79, 81, 98, 101, 206; march to Vitoria, 70, 72; pay arrears of, 72–3, 76, 84–9, 95, 98, 102–3, 108, 112, 114, 116, 205, 228n; privations of, 73, 75–8, 102–5, 112, 205; wastage rate of, 73, 79, 98, 103, 111; indiscipline in, 74–5, 78, 85–6, 89, 104, 112, 114, 205; inadequate accounts of, 76, 84, 89; Light Brigade of, 79; Irish Brigade of, 80; at battle of San Sebastian, 79–81, 115; lack of numbers, 81–2, 87, 95, 98–9, 114, 205; artillery of, 82–3, 95; at battles for Passages, 82, 87; at battle of

Index

Fuenterrabia, 83; at battle of Hernani, 93, 104, 205; rôle in Spain, 95, 98, 103, 114, 205–7; captures frontier towns, 96–7, 115, 207; criticised in Britain, 97–8, 101–3, 106, 108, 110–15, 120, 206; flogging in, 102–3, 105, 111–12
Le Marchant, Brig.-Gen. J. G., 89
Le Marchant, Sir Denis, 51–2
Lewis, Sir George, 192–3
Lichfield House compact, 62
Lieven, Prince, 33
Limerick, 1–2
Liprandi, Gen., 160
Literary Association of the Friends of Poland, 32
Liverpool, 67, 118, 189
Llanos, Don Mateo, 88, 95
Lockyer, Capt. Nicholas, 11
Lombardy, 135
London, 33, 44, 59, 62, 64, 67, 120, 164; press, 29, 38, 52, 102, 186; City of, 108, 118–19, 131–2, 134
London and Westminster Review, 104
Londonderry, Lord, 102, 105, 116
Louisiana, 11
Lucan, Lord, 173–4, 177
Lushington, Charles, 131–3, 139, 141
Lyndhurst, Lord, 49–50
Lysons, Maj. Daniel, 155–6
Lytton, Lord, 32

MacDougall, Gen. Sir Duncan, 6, 75–6, 80, 85, 180, 182, 188, 213n
McHenry, Fort, 10
McNeill, Sir John, 172–3, 175, 177
Madison, President James, 8
Madrid, 63, 84, 94, 97, 101; Carlist threat to, 66, 70, 96; intrigue in, 67; Spanish government in, 72, 75–8, 86–7, 89–90, 95, 113, 116, 200, 205; rebellion of 1841 in, 123
Mahmud II, Sultan, 19, 36–8
Mahon, Viscount, 64
Malcolm, Sir John, 3, 25–6; criticises Evans, 28–9
Malta, 20, 162, 167, 187
Maidstone, Lord, 140, 142
Manchester, 56–8, 62, 116, 124, 145
Mandeville, Lord, 131–3
Manners, Lord Charles, 4
Mansfield, Maj.-Gen. Sir William, 194, 204

Maria, Queen, 36, 49
Marines, Royal, 6; rôle in Spain, 78, 82–4, 91, 93, 98, 104, 115, 205; rift with Legion, 84–5; in the Crimea, 160
Marlborough, Upper, 8
Marylebone, 131, 135–6
Mathew, Capt. G. B., 113
Mauritius, capture of (1810), 3–4, 198
Maynooth Grant, 125, 131, 201
Mazzini, Giuseppe, 135
Mehemet Ali, 35–8
Melbourne, Lord, 58, 60, 109, 113, 121; government of, 62, 67, 88, 116–17, 119–20
Memoranda of the Contest in Spain (1840), 114–15
Mendizábal, Juan, 86; and Evans, 64, 78, 88, 98; government of, 67, 77, 82; neglects Legion, 74–6, 89, 95
Mentschikoff, Prince, 155
Metropolis Water Bill, 137
Metropolitan Anti-Corn Law Association, 116, 123
Metropolitan Internments Bill, 137
Metropolitan Police, 51, 57
Metropolitan Political Union, 48
Meyendorff, Baron, 23, 25, 27
Middlesex Registration Association, 121
Miguel, Dom, 36, 49, 63–4
military education, 3, 173, 179–82, 184–5, 210–11
Militia, 49, 168, 184; proposed reform of, 138–9, 200
Mill, John Stuart, 197
Miller, Samuel, 40–1
Milltown, townlands of, 1–2
Miranda, de Ebro, 70, 72, 77
Mirasol, Count, 70
Mississippi, river, 11–12
Mobile, 13
Molesworth, Sir William, 143
Morley, Samuel, 167
Morning Advertiser, 53, 62, 112, 139–40, 176
Morpeth, Viscount, 32
Muraviev, Capt., 23, 25
Murray, Sir George, 106–8, 120

Napier, Sir Charles, 188
Napoleon, Emperor, 13, 22
Napoleon, Louis (later Napoleon III), 138, 162, 189; foreign policy of, 188, 200

Napoleon, Prince, 153
Naples, government of, 135
National Political Union, 48
Navarino, battle of (1827), 19
Navy, Royal, 20, 36, 38, 135, 140, 204; in War of 1812, 6, 8–12; and Spain, 64; officers in, 130; and Crimean War, 145
Neill, Brig.-Gen. Sir James, 186
Nervion, river, 70
Netherlands, see Belgium, Holland
Newcastle, Duke of, 146, 148, 162–4, 203
New Orleans, battle of (1815), 11–13, 17
New Reform Movement, 134
Ney, Marshal M., 13, 16
Nicholas I, Tsar, 19, 36, 38, 145, 171
Nicholson, Brig.-Gen. John, 186
Nightingale, Florence, 192
Nivelle, battle of (1813), 4
Nolan, Capt. L. E., 155, 159–60
noncommissioned officers, promotion of, 166
Norcott, Maj. William S. R., 202
North West Frontier, 25–6, 38, 201
Northcote, Sir Stafford, 167

officers, 174; promotion of, 5, 16, 49, 166, 177–80, 192–3, 199, 209–10; rewards for, 129–30, 182, 186; in the Crimea, 164–5, 167, 175, 179, 186; expenses of, 180; education of, 184; staff, 184–5; in Indian Mutiny, 185–6; in politics, 198–9
On the Design of Russia (1828), 19
On the Practicability of an Invasion of British India (1829), 24
Oraa, Gen. Marcelino, 90
O'Connell, Daniel, 59, 62, 124; on Poland, 31, 35; and Evans, 54, 109, 123
O'Connor, Feargus, 59, 136
Ordũna, 70
Orsini, 188
Orleans, Duke of, 101
Oriamendi, fort of, 93, 96
Orthez, battle of (1814), 4
Osborne, Capt. R. B., 138
Ottoman Empire, see Turkey
Owen, Col. John, 115
Owen, Robert, 141
Oxford University, 166
Oxus, river, 20, 25, 28

Oyarzun, 90, 92, 96, 115, 207

Pack, Maj.-Gen. Sir Denis, 16
Pakenham, Maj.-Gen. Sir Edward, 11–12
Palmerston, Viscount, 179, 185, 187, 190; on Poland, 30–4; foreign policy of, 35–8, 61, 63–4, 134–5, 168, 200; and the Legion, 68–9, 74, 76, 81, 89, 97–8, 113, 116, 206–7; and Evans, 82, 84–5, 87–8, 90, 109, 110, 176, 202–3; Militia Bill of, 138–9; governments of, 164, 166, 169, 176, 183, 189, 194–5, 197, 206; and Crimean Commission, 174, 177; and purchase reform, 178, 191; on the Indian Mutiny, 186
Pamplona, 76, 90–1; siege of (1813), 5
Panmure, Lord, 176, 185–6, 190; on Crimean Commission, 174, 177; on purchase, 178–9, 181, 209; on Indian Army, 194
Paris, 13, 57, 101, 162; treaty of (1856), 171
Parliamentary Electors and Freemen Bill, 128, 134, 142
Parliamentary Voters (Ireland) Bill, 136
Parque, Fort del, 96–7, 207
Passages, 81–2, 91; battles of (1836), 82, 87
Patapsco, river, 10
Patuxent, river, 6
Pechell, Capt. Sir G. R., 125, 130
Peel, Frederick, 174–6, 178
Peel, Sir Robert, 46, 60–1, 119, 125, 148; on Poland, 32; government of, 62, 121, 128–9; budgets of, 121–2; splits Conservative party, 125
Peel, Gen. Jonathan, 169, 185, 190, 194–5
Peelites, 138, 142
Pelham, John Cressett, 34
Pemberton, Thomas, 45
Peninsular War, 4–5, 16, 64, 68, 103, 110–11, 148
Pennefather, Maj.-Gen. John L., 149, 153, 156, 161, 165, 208
Persia, 3, 22, 25, 27–8, 33–4
Peshawar, 26
Peterloo massacre, 46
Peyton, Capt. W., 86
Philippart, Sir John, 130, 164, 186
Philippe, Louis, 101
Philips, Mark, 124

philo-Polish movement, 32, 38; political weaknesses of, 34
Phoenix, 80, 82
Picton, Lt.-Gen. Sir Thomas, 14–15
Pitt, William, 55
Place, Francis, 51, 55
Poland, 22, 30–6, 170, 200; revolution (1830–1), 29, 31, 33; exiles from, 35
Ponsonby, Sir William, 14–15
Poor Law Amendment Bill, 60
Poor Law Board, 137
Poor Man's Guardian Society, 129, 131
Portugal, 16, 36, 49, 63–4, 68; Legion of, 78
Portugalette, 72, 87
Preston, 44
Prevost, Lt.-Gen. Sir George, 5, 10
Prout, Thomas, 51, 164
Prussia, 13, 30; army of, 13, 185; foreign policy of, 31
Punjab, 25
purchase system, 16, 169, 179; abuses of, 5, 180–3, 190–2, 210; effects of, 49, 130, 166–7, 199; abolition sought, 173, 177–8, 181–2, 185, 191–3, 202, 209–11; advantages of, 181–3
Pusey, Frederick, 41

Quadruple Alliance of 1815, 18; of 1834, 35, 63
Quartermaster-General, staff of, in Peninsular War, 5, 64, 205; in War of 1812, 8–9, 12–13, 205; at Waterloo, 13, 205; in Legion, 89; in the Crimean War, 167, 173–4
Quartre-Bras, battle of (1815), 13–14

Radicals, 198, 204; on Poland, 32–3; limited parliamentary influence of, 46; rift with Whigs, 56; realigned with Whigs, 60, 62; in election of 1837, 108–9; and flogging, 112; on Corn Laws, 122, 124; on Ten Hours Bill, 128; split over military policy, 130, 138–9, 203; split on Crimean War, 145
Radnor, Earl of, 126
Raglan, Lord, 146, 148–9, 155, 157–62, 169–70; and Evans, 150, 152, 162, 164, 167–8, 171, 176, 208; tactics of, 152–3, 159
Rait, Lt.-Col. James, 82
rank and file, 41; in War of 1812, 8, 11–13; in 5th Division (1815), 14; recruitment of 59, 63, 209; promotion of, 63; education of, 129; drunkenness of, 129, 149–50; in Crimean War, 152, 158, 163–4, 173–5; living conditions of, 173, 209; pay of, 209
Redan, 169–70
Reform Bill, movement for, 42–4, 48, 61; first Bill, 29–30, 43–4, 201; second Bill, 50, 60
regiments, 22nd Foot, 3; 3rd Dragoons, 4–5; 51st Foot, 5; 4th Foot, 5; 44th Foot, 5; 85th Foot, 5–6; 21st Foot, 6; 5th West India, 13; Royals, 14; Scots Greys, 14; Inniskillings, 14; 7th Dragoon Guards, 45; 21st Royal North British Fusiliers, 144; 30th Foot, 149, 156, 160; 55th Foot, 149, 156; 95th Foot, 149, 155–6, 158; 41st Foot, 149, 155; 47th Foot, 149, 155–6; 49th Foot, 149, 155, 160; 7th Foot, 155; 5th European, Indian Army, 194; 15th Hussars, 210
Reid, Brig.-Gen. William, 68, 80, 83
Report on the Organization of the Civil Service, 167
Reynolds's Newspaper, 163, 178, 182
Ricardo, David, 25
Rich, Henry, 169
Richard, Rev. Henry, 139
Richards, A. B., 188
Richardson, Maj., 104
Rodgers, Commodore John, 10
Rodil, Gen. Ramón, 87
Roebuck, John Arthur, 59, 108, 128; on the Crimean War, 164, 167, 169, 174, 204
Romanov Empire, see Russia
Rosa, Martínez de la, government of, 66–7
Rose, Maj.-Gen. Sir Hugh, 194
Ross, Maj.-Gen. Robert, 5, 6–11
Rothschild, Baron Lionel Nathan de, 134
Rous, Capt. Henry John, 117–20, 125–7
Royal Commissions, on Military Punishments, 62–3, 103; into the Supplies of the British Army in the Crimea, 172–5, 177; on Purchase, 178–83, 185, 191–2, 197, 211; on national defences, 189; on Indian Army, 194–5
Royal Oak, 6
Russell, Lord John, 60, 62, 129–30, 132,

164; on Corn Laws, 119, 125;
leadership of, 121–2; government of,
128, 133–5, 138; on the Militia, 138–9
Russell, William Howard, 152, 162–3,
171, 208
Russia, 13, 135, 200; army of, 2, 20, 22,
24–9, 31–2, 36, foreign policy of,
18–20, 22, 27, 29, 33, 36–8; trade with
Britain, 18, 23; depleted finances of,
19–20, 27–8; navy of, 20, 23, 36–7;
vulnerabilities of, 22–5, 201;
suppresses Poland, 30–5; and the
Crimean War, 145, 150, 171, 203; her
army at the Alma, 153, 155–7, 208;
and defence of Sebastopol, 158–60,
170; her army at Inkerman, 161
Russophobia, 18, 29, 39, 135, 144, 200,
212n
Russo–Persian War (1826–8), 19, 27, 29
Russo–Turkish War (1828–9), 19, 22,
25, 27, 29; (1853–6), 144–5, 148
Rye, 43; Evans as M.P. for, 30, 45, 49,
198, 201, 211; a freeman borough, 40,
42; Independent Association of, 40,
42, 44; elections (1830), 41–2; (1831),
44–5; (1832), 50

Saarsfield, Gen. Pedro, 98, 115; tactics
of, 90–1, 99; his indecision, 91–3
St Anne, parish of, 54, 56, 104, 107,
118–19, 127, 133–4
St Arnaud, Marshal, 153
St Clement Danes, parish of, 54, 107,
118–19, 127, 133
St George, parish of, 52–4, 61, 105, 107,
118–19, 127, 132–3
St George's Volunteer Rifle Corps, 189
St James, parish of, 54, 56, 107, 118–19,
127, 133
St John, parish of, 54, 107, 118–19, 127,
133
St Margaret, parish of, 54, 107, 117–19,
127, 133
St Martin in the Fields, parish of, 54, 60,
107, 117–19, 127, 133
St Mary-le-Strand, parish of, 54, 107,
118–19, 127, 133
St Paul, parish of, 54, 107, 118–19, 127,
133
St Petersburg, 22, 26–7, 35, 145
Salamander, 80, 82
Sandhurst, Royal Military College, 179,
184

Sandon, Viscount, 32, 34
San Sebastian, 67, 69, 84, 90; siege of
(1813), 5; battle of (1836), 79–81, 99,
115; defences of, 81–2; Legion's base
at, 91, 93, 95–9, 102, 104, 110, 114,
206
Santander, 67, 73, 79
Sardinia, 200
Saussaye, Col. Richard de la, 75, 80
Savoy, parish of The, 54, 107, 118–19,
127, 133
Scarlett, Sir James, 180
School of Musketry, 143
Scinde campaign, 146
Scotland, 56, 186, 189
Scutari, 167; barracks, 148–9; hospital,
163
Seaton, Lord, 143
Sebastian, Don, 93
Sebastopol, 158, 160, 169–70, 175, 208;
march to, 152, 157–8; siege of, 163
Segastibelsa, Gen., 79
Select Committees, on Army before
Sebastopol, 152, 167, 169, 175,
208–9; on Sandhurst, Royal Military
College, 184; on East India (Transport
of troops), 187; on Military
Organization, 189–90
Seoane, Gen. Antonio, 96
Shaw, Brig.-Gen. Charles, 74, 80, 83,
85–6
Sheil, Richard, 37
Shelburne, Earl of, 125
Shelley, Sir John, 139–40, 142, 164–5
Sheridan, Richard Brinsley, 54
Shirley, Henry, 43
Sidmouth, Viscount, 69
Sikh War (1845–6), 130
Simpson, Lt.-Gen. Sir James, 170, 176
Singh, Runjeet, 26
Sinope, battle of (1853), 144
'Six Acts' (1819), 69
Smith, Benjamin, 42
Smith, Gen. Sir Harry, 6, 9, 13, 16, 130
Smith, Maj.-Gen. Samuel, 10
Somerset, Duke of, 191
Somerville, Private Alexander, 68, 74,
111, 114, 228n
Sorauren, battles of (1813), 4
Spain, 85, 106, 120, 131, 162; army of,
2, 38, 68–9, 74–5, 84; northern, 4,
102; Evans's service in, 5, 107, 141,
165, 198, 203; revolt of 1820, 18;

foreign policy of, 20, 35, 64, 206;
constitutional cause in, 64–66, 88,
100, 103, 105, 200; government of,
65–7, 72, 74, 94–5, 103, 111, 114–15;
financial weakness of, 67, 76, 89, 116;
political instability in, 67, 70, 82, 86;
neglect of Legion, 75, 88–9, 98, 104,
112–13
Spencer, Brig.-Gen. the Hon. A., 180
Staff College, 186
Stanley, Lord, 142, 178–9, 193–4
Steele, Col., 157, 196
Stewart, P. M., 34
Stricker, Brig.-Gen. John, 10
Stuart, Lord Dudley, 32, 35, 136
Sturge, Joseph, 138
Sullivan, Sgt., 202
Sussex, 45, 49; protests in, 30, 48

Tamworth Manifesto, 61–2
Tarbes, battle of (1814), 4
tax, 118, 119; house, 51–6, 137–8, 142;
  window, 51–6, 137, 141; income, 121,
  132, 141
Ten Hours Bill, 128
Tchnernaya, river, 158–9
The Courier, 85
The Daily News, 152, 167, 178, 192–3
The Examiner, 23
The Freeman's Journal, 53
The Globe, 59, 192–3
The Inquirer, 136
The Morning Chronicle, 44, 115, 117,
  124; on Evans, 23, 60, 104, 108, 110
The Morning Herald, 36–7, 163
The Morning Post, 29, 126; on the
  Legion, 101; on Evans, 102–3,
  110–11, 165, 171, 176, 178: on
  purchase, 178, 192
The Naval and Military Gazette, 130,
  144; on Evans, 163, 168, 176
The Nonconformist, 141
The Patriot, 141
The Quarterly Review, 23
The Spectator, 136
The Standard, 23, 29, 110, 126, 168, 182
The Times, 118; on Russia, 22, 29, 144,
  201; on Evans, 22, 103–4, 108,
  110–11; on the army in the Crimea,
  146, 152, 163, 168, 170, 176; on army
  reform, 167, 182–3, 192–3; on the
  Indian army, 186, 195
The United Service Gazette, 177

Thompson, Lt.-Col. Thomas Perronet,
  124, 136, 138, 143, 199, 202, 204
Thornton, Col. William, 8, 11–12
Tolpuddle martyrs, 58–9
Tonnant, 6
Tooke, Thomas, 23–4
Toreno, Count de, 67
Tories, 36, 42, 44, 46, 50, 61–2, 118,
  141, 199; and Poland, 32–4; and
  Spain, 64–5, 69, 94, 101–3, 105, 108,
  115, 206
Toulouse, battle of (1814), 4
trade unions, 59; growth of, 42, 58
Treasury, 167, 195
Trevelyan, Sir Charles, 167, 181–2
Tulloch, Col. Alexander, 172–3, 175,
  177
Turkey, 19–20, 22, 28, 33–8, 135, 166,
  170, 200; army of, 150, 155, 160, 162
Turner, Capt. John, 155–7

United States of America, 5, 20, 45; army
  of, 5–6, 185; gunboats of, 6, 8, 11;
  artillery of, 8
universal suffrage, 41, 134, 140, 188
Unkiar–Skelessi, Treaty of (1833), 36–8
Urquhart, David, 39
Urumea, river, 79–80, 82, 92, 96
Uxbridge, Earl of, 14

Vaillant, Marshal, 162
Valencia, 66, 82
Vandeleur, Maj.-Gen. Sir John, 15
Varna, 149–50, 152, 167
Vernon, Capt. Leicester Viney, 192
Victoria, Queen, 107, 148–9, 177, 184,
  190–1; on Evans, 174; and purchase,
  178; on the Indian army, 194–5
Vienna, Treaty of (1815), 30–1
Villafranca, Peace of (1859), 189
Villiers, George (later Earl of
  Clarendon), 63, 77–8, 92, 96, 100; on
  the Legion, 68–9, 74–6, 81, 95, 97;
  assists the Legion, 72, 79, 81–2, 84,
  87, 89–91; on Evans, 74–5, 84, 89, 94,
  108–9, 203
Vitoria, 81–2, 91; battle of (1813), 4;
  Legion's march to, 70, 72; Legion's
  base at, 73–4, 76–9, 90, 98–9, 102,
  104–5, 112
Vivian, Sir Hussey, 16
Volunteers, 49, 138–9, 188–9

Wakley, Thomas, 128
War Office, 190–2
War of 1812, 5–6, 8–13, 16
Warren, Col. Charles W., 156
Warsaw, 29–32
Washington, George, 107, 135
Washington, D.C., attack on (1814), 6, 8–9
Waterloo, battle of (1815), 13–16, 18, 148
Wellington, Duke of, 4, 13–15, 64, 110, 145, 198; on India's defences, 26; government of, 42–3; and Evans, 49–50, 60, 143, 172, 206, 241n; and the Carlist War, 63, 68; on the Legion, 68, 101; and military discipline, 75, 99; on army reform, 130
West, Col. Lord, 180
Westerton, Charles, 183
Westminster, 44, 74–5; protests in, 30–1, 60, 135; elections (1832), 50–2; (1833), 52–4; (1835), 60–2; (1837), 101, 104–8, 117, 165; (1841), 117–20, 201; (1846), 125–6; (1847), 131–3; (1852), 139–42; (1857), 183; (1859, 188; Tories, 52, 61–2, 101, 105–8, 117–20, 126–9, 131, 141, 183, 201–2; Radicals, 52, 101, 103–5, 107–9, 118, 140–1, 201–2; tax burden of, 56; Whigs, 60, 62, 106, 201; and Evans, 65, 75, 87, 89–90, 97, 103, 112, 123, 198, 201, 211; Liberals, 106–7, 117–18, 121, 126, 131–2, 141, 196–7; Chartists, 118, 201; Reform Society, 125–6, 131, 134, 139; demographic changes in, 127
Westminster, Marquis of, see Grosvenor, Lord Robert
Wetherall, Lt.-Col. Charles, 108
Whigs, 42, 62, 110, 138, 141, 198–9; and Poland, 32–4; government of, 43, 46, 49, 52, 56; funds of, 44; split with Radicals, 56–7; realigned with Radicals, 60, 62; conversion to free trade, 118–19; and Spain, 64–5, 206; after election of 1837, 109; in opposition, 121–2
'white mutiny', 194–5
Wielopolski, Marquess, 30
Wilde, Sir Thomas (Sergeant), 47
William III, King, 107
William IV, King, 34, 42, 44, 48, 50, 60, 97, 219n
Wilson, Sir Robert, 18
Winchelsea, 43, 50
Winder, Brig.-Gen. William H., 8
Wood, Sir Charles, 137
Woolwich, Royal Military Academy, 3, 116, 179, 184
Wylde, Col. William, 72, 74–5, 81, 91; on Evans, 74, 89, 94; on Legion, 89; and Espartero, 94–5

Yeomanry, 46, 49
York, Duke of, 4
York (now Toronto), sacking of (1813), 9
Yorke, Maj.-Gen. Sir Charles, 180

Zumalacárregui, Gen. Tomás, 63, 66, 102

DATE DUE